LETTER OF PROCEEDINGS

Origins, Childhood, Four Careers

Jock Ritchie

MINERVA PRESS
ATLANTA LONDON SYDNEY

LETTER OF PROCEEDINGS:
Origins, Childhood, Four Careers

ISBN 0 75410 590 3

First Published 1999 by
MINERVA PRESS
315–317 Regent Street
London W1R 7YB

Printed in Great Britain for Minerva Press

LETTER OF PROCEEDINGS

Origins, Childhood, Four Careers

To my grandchildren, Victoria Smith, James Maby, Anna Wood, Henrietta Wood and Angus Wood

for whom this letter of my life's proceedings was first undertaken

Acknowledgements

Many people, in many ways, have helped me during the four years it has taken me to write this book. Memory dims across the years, but luckily that which I had forgotten has often been stored in others' brains and written records. It would be impossible to list all who have recalled a name or a date, but I must mention some names. My cousin, Rear Admiral Steve Ritchie (himself an author) and his wife, Disa, read all of my naval passages, put me straight on nautical matters where my memory had faded, and Steve extracted from the Hydrographic Office (of which he had been head for five years) wartime charts showing the area (including the mineswept channels) in which HMS *Rockingham* was sunk. Selwyn 'Chidge' Chidgey, in Australia, produced a treasure trove of naval records and photographs. Sir Leslie Froggatt fleshed out my own papers of the Shell European 'Marketing Teams'. Abel Carparelli and Edith Goemans, colleagues in Shell Brasil, helped greatly in my recounting of what we did there. About Asiatic Petroleum, Tom Pryor, Mike Lorenzo, Arnie Pollard and two successive secretaries, Rita Gerhart and Edna Gampert, were invaluable. Joan Bok, until very recently Chairman of New England Electric System, and her predecessor in that office, Guy Nichols, reminded me of much of my business dealings with, and then service as a director of that organisation. Dick Woolbert, Executive Vice-President of McDermott International, and Henry Zarrow, Chairman of the Board and majority owner of

Sooner Pipe and Supply filled in the gaps of my memories of my work with these two companies. Geoffrey Lumsden and his wife Yvette read the whole book in pieces as they came off my word processor, and their frank comments were most useful. Geoffrey used his capacity as a Reader in the National Archives to dig out names of ships and shipmates from Navy Lists of the war years, and much other arcane information. But beyond this, he has been my literary mentor, and guided me in fields (such as publishing) of which I had no knowledge. Finally, my wife, Billie, encouraged me in the dark moments when I was tempted to give up. She proof-read every word I wrote with the skill she acquired as secretary to a British ambassador during World War II. She has served me as Dr Johnson's advice to a young author: 'When you read through your work, and come to a passage you think particularly fine – strike it out!' She rid my text of my pomposities, awkward adjectives, and infelicitous phrases, to say nothing of innumerable typographical errors. I can truly say, '*Sine Billie, nihil.*'

Contents

Part Three

First Career, the Royal Navy

Part Four

Royal Dutch/Shell Group

Introduction

The Captain of any of His Majesty's ships was,[1] whenever his ship had been involved in anything out of the ordinary, required to write to his commanding officer a 'letter of proceedings'. The style was formal: 'Sir, I have the honour to submit the following letter of the proceedings of HM Ship – under my command on [date]...' And you closed: 'I have the honour to be, Sir, your obedient servant...' I have had anything but an ordinary life, which explains my title.

For most of my working life I was an expatriate, and when I retired from my full-time job we had become residents and then citizens of the United States. So I have, alas, had much less contact with my grandchildren than I would have liked. For this reason my initial purpose in writing this book was to put on record what may interest them about me and their earlier ancestors, and about the places where I have lived, and the sorts of job that I have had. My secondary object was introspective; to see if I could trace the events and circumstances that have shaped me into what I am. And perhaps, when I have finished, I may offer it to a wider readership.

In the mid-Victorian era people were much preoccupied with the extent to which, by the exercise of will and self-teaching, you could mould your character. My favourite psychologist, the late Dr Charles K. Ferguson held that,

---

[1] I write in the past tense, because I believe this admirable custom has fallen into desuetude.

while you cannot change character, you *can* change behaviour. Under the influence of Samuel Smiles's 'self-help' and the torrent of writings that followed it, the question of whether character and conduct (or behaviour) were the same, and the extent to which either was susceptible to change, engaged much thought and discussion in Victorian Britain. In his book *Plain Living and High Thinking*, two decades after Smiles, Davenport Adams wrote: 'The world judges us by our conduct; it has neither the time nor the inclination to study our character; moreover, it assumes our conduct is necessarily the reflex of our character'. In the hope, presumably, of improving the conduct of their sons (daughters were less important!) parents of the late Victorian era and a couple of generations after them, were anxious to see included in the educational curriculum of boys a strong element of 'character building' – boxing, competitive games, cross-country running, religious services or organised prayers fifteen times a week, and brutal corporal punishment, often administered by the same men who conducted the prayers. What practical effect this had I don't know; though it is all too easy to see, in the United States at any rate, that discipline early in life is essential for the quality of education and of society.

I have often wondered whether I would have been different if, for example, I had failed to get a scholarship to Eton, if my eyesight had kept me out of the Navy, if I had gone to university, if... if... and if. But since the ifs of history are not subject to rational analysis, I can only go on wondering. What I do believe is that we all have facets to our characters, and that different people see different facets, and that in different circumstances we show different ones. Try this little experiment. Cut a cork in half lengthways, so that you have a cylinder roughly as long as its diameter. Draw a diameter across one of the ends, and, with a sharp knife cut from that line at an angle such that the cut will reach the other end at a tangent – that is without encroaching on the circumference of the bottom end. Turn the piece one hundred and eighty degrees, and cut from the original diameter that you drew, again down to a tangent to the bottom end. You now have a fascinating shape – a solid bounded by a circle (the bottom), two semi-ellipses meeting in a chisel point, and two parts of the surface of a cylinder. Now hold it up and look at it from the bottom: you see a circle. Look at it along the line where the two cut sides meet: now you see an isosceles triangle. Rotate it through ninety degrees and you see a rectangle, and in between are all sorts of variations. I believe that (with the lawyers' caveat, that all analogies are false!) this is a sort of analogy for character – that a lot depends upon the point of view of the observer, and on how the observed wishes – consciously or unconsciously – to be seen. I also believe that, as we learn from the example of others and our own experiences, our characters are indeed modified. At the very least, our behaviour has been sufficiently altered for it to appear that character has been changed, too.

What I will try to do in this book is (without too much introspection) to identify those places, people, institutions and experiences that I believe have changed me into what I am – recognising always that I can never know what I might have become in their absence.

Part One
Origins

Chapter One

Collieston

A newborn child acquires its nationality either from its father (and sometimes mother) who is a national of a particular state, regardless of where the child was born, or by being born in the territory of a state, regardless of parentage. Legally these two ways are known as *jus sanguinis* (the law of the blood) and *jus soli* (the law of the soil). Countries such as Britain, which have generally been colonisers and exporters of population, used to adhere to the first. (Let the *people* go, but hold on to their allegiance and that of their children, and hope they will remit lots of money back home, or maybe just for the reason that my father put into the words: 'If you'd been born in a stable, would you be a horse?') Receiver countries – the United States, Brazil and Argentina for example – espoused *jus soli*, for they needed citizens to populate comparatively empty lands.

Both my grandfathers and my maternal grandmother were born in Scotland, but my paternal grandmother was English and my father was born in England, as was I in my turn. *Jus soli* would make me English, but since at that time the prevailing *jus* in Britain was *sanguinis*, we did, as a family, consider ourselves Scots – and still do. Which explains that, while I was christened John, I have, ever since I was a very young baby, been called 'Jock' (the Scots equivalent of the English and American 'Jack').

It also explains why I start my story in Scotland, and more precisely in Collieston, the village from which my paternal ancestors came. It lies in the parish of Slains, the south-east corner of Buchan, one of the historic earldoms of Scotland, which occupies the north-east corner of Aberdeenshire, bounded on the north and east by the North Sea, on the west by the River Deveron and on the south by the River Ythan.[1]

To describe Collieston I can do no better than to quote from a letter of T.E. Lawrence ('of Arabia') written in September 1930 to F.N. Doubleday.

> Come with me northward many miles above Aberdeen, and then strike towards the sea across the links, which are sand-tussocked desolations of charred heather and wiry reeds, harbouring grouse to whirr up alarmingly from under-foot, and rabbits so lazy that they will hardly scuttle their snow-white little tail-flags from the path. Add a choir of larks and a thin high wind piping over the dunes or thrumming down the harsh stems of heather.
>
> They are three miles wide, these links, and ever so desolate, till they end abruptly in a rough field whose far side is set on edge with a broken line of cottages. Behind their roofs seems to be pure sky, but when you near them it becomes sea – for the cottages have been built round all the crest of the grassy sea-cliff and down it too, cunningly wedging their places into its face wherever there was a flat of land as wide as two rooms. Almost to the beach the cottages fall.

The village today has not changed much from Lawrence's time, except that most of the houses have been enlarged

---

[1]Pronounced 'eye-than'.

and improved. Other than in a summer gale or winter storm it is a quiet, peaceful place. Look down on it at low tide from the brae head (the top of Lawrence's 'grassy sea-cliff') and you see a small cove of firm yellow sand – so firm that you can ride a bicycle on it – its entrance a narrow channel between the Pier, a concrete breakwater, on the north-east, and a straight line of rocks on the south-west. Within the harbour, the beach is divided into two by an isolated outcrop of low rocks. There are maybe half a dozen boats, none longer than four metres or so, hauled up on to the grassy brae on the southern side, clear of the beach and out of reach of the sea. There may be one or two others, moored in the right angle of shelter between the narrower arm of the Pier and the broader seaward part, a fifth of the total length, which covers the rocks that used to be known as the Dulse Craig and the Black Rig, part of which latter still projects from the concrete as a natural extension of the Pier. The north and wider side of the beach is, in good weather and when the tide is low, occupied by playing children and energetic dogs taking advantage of the firmness of the sand.

Yet, if you had looked down on that same cove before the mid-1880s there would have been no pier and no sand, just a natural harbour with water a couple of metres deeper than today, sheltered by islets of rock, home port to sixty-four boats, manned by one hundred and seventy fishermen. Thirty years earlier still there were two hundred and fifty fishermen, and five of the boats were 'first class', over ten metres long, and able to take part in the herring fishery as the shoals of 'silver darlings' moved down the east coast in summer.[2] When I knew Collieston first, as a young boy in the Twenties, no more than a dozen boats were left, with a

---

[2]Peter Anson, *Fishing boats and Fisherfolk on the East Coast of Scotland*, Dent, 1930.

score of fishermen, mostly in middle age. In other ways the village was little changed since the turn of the century.

Most of the houses (in fact probably all but the Manse, the post office-cum-general store run by Geordie Forrest, and Seaview, the house built by my grandfather for his parents, and at that time owned by my father) were the traditional Scottish 'but and ben'; two-room cottages without plumbing and with only fires for cooking, warmth and heating the water for washing clothes and bodies (the latter in a tin tub in front of the fire, once a week at the most). There existed, until after 1920, a score or so of cast-iron pumps around the village from which one could draw water, and some of the families had earth closets. Those that did not had one public earth closet available to them, or they relied on the open spaces – preferably those that would be flushed twice a day by the tide. (An English visitor, in the early Thirties, asked one of the fishermen, 'Can you please tell me where the nearest public lavatory is?' The fisherman's reply was to stretch his arm out horizontally and, without a word, wave it round in a semicircle, from north round to south!) Our house had its outside closet converted to a water closet soon after World War I – the first house, other than the Manse, to enjoy this attribute of civilisation – but it was not until the Thirties that one of the upstairs bedrooms was turned into a complete indoor bathroom. There was no electricity, and light came from oil lamps or candles.

The door of the but and ben gave on to the but end, which served as the kitchen, while the ben end was the parlour and the bedroom. The greeting to a visitor was (and even today, among the 'auld folks', still is) 'Come awa' ben the hoose' – 'Come on into the parlour'. In the summer of 1993 there was only one but and ben surviving essentially unaltered (though it had plumbing) and its owners were on the point of starting to modernise and improve it. Luckily they had a plan of the house as it was, and from this they gave me the measurements, which I have compared approximately with others that have been altered and enlarged, by pacing out their sides and ends, so that I can be reasonably sure that it is typical – twelve metres long, six metres wide, making a floor area of seventy-two square metres, and two metres high on the inside wall.

The unimproved but and ben would have a fireplace at the centre of each end wall, and a corresponding 'lum' (chimney) at each end of the roof. The front wall was pierced by two windows, one either side of the door, and there might be a flat skylight window (or sometimes two) in the roof. The back wall had no windows, for its surface was occupied by the box-beds. These were wooden structures, each about two metres long, separated by a wooden wall, with a platform for the 'kaff-bed' (a mattress made of a ticking bag filled with chaff from a flour mill). This platform was about seventy-five or ninety centimetres above the floor, with a depth of 1.4 metres, and the space below was occupied by drawers or cupboards for storage. Along the top ran a narrow architrave behind which were rails for the curtains, which at night completed the enclosure into a warmth-conserving compartment for husband and wife, plus a young child or two, while as many as six children might have to share another bed. Thus a ben could accommodate three beds, and a large family might have to have beds in the but as well.

The fire grate was small, maybe forty centimetres wide, with a hook above to hang a pot or a kettle, and trivet to hang on to the fire bars to add to the cooking space. Fuel would be peat, which had to be bought in the countryside, where it was dug out of the peat bog and dried, or 'spreath', driftwood gathered along the seashore. This was free in cash terms, but involved the time and labour of collection, by men, women or children whenever there was time to spare from other tasks, usually when bad weather prevented fishing. Kitchen utensils were few and simple – a kettle to make tea; a pot for porridge or 'tatties'; a 'brander', a grill of heavy steel wire for broiling fish; and a 'girdle', a round, slightly convex piece of sheet iron with a half hoop for a handle, on which to bake oatcakes and drop scones.

The better-off families might add a third room, if their land allowed, but this was exceptional; only the three houses that I mentioned above had more than one storey. Our house and the shop had two, and the Manse three. It says a lot for the social stability of the time – and the place – that the disparity between the Manse, for the one minister, and the but and bens of the few hundred people who supported him was accepted, and caused no (overt at any rate) resentment.

The fishermen always regarded themselves as vastly superior to those they referred to as the 'gypit[3] country folkies'. They were Presbyterians, and so had no clerical hierarchy to suggest class structure though 'the meenister' was always a man of authority and worthy of respect. They were educated in the three Rs, the Bible and the practical skills of seaman and fisherman.

They were poor, but their poverty was not a grinding one, and they were their own masters. They lived hard lives and faced the dangers of the sea every working day; many of the men were lost in comparative youth. But they were sturdy, determined and independent, and had an inborn shrewdness which enabled them to follow their fathers into the profession with open eyes and a clear view of the risks and rewards of their choice, coupled perhaps with resignation to the fact that there were few alternatives, other than emigration.

They fished by the 'long-line' method: each line was one

---

[3]Stupid.

hundred metres long, and had one hundred hooks, each on a short side-line, half hemp ('sneed') and half twisted horsehair ('tippen'), to which the hooks were 'beeted' – attached with linen thread. Each man of the partnership, of two or – rarely – three, which operated a boat would provide and prepare his own line, or very often two. When the boats came in after the early morning fishing the men breakfasted, maybe got a little sleep, and then prepared for the following morning. The lines had to be 'redded' – checked for missing hooks and other damage and set into order – and then the hooks baited with mussels, which had first to be shelled. Mussel shells were not wasted; they became the standard paving material for footpaths and for the 'shally braes' – the steep paths that led down the grassy brae, the cliff side, from the High Town to the Low Town and The Bog.

Meanwhile, the fish was turned over to the wives. In The Bog there is an ever-running spring – the Bog Well – the temperature of which never varies from midsummer to midwinter. This water runs down on to the shore, and provided for the washing of the fish, as the wives gutted and cleaned them. The flatfish (flukes and plashies) were set aside to be marketed fresh. The round fish were split, and then ranged on a wooden board in circles, tail in. Each complete ring was sprinkled with sea salt, and other rings added on top until they formed a cylinder twenty to thirty centimetres high. They were left in salt for a day, and then ranged out on the rocks or frames of wire netting to dry for about three days in the sun and the wind. Their original dead white colour turned to ivory, and the soft, floppy flesh became, not quite as hard as a board, but rigid. Thus were haddock and whiting turned into that delicacy for which Collieston was famous – the spelding.

The wives' work was not yet done, for the fish had to be taken to market, carried, sixty or seventy pounds at a time, in creels, U-shaped baskets with shoulder straps, on the backs of the 'fishwives' (who would not necessarily be wives, but might be mothers, sisters, daughters or no relation at all) to Ellon, the nearest market town, for sale: and all this over and beyond the bearing and raising of the families. As a little boy I remember clearly my great-aunt Jean doing this chore at least once every week. Always known as Jean, she was really *Jane* Ritchie; she had married an unrelated John Ritchie and had three children, two sons and a daughter. She had lost her husband at sea, but at the time I remember her, her younger son was fishing from Collieston and Jean was acting as his fishwife. She and her daughter, Nellie, lived in Seaview, and helped to take care of us while we were there, and cared for the house – which after all was built by her brother for her father and mother.

The creel of speldings was too heavy for her to lift on to her shoulders alone and she needed the help, usually of Nellie, to get the burden into place. Then she set off to trudge the seven miles into Ellon, in her black skirt, black blouse or jersey, and a black shawl over her head and around her shoulders. With the proceeds of the sale of the fish, the fishwives would buy whatever their households needed (but was not obtainable at Geordie Forrest's shop in Collieston) and walk back home.

A day that I remember very vividly must have been in the summer of 1922. It was a lovely sunny day, and I was playing on the lawn at the back of Seaview, making a representation (the resemblance was not close enough for me now to call it a model!) of a steam fishing trawler – one of those ships that passed by not far offshore every day – out of the materials I had at hand; a herring box picked up as driftwood, bits of narrow plank, a cardboard box for the wheelhouse, and rolled-up paper for the smokestack. Late in the afternoon Auntie Jean arrived back, with her creel, now much lighter than in the morning, still on her back.

She was extravagant in her praise of how realistic my trawler was, and to this day I can feel the pride that rose within me – until it was overcome by a much stronger emotion. Out of the top of her creel she took a largish parcel, wrapped in brown paper and tied with string, which she unwrapped to disclose a wooden toy wheelbarrow, painted bright red and bright green, which she proceeded to give me.

My heart almost burst with joy, and I was quite incapable of speech until my mother said, rather crossly, 'Well, shouldn't you say "Thank you" to Auntie Jean?'

Fishing was the main economic activity, eked out in the summer by holiday and weekend visitors, and there were the support businesses – the dairy farm, Kirkton (the church farm), Geordie Forrest's shop and post office, the blacksmith at Little Collieston. There was, however, one other activity: the shooting.

Until 1970, land tenure in Scotland was still almost wholly feudal, and a grant of land from one person to another was subject to the payment of an annual 'feu-duty'. All the owners of houses in Collieston would have had to pay feu-duty to their over-landlord, the Cluny estate, which (subject always to the payment of feu-duty to the next level up, ending with the Crown, as original grantor of the land) continued to own all the land not granted by it to others. This included the large area of the links and the right to hunt or shoot game on it.

In my childhood the shooting, and with it the Shooting Lodge, was leased every year to Lorna, Countess Howe. She used to have a number of guests for the shooting, but her full-time interest was her black labradors. She was a well-known breeder of these dogs, and they were exercised and trained as retrievers on the links south of Collieston. So it was not at all unusual to come round a bend in the main street (the 'Muckle Reed') and find that you had to allow three dozen shiny black dogs to flow past you before you again had the road to yourself.

Otherwise, one was hardly aware of Lady Howe and her guests, for they scarcely mixed with the villagers or the other visitors. There was one notable and noble exception – the Earl of Chesterfield. You would often see him sitting in a sunny corner on a bench deep in conversation with two or three fishermen. The Earl might be smoking a cigar, while the others smoked their pipes, filled with the favourite tobacco, Bogie Roll, so-called because it came as a black roll, finger thick, which had to be cut with a pocket knife into paper-thin slices and then rubbed between the hands before it could fill a pipe. I occasionally made use of the invisibility of a silent child to eavesdrop on these talks. That was a time when (though in Scotland less than in England) class-consciousness was strong, so it was fascinating to listen to the ninth Earl in deep and serious discussion of politics, world affairs and the fishing with Tammy Buthlay, Cotie and Doddie Sangster, without any condescension on the one hand or awe on the other.

From the few fishermen left, and the other able-bodied men of the village – the shopkeeper, the baker, the carpenter – there was formed a Rocket Rescue Company. The coast to the north and south is rocky and treacherous, and wrecks were all too frequent. When a ship went aground, the Rocket Company was called out and led by the coastguards, of whom a detachment lived in the village. A rocket carrying a light line was fired over a wreck, until the crew could get hold of it and haul it over to the ship, pulling a much heavier hawser and a pulley block through which the loop of a lighter rope was rove. The crew of the ship fastened the hawser to a secure place in the wreck, as high above water as they could. Once the ship end was secured, the company on land used a big block and tackle hitched to an anchor on the ground to haul taut the hawser, which was kept off the ground by a sheerlegs.

Then a snatch-block was hooked over it to suspend a breeches-buoy, a pair of heavy canvas breeches whose 'belt' was a standard cork lifebuoy. To this were attached both ends of the looped rope, so that the breeches-buoy could be hauled out to the ship and back. One man at a time climbed into the breeches-buoy and was hauled back to shore, suspended in the breeches, and, if there was too much sag in the hawser, kept afloat by the lifebuoy as he was hauled through the water.

There were Rocket Companies all around the coasts of Britain, where the formation of the land made this method of rescue the best, where for example a lifeboat could not approach a ship grounded on jagged rocks with heavy seas likely to be breaking over them. The Collieston Company was among the most honoured for its collective and individual gallantry, and in 1932 its members all went to Buckingham Palace to receive from King George V the shield awarded each year for the most successful company in its rescue efforts, and over the years a number of individual members were awarded medals for gallantry.

Skill in this form of rescue demanded training and discipline, and total teamwork. So periodical practices had to be held, in the presence of a senior officer of the coastguard. There was a part of the links where a dip in the ground could do duty for the watery gap between a wreck and the cliff top. On the far side was a mast which represented the wreck, and the company carried out a mock rescue with a genuine rocket firing. This was an exciting event with the great rocket blazing across a quarter mile of the links, and most of the village and visitors turned out to watch. After a 'shipwrecked mariner' was safely hauled back, the inspecting officer would examine the members of the company in other aspects of life saving, especially artificial respiration. At that period mouth-to-mouth resuscitation was not yet used, and the prevailing technique was the Sharpey-Schafer method of alternate pressure and release of the lungs from the back of the ribcage, in which all members of the Rocket Company were required to be proficient.

The 'rocket practice' was not all earnest drill, however; Collieston folk would enliven any activity with a bit of fun. One year the inspector picked on 'Aul' Rossie' (whose real name was Robertson) for his first question. 'Mr Robertson, if you found a man who appeared to have died from drowning, what is the first thing you would do?'

Instant answer from Rossie: 'I'd rape his pockets!'

For many decades the majority of the fisherfolk carried one of four surnames – Buthlay, King, Ritchie and Walker. Inevitably, they intermarried, and just as inevitably the original families became cousins of such remoteness that they became separate – so separate that I, Jock Ritchie, would have had to spend days researching the parish records to find how I was related to the several other Jock Ritchies. And since immigration from, or emigration to neighbouring parishes and the city of Aberdeen was common, a connection might be impossible to find. The search would be the more difficult because given names tended to be chosen from a small list of traditional ones. My great-grandfather and my father were both George, my grandfather and I both John. My grandfather's brothers were Alexander, Andrew, Thomas and George, and those names were shared with half the men in the village.

This hewing to tradition (or lack of imagination at the font) led to the need for bynames or T-names: Alexander became Alex, or Alec or Sandy; Andrew became Ondy; Thomas, Tam or Tammy; George, Doddie or Geordie. Even these were not enough; in the Thirties there were at least three Thomas Walkers who were distinguished as Tam Walker, Tooley, and his son Tom (pronounced

Tawm), while my best friend among the fishermen, Alexander Ritchie (no, or at best a very distant, relation) bore the name 'Cotie', because he was born at the farm of Cotehill, a mile from Collieston on the road to Ellon, when his mother couldn't make it back home from delivering fish in time to deliver her baby! Many of the T-names had obvious, or not so obvious origins, but how Jimmy and Doddie Sangster got to be Gibberlin and Toony Sot, I have never been able to fathom.

The tombstones in the kirkyard are eloquent witness to all the many intermarriages, and also to two other characteristics of Collieston folk – the first that they emigrated; there are stones that record deaths at places as distant as Baffin Bay and South Africa, and today we have fairly close relatives in Kenya, New Zealand, Australia, Canada and the United States.

The second is that illegitimate births were not uncommon. My friend Cotie used to say that only in winter did he get a foretaste of heaven. I asked him why and he answered, with a nostalgic smile, 'Glass [barometer] at twenty-nine,' – indicating stormy weather, and so no fishing – 'dark at four o'clock, four pints of ale, and a lass!'

Whatever the Church may have thought, there was on the part of the majority in the community no stigma attached to lasses who gave birth to bastards. But there were two rules: the woman never disclosed the identity of the father (he might be married already, or be recognised as committed to another lass), and the father contributed to the care of the child. Of course, the first of these rules was sometimes unavailing.

After Billie and I had bought the old bakery, Robert Wood, my son-in-law, and I were up ladders replacing the gutters, when my friend from my earliest youth, Dickie Ingram, came by, and started telling us about Sandy Walker, the baker who used to own it.

'Of course ye ken that Sandy was the father of your auntie Jean's illegitimate dochter?'

'No, Dickie,' I said, 'I thought that that was something naebody ever kent.'

'Och!' said Dickie, 'The whole village kent. Ye'll remember that Sandy used to take orders for rolls for breakfast, and deliver them round the village. Well, Seaview's order was for just two rolls, and it took Sandy forty-five minutes every morning at Seaview to deliver them – two rolls: forty-five minutes!'

During the summer, Collieston became, as it still becomes, what the old people would have called a 'stirry place'. By the time of the autumnal equinox, however, the last of the summer visitors leave, and the weather begins to get too bad for small-boat fishing, so the pace slows down, until between Hogmanay (31st December) and Burns's birthday (25th January), both of which are celebrated in a fashion that any Scot could be proud of, the place is dead.

Chapter Two

Ancestors – Ritchie

Except for my father and his mother, all my male paternal ancestors back to the 1700s and their wives were born in Collieston, and most of the wives came from the Buthlay–King–Ritchie–Walker nexus of families. My paternal great-grandfather, George Ritchie, born in 1827, became 'tacksman', or water bailiff, to the Waterside estate on the north side of the estuary of the Ythan, hence his byname, Waterside Doddie, and lived not in Collieston but in Newburgh. One of his duties as 'tackie' was to collect the annual tax or fee of three pounds for each fisherman under sixty-five, and two pounds for those older, for the right to collect mussels – the principal bait used by the long-line fishermen – and to enforce the regulation that allowed fishing only on two days of the week, to prevent over-harvesting of the mussels. From his job, therefore, he knew all the Collieston fishermen, and probably many of their wives, who would have had delegated to them from time to time the task of collecting the mussels and carrying them home in creels on their backs.

It is not surprising, therefore, that in September 1853 George married Janet (always known as 'Jinsie'), daughter of a Collieston fisherman, Robert Walker. At her insistence – Collieston women were, and are, strong-minded – Waterside Doddie lived the rest of his life in Collieston and, I imagine, joined the fishing. To this marriage was born in 1854 John Walker Ritchie, eldest of eight children, and my grandfather.

J.W.R. got his basic education in the school in Collieston, a private enterprise run by Geordie Tough, with the moral (if not financial) support of the minister and the elders of the kirk, including the owner of the village shop, who served as school visitors and conducted examinations in 'the facings' – otherwise known as the three Rs. The students – boys only; girls got what education they could from parents or elder siblings – paid for their tuition by taking to school each day one peat, one square block of combustible decaying vegetable matter, roughly equivalent to wood in calorific value, and the commonly used domestic fuel of then and there.

Grandfather's education must have been a success, for at age fifteen or so ('while a young lad' says an obituary notice) he left home and 'began a mercantile career at Aberdeen'. In fact he went to work in a draper's shop. This job must have given him an interest in cloth, in 'yard goods', for at the age of eighteen (that is in 1872) he went to Manchester, the hub of England's cotton weaving industry, and got into the manufacturing side of cotton cloth. In a few years he started a business for his own account as a 'manufacturer of dyed and white cotton goods' and later formed the partnership of Ritchie & Eason. In this firm he invented (but failed to patent) tracing cloth, which, before the days of photocopying machines, was much used for property surveys and working drawings of machines and buildings, and from which blueprints were made. Another invention was a process for printing, on a suitable length of cotton fabric, the pattern for the common undergarments, which at that time were not factory-made but sewn at home. Paper patterns were not yet in general use, but a woman could go into the draper's and just say, 'A yard and a half of Ritchie & Eason's calico bloomers, please!'

Outside his business he had many charitable and cultural interests – the Congregational Church, the Jackson Street 'ragged school', the YMCA, the local Literary and Philosophical Society, and the Shakespeare Society of Owens College in Manchester, where he had furthered his education in evening classes.

In his early twenties he married Mary, daughter of John Southern, a solicitor in Burnley, a grey and grim cotton weaving and coal mining town in north-east Lancashire, of which his son Walter was town clerk. Of this union were born one daughter, Nellie, and three sons, George (my father) born on 16th January, 1881, Harry and Douglas. By this time Grandfather was clearly prospering. The family had moved to the fashionable suburb of Heaton Moor in Cheshire, where he planned to build a house for them. He had already built, in 1883, a house for his parents in Collieston – Seaview, which we have already met, and which, since it was the largest in the village, was familiarly known as 'the Muckle Hoose'. And to Collieston he went every summer to spend a holiday with his wife and family.

In 1889 he bought a sailing boat in Peterhead, the big fishing and boat-building port fifteen miles north of Collieston, and he and his father used to spend the forenoon of every day, given good weather, sailing off Collieston. It was this pleasure that cost him his life, for in July 1890, he, together with his father and a fifteen-year-old boy from the village, was drowned when his sailing boat, last seen 'sailing along under a spanking breeze with all sails set', drove its bows under water and sank instantly with the loss of all three lives.

Grandfather's death left Granny a widow – albeit a comparatively wealthy one – with four children between the ages of eleven and five. She continued to live in the Cheshire residential suburbs of Manchester, and turned, naturally, to her brother Walter Southern (who by then had ceased to be town clerk of Burnley, and had taken over, as sole partner, the oldest firm of solicitors in the town) for support and advice. He persuaded her that there was not much future in Ritchie & Eason's business, and she sold her share in it to Eason for forty thousand pounds – worth about one and three-quarter million pounds in today's money. With the wisdom of hindsight the family always felt that Walter's was bad advice, since Eason, even without Grandfather, substantially increased the equity of the business to a value of more than twenty million of today's pounds by the time he died in the late thirties.

There were some in the family who felt that we should try to get part of that wealth back by arranging a marriage between Eason's son and the most beautiful of my generation in the family, Uncle Harry's younger daughter, Betty. But alas, this never got beyond chatter over dinner!

Nevertheless, Granny was able to educate her three sons at Manchester Grammar School, which is still one of the best of the non-boarding public schools, and live comfortably for the rest of her life.

Chapter Three

My Father

As Granny's children grew up, and the town of Burnley was growing in population (doubling every twenty years) and importance, Uncle (really Great-Uncle) Walter's law practice grew with it, and it was not surprising that he should want to bring his nephews into the firm. So in due course my father and Uncle Douglas were taken in as 'articled clerks', the usual way in which solicitors learned their profession at that time. Both were admitted to the practice of law on the Roll of Solicitors of the Supreme Court, in my father's case on 11th April, 1902, and Uncle Douglas presumably four years later. Only Uncle Harry escaped, and became a civil engineer; I use the word 'escaped' advisedly.

A mile and a bit south of Collieston is Hackley, one of the most beautiful bays I have ever seen, where we as children, and the previous generation in their time, used to go and swim. (How we ever did it I cannot now imagine, for the last time I put my toes in the water there I thought I would freeze up to my knees – maybe we were all hardier in our youth.) My father's feelings about Burnley were expressed in a sonnet he wrote in the autograph book of Elma Ogilvie, daughter of the then minister in Collieston, and shortly to marry Harry Ritchie. Pasted on to the page were a postcard of Whittlefield, one of Burnley's most ghastly industrial areas, and a photograph of Hackley with, on the sand, a group of people including Elma and Harry and both their mothers. My father gave it the title 'Consolation', and wrote:

> The day is dark, and muddy drops are blown
> From window-frames: a drizzled wilderness
> Of chimneyed roofs – a prospect nothing less
> In ugliness than that on postcards shown
> Of Whittlefield – confronts me where alone
> I stand; yet now my flying thoughts the stress
> Of present things escape, and richly bless
> The mind with memories sweet of Collieston,
> Where oft the sunlit morn has heard us sing
> Like vocal skylarks with excess of joy,
> And oft the affrighted merman with his coy
> And bright-haired daughters, all abandoning,
> Hath seaward fled our strange approach. Employ
> Ye Gods, oft such days to bring.

Nor was it only the awful ambience that made Burnley a less-than-ideal place in which to pursue his career, but, though my father never articulated it, Uncle Walter was not the easiest of men to work for. Nevertheless, in 1908 my father became a partner in the firm, as did his cousin, Walter's son Guy, shortly afterwards.

On the outbreak of World War I in 1914, my father joined the army as a private soldier in The Universities and Public Schools Battalion. No one then expected the war to last long ('It will be over by Christmas'!) so the idea that there might be something better for educated men to do than become infantrymen never seems to have occurred to the powers that be – at least not for a couple of years. He moved on from the infantry to the Machine-Gun Corps, and then to the Tank Corps. He soon became the Captain of a tank ('Gulliver' of the G or 7th Battalion). In this he took part in the first Battle of Cambrai, in late November, 1917. For his gallantry in this, the first real tank battle, he was awarded the Military Cross.

His sister and both brothers were all three married by the outbreak of war, and while he was on leave in 1915 he went to spend some time with Uncle Douglas, himself on leave from the Gordon Highlanders, at the home of his wife, Peggy, born Allan, in Methlick, Aberdeenshire. They had staying with them Bessie Duff, a close friend of Peggy's at Aberdeen University, and who had become a Master of Arts in the classics and modern languages – a combined degree created especially for her – and was then a schoolteacher.

My father was fluent in Latin; indeed, he often said that half the world's troubles began when educated men, of whatever country, could no longer communicate with one another in Latin. With this common interest his friendship with Bessie obviously ripened, for in September 1915 he gave to my mother a beautiful copy of the works of Horace in Latin, with a dedicatory inscription likewise in Latin, and during the courtship that followed they carried on at least some part of their correspondence in this same dead language.

Chronologically, the next piece of evidence is a postcard, in reality just the back of a photograph of my father standing in front of one of the colleges of Cambridge, in army uniform with a white band round his cap, indicating that he was in training to become an officer. It is postmarked 15th July, 1916, addressed to his mother, and just says: '*We have provisionally fixed the 26th of August. G.*' Their plans must have had to be changed – presumably because my father had been sent back to the front in France – for they were married before the month of July was out.

My grandparents had been strict Nonconformists, and demanded very high moral standards from their children; and 'moral' included care for your body as well as your soul. My father trained himself to be hardy, and he sincerely felt that to be ill was your own fault – a sin, almost. He never owned a car, and walked to and from his office (and everywhere else) every day, rain or shine, hot or cold; and, even on the coldest, dampest days (and in Burnley, days could be penetratingly cold and damp!) he never wore gloves. He had gloves, but only lavender-coloured ones, to be worn with formal morning dress for weddings and such. His weight at the end of his life was the same as it had been when he was weighed to join the army in 1914, and an evening tailcoat made for him in 1910 still fitted him perfectly when he wore it at a dinner given for him in 1952 to celebrate the fiftieth anniversary of his being admitted a solicitor. He had a cold bath every morning, dried himself on an especially rough kind of towel, and before getting dressed he did ten minutes of exercises. While he lived at Rosehill, he did these on the roof of the house, on the leaded surround of the big central skylight, which had roofs sloping down to it on all four sides, and so assured him of privacy. He always slept with his bedroom window wide open, and, of course, there was no heating in the room – the great big house had a total of two centrally heated radiators! I remember going in to see him before he got up one morning; I was leaving early to go back to school or my ship. It had snowed during the night, and under his open window was a pile of snow four inches deep.

He was scrupulously honest in everything, I remember him getting very annoyed with my mother once because she had floated off, and was going to reuse a stamp which had escaped the post office's cancellation. Honesty for him was absolute, and never a function of the amount involved, and his clients all knew this.

My father's great love, however, was the English language, words and style. He loathed legal jargon, because it got in the way of clarity; his will occupies less than a foolscap sheet of paper, and contains not one 'whereas' or 'inasmuch'. He once wrote about some lengthy document: 'For this practice (suggesting a hesitancy to believe that the Act can really mean what it very plainly says) there would appear to be no ground in reason whatsoever, since in assurances on the sale (not being documents rewarded according to their length) there seems no virtue in superfluous words.'

In this matter he was on particularly strong ground because, when Parliament was preparing the Law of Property Act of 1925, not only was he consulted on the law and practice of land tenure by copyhold,[1] but was also invited to draft large sections of the Act, so that 'what [the Act] very plainly says' was his own drafting. Another couple of examples are worth quoting. He was the legal adviser to the Burnley Building Society (and a member of the National Legal Panel of the Building Societies Association) and one day he was asked by the General Manager of the BBS to draft for his signature a letter to a firm of solicitors in Leeds. The letter he wrote is evidence of another characteristic of my father – he didn't suffer fools gladly:

> *Dear Sir,*
>
> *The protest your client has instructed you to make leads us to suspect that he has not been properly advised. And we suggest that you inform him – as you can scarcely fail to know – what the practice of building societies is in relation to the dispatch of deeds in your particular circumstances.*

---

[1]W. Ashworth, Southern Jobling and Ashworth – Solicitors 1792–1992.

To the last ten paragraphs of your letter we attach no importance whatever.

Yours faithfully,
General Manager

And his letter to another – procrastinating – solicitor:

Dear Mr Cool,

Please, PLEASE, PLEASE *reply to our letter of — 194—*

Yours faithfully
Southern, Ritchie and Southern

When I was at school we had 'holiday tasks' in the form of a book to read and study, on which we would be examined when we went back after the holidays. I was lying on the floor of the sitting room of Rosehill, behind the armchair in which my father was sitting, resting on my elbows with the open book on the carpet in front of me. It was Shakespeare's *Julius Caesar*, and I was puzzled by a couple of lines (I cannot now remember which they were). So I asked him to help, and read the lines to him. He thought for a moment, and asked: 'That's the New Temple edition, isn't it?'

I looked at the front of the book and, sure enough, it was. I asked him how he knew, and he recited the whole scene to me, and went on to tell me how the passage was in the First Folio, and in many of the subsequent editions. He told me which reading he preferred, and why.

'You know the whole scene by heart?' I asked.

'I know the whole play,' he answered, and went on to tell me that he knew certainly all three of his favourites, *Antony and Cleopatra* and *Midsummer Night's Dream* as well as *Julius Caesar*, and, probably with some hesitations, several others.

'How do you come to know them by heart?'

'Well, I've *read* them.'

I then asked him whether there was anything in the theory that the plays were written not by Shakespeare, but by Francis Bacon.

With more contempt in his voice than I had ever heard before, he said: 'Anyone who believes that that dry as dust lawyer could have written any of Shakespeare's works has no sense of *style* whatever.'

He himself had a scarcely believable sense of style. During World War II *The Times* was not easy for the casual buyer to find – you needed to be a regular customer. He loved doing the crossword puzzle, and so did I. But when on leave once I was staying with my parents in Burnley, and rarely found a copy of *The Times* for myself, so my father said that he'd do the crossword first without writing in the words, so that I could do it when he brought the paper home in the evening. I was challenged by this and said that I would do it without writing it in every other day, so that he could have it clean in the evening, which was when he liked to do it, and ever since then I do *The Times* crossword without writing in the words. One evening I got the puzzle just after my father came home, and before he had done it. He was sitting by the fire, reading, when I came to a clue that I couldn't answer. In those days *The Times* would sometimes have as a clue a quotation, in quotes and with a blank in it, but without helping you by giving (as it does now) the name of the author. So I read it out to my father – it was a complete, but not long sentence – and asked if he knew it.

'No, I don't,' he said, 'but it will be by... er... George Meredith.'

'If you don't know it, how *do* you know it's by George Meredith?'

'By the style.'

'Do you really mean,' I asked, 'that you can tell from the style of one sentence, with no proper names to help, who the author is?'

'Yes,' he said, a little hesitantly, 'I think I could do that for any of the English authors I read as a young man. Anyway, they're all in the bookcase behind me: pick a book at random and read me a sentence that doesn't contain any hints, and I'll tell you.'

The bookcase indeed contained collected editions of Walter Scott, R.L. Stevenson, W.M. Thackeray, Thomas Hardy, George Eliot, George Meredith and several others. So I picked out three books in turn and found in each an appropriate sentence. He was as good as his word! I related this to someone many years afterwards, and expressed my amazement at this feat.

'No,' said my friend, 'I'm a music lover, and I could almost always identify the composer of no more than three bars of the music of any of my favourites.'

Moreover, my father didn't keep his literary knowledge and perceptions to himself. I have in my possession a number of papers he wrote to be read to the Burnley Literary and Scientific Society, the Burnley Rotary Club and other audiences. The subjects include 'Words', 'Autobiography', 'Some Sonnets', 'Sir Walter Scott', 'Edward Gibbon', 'Oliver Goldsmith', and the one I like best of all (and have myself plagiarised and adapted to read to the Fort Pierce Rotary Club in Florida) of which I have two versions. Of the older, entitled simply 'The First Folio', I have only a manuscript text, in my father's hand, neat, steeply sloping and difficult for one not in practice to read. It demonstrates the truth of some words which he uses, that '*...the practice of writing [is] a laborious business – a cycle of experiment, emendation, revision, deletion and beginning again*', and was illustrated by slides. I believe this was written for the three-hundredth anniversary of the publication of the First Folio, a few days after it was entered at Stationers' Hall on 8th November, 1623. Of the later version I have a typed copy, but even that has considerable manuscript emendation. He had changed the title to 'The Mortal Bard', on the grounds that the First Folio was '...the means whereby this mortal put on immortality', and that 'Without the work of collection and preservation accomplished in 1623, the greater portion of Shakespeare's writings might easily have been lost, including some things of price beyond reckoning that have place among the highest achievements of the human mind'.

It was not only great literature that engaged my father's mind. He was the only person I have ever met who actually used the proverbial back of an envelope for 'back-of-the-envelope' calculations and rough drafts. For he used to keep in his jacket pocket (and in his time no gentleman ever went out without a jacket) a number of used envelopes, slit along the top and down the sides to give him an instantly available clean piece of paper to write on, or to give to one of his children in need. Sometimes he would notice, or remember, some little incident which amused him or which he thought worthy of comment. A little secret smile came to his lips, he would muse for a few seconds and take out the back of an envelope and write, usually in verse, his thoughts.

He usually had lunch, on working days, with a group of friends, professionals and businessmen, at the Savoy Cafe in the centre of Burnley. One of these was the coroner, Harry Ogden, who took his office (and himself) very seriously – to the point that one day a cotton merchant said to him, 'Harry, if I could buy thee at my valuation, and sell thee at thine, I'd make a bloody fortune!' (The use of the true second person singular was still alive and well in Burnley in the Twenties and Thirties). This provoked my father to an elegant, but none the less damning, comment in verse, entitled 'Crowner's Quest'.

He sought each mid-day to initiate
Some conversation leading to debate
On things of moment – questions of the hour
Or points of principle – the Abuse of Power,
War crimes, Jus Gentium, Democracy,
National proneness to hypocrisy,
Chaos in Europe, Reconstruction, Coal,
Social Insurance, Government Control,
The Rights of Man – but meeting no response
From those with whom his lot was for the nonce
To be consorted, he would seize his hat
And (making noises as of one who spat
Shreds of tobacco from his tongue) depart,
Not having any longer any heart
To hear his crack-brained lunch companions laugh
O'er crossword nonsense in the *Telegraph*.

He chose the sonnet form for a comment on the failure (perhaps not yet absolute) of the marriage of a couple of friends:

Rest-Cure

Shock-headed woman and sore-headed man
Was all that each could in the other see;
The married years had brought them but to be
Medusa keeping house with Caliban.
Parted; antagonism ceased to fan
Exasperation's flames, and he and she

The vanished spouse (like widowed Antony)
To think upon as 'good, being gone' began.
Since absence shews some promise to repair
Cohabitation's ravages, and tune
Discordant hearts to sing again – too soon
'Twere yet to end it, and apieces tear
The web of dreams illusion's honeymoon
Now weaves for each about an empty chair.[2]

My father always wore very conventional clothes: off-white wool taffeta shirts with gold cuff links, starched collars, dark ties and dark blue or grey suits during the week; during the weekend and on holiday plus fours (does anyone remember that garment now?), but always the same stiff collar. The furthest he got from formality was in Collieston when he would wear his plus fours without stockings, but even to walk to Hackley for a swim he would have on a stiff collar and a tie.

He was a moderate man in all things, and conservative in his tastes. My cousin, Pat Waters, elder daughter of Uncle Harry, and in age the second of my generation, was the most glamorous person that we, as children, ever met. Several years older than I, she had, as a young woman, a job as a fashion model, and, as such, wore make-up. This was then regarded as being rather daring, if not outré, and we could hardly believe our eyes when she appeared one day when she was staying with us, wearing sandals and with her fingernails and toenails lacquered black. After she had gone, my mother asked my father if he didn't think that Pat was a very beautiful girl, only to get the reply, 'I don't know; I've never seen her with her face washed.'

He was a great reader, and liked to spend his evenings in

---

[2]Spacing and spelling are G.S.R.'s.

an armchair, in front of the fire if the weather demanded, doing the crossword and then reading a book, smoking a cigar (always a Romeo y Julieta from Havana) and drinking a glass of whisky, barely diluted with water. The whisky was always a single malt, called Very Old Highland, from a grocer and wine merchant in Aberdeen called Andrew Collie & Sons. It was kept behind the books – the taller ones on the bottom shelf of the bookcase – not for fear of pilferage, but just to have it handy.

He would never flick off the ash from his cigar, because he believed that a long ash cooled the smoke. So inevitably, halfway through the cigar, the ash fell off on to his waistcoat. He would put down his book, hold the cigar in his mouth, rise from his chair, hold up the points of his waistcoat as if it were an apron, walk over to the fireplace and brush off the ash with the back of his hand.

He never had a headache in his life – he once asked me what one felt like – and seemed to enjoy almost uninterrupted good health. In about 1951, however, he was diagnosed as having diabetes. He told me that his doctor had advised him to give up sugar and starches, and inject himself with insulin every day. It was his custom to eat porridge for breakfast every day, and he was very fond of potatoes and good brown bread, all of which would have been on his doctor's 'give up' list. He said that he had already reached that span of threescore years and ten allotted to our life by the Ninetieth Psalm, that life on those terms would not be worth living, and that accordingly he did not intend to change any of his habits.

Inevitably the day came, in March 1954, when he had to leave his office early, and call in to see Dr Claude Bruggen on his way home. Dr Bruggen was appalled by what he found, and could hardly believe that my father had walked to his office that morning and was now walking home again, for he had diabetic gangrene of his leg. The doctor dressed the gangrene and sent my father home to bed. A couple of nights later he died, and my mother found him in the morning with his glasses still on his nose, and his gold pencil and the half-finished crossword puzzle lying on the floor beside him. In his office they found everything in order, and all unfinished bits of business with notes telling what needed to be done next clipped to them. If pride had been in his nature, he would have been very proud of the way he departed his life.

Chapter Four

Ancestors – Duffs, and my Mother

I know much less about my mother's family than my father's. Her father was Thomas Alexander Duff, whose parents were William Duff, a farmer, and Elizabeth, whose maiden name was also Duff. Grandfather lived, and had his office, in No. 4 Meadow Street, Huntly, in Aberdeenshire, about forty miles west of Collieston, and though it is at the confluence of the rivers Deveron and Bogie it is outside Buchan. 'Gappa', as we called him, was, I think, a lawyer by profession, and for most of his working life the factor (estate agent and manager) of the Huntly estates of the Duke of Richmond and Gordon. He married Mary Gordon-Tawse, and they had four children, all born at 4 Meadow Street. Of these my mother, Elizabeth Helen – 'Bessie' – was the second; her older sister was Florence, the third was William and the youngest Sarah, who never escaped from her nickname of 'Baby'. Grandmother Mary Gordon-Tawse died while her children were still very young, and Gappa married a second wife, Janet, after whom my sister Danny was named.

The Huntly estate was not known for its open-handedness – it was said never to give anything away. So one is entitled to presume that Gappa served his employer very well, for on his retirement he was given a small farm,

Burnend, a mile and a half from Huntly, which provided him with a new interest in life (and, I suppose, some retirement income as well) and gave his grandchildren a wonderful place to stay. Until the late Twenties we usually went from Collieston to spend about a week of each summer at Burnend, and in 1923 while Danny's birth and the move from Parkfield to Rosehill had my mother confined to Burnley, we stayed there for about a month.

Janet was a wonderful hostess to children, an accomplished gardener and an experienced bee-keeper. Her garden was in the formal style, with low privet hedges dividing the plantings. I cannot, to this day, brush by a privet hedge without the scent reminding me vividly of Burnend and its chatelaine. She showed us how you could pacify the bees by puffing smoke, and how, protected by gloves, a wide hat and a veil, you could then take the honey out of the hive. And, on one particularly lucky day, we were able to watch her recover a swarm from a tree just outside the garden fence, and get it settled into a hive.

Gappa, too, could provide excitement. One morning we were in the dining room having breakfast when he spotted a largish flock of crows eating the ripe barley in the field just fifty yards away from the house. 'I'll teach those greedy birds,' he said, and opened the top half of the window wide. He went out of the room and came limping back (he was injured by a cricket ball in his youth) with his shotgun (broken open, of course), leaned out of the window, snapped the gun closed, and with a left and right shot two crows. After we had finished our meal, he and one of his farm men – there were two – took me out into the field. There we (I mean 'they', for I was not of a physique to be of much help) drove two stakes into the ground, about twenty feet apart, and tied one of the two corpses to the top of each. Sure enough, they worked as 'scarecrows' and, during the rest of our visit, no crows came back to that field.

Gappa used to take me for walks. Because of his lameness he walked with a stick, with which he also lopped off the heads of thistles in the hedgerows, explaining that if you got the heads of thistles while they were still flowers, before they had turned to seed, you helped to reduce the number of new thistles that would grow. The emblem of Scotland it is, certainly, but none the less a pesky weed. One day, as we were engaged in this activity along the road to Huntly, his whacking down of a bunch of thistles disclosed an ancient milestone, with no legend but a bald '64' engraved on it. He found a nice round pebble on the roadside, and placed it on the top of the milestone, to see whether anyone cutting the grass and weeds along the road ever got close enough to the stone to knock it off. It certainly survived for at least two years, since he would always sign his letters to me with a little picture of stone upon stone, to show that it was still there.

The house at Burnend in which Gappa and Janet lived was a modern bungalow. Behind it, in an old two-storey farmhouse, presumably the original one of the property, lived 'Grandfather', my Duff great-grandfather, looked after by a cook-housekeeper. He was getting pretty old at the time we knew him, and he didn't stir much from his chair, except on very special occasions when he would lift down from the wall one of his two fiddles and play to us. These were both 'fiddles' to me then, although Id[1] tells me that they were violas rather than violins. One lived in a fiddle case of the conventional shape, following the line of the instrument; the other, and from its appearance evidently the older, had a plain rectangular case. He didn't seem to make a favourite of either one, but tuned and played them both.

---

[1]My sister Elizabeth.

Grandfather lived in the kitchen (indeed I don't know if there even was another living room) and his housekeeper cooked and served midday dinner to the two farm men at the big kitchen table. There were chairs there, but the two men never sat down. The meal was always the same – a big plate of Scotch broth, made of mutton stock and vegetables from Janet's garden, with two big boiled potatoes in each plate, and home-made oatcakes on the side. I spent a lot of time with the two men (though one, Wullie, was my special friend) and sometimes I would go and sit with Grandfather while they ate their dinner. As children we were never allowed to eat unless properly seated at the table, so my curiosity was excited by these two never sitting. So one day I asked Wullie why.

'Laddie,' said Wullie, 'a standin' sack fills best.'

This seemed logical, but I was puzzled why it didn't apply to us – or to any of the other people I had ever seen eating.

The logic of filling sacks wasn't, however, all that I learned from Wullie. If one of the horses was pulling a cart, he would let me take the reins and drive. And he would lift me on to the bare back of a horse and let me ride it.

But the most exciting thing of all was learning how to tickle a trout. Burnend was not so-called for nothing, for it was bounded on one side by a burn[2] which flowed in a culvert under the road to join the River Bogie. This is one of the best trout rivers in Scotland, and the burn was also home to many fish then. It ran down a gentle slope towards the Bogie, along the grassy edge of a field, and was a metre or perhaps one and a quarter wide, with clear but peat-brown water, a sandy bottom and undercut banks. It was not difficult to see trout, and Wullie taught me the art of catching them by tickling. You found one that was under

[2]Stream.

the overhanging bank, and swimming through the water at just the speed of the current, so that relative to the bank it was stationary. You then lay down, full length, on the grass a little back from the edge, and a foot or so behind the fish. Very slowly you edged closer to the bank until you could just see the fish (because you were behind it, it couldn't see you). Then very, very gently you lowered your hand, in the shape of an inverted U, over the back half of the fish's body. Waiting still for a few seconds, you gradually closed your fingertips towards your thumb until you barely touched the fish's belly, and stopped. Soon you could feel that he was relaxing, and you started to tickle him, and gradually closed your hand around him a little more, until, wham! You grabbed him behind his gills, and with a forward motion and a sense of triumph you whisked him out of the water and on to the grass.

Of course, you couldn't always find a fish obliging enough to start in the right position, and not to get scared by any sudden movement, but in the weeks we were at Burnend waiting for Danny and Rosehill to be ready to receive us I caught at least three, and had them fried for my breakfast.

In the early Sixties Billie and I lived in Richmond, in a flat that was a few yards from Richmond's justly celebrated Terrace Gardens, in which we used to walk several times a week. Just inside the gate at the top of the gardens there is (or at any rate was) a fountain surrounded by a basin in which there were about a dozen big fat goldfish. Watching these one day I remarked to Billie that they would make a good reserve breakfast if ever we got hungry. She asked me how I'd catch them without exciting the vigilance of the garden-keepers by carrying in a net. 'By tickling them' I told her. She was totally incredulous, until (it was a cold winter's day, with practically no one about) I lay down, and re-enacted Wullie's lesson of forty years earlier – and caught one!

But back to my mother. Bessie was educated at Huntly Gordon Schools (I never knew why it took the plural), an educational establishment which was, even by the excellent standards of Scotland, of the very highest quality. She studied Latin, Greek, German and French as well as 'Natural Philosophy' (which nowadays we would call science), mathematics and religion, and achieved such high standards that she was granted a scholarship at Aberdeen University. There she excelled, and on her graduation, in 1914, she was granted a research scholarship into the Romance languages, her work to begin in France. She went there, but barely had time to find somewhere to live, before Archduke Franz Ferdinand was assassinated in Sarajevo. On 23rd July a harsh ultimatum was presented by Austria to Serbia. This was the first event of a chain reaction which led, on 3rd August, to Germany's declaration of war on Britain's ally, France, and on the following day Britain's ultimatum to Germany. Germany declined to answer, and at midnight of 4th August Britain was at war. Bessie Duff had to return home, and her career as a research scholar ended.

After she and my father were married in July 1916, she went to live with her mother-in-law in Burnley, where I was born on 6th June, 1917. My mother was very fond of Granny, and they lived very happily together for the rest of the war, though it was over a year before my father came home, and met his year-old son.

She was very erudite, but had not my father's gift of communicating her erudition to children; she had been, and in many ways was all through her life, a schoolteacher at heart. Until I was aged about ten, she seemed to me a warm person; she would play the piano to us, and sing, though the pleasure of this latter was diminished for me because so many of her favourite songs were in languages other than English. I think the earliest song I learned from her – though I knew it by heart in German it was many years before I understood the words – was '*Die Lorelei*'. She told me the story, and it left me with a longing to see this maiden on the Rhine, combing her golden hair with a golden comb, and luring mariners to be shipwrecked on her rock. The longing was not assuaged until 1974 when I was on a Rhine passenger ship, in the process of being persuaded by two friends to take on the job of trying to co-ordinate the two parts, European and American, of the International Road Federation. One of them, Bob Swain, the President of IRF, had been in the US Army Corps of Engineers at the end of and after World War II, working on restoring the Rhine crossings, and he knew this part of Germany well. So, as we passed it, he pointed out the Lorelei to me. It was difficult to distinguish that rock from any of the surrounding ones, and guess how the legend could have started, except that the human imagination is almost unlimited.

My progress at school was not outstanding, but I got by. However, my mother obviously hankered after a son who could emulate her academic success, and in the classics, which failed to excite me. So she was for ever detecting lacunae in my learning of Latin and Greek, which could be remedied by some extra coaching from her. This meant that I had to spend an hour out of nearly every day of my holidays being tutored by my mother. I don't think she ever perceived my resentment at this, but if she did, she wasn't going to give up her schoolmistressly duty. In due course I arrived at the point at Eton where I had to decide in which subjects I would specialise, and I picked science. This was too much for my mother and she came post-haste down to Eton to try to get me to change my mind. She was invited to stay with the vice-provost, and tried to enlist his help in the task of persuasion. She failed, and someone, m'tutor[3] perhaps, who became privy to what had passed between them, told me that the vice-provost had suggested to her that she should try no further, on the grounds that, if she succeeded, I would at best be a reluctant convert, and at worst a rebel. 'Let the boy take up what he prefers – at least then he'll be an enthusiast.' This incident finally cut the apron strings. But I don't think she ever quite forgave me!

During the latter part of World War II my mother got a job in which she could make use of her language skills, in the censorship organisation, which made her a temporary civil servant. After the defeat of the Axis she was offered a similar job in Germany, in a letter which said, in part: 'If, however, you should decide not to accept this offer, you will still be eligible for promotion at a later date.' But, promotion or not, she didn't accept the offer, and decided to stay at home.

After my father died, in March 1954, she joined the British Institute in Naples, as a teacher of English to Italians. What progress they made I don't know, but she came back several years later speaking fluent Italian – with a strong Neapolitan accent!

She had given up the house in Burnley when she went to Italy, and when she came back she bought herself a house in Edinburgh, very close to Danny and her family. Like most British houses, it totally lacked insulation, and relied on open fires for warmth, until Billie and I gave her, as a birthday present, roof insulation and double glazing, which, she said, made all the difference in the world.

Her interests were intellectual, she depended for her pleasure and stimulus on the radio for music and intelligent commentary on the goings-on in the world, and on books. But sadly, she had degeneration of the maculae in both

---

[3]See p.108.

eyes, and slowly her sight faded from the centre of her vision outwards, until she had minimal peripheral vision. Nevertheless she still kept house, claiming that she knew where everything was, and could do her cooking by feel and memory. You realised, however, when you went to stay with her, that she couldn't tell which cup was clean, and which dirty! But she couldn't read, and claimed that talking books were too difficult to operate, and that anyway, she didn't like the voices in which they were read. This rang hollow, for the talking book player had very simple controls, and she could fill a kettle at the sink, put it on the gas stove, which she lit with a match, and make herself a cup of tea or coffee, despite the fact that she was having increasing difficulty in using her hands, caused by what I think is called Dupuytren's contraction – her fingers began to curl into her palms and not be able to straighten. This was the first sign of her beginning to give up, and to make matters worse, she began to go deaf, to the point where she could just sustain a conversation, but not hear – adequately – a symphony on the radio. She was always an early riser and early goer to bed, and one evening she went to bed and took an overdose of sleeping pills. As luck would have it, Danny came round to see her during the evening, saw what had happened, and called the emergency services, and Mum was taken to hospital, stomach pumped out, and her life saved. She was, however, submitted to the kind of indignity which she loathed: she was admitted to a mental hospital where she was kept for two or three weeks.

Soon after she was released, my sister Id found for her a very nice home in Cirencester, where she was well fed and looked after, and had company. But the sands of the enjoyment of life had run out for her, deprived of sight, and with very limited hearing. The last time I saw her was there, and we sat on a bench in the garden, and made awkward conversation, while she held my hand – a gesture very unlike her, for she disliked physical contact. She told me that she was just waiting for the end (and there is nothing convincing that anyone can say to that). Not many weeks later, she tried to cut the arteries in her wrists with a razor blade while she was in a warm bath. She failed to cut deeply enough, however, and was again taken to the emergency room of a hospital, and from there, when her wrists were healed, to a mental hospital. Despite her failure she didn't lose her sense of humour; while she was in the ambulance being driven to the emergency room, she asked the driver (presumably as a rhetorical question), 'Why didn't I manage to kill myself?'

'Because you made such an amateur job of it,' answered he, to which Mum riposted; 'You mean there are professionals at this sort of thing?'

On 5th January, 1981, Id's ex-husband, Sam Haighton, committed suicide by shooting himself with his shotgun – he had multiple sclerosis, and told Id that he was not prepared to get to the stage where he had to be handled. Two days later, Id told Mum, who got very excited and eloquent in the expression of her dislike for Sam. At almost the same time she must have heard – it was difficult not to – that an IRA prisoner in Ulster, Bobby Sands, had succeeded in starving himself to death. I think that Sam had restored her resolution, and Bobby Sands had shown her the means, because she just stopped eating. A week later Id could get no response from her, and was told by the doctor that she had lost her power of speech. Very shortly before the end, Id and her neighbour and close friend, Anne North-Lewis, had gone to see her and were trying to persuade her to eat something. Mum wouldn't reply to any suggestion, until at last Anne said, 'Is there anything you *do* want, Granny?'

In a strong, determined voice, Mum answered, 'Peace – and freedom!' A few days later, on 22nd January, 1981, in her eighty-ninth year, she was dead.

Mum's suicide, at the third attempt, had a profound effect on my views on a person's right to end a life that has ceased to become worth living *in the view of the only person who has the right to come to that conclusion.* Her two unsuccessful attempts to end a life that had lost most of its meaning to her led to her being treated as if she were mentally ill, and subjected to treatment to try to cure her 'illness'. Though many religions consider *felo de se* as just that – a felony – I can only regard that attitude as cruelty. If ever I arrive at the point where I decide that enough is enough I hope that I shall be able to kill myself successfully, and, please, let no one hold me back! I saw what happened to my mother.

Part Two

Childhood

Chapter Five

Collieston Childhood

It was in Collieston that my two sisters and I spent our summer holidays: eight weeks in those days. We played with the village children of our age; we walked on the links, or round the Sand Loch; we bathed at Hackley or on the shore. We made sandcastles, we dammed the little streams that ran down on to the beach, and made elaborate hydraulic works and fortifications. We took picnics to the Sand Hills or the Aul' Castle. The former is a patch of dunes almost totally bare of vegetation and with slopes made by nature for children to roll or slide down, and folds where you could have your picnic sheltered from the breeze, invisible to the world, and with no view but the yellow sand and the blue sky. The latter is Old Slains Castle, the remains of the ancient fortress castle of Francis, eighth Earl of Erroll, Lord High Constable of Scotland, who took the wrong side in the uprising of the Earl of Huntly against King James VI of Scots (and later James I of England). All that is left of what must have been a large and formidable castle are two sides of a tower, twenty-five metres high, two and a half metres thick and perhaps ten horizontally, with a passage and steps in the thickness of one of the walls. It stands on a bold, precipitous peninsular rock, almost one hundred metres above the sea. It was probably built in the second half of the twelfth century, and was destroyed, to 'bring the Earl of Erroll to obedience', on

15th October, 1594, by order and in the presence of James VI. He used a quarter of a tonne of gunpowder, requisitioned of the city of Aberdeen, at a cost of £213.

It was a wonderful place for a picnic because the ruins, and especially the passage in the wall, enabled children to imagine all kinds of adventures, battles and derring-do. Alas, the present generation is warned off from approaching the castle too close, never mind from playing in it.

While we were small children, we shared Seaview in the summer with Auntie Jean, her daughter Nellie and granddaughter Cathie. Cathie is between Id and me in age, but at that time she was infinitely more knowledgeable about life – she lived much closer to the earth than we did. So it was from her that I was first exposed to 'the facts of life' (even if I didn't understand any of the implications). One day the three of us had been out on the links and were walking back, at the end of the afternoon, by the back road that came into the dairy, next door to Seaview. We were passed by a couple, a young man and a young woman, both known to us, with their arms round each other's waist, walking towards the links. After they were out of earshot, Cathie stated, 'Ye ken whaur they're gauin', dinna ye?' When we said that we didn't, she said; 'They're gauin' oot on the links, fuckin'.'

We were both nonplussed by this answer, and asked Cathie what she meant. She must have spent several afternoons by herself on the links, hidden by a patch of heather or bents, watching such goings-on, for she gave us a vivid description of what that strange word meant, including the prior contraceptive precautions. But I don't think she understood the relationship between what she had observed and the arrival of babies, and I (and, I imagine, Id, too) was left in total puzzlement at yet another example of the incomprehensible things that grown-ups did.

We were both very fond of Cathie, and when her mother married Billie Davidson (son of Geordie, carpenter, undertaker and precentor of the kirk) and with him moved to another part of Scotland, she left a big hole in our Collieston family.

We helped with the housework, and we did chores (little ones while we were young, and then, as we grew stronger, larger) for neighbours. I spent a lot of time hanging around the fishermen, being useful when I could, and learning all the skills of the craft, from shelling mussels to splicing lines that had got worn from being dragged over a rocky bottom. For Cotie, who came more and more to monopolise my time, I ran errands ('messages' in the Doric) to the shop, often for an ounce of Bogie Roll for his pipe and for his sweet tooth a stick of 'Cow' candy – it had a picture of a cow on its wrapper, presumably to suggest milk as one of its ingredients. (It was a heart-warming surprise, only last summer, to find 'Coo Candy' still available!) In groups of little boys who played together, it was the unkind custom to send the youngest off on 'messages' which would make a fool of him when he got to the shop, and innocently asked for a packet of straight hooks, or two-pennyworth of pigeon's milk. This practical joke, however, had two drawbacks; first, it was a single-shot one – none of our friends was fool enough to fall for it twice; and second, you had to give the messenger the twopence, and couldn't, in decency demand it back!

From about the age of thirteen, I became Cotie's helper at the fishing, getting up at whatever early hour of the morning the tide demanded (though not, I must confess, every morning without fail!) and rowing one oar on the way out to the chosen fishing ground, and both oars while Cotie 'shot' the line, and again when he hauled it back in. Once, or maybe twice, each season Cotie would set a net for herring, and for this he needed a helper – usually me.

And when we brought back our catch, I helped him clean the fish, and then carried them around the village to sell. Our biggest catch was over one hundred and twenty, and to get all those sold in the little village was a not inconsiderable marketing job, particularly since I'd been up since four in the morning, and had nothing but a cup of Cotie's tea for breakfast. But there can be few midday meals more satisfying and delicious than two herrings fresh from the sea, fried in oatmeal, and which you have sold, not given, to your mother.

Until about the early Thirties, Uncle Douglas, Auntie Peggy and Steve also came to Collieston for part of the summer (the rest they spent in Somerset, in country pursuits, riding and shooting among them). So one summer, my father and Uncle Douglas between them bought a little boat for Steve and me. It was ten feet long, double-ended, clinker-built and cost four pounds. The Royal Naval College at Dartmouth had a yacht, *Amaryllis,* in which the cadets could get sailing experience. Steve, who was such a cadet, being the senior partner in our venture, arrogated unto himself the right to name our boat, and she became *Amaryllis II.* This wasn't a good choice for Collieston, because few of the folk recognised the name, either as that of the lily, or of Virgil's shepherdess, sporting with whom in the shade Milton clearly regarded as a worthwhile activity. Inevitably, therefore, and almost instantly it was corrupted to *Mary Ellis.* We must have been quite young when we acquired *Amaryllis* (the '*II*' was soon dropped, except on the boat's name board) because we weren't allowed to go out of the harbour unless accompanied by one of our fathers. That restriction didn't last long, because we both quickly became more competent seamen than either Uncle Douglas or my father, and we were soon rowing, on calm days, as far as Hackley to the south or the Aul' Castle to the north, and we fished for mackerel and saithe just offshore. Alas, soon after our partnership began, Steve ceased to come to Collieston at all in the summer, but I soon found a new soulmate. He was David Wallace, son of an Edinburgh-based Scottish civil servant, of the Highlands and Islands Medical Board, and we quickly became inseparable, hampered only by the fact that Scottish schools had their holidays earlier than English, so our coincidence in Collieston was not total.

In Seaview one summer I found a book called *A Manual of Sailing*, with on the flyleaf the name of Auntie Jean's son, John Ritchie, who had by then emigrated to Australia. This contained descriptions of every kind of sailing vessel, from standing lug yawl to full-rigged ship, and clear descriptions of the art of sailing – how you run before the wind, how you sail close-hauled, tack, jibe and heave to, and the difference between the true and the apparent wind – indeed, all you needed to know to be able to start to sail, though you could no more learn to sail from a book than you could learn to ride a bicycle.

Many parts of fishing gear required floats, and some were slabs of cork, about twenty-five centimetres by twelve by five thick. From a good one of these several of the fishermen, and notably Doddie Sangster, could carve out model boats for wee laddies. We used to flatten a short piece of barrel 'gird' (the steel hoop that holds the staves together) and stick it into the bottom of the boat as a keel, and a shorter piece into its stern as a rudder, while seagull wing feathers made combined masts and sails. One of the uses to which we put our cork-boaties was ocean exploration. You wrote a message '*To whoever finds this boat…*' with your name and address and the date, and then waterproofed the paper by soaking it in melted candlewax. You put the message in a tobacco tin, which was about eight centimetres by five by two centimetres, waterproofed that also with wax, cut a shallow well in the deck of the boat into which the tin fitted tightly, and then held it down by a brass wire, threaded through a hole across the hull and its ends twisted together. On the next day with a good westerly wind you launched it, and watched it until it disappeared from sight on its journey – you hoped over the North Sea. One year I launched two such adventurers: one was picked up about twenty miles up the coast; the other reached the coast of Norway near Christiansand after a five-month journey.

If, however, you weren't prepared to let your boatie (the Scots requires the diminutive!) go off on a one-time journey, then you got the whole thing adjusted, and it would sail very well across the wind on one of the 'pots' – the miniature fjords which split the rocks – or even on the Sand Loch, and you had something to play with for a long time. Thus, on a miniature scale, I learned in practice how the sailing I had learned in theory from John's book worked, and I became discontented with *Amaryllis* as no better than a rowing boat.

From somewhere I found a spar that I could rig up as a mast, and out of old flour bags I made a rudimentary triangular catboat sail, and David and I started to do a little sailing. But *Amaryllis* had no keel, and therefore made too much leeway to be able to make progress against the wind by tacking. But with the wind, and across it, we saved ourselves a lot of rowing. This was the summer that my mother decided that my Latin (or was it Greek?) wasn't up to standard, and she engaged an undergraduate from Aberdeen University as a resident tutor for the summer.

David and I used to take this young man out in *Amaryllis* with us, and though he clearly would rather have been on dry land, he didn't want to seem too scared – until one day. We had been away outside the harbour in a brisk south-easterly breeze, and turned to run before the wind back home again. The tide was ebbing, and the water in the harbour entrance was getting shallower, and as we got into the narrow mouth between the Pier and the rocks, the waves were breaking over the rocks in a way that looked quite fierce, and my poor tutor began to go green and say that we were all going to be drowned, and he wouldn't let two fifteen-year-olds comfort him – he evidently just didn't trust our seamanship. In fact there was no danger, and in five minutes we were safely in the lee of the angle of the Pier, and he was able to clamber up to dry land. But the experience was too much for him, and that evening he resigned his office as my tutor. I think that my mother at any rate half suspected that it was all done on purpose, but she had no evidence and so could take no action. My sister Id is less charitable, and is sure that it was all deliberate; in fact, she says that between us one day we pushed the boat away from the ladder just as the tutor was about to step into it, so that he fell into the harbour with a big splash. This would suggest cumulative malice, and I can honestly state that I have no recollection of such an incident. Anyway, it was good riddance!

During the next year at Eton, I was able to buy, for next to nothing, from one of the boatmen at Rafts (which were just that – rafts between the school boathouses and the river, from which you launched and then got into the boat in which you were going to row) a lug sail, with a beautifully made belly, and properly roped and grommeted, with a bamboo (and therefore lightweight) yard and boom. And one of the instructors at the School of Mechanics to whom I had been telling of my problem with *Amaryllis*'s leeway, suggested a false keel.

That summer David and I fitted a false keel. It was a simple job. We bought a piece of oak, one and a half metres long, twelve centimetres wide, cut off each end at an angle and waterproofed it with three coats of linseed oil. *Amaryllis* had a steel protective strip along the keel, out of which we cut a piece long enough for the false keel. We drilled holes every fifteen centimetres through the false and real keels, and riveted the two together with quarter-inch copper rod and copper washers top and bottom. It wasn't pretty to look at, and when pulled up on to the beach the boat had a pronounced list, but she would sail! The Eton sail was, however, a little small, and we plotted how to do better. David came to stay with us in Burnley for the next Easter holiday, and on my mother's sewing machine we made a Bermuda rig sail out of Burnley 'grey cloth', or unbleached cotton, which cost five pence a yard. When I got to Collieston I bought a spar from a timber yard – just a young pine tree, four metres long and tapering from a diameter of eight centimetres or so at the bottom to a very thin top. I also bought a draw knife, and with this we sliced off the protrusions where the branches had been until we had a fairly smooth mast, which we varnished. In a few days we had everything ready for a trial and our new rig worked much better than the old one, though from our inexperience we hadn't cut the sail with enough belly to be really efficient. Collieston men were not familiar with the Bermuda rig (a tall triangular sail needing no spar above the level of the boom) and were horrified when they saw it. They were sure that the least puff of wind with the leverage of a mast that tall would just blow it over, and were not to be convinced by pictures in yachting magazines, nor by my descriptions of the International fourteen-foot racing dinghies that Eton (with my encouragement) had managed to borrow from the Oxford University Sailing Club for the end of the summer half. I was chased around the village by 'Awa', laddie, an' tak half o' yon mast oot o' yer boatie, afore ye're droont like yer grandfaither', or variations thereon. It took a couple of weeks of watching us sail with impunity before, reluctantly, they piped down.

Among many things I learned from the Boy Scouts at

Eton was life saving for swimmers in danger of drowning, and I reached the level of the bronze medal of the Royal Life Saving Society, as well as the Scouts' badge of proficiency. One day, while the tutor was still with us, we were swimming in the harbour, and my mother, who was a strong swimmer, was swimming out towards the open sea (it was a day of flat calm) when she suddenly got almost total cramp, and had just time to yell out for help. Luckily, I was on the Pier and could run close to her and dive in. By the time I got to her she was floundering dangerously, but I was able to perform as I had been taught and keep her head above water, and then tow her into shallow water. Her cramp eased on the way, and she was finally able to stand up and walk to the shore. This may have accounted for the lack of an angry reaction to the circumstances of the departure of the tutor!

In the summer of 1934, David Wallace and I signed on for a couple of days as supercargoes in a herring drifter working out of Peterhead. The drifter shoots its net, a curtain of light net, as much as three thousand metres long, with floats along its upper edge. The art of drift-net fishing resides in knowing where, at what time and in what direction to shoot the net. The ship then stops its engine and drifts – hence its name – with the net acting as a kind of sea anchor, and with a triangular sail on the mizzen-mast keeping the ship's head into the wind. These drifters were steam powered and coal-fired, and the boiler room was thick with coal dust. But it was warm, and so, during the hours of waiting for the time to haul the net, David and I found a space where we could doze protected from the cold outside. Though it was August the breeze in the open sea and the middle hours of the night was bone-chilling unless you were working. As if the cold weren't enough, the ship, with no way on to give some stability, rolled so that we were both very seasick!

We were employed for short periods as stokers, shovelling coal under the boiler when it needed it; we did tricks at the wheel, and helped generally where a hand was needed, and when we got into Peterhead in the morning we helped unload the night's catch of herring, and then get the ship ready for the next night's fishing. After two days of this, without the opportunity of a bath, and having slept in the coal dust of the boiler room, we were two pretty unsavoury-looking people. We hitched a ride on a lorry most of the way back to Collieston, but had to walk the last few miles. We managed not to meet anyone we knew until we got home, and were greeted with loud horror by my mother; why hadn't we bathed before we arrived in the village in this disgraceful state, and what *would* people think of us? Explanations that the drifter didn't have any washing facilities cut no ice: couldn't we have at least found a stream in which to wash our faces? Well, Seaview had a bathroom with hot water, and we did finally get clean, but I was for ever grateful that I never had to go to sea in a coal-fired ship again.

That escapade was the end of my childhood. Three weeks later I donned my naval cadet's uniform for the first time, and set off for Chatham to join my first ship.

Chapter Six

Collieston Now

There are about 110 houses (and 205 inhabitants) in Collieston now, including the Barratt Houses, so-called for the developer who fashioned them out of the stabling of what was once the Whiteness Hotel, and then became the Shooting Lodge, so that people now live in what used to be home to Lady Howe's labradors. The lodge itself has been turned into flats, reassuming the Whiteness name, and the post-World War II council houses are now mostly in private ownership. The old cottages have been added to; some have an upper storey, some an extension at right angles, and some must be contented with just replacing an original small window by a bay.

Today there is not one professional fisherman left, but yet Collieston thrives; indeed, is as flourishing a community as you could wish to find anywhere, when it could easily have become one with so many other ghost villages on the east coast of Scotland, as fishing ceased to be a craft and became a technology-driven industry.

How this came about is a combination of the character of the people, and the story of a well-intentioned improvement which became, first, a disaster, and then the salvation of Collieston.

Three traits seem to have survived in the Collieston families' genetic progression: we have a strong sense of community (I and many of my cousins still think of

Collieston as home), we are independent-minded, and the sea is in our blood. And although there are very few of the original families now left, the sense of community, at any rate, seems to survive.

The history of Collieston is inextricably linked to the Pier. The port, as nature made it, had two entrances, the North Haven, the most commonly used, and the South Haven, separated by an island of rock. The tidal stream was thus able to flow through the harbour and scour out the sand and silt, and one haven or the other was usable almost whatever the direction of the wind. Nevertheless, the boats had to be hauled out of the water, at any rate when the weather was, or threatened to become, bad. As neighbouring ports began to use larger – and decked, as opposed to open – boats, a harbour usable at all states of the tide, and where the larger boats did not need to be hauled out of the water, was essential to Collieston's survival. The community had for years tried to persuade the fishery board to do something, but to no avail until the Collieston Harbour Committee, under the vigorous and persistent chairmanship of the minister, the Reverend George Greig, did two things: in October 1891 it addressed a 'Memorial and application' to the fishery board, and, to back it up, raised, by public subscription (from a population of Collieston and Old Castle together of 514 people) £1,600, equivalent to seventy thousand pounds of today's money. In April 1894 the fishery board voted £4,400 for the project, and commissioned a survey of the existing natural harbour, and a study of how it could be improved.

Two general plans were studied – to close either the North or the South Haven, with the idea of making a protected harbour in which the boats could be kept afloat most of the time. The decision taken was to close the North Haven, and incorporate the islands of rock into the fabric of a concrete breakwater along the north side, with a second breakwater at right angles to the rock wall on the south side, reaching out to leave an entrance fifty feet wide between them. At no stage of the proceedings, it seems, were the views of the locals sought, but in due course the plan was announced to a meeting of the fishermen, whose reaction was summed up by a man at the back who yelled out: 'If ye're ga'in' to block the North Haven, ye can shove the Sooth Haven up yer airse.' His comment, albeit inelegant, was none the less an accurate forecast of the eventual result of the work; the tidal scour was stopped, the cove filled up with sand and the South Haven became so shallow that at low water, spring tides, you might walk across it. Ironically, one of the reasons for the choice of the plan was that the natural North Haven allowed the harbour to be choked by the sand that entered through it!

On 17th October, 1894, almost half of the northern breakwater was complete, and the official foundation stone was laid, with much pomp and ceremony, by the laird of the Cluny estate, Lady Gordon-Cathcart, who laid beneath the stone a casket (what today we would call a 'time capsule') containing British and American coins, some of the day's newspapers, and a handwritten account of the enterprise. I called this a well-intentioned improvement which became a disaster. Within less than ten years, only sixteen boats were left, and the younger families had moved to Torry, a drab housing complex in Aberdeen, purpose-built for fishing folk, and the men went to work on steam trawlers, or emigrated.

The building of the Pier, however, only accelerated a change that would have happened anyway. In 1871 the first steam-powered fishing boat was built in Aberdeen, the technology of fishing was changed for ever, and within half a century the days of the open fishing boat, propelled by sail or oars, operating out of a small, shallow-draught port, were gone for ever.

My uncle, Sir Douglas Ritchie, was Vice-Chairman of the Port of London Authority until concern about his health caused him to take early retirement in 1955. He retired to Seaview (which by then belonged to him) and dedicated his great administrative skills and leadership to the betterment of Collieston. As means to this end he formed the Amenities Committee, of which he was Chairman for thirteen years.

About twenty years ago the system of local government in Britain was changed to one of three tiers. In the north-east of Scotland the old counties – Aberdeen, Kincardine, Banff, Elgin and Nairn – became the Grampian region, while district councils were established to cover the various areas within the region, Collieston being in the Gordon district. Small towns such as Ellon and Newburgh were to be controlled by elected community councils. Collieston, being content with its Amenities Committee (and of a piece with its spirit of independence!) declined to form such a council.

In The Bog the Amenities Committee has made (and maintains in splendid condition) a children's playground which would do credit to any big city park. The public benches (many of them placed in memory of now-dead residents) are secured to the ground against the possible ravages of winter gales or, perish the thought, vandals, and surrounded by a neat rectangle of pink Peterhead granite chips. The old 'shally' (mussel shell) brae paths are now wooden steps, and the tracks along the head of the braes to the south are pink-gravelled, their grassy verges clipped and trimmed, all by volunteers. But the committee's greatest triumph was the salvation of the Pier.

After enduring almost a century of the terrible winter storms, and one especially bad one in 1988, bits of the end of the Pier and the back sea wall, and some of the underwater foundations were crumbling, to the point where it was not unimaginable that the North Haven would again open itself.

The upper and middle levels of local government had each some part of the responsibility for the upkeep of the Pier, but since it had long since ceased to serve the purpose for which it had been built, and was now only one of Collieston's tourist attractions, the regional and district councils agreed that they would only bear their shares of the approximately one hundred thousand-pound cost of the necessary repairs, on the condition that the village itself raised, by the end of the following year, thirty thousand pounds – three hundred pounds per house, many of which were rental houses and did not represent full-time inhabitants. One can imagine them, as the door closed behind the departing Collieston delegation, rubbing their hands and saying, 'Well, that'll be the end of that!' But they reckoned without the Amenities Committee, and the community spirit of the village.

The chairman of the committee at the time was my first cousin, Steve Ritchie, retired Rear Admiral, Royal Navy, son of the founder of the committee over thirty years earlier. Steve had a full career in the Navy, and then spent ten years as head of the International Hydrographic Office in Monaco – in other words he had some experience of taking on daunting tasks and organising to get them carried out!

The committee set in train every conceivable sort of fund-raising effort, from bumper stickers, T-shirts, raffles, to sports days, dances and a summer gala. John Robertson wrote verses and Paul Ritchie produced an edition of etchings of the Pier in a storm to be sold. And there was one that caused me to make a very expensive mistake.

We were living in Stone Ridge, in New York State, at the time, and one day I received a telephone call from Steve. The conversation went something like this:

STEVE One of the things we're going to do to help the Pier Fund is to have a sponsored walk – so much a mile – along the sands and links from Belhelvie to the point of the Pier. It's nine miles as the crow flies, and those are the miles we'll count, though if you cross the Ythan by the bridge you have to walk an extra mile upstream, then back to the coast across the links – but we have some enterprising people with boats who will, for a fee payable to the fund, ferry people across the mouth of the Ythan and so avoid the detour. Will you and Billie sponsor me?

MYSELF Yes, of course we will.

STEVE How much?

MYSELF How about one hundred pounds? [*Intending that amount for the whole nine miles.*]

STEVE That is pretty generous – are you sure you want to go that high?

MYSELF Yes, because I don't think you can do it. [*Steve is two and a half years older than I, and carries a belly that is a tribute to his lifelong fondness for beer.*]

STEVE Done! For one hundred pounds a *mile* you bet I'll do the whole distance or die in the attempt! But suppose I did die of a heart attack on the way?

MYSELF [*Swallowing hard, because I realised I'd committed myself to nine times what I'd intended.*] Well, we'll come over for your funeral.

STEVE No, I mean what about the money?

MYSELF Okay, one hundred pounds per mile or per part of a mile completed, even if you do die in the attempt.

Well, he did it, and was met at the top of the village by a bagpiper who piped him all the rest of the way to the finish, where in due course he was presented with an award for the oldest walker to complete the distance. With Steve's help, and that of many other contributors of money (notably a very generous contribution from the laird of the local Slains estate), things to be auctioned or sold, or just their time and effort in fund-raising, the village raised its thirty thousand pounds and a little bit over by the year end. So, over the next two summers the Pier was restored, and part of Collieston kept alive.

Chapter Seven

Childhood – Burnley

Since my father's practice was in Burnley, there we lived, though happily sheltered from much of the horror of the town, for Burnley, amidst all its industrial grime and smoke, had then two superb parks, Towneley and Scott, oases of greenery, flowers and peace.

The house in which I and later my sister Elizabeth were born was at the end of Fern Road, a short cul-de-sac ending at the huge iron gates of Scott Park, one of three houses in a row at right angles to the road, separated from the park only by their own access driveway. With not much imagination, the house was called Parkfield; it had been my father's home when he was a bachelor, and his mother had lived there with him.

My earliest memories are from Scott Park and Parkfield. One day, when I was about nine or ten, I suddenly asked my mother about something I thought I remembered – was it really a memory, or something I had dreamed or imagined? I told her that I seemed to recall being, as a very young child, pushed by my mother in a perambulator, holding a flag in my hand, and my pram being just one of a procession of others all with children in them waving flags, and of there being flags all around us. My mother looked very surprised for a moment or two, and then said: 'I can't believe it, but yes, that actually happened. It was Armistice Day, 11th November, 1918, the day that World War I ended. All the mothers of the neighbourhood, and lots of other people too, were in Scott Park, celebrating. You were very excited, and kept on saying "A fwag… and a nunna fwag… and a nunna fwag!" over and over again!'

Whether it really was Armistice Day itself (which I doubt, because the German surrender was only signed at 11 a.m. that day) rather than an arranged celebration a day or two later, I would have been scarcely seventeen months old, and only a very profound communication of emotion from all the people there could possibly have imprinted the scene on so young a memory. If I close my eyes now I can still see that scene, though it may be a memory refreshed by my mother's confirmation of my childish memory. Whatever, *I know* that sixty-five years or more ago I did remember an event of my very young childhood.

My next memory was an incident of enlightenment. It happened well before Janet ('Danny') was born so I was probably five, and Elizabeth (whose own baby name for herself, 'Iddy', or even just 'Id', had become her appellation within the family) barely three. We had a nursemaid who regularly took us for walks in the park, where we would meet other children of our ages. I had absorbed the idea that not all children urinated in the same way, that some sat down to do it, while others, myself included, could do it standing up, and that the public lavatories in the park were designed to accommodate this difference. I also knew that some children were boys and some girls, but I had never made the correlation between these two facts – until one day when we were with the nursemaid and two or three other children in the park and all of us had to go, or were ordered to by the nursemaid. One of the group was my friend Douglas Lancaster, of almost exactly my age. He and I, the boys, went into what I knew was the stand-up department, while Id and her friends, all girls, went into the other. And while I was in the act, the truth suddenly dawned on me – that all those who stood up were *boys* and those who sat down were *girls*! And in the same moment another correlation came to me – that the difference between boys and girls was anatomical.

A third memory is one I am not proud of. Just before the time of Danny's birth my parents moved out of Parkfield into a much larger house, Rosehill, which my father had bought from Uncle Douglas when he moved on from the town clerkship of Burnley to become secretary and solicitor to the Port of London Authority. Parkfield was sold to the vicar of one of the local churches, and soon after he and his family settled in they gave a children's party to which Id and I were invited. Of course the two of us knew the house much better than even its new owners. The bathroom had, behind the enormous bathtub-cum-shower, a very deep airing cupboard, which contained the hot-water tank. In front of the tank there were slatted shelves for the sheets and towels being aired, but Id and I knew that you could scramble under the bottom shelf and find room at the back to stand, or maybe sit, virtually invisible to anyone who looked in.

Our hosts got us all into a game of hide-and-seek, and Id and I went into the airing cupboard. Of course none of the other children found us, and when, at length, all the others were found and accounted for, the grown-ups started to worry about the two of us. We could hear them opening doors and searching from room to room, and at least twice they came and looked into the airing cupboard, but saw nothing, and since we kept completely quiet, they heard nothing either. Id, recalling this prank in adult life, has often commented that she doesn't know how on earth we managed to keep quiet – we were probably in there for at least fifteen minutes. Finally, however, the growing desperation of the grown-ups must have communicated itself to us, for, waiting until the footsteps were not near, we came out and quietly made ourselves visible. Whether relief or anger triumphed I cannot now remember, but certainly we were never invited to that house again.

Even when we moved to Rosehill we were close to Scott Park, though to its other side, so we went in at a different gate, and I used to go there and play with my friends. I was small for my age, and slight in build, so I tended to be the victim rather than the aggressor when games got rough. But I had an inward secret that allowed me to feel that, in the final analysis, I had one up on my friends. At each entrance to the park there was a large noticeboard with the rules and regulations for visitors. There were no portable radios then (indeed very few of any kind) so today's standard admonition for visitors to parks, NO RADIOS, was not among them, but there were still perhaps three times as many commandments as Moses brought down from Sinai for the whole government of the human race (and all in the same negative form – 'Thou shalt not…'). At the bottom were the words 'By order of the Council, J.D. Ritchie, Town Clerk'. I always felt that, if my friends' actions got beyond the limit of the tolerable, I could scare them off by threatening 'I'll tell the town clerk about you.'

At the age of five we each in our turn went to kindergarten and three years of primary school at Mrs Kelk's Woodfield School, which was about ten minutes' walk from home. The education we received there must have been above average because, when I went on, at nine, to preparatory school, I was academically ahead of most of my companions.

Only three things stand out in my memory of Woodfield: one, being asked on my first day there if I was 'Church or Chapel' – meaning Church of England, the established Church, or Nonconformist. Since we never went to church, except in Collieston (neither of our parents professed any organised religion), I was terribly embarrassed to have to answer that I didn't know. I can't remember now what difference it would have made, since churchgoing was not part of Woodfield's curriculum, though we all, Church and Chapel indifferently, said prayers and sang hymns every morning before school began.

The second was Mrs Kelk's more-than-usually keen sense of smell. For some reason she did not permit the wearing of what are now called sneakers (but then, gym shoes) in school. It was part of her management style to walk randomly into a class, and stand at the side for a few minutes, usually in silence. But sometimes she would sniff suspiciously, and ask, 'Who's wearing gym shoes?' and some miserable five- or six-year-old would blush painfully and have to own up that, yes, he or she was.

'Tell your mother that I don't allow them, and *never* to let you come in them again,' was the terrible rebuke, in tones that often reduced the wretched miscreant to tears.

The third was an injustice that I feel to this day. Kindergarten was taught by Miss Hallard, of whom I was very fond, and who was – I could sense it even then, because she made learning to read and write fun – a good teacher. One day she divided the class into pairs, gave us some modelling clay and told each pair to make something. Other pairs made cows, or cats or flowers, and pretty crude representations they all were. I was paired with Reggie Clarkson, who was, and remained for years, a close friend. Reggie and I made a horseshoe magnet – just a flat strip bent into a U-shape – and a lot of ball bearings, little pieces of clay rolled in our hands into almost perfect balls. The others' cows didn't moo, their cats didn't purr, their flowers had no scent, but our magnet, just like a real one, picked up the balls with a touch. When Miss Hallard came round the class to see what we had all done, she had only contempt for our efforts, and let the whole of the rest of the class know it, to the terrible chagrin of Reggie and me!

Rosehill was in fact only half a house; a very big one. The original drive of the complete house had made an arc of a circle off Manchester Road, with imposing cast-iron gates at each entrance, so that each half of the divided house had its own entrance and drive. The other half was occupied by Sam Taylor, who was a town councillor, and although we children knew him by sight, in no other sense did we know him or his family. We lived back to back, both physically and metaphorically; we went out by the north drive and they by the south, so we very rarely even met, and I don't think I was ever actually inside their house. The strangeness of this impressed me at the time, and puzzles me still, for in general Burnley people were friendly, particularly neighbour to neighbour.

The two halves of the house have now been reunited and turned into a hotel, and the red sandstone of which it is built has been restored to its original pristine colour. The front door – our half had the original – occupied a beautifully made Gothic arch, and on the wall above and to the left of it was a coat of arms carved into a plaque of sandstone with, below, the motto '*Perseverando*'. You didn't need much Latin to understand the meaning of this, but my father made a little joke of it, claiming it to be the name of the man for whom it was built, an Italian called 'Percy Verando' – silly, but it still amuses me!

Once inside you found yourself in a large square hall, two and a half storeys high, with a very fine staircase of natural carved oak, with wide and shallower than usual steps, going up on your right to a halfway landing where the stairs turned left up to a gallery, as wide as the stairs, which occupied the remaining two sides of the square. The hall was lit by a large skylight shaped as a shallow pyramid on vertical side walls. In the fashion of the times of its construction, much of the glass was coloured in rather crude shades of red and blue, so the light that it might have given was a little dimmed and tinted. The right-hand wall (as you came in) of the hall was that which divided us from Sam Taylor, so that our rooms lay to the left of, and behind the hall.

On the ground floor were our living and dining rooms, both grand rooms, and beyond them what had been a ballroom – probably ten metres long and five wide, with a floor of polished oak strips. This room had not been redecorated when we moved in, and its walls were papered in an unpatterned maroon wallpaper with a matt surface. It was lit by four huge sash windows of plate glass, from a foot above the floor to a foot short of the ceiling, three on the side and one at the end, and since dances weren't likely to make many demands on the room, it became the children's playroom, with the great advantage that it didn't really ever need to be tidied. And the red walls were perfect surfaces for graffiti! The side windows looked out on to the front garden, which was embellished by a red sandstone fountain with a two-metre diameter basin on a stout column, surrounded by a hexagonal carved rail, with a shallow basin between it and the column, which was better than nothing as a place in which to sail toy boats.

Fountain apart, the garden didn't amount to much, because the earth was totally soured by the soot which had turned all the stone of the house almost black, and it would have needed more enthusiasm for gardening than either Father or Mother possessed (to say nothing of the time) to undertake the task of liming, fertilising and tilling that would have been needed to make it grow anything but dirty green grass and sad laurel shrubs. Only when the Great Depression really started to squeeze did we, as a family, attempt to get any economic advantage from it. The Taylors next door kept a few hens, and one day my father suggested that we (meaning, in practice, my mother) should follow their example; Sam Taylor had told him 'It's a nice 'obby, is a few birds,' and maybe it would be nice to be able to enjoy fresh eggs at a very low marginal cost. So part of the garden was fenced off by wire netting, and a dozen Rhode Island Reds moved in. Alas, such 'obbies didn't really suit my parents, and the project didn't last long!

Of course it was not only surroundings and neighbours that were new to us – the big difference was that we had a new sister. It was 1923 when we moved in, and times were still fairly prosperous, so we had two Irish women as cook and housemaid and an Aberdeenshire lassie as nursemaid for the baby, but Id and I still got roped in to help with Danny, presumably on the nursemaid's night off, or maybe it was even after she had left as the economic recession was closing in.

Behind the bedrooms on the first floor of the 'grand' part of the house was the 'morning room', which had presumably once been a bedroom, looking out over the back garden, and which had a bathroom next door to it. It was warmed by a gas fire with a protective fireguard around it. Here, in late afternoon, Danny used to be left in our care. The fireguard and the gas fire within did double duty; it warmed the room, and recently washed baby clothes and nappies were draped on it to get thoroughly dried and aired, while Id and I used to play with our own toys on the floor. Id's was a favourite doll, called by its makers 'Queen of Hearts' (she was appropriately dressed) but known as Queenie Artz from Id's first approximation to her name, and mine probably a clockwork train.

Danny was just starting to crawl, and of course we didn't keep her under constant observation, so that, sooner or later she would get, unobserved, to the fireguard, and grab the end of some drying garment to try to hoist herself up. The stability of the fireguard, alas, was not enough for this load and she would manage to pull guard, clothes and all, down on top of herself. She didn't get hurt, but she did get scared, and would dissolve into uncalmable howls. Id and I would both see what was happening before the fireguard had completed its fall, and would rush to pick up Danny and try – vainly – to console her. Only when my mother finally heard the crying would she come and rescue us, or rather, rescue Danny from our neglect of duty. There can be few frustrations in life greater, for a seven-year-old, than a howling one-year-old sister whom you cannot get to stop crying, and whose mother, when she arrives to take over the problem, and very quickly succeeds, looks at you in a way that clearly says 'It's all your fault.' How many times this happening actually repeated itself, heaven only knows, but I know that I dreaded those evenings in the morning room. They were not, however, the only occasions on which poor Danny was exposed to physical danger by me.

Children in the Twenties were not, as today's are, protected by the regulations of a benevolent government from dangerous, perhaps even lethal weapons, and misguided friends or relations had provided me with at least two: an axe and a bow and arrow. The former was fairly sharp and the latter not a bad small copy of Robin Hood's. There were, of course, no deer in Rosehill's back garden, and few alternative targets for my arrows, so what I learned to enjoy was to shoot my arrows vertically up into the air so that they fell to earth I knew where – to plunge deeply into the lawn. Danny was at the age where she had an afternoon sleep in her pram in the garden, parked in the middle of the lawn. But she was active enough to be able to pull herself upright in the pram and tumble out on to the grass without hurting herself, and without making any noise. Which was just as well, because one day I shot my arrow into the air, and it came down right, thump, into Danny's pram – out of which she had providentially just fallen. If she had been where she was supposed to be she could not have avoided serious injury at best.

With the axe, on the other hand, I was purely passively guilty: I had left it lying on the floor of the big playroom downstairs. Danny was still only crawling, but was widely mobile; she was in the playroom and found and picked up the axe. She was unobserved, so her actions can only be deduced from their results, thus; with the axe, she went over to one of the big, plate glass windows, and hit it a sharp blow which punched a hole, five centimetres in diameter, in the glass. Then she put one hand on the floor (the bloodstains showed this) and hit one finger with the axe. She missed all her bones and her nail, but sliced almost through the tip of one finger. Crowing with delight at her success, she crawled through to the kitchen, leaving a trail of blood along the way, to show off, with evident pride, her bleeding finger to her mother. I don't think that after these two incidents either axes or bows and arrows could have been found in the inventory of my toys for many years.

Burnley was of necessity our home, but from the age of nine my sisters and I went to boarding schools, and the summer (and sometimes the Easter) holidays we spent in Collieston. Looking back on my childhood and teenage years, the time divides naturally into three: in Burnley, we existed, in school we survived, but in Collieston we *lived*! We had friends in all three places, of course, whose accents, in Lancashire and Aberdeenshire, were not those of the 'received pronunciation', that nineteenth-century ecclesiastical version of English which was taught in public schools, and which our parents demanded of us. I say 'parents' but it was our mother who was the driving force. My father still had some traces of his Manchester boyhood in his accent; he pronounced the 'a' in words like grass and bath short, rather than as 'ah', while my mother had rid herself of every vestige of her Aberdeenshire childhood voice. The right accent was, in those far-off days, very important as an indication of one's class, which seemed to matter then.

Luckily, Id and I were – we still are – natural mimics, so when we played with our Burnley friends we could talk as broad a Lancashire (not only a question of accent, but of vocabulary too) as they, and in Collieston we spoke the real 'Buchan Doric'. This was (and I have to use the past tense, because it is, alas, dying out) the dialect of Buchan. Lancashire was to some extent understandable to ordinary English-speakers, but the Doric was – and is – far from it. So we had, Id and I, the means of talking to each other in public places in a language that those around us could barely understand. And didn't we have fun making use of that ability!

Uncle Walter also lived in Burnley, with his wife, Lucy, and two unmarried daughters, Peggy and Dolly (Dorothea). Their home, Palace House, was about two kilometres from us, and we, my father, Id and I, used to walk, or if it was raining, take the tram over there after an early supper on most Sunday evenings. At any rate in the early years, Danny didn't come with us; she couldn't yet walk the distance and my mother stayed at home with her.

Auntie Lucy was the sweetest person, with the great gift of making children at ease, whereas I remember Uncle Walter as one of the dourest people I have ever met. I avoided speaking in his presence whenever I could, and while he made one of the company there were no smiles and little conversation, and even Auntie Lucy's charm was blanketed. Luckily, Uncle Walter liked to go to bed early (and I suspect that he didn't find the company of children of our ages at all agreeable). So after we had been there for half an hour or so, sitting in gloomy silence or listening to the forced conversation of our elders, he would rise solemnly to his feet, ignore the rest of the company, say, 'Well, goodnight, Mrs Southern,' and go off upstairs. As soon as we could no longer hear his footsteps, the atmosphere lightened, Dolly went off to the kitchen to make tea and bring the biscuits, Peggy might go and get her cello and play to us, and Auntie Lucy got us all talking and laughing (not, of course, loudly enough to disturb Uncle Walter!) and the rest of the evening passed happily and all too quickly.

These walks and tram rides were occasions for me to get to know my father. He was a quiet man, not self-assertive unless his principles were engaged, with an enormously wide general knowledge, and (though it was later that I really got to know and appreciate this) a very deep knowledge of the English language and literature, and with a natural affinity for children. He never talked down to us, and when he laughed at some childish error, it was laughter that you absolutely knew had nothing of criticism in it. I remember soon after we moved to Rosehill, and I was just learning to spell, an occasion when my mother and father were sitting in front of the fire in the sitting room. I came in and announced: 'I'm just going upstairs to *w-o-s-h* my hands.'

Both parents laughed, and my father said, 'You mean *w-a-s-h.*'

I riposted, 'No, that would be *wash,*' (to rhyme with *ash*), so my father explained that, alas, English wasn't necessarily bound by what seemed to be the rules, and gave me some other examples, like *woz*, but *haz*, which, by opening my eyes to possible traps, helped me take a big step in the art of spelling!

He had lived many years as a bachelor in Burnley, and he was a great walker, so he knew all of the surrounding countryside within a radius of fifteen miles or more (because one could take the bus to get to a starting point away out of Burnley). Unlike the town itself, much of the surrounding country is beautiful, and there are lovely walks. What we enjoyed most were those that were divided into two by lunch at a pub – the Waddington Fell Inn and the Devonshire Arms at Bolton Abbey (then just a coaching inn, but now transformed by the Duchess of Devonshire into a modern hotel) were our two favourites!

Before we were too far on our way he would go into one of the small tobacconist-newsagent-confectioner's shops that were open on Sundays, and slip into his pocket a half-pound slab of chocolate, sometimes Terry's bitter for his taste, but often, for Id's, Cadbury's milk chocolate with Brazil nuts. He would ration this out among us, so that by the time it was finished we were nearing home – or at least the bus stop for the homeward journey. (It was the price of this chocolate that first brought home to me what I now know as the deflation caused by the Depression. In 1926 a half-pound of chocolate cost a shilling; by 1933 this had come down to eight pence – a reduction of one-third; the retail price index fell from 6.3 in 1926 to 4.9 in 1933; most personal incomes came down by a much larger fraction.)

While we walked, he would recite poetry, of which he had a huge store in his memory. Our favourite was George Canning's satirical 'The needy knife-grinder and the Friend of Humanity', written in Sapphic stanzas. This is in the form of a theatrical dialogue, of which my father played the parts of the stage directions and both characters. I haven't seen or heard the poem for years, but I can listen in my memory to my father's voice, and see him making all the appropriate gestures, jumping from one side of us to the other as he switched characters, without noticeably retarding the progress of our walk.

It was in a tram going down Manchester Road with my father on our way to go for a walk somewhere that I learned more about the Depression. In 1930 there had been three hundred chimneys from coal-fired mills and mines – Burnley had been the largest cotton weaving centre in the world before World War I – and they all burned Burnley-mined coal. The slump that began with the General Strike in 1926 started to reduce the number of working mills and, in parallel, the coal mines – or 'pits' as they were called – that fed them. The onset of the Depression accelerated the decline until there were perhaps only a couple of dozen chimneys still alive, so that the amount of sooty smoke discharged into the atmosphere was much lessened.

Manchester Road is a steep incline down into Burnley Centre, so from the tram you could see into and across the town. This was a beautiful early spring day, and behind Burnley, Pendle Hill bathed in sunshine looked glorious. I said to my father, 'Dad, isn't Pendle Hill a beautiful sight today?' The trams on this route were single-deckers, with one long wooden seat along each side. There were not many people in the tram, but a few feet down from us on the other side was a man, from his clothes a typical weaver (dark, coarse woollen jacket and trousers, flat cloth cap, collarless shirt with a scarf round his neck, and clogs – leather uppers on wooden soles with steel 'clog-irons' underneath to reduce wear on the wood).

He turned on me and said, in a voice full of despairing anger, 'No, it's bloody well not beautiful. You shouldn't be able to see that for t'smoke. All them bloody chimneys should be belchin' out black, because that'd mean that there'd be men workin' – and to 'ell wi' Pendle 'Ill.'

Tram rides, and other occasions of close proximity with one's fellow men, made one all too aware of another effect of the Depression – that people couldn't afford soap, so that bodies at best got washed in cold water, and clothes not at all.

Down at the bottom of Bridge Street was a shop I used to pass every now and again. It sold working people's clothing, and in its window displayed small piles of underwear of the cheapest kind – long underpants and undervests for men, and their equivalents for women. Cheap cotton then had a sort of pale grey colour tinged with pink, but the piles in this shop were acquiring a coating of sooty dust, which week by week got noticeably worse. At the depth of the Depression Burnley's level of unemployment was one of the highest in the country, and poverty was extreme. Faces were grey and hopeless, limbs were wasted, and nobody whose family was hit by unemployment could afford to buy new underwear, indeed, nothing beyond shelter and food. In some of the economic recessions that we have been through since 1945, I have heard people say: 'This is getting to be as bad as the Depression,' and it makes me mad! Until you have smelt those unwashed people, seen their hunger and felt their loss of hope – and often, with hope, their sense of self-respect – until you have seen the little children running about with bare bottoms for want of knickers, like the TV pictures from Haiti, *no one* can have any idea of what the Great Depression was like. And I passionately hope that no one of the generations younger than I ever will have.

It was the working people, who had no financial reserves, that were hardest hit, of course, but very few at any economic or social level escaped. Our own standard of living dropped very quickly. My father's was essentially a family practice, so its principal source of income was from conveyancing, and during a depression virtually no properties, private or commercial, change hands. Moreover, many bills incurred before the worst of the times remained unpaid, and (while trying to enforce payment in any case would have been trying to get blood out of a stone) it was not in my father's nature to press too hard – the defaulters were probably worse off than he was. But he told me later that his income essentially ceased in 1930, and that for several years we lived on his capital. But there were no more servants, no luxuries, and repairs to the house were just postponed. One very cold winter night a water pipe froze above the ceiling of the bedroom in which I slept, and a drip came through the plaster. My father went up to try to stop the leak, and his foot slipped off the rafter in the attic and went through the sodden plaster. Neither that hole nor the one that Danny made in the playroom window got mended as long as I lived in the house. All this notwithstanding, our parents did their best to shield their children, and (though pocket money was short) we remained in our boarding schools, and never missed a summer in Collieston.

Chapter Eight

Boarding Schools

It was an American who said, 'Oh, yes; you British upper classes, you keep your dogs at home and send your children away.' We were not, of course, of the upper classes as Dickens or Trollope would have known them; we were upper middle class, and the time had vanished when solicitors would not be included in the definition of 'gentlemen' (whereas barristers were), but we aspired to that level of education and manner of speech that at any rate opened the upper levels of the job market. And two generations ago the accepted way of achieving these was by going to a boarding school, and not just *any* boarding school, but one of those one hundred and fifty schools which were represented at the Headmasters' Conference, and thus entitled to call themselves 'public' schools. This is essentially an English institution. There are a few Scottish public schools, but they really used to exist to de-Scotticise Scots children to make them better able to compete with the English, which, except when a 'correct' accent was important, any Scottish school could do. All societies have classes of some sort, and most have ways of speaking that denote geographical origins. And alongside the regional differences are others which indicate, to some extent, a level of education. How, otherwise, could *My Fair Lady* (of which the basis is that 'It's "Aow" and "Garn" that keep her in her place') have been so successful in places as diverse as

Austria, Brazil and Japan? But England is (maybe *was*) alone in producing a class whose speech had lost any trace of regional identity, and instead set you apart as having been educated in a certain kind of school. I have often wondered that this could still be a desideratum, when in every economic activity communication is so very important. I have often wished, when a naval officer and later a manager in industry, that I spoke in the same way as the petty officer or foreman that I was trying to persuade to strive for promotion, when from his point of view he must have seen the accent difference as 'Between us and you there is a great gulf fixed.' I wonder if this is not one of the reasons why I have enjoyed passing a lot of my working life in countries where *my* accent was the odd man out.

Digressions aside, it was the culture of the time of our youth that these things were of supreme importance, not only the question of how you spoke, but the belief that the public schools were essential for 'character-building', and that really only those that were also boarding schools did this part of the job properly, so this was the course on which we were launched at the age of nine. Nine, because the door into the public school system led through 'preparatory schools', in which you spent four years preparing for greater things.

The school to which I was sent, Mill Mead in Shrewsbury had, like all private schools then, a list of the clothes which every boy must have, and a recommended shop from which they could be acquired. Not surprisingly there was only one which found it worthwhile to stock items of uniform for which the market was fifty boys, and which therefore could charge prices that inevitably represented some degree of monopolist's profit. By the beginning of the school year in the autumn of 1926 the family was beginning to feel some economic tightness; the General Strike of early May had caused the loss of over

160 million work days nationwide, and Burnley was hit particularly hard. So my mother decided that, rather than buy, she would make me some shorts by cutting down a cast-off pair of my father's trousers, and knit me the required white sweater. Though my mother was normally a good seamstress, these garments must have been designed to allow for ten years of growth – the shorts were too long and too wide, and the sweater, after its first wash, reached my knees. She was, alas, totally insensitive to the need of children not to be different from their peers! I was very homesick for my first few days away from home – nothing unusual in that – but my embarrassment at these dreadful clothes was painful in the extreme. I imagine that the headmaster (or the matron) must have written to my mother to advise her of this problem because, in some way that I cannot now remember, the offending garments were replaced by shop-bought ones, and my misery was almost ended – almost, because (little boys being what they are) it was some time before my schoolmates allowed me to forget what I had had to wear.

Once the first few weeks of homesickness and humiliation were behind me, I enjoyed the school, and I learned much from it. It was small; we were fifty boys, divided into four forms, numbered upwards from fourth to first, the opposite direction from public schools which usually started from third and went on up to sixth. The curriculum included English, French, Latin (and in the last year, the beginnings of Greek), history, ancient – Latin and Greek – history, and scripture, for our minds (and, in the case of the last, our souls). Our bodies were taken care of by games: soccer in the winter term, hockey in the spring, cricket in the summer. All year round we had boxing (which I hated), gymnastics, and in the summer, swimming. There were some extra subjects, which you could take for an additional fee; among these were carpentry, which I took, and piano, which I started. This latter was taught by a middle-aged man, who chain-smoked cigarettes, which, once lit, he kept between his lips, to one side of centre. His hair, his eyebrows and his moustache were grey, except that where the smoke drifted upwards it left brown tobacco smoke patches on all three, and on one of his nostrils. He (and I don't think he was by any means unique among his kind) made no effort to let us see that pianos could make music, and we learned scales, repeated *ad nauseam*. They were made even more nauseating by the fact that he hung over you, watching your fingering, and from time to time the ash fell off his cigarette on to the keys, and he would take out his handkerchief and flick it off on to the floor, some inevitably not getting past your trousers. One term was enough of this for me, and it put me off music as an active affair for the rest of my life – I became an exemplar of what Sir Thomas Beecham said of the British: 'They know nothing about music; they don't understand it, but they just love the noise it makes.'

Every Sunday we went to the huge, ugly Victorian parish church of St Giles for morning service. The vicar, who was the normal preacher, was very dull, and so we had lots of time to read in the early pages of the Book of Common Prayer such fascinating things as how to find the date of Easter, the Thirty-Nine Articles (of the Protestant faith) and the 'Table of Kindred and Affinity…' which laid down that 'A man may not marry his grandmother' or, later, 'his granddaughter'. On the other hand, we heard virtually the whole Bible read as the lessons, and we learned by heart the Canticles and the best hymns and psalms. Much of this has stayed with me, and I am still sometimes surprised to find that I know more of the Bible than even, sad to say, some of my clergymen friends.

The school was a private enterprise of two partners, F.F. Sandford and A.T. Bennion. The former, the headmaster, was a short, balding, dumpy man with a strong facial resemblance to Mr Punch (a hooked nose and a protruding chin that looked as if they would soon meet) so he of course was known as Punch. Bennion was tall, spare, almost stringy, and always – apparently at any rate – in a bad humour. He was known by a play on his initials as 'Batey B.' (Has the meaning of 'bate' as 'anger' fallen into desuetude? It's years since I heard it used, perhaps not since I left Mill Mead.) They both taught, and presumably shared the administration and profits of the school between them, while three 'assistant masters' (recent graduates from universities) did the rest of the teaching and organised and oversaw the games. A retired army sergeant taught boxing and gymnastics, and a matron took care of our health and hygiene and made sure our wardrobes were up to standard.

Punch and Batey B. were both wielders of the ultimate disciplinary sanction; they both kept canes in reserve and we all knew that egregious misconduct could earn up to six strokes on the bottom. But either they were unusually tolerant for men in their positions in those days of 'spare the rod and spoil the child' or we were unusually well behaved, for I cannot remember more than five or six boys getting caned during the four years I was there. But, just in case, Punch kept a couple of canes hanging on the corner of a cupboard in his study, right in the line of sight of any boy who was summoned there, so perhaps that warning was awful enough.

I was never any good at organised games, though I did learn to swim well, but the contempt with which I and my ilk – I wasn't alone – were held by those who could score goals and hit boundaries was moderate, and didn't bother me much. And as I began to do noticeably well academically, friendships formed across the lines of our different talents, and hobbies and taste in reading became stronger bonds than cricket.

My father had a barely detectable but nevertheless real stammer. So I imagine I had some sort of hereditary tendency in this regard, for when I was at Mill Mead I developed one of my own, which was, for a few years, a bad case. And of course, the embarrassment caused by the disability only makes it worse. However, one learns to cope; breathing, adding a vowel sound before the 'trap' consonants – for me, D and R particularly – singing, or shouting. They say that stammer or stutter starting in mid-childhood is probably of psychogenic origin, even when it builds on heredity. I spent eight years at boarding schools, and for the most part enjoyed them, but I cannot help feeling that parents, particularly those that have not themselves been to boarding schools, simply do not appreciate the stress that being cut off from one's family and being subject to a totally strange form of regulation of one's life can inflict on a nine-year-old, and that this stress may manifest itself in the form of a speech impediment.

Let me not seem in any way to be blaming my parents; they were doing what they very sincerely felt would be best for me, and in the outcome probably was: 'the ifs of history' again! Looking back now, and seeing the sorts of life my grandchildren enjoy, I have a slight sense of being short-changed in *family* life – and I wish my mother had been more sensitive. But experiences in life, like persons, come in whole packages, and you cannot have the good parts without the less than good. Anyway, I have no reason to complain, since my stammer gradually went away, and now manifests itself to me – it has long since not been detectable to others – no more than a few times a year, and it has never affected my various careers.

Scholastically, I did well at Mill Mead, though it was only a very small pond, and I won the form prize in each of the four years I was there. This (in discussions to which I was not privy) led to the conclusion that I ought to be able to get a scholarship to a public school, which I imagine was almost a necessity in the economics of 1930, if my education was to continue at a boarding school. My parents, presumably with information and advice from Messrs Sandford and Bennion, entered me in the competition for a scholarship to Marlborough. Then Uncle Douglas persuaded my father that I should also make a try at Eton, which was, and probably still is, regarded as the quintessential public school, offering all the intangible advantages of such establishments in the highest degree. Thus it came about that, towards the end of the summer term of 1930, my mother took me to London (it was the first time in my life I had been south of Derbyshire) and on to Eton for the interview that was part of the process of the election of King's Scholars. I suppose that we went to Marlborough as well, and somewhere I sat for two written exams.

Before I left Mill Mead there was still one ritual to go through. We all became aware that this was in store, but we all – well, maybe not all, but I for one anyway – were totally ignorant of what it was to be. It was known as 'Punch's pi-jaw', and was Punch's pathetic effort to warn us of the potential dangers of homosexual advances from older boys at your public school. There was no such thing as sex education then, and since very few of us had reached puberty, it was very difficult for a headmaster with the best will in the world to get his story across if he was unwilling to explain what his elaborately encoded words and phrases really meant, and I came out after half an hour in his study not one whit the wiser than when I went in. And since we were absolutely forbidden to discuss the subject of the pi-jaw with any other boy, ignorant I remained for a long time.

Jumping ahead in time, but on the same subject, during my last year at Eton the master in college, J.C.V. Wilkes, came into my room one night to find me reading Havelock Ellis's *Studies in the Psychology of Sex* which I had borrowed from one of my older and more worldly-wise friends, John Waterlow. I was unable to hide the book in time, and Wilkes said, 'Oh, so that's what you're reading. I had been intending to talk to you about that subject, but I see I'm too late.'

Eton, or to give it its full name, The King's College of the Blessed Mary at Eton beside Windsor, was founded in 1440 by King Henry VI for four purposes: to fill the gap in education left by the decline of the monasteries; to counter such influence of the Lollards as might escape his grandfather's statute *De Heretico Comburendo*;[1] to be a place where masses might be sung for the soul of his father, Henry V, and an almshouse. His original foundation consisted of a provost, ten sad (in its archaic meaning of 'serious') priests, four clerks, six choristers, twenty-five infirm beadsmen (who received alms for saying prayers as they told their beads) a schoolmaster and twenty-five poor scholars. Four years later, he revised this to an even more overhead-heavy constitution – a provost, one hundred other priests, ten chaplains, ten clerks, sixteen choristers, thirteen poor infirm men, a schoolmaster, an usher (assistant schoolmaster) and seventy poor scholars. It was Henry's intention that his scholars should all take holy orders, and in the year after the foundation of Eton he founded King's College at Cambridge. To this college Eton scholars had preferential entry, and for centuries, if you played your cards right (you supported the king's religious views, you remained unmarried and avoided too flagrant fornication and peculation), you could progress from King's Scholar at Eton to scholar of King's, then by way of classical tutor at Eton to fellow of King's, and have board, lodging

[1]That the heretic is to be burned.

and a stipend for your lifetime.

But King Henry from the start wished his school's education to be cast more widely than just to his scholars, and so his statutes provided that it should be extended to not more than twenty 'commensales' – sharers of the table – who would have to pay. By today, of course, the modern descendants of his commensales, the Oppidans, or town boys, outnumber the collegers by fifteen to one.

Henry never managed to finish the great church he had planned as the heart of his school, and even what was intended as the choir (and is now the school chapel, with room for eight or nine hundred worshippers) was not finished when Henry was for a time supplanted on the throne by Edward IV – indeed not until more than a decade after Henry's death. Henry endowed the school very richly with lands, most of which form part of what is now east London, so the value of the income has pretty well kept pace with the rise in the cost of education. This endowment was supplemented in the early days by the grant of papal indulgences and dispensations to penitents who went to Eton on the Feast of the Assumption, and the grant to the provost of the power to hear confession and grant absolution – clearly, in accordance with the custom of the times, against some payment to the college – and by the confiscation of the revenues of the English subsidiary 'cells' of some Norman priories.

The number of *seventy* poor scholars had been strictly adhered to since that time, except in some low periods of the school's fortunes, when sufficient candidates could not be found, until very recently when some flexibility at the margin has been introduced to admit a very desirable candidate or reject one whom the strict numbers would have let in, but did not seem quite up to standard. While the largest number of boys leaving in a year did so at the end of the school year in July, some also left in December and April. Scholars are elected by the provost and fellows, on the basis of an examination, and the interview referred to above. But, since the number of boys who would leave during the year to come was never precisely known, the number who could be admitted was also unknown. Most boys spend four or five years at Eton, so each Election consists of somewhere between fourteen and eighteen boys. Whatever number the 1930 Election actually had, I was, in the summer, two below the cut-off point on the list.

Accordingly we (my parents, rather than I – I was a passive participant only) had to settle for our second choice, and at Marlborough I had won a scholarship with no ifs and buts, so in September there I went. I didn't like Marlborough. It was founded in the mid-nineteenth century as a school for sons of the clergy and its culture was much influenced by the ideas of 'Muscular Christianity'. It laid great stress on the 'character-forming' part of education, perceived as vigorous games, cross-country runs and little if any heating in the premises. It was academically successful, despite (or perhaps in part because of) the fact that it believed in corporal punishment as an aid to learning. I was summoned one evening by my housemaster and hauled over the coals for not being good enough at my Latin verses, or Greek verbs or something, and then made to bend over the chair and submit to three strokes of the cane. This was, of course, in conformity with the long traditions of English education, though I couldn't understand then, and still can't, how leaving three weals on a boy's bottom, the hurt of which took a week to pass completely, could possibly have an advantageous effect on his capacity to learn.

Marlborough only lasted two terms, however (by which time of course I was beginning to dislike it less), for during the spring term I received the news that two boys hitherto not taken into the calculation at Eton would be leaving, so therefore I (and one other) had places in the 1930 Election, and would be going to the school at the beginning of the summer 'half' (as the school term of one-third of a year was called at Eton). In anticipation change always has its downside; the unknown is in some way to be feared, and suddenly I would have preferred familiar Marlborough to frightening Eton – the Spanish saying has it that *'mas vale malo conocido que bueno por conocer'*.[2] Moreover, though I didn't appreciate this until much later, its education at that time was broader than that of Eton: maths, science, history, geography and modern languages got a bigger share of the available time, and music (in the form of choral singing, at any rate) was not, as at Eton, just an extra subject. I have no musical sense – I cannot sing in tune – but in my first few days at Marlborough I passed a test in singing (to the Spanish this kind of unlikely occurrence is known as 'the donkey played the flute'!) and became part of the treble section of the choir. We were preparing the first part of Handel's *Messiah* for a performance later in the school year, and sang some of the sections in chapel. It is still one of my favourite pieces of music, and I know large bits of it by heart, if not in exact tune!

At Marlborough our uniform was not too far distant (in shape, if not colour) from everyday clothes; Eton boys wore, until they were five feet four inches tall, a short black 'Eton' jacket – a 'bum-freezer' – and waistcoat, striped trousers, and a white shirt with a black tie in an 'Eton collar' – the frustum of a starched white cone, open at the front, of which the narrow end fitted round your neck and the wider rested outside your jacket. When you had grown tall enough, this garb was replaced by nineteenth-century morning dress, consisting of a black cutaway tailcoat and waistcoat, striped trousers, white shirt and a starched collar

---

[2]The bad you know is worth more than the good yet to be known.

with, between its two points, a space about four centimetres wide, occupied by a narrow bow tie, made of white cambric, folded on the bias to a finished width of two centimetres, with its two ends tucked under the points of the collar.

Both these outfits were crowned by a silk top hat, and if you were 'in college', that is to say a King's Scholar, you wore, to chapel and to classes, a black broadcloth scholastic gown down to your knees, and for chapel on Sundays a white surplice. For games, of course, you wore appropriate clothes, with a cricket-type cap to identify your athletic achievements, if you had any, and otherwise a cap that marked you as a 'scug', one who had no school or house colours. There were geographical limits (and, I'm sure, day of the week ones too) on the wearing of various degrees of formal or informal wear. The boundaries were Barnes Pool Bridge, by which Eton College was separated from the town of Eton, and Windsor Bridge, across which you were in Windsor, and Berkshire rather than Buckinghamshire. Memory is dim as to exactly what the distinctions were, but it went something like this, for a colleger. North of Barnes Pool Bridge, a tweed jacket instead of the tailcoat of the uniform, with a cap instead of a top hat. South of it, tailcoat and gown; in Windsor, both gown and top hat.

The heart of Eton is the college, two contiguous quadrangles of buildings, of which the western, School Yard, is the larger, presided over by a bronze statue of the founder in its centre. The south side of School Yard is the chapel, the west is pierced by the gate which shuts off the school from Eton High Street, and has as its upper storey Upper School and the headmaster's rooms. The north side's ground floor is the original schoolroom, and over that is Long Chamber, in which all of Henry VI's seventy scholars slept – and not even with a bed each! Now the fifteen most junior members of college sleep in the left half of it, each in his own cubicle divided from the central passage by curtains. The rest of the old Long Chamber, and the century and a half old New Buildings at right angles to it to the north, provide living quarters for the remaining fifty-five collegers, each in a study bedroom of his own. The furnishings of the cubicles in Chamber and in the rooms were essentially the same; a bed that folded up against the wall and behind a curtain, a 'burry' (drop-leaf desk), a Windsor chair (and in rooms, a wicker armchair), drawers and hooks for your clothes, a washbasin with cold running water, a painted tinplate bath hanging on the wall, and a hot-water can, also of painted tinplate, of a design familiar to anyone who has seen on television a Victorian housemaid carrying hot water upstairs. We were better off than Victorian maids; we had ample supplies of very hot water only a horizontal carry away. With a canful of this, diluted, with the aid of a small-diameter rubber hose known as a siphon, by cold water from your basin, you could bathe not uncomfortably in your room. Once (or was it twice?) a week you had your turn to use the very large tub baths in the bathrooms, and when you came in from games there were showers, with roses a foot in diameter, under which, at a pinch, three boys could shower at the same time.

The east side of School Yard is dominated by the architectural feature most portrayed on postcards of Eton – Lupton's Tower, built by Roger Lupton, who became provost in 1504, and through the arch of which you pass into the Cloisters, and on the right the broad steps that lead up to College Hall. This is a splendid medieval building, with stone walls, and a huge stone fireplace set in an elaborately carved oak-canopied screen at the end opposite the door, where the floor is raised to make a dais for the high table. The kitchens are off the main hall to the left of the high table – perhaps so that the great ones who sat there could receive their dinner hotter than the hoi polloi. There had been times when the provost and fellows systematically misappropriated the funds destined for the feeding of the collegers, who were reduced to a diet of one meal a day, always the same: mutton, bread and beer – the last brewed in Brewhouse Yard behind College Hall. By the Thirties, however, our food was always good, and not only good, but varied and plentiful, and when I used to hear from friends at other schools of food that vied with that of hospitals, it was difficult to resist the temptation to be smugly boastful about Henry VI's legacy to our appetites!

So, at the end of April 1931 I became a resident of Long Chamber – the 'Long' is usually omitted – and a wearer of a bum-freezer and an Eton collar. I was in the lower half of the fourth form, with a programme of education based largely on the classics, and I was bound in servitude as a 'fag' to a boy in the sixth form called Peter Blundell, and to any other member of the sixth form who wanted some menial task done for him and called out 'Here!' – in Oppidan houses the summons was 'Boy!'

Looking back, I believe that, at any rate in what Eton should have excelled in, we were very badly taught; too many of the masters were 'lost in the mists and quagmires of medievalism', and we studied four dead languages – Latin, Greek, Chaucerian English and French. I know that French (despite some of the efforts of the Académie Française) is not a dead language, but you would never have guessed it from what we were taught. Learning slugs of stuff by heart, knowing the verbs and the grammar, 'unseen' translations and writing verses were what mattered. Never did we think about the beauty of the *Odes* of Horace, the fun of the comedies of Aristophanes, the 'surge and thunder of the *Odyssey*', nor of the possibility that you could actually communicate with other people in French. Not even did we learn what constitutes a Greek tragedy; I found that out by my own reading later on in life. Thank heaven, for the sake of the utilitarian side of education, mathematics and science were better served.

Eton differed (and I believe still differs) from most other public schools in two principal ways. First, an Oppidan boy will have two masters to whom he refers as 'm'tutor'. One of these is his housemaster, the other his private tutor (the colleger's equivalent of housemaster is the master in college, who isn't referred to as m'tutor, so the colleger has only one tutor).

A boy is taught different subjects by various masters, but he has also special relationships with his tutor or tutors. His housemaster is, first of all, his boarding-house keeper – he supplies him with room and board – and then his moral guardian, and the general supervisor of his behaviour and progress in the school. But he has no direct disciplinary role. A boy's private tutor is his educational guide and counsellor; and sees to it that work that has to be prepared before a class is done. For this purpose a tutor holds 'pupil-room' (or 'puppy-hole') in which junior boys will have to do their preparation under his watchful eye, while more senior ones are left to do it in a place and at a time of their own choosing – though m'tutor would always be available for help. This system, which I calculated left me, after my first year, to do half of my work in my own time, was a very valuable bit of learning for later life. The private tutor also saw his boys once a week for 'private business' in which something outside the general curriculum would be studied in depth or width at the tutor's discretion. The master who taught you Latin, for example, would send to your tutor, by you as messenger, a report card of your place in class and so on, or if he thought that you were not doing well enough by your own fault, a complaining 'ticket'. It was then up to your tutor to try to get you back on the rails. Before I became a science specialist, my classical tutor was H.G.C.

Streatfield, who sent for me one day to tell me that I was spending too much time at the School of Mechanics. This, now called the School of Technology and Design, was a voluntary extra-curricular activity, where from three extraordinarily good teachers you could learn woodworking, metalworking and electricity and electronics, which at that time meant radios and radiograms (though we had one boy, absolutely hopeless academically, who built a primitive television receiver operating on the Baird system).

'Ritchie,' said m'tutor, 'you spend too much time at the School of Mechanics.'

'Yes, sir,' I replied aloud in a tone of contrition; and under my breath I added, 'yes, sir, three bags full!' And I resolved that I would in future observe the sailor's eleventh commandment – 'Thou shalt not get found out'; that I would just make sure that my school work was of a high enough standard for me to get by and go on spending as much time as before at the School of Mechanics.

I said that the teachers there were extraordinarily good. One had to do a year confined to wood and to complete a test piece before you were allowed to graduate to metal. Although there were tools available for common use, we were encouraged to acquire our own basics – a plane, three chisels and a gouge, and a tenon saw – and were taught how to keep them sharp; learning on the way the fact that blunt tools are far more dangerous than sharp ones, and that while you keep your own tools sharp, nobody has the responsibility for common-use ones. We were taught how to use all the usual tools, how to make joints, how to glue, and how to sand to a smooth finish.

I cannot now remember what the woodworking test was, but I know that at some stage (with help and supervision) I made out of mahogany – although a 'hard' wood, very easy to work – a box, about ten inches by eight by four with secret dovetail corners. These are time-consuming to make, and require accurate workmanship, and you learn to observe the woodworker's first rule – 'Measure twice, and *then* cut once' – but when done are a source of great satisfaction, mostly because they *are* secret. They are made by cutting dovetail joints in the two thirds of the thickness of the wood that will be the inside of the box, and cutting the remaining third at forty-five degrees, so that when you fit the dovetails together, the chamfered edges meet to form a right-angled corner so that you cannot see the dovetail joint either from inside or out.

When my box was made, I was encouraged to veneer the whole of the outside of the box (completed with a top and bottom of wood thinner than the sides, and then sawn into two parts to make box and lid, hinged together and fitted with a mortise lock) and finally to French polish it.

When you had reached a sufficient level of competence with flat wood, you could start on the lathe. To put between the centres a length of wood, sawn roughly to an octagonal section, start up the lathe and tentatively ease the cutting edge of a turning gouge into the wood and, as the cuttings cover your apron, slowly draw the tool along the length of the workpiece, see it become a cylinder – that is to know just what Keats meant when he '...felt... like some watcher of the skies/When a new planet swims into his ken'. And to go on from there and turn the raw cylinder into a spindle of swelling curves and sharp grooves, which can be bored down the middle and matched to a base turned, not between centres but on a faceplate, to become a table lamp, and a Christmas present for someone – that is joy indeed.

One year I made two coffee tables, of the kind that has a round top fifty centimetres in diameter supported on a turned spindle, which in turn stands on three curved legs. One was mahogany and the other walnut, and I gave them as Christmas presents to my mother and Auntie Peggy.

Our woodworking instructor also helped me develop another skill: carving. I thought it would be fun to make a figurehead for my little boat in Collieston. He introduced me to yellow pine, the pattern-maker's wood; soft, easy to cut, not prone to splitting and which would hold a sharp edge. Out of a piece of this we made, during my last half, a female head, chin up and long hair streaming back. Alas, I didn't have any measurements of the stem-head of the boat at Eton, and in Collieston I didn't have the tools to do the fitting, so *Amaryllis II* never got her figurehead, but I had learned to carve.

The metalworking test piece was deceptively simple. You started by cutting, with a hacksaw, a ten centimetre piece off a length of rolled steel bar five centimetres by two centimetres. This alone took some learning; the natural tendency is to try to push down too hard and to saw too fast, when slow, deliberate and straight, without rocking, is the correct technique. This lump of steel had no plane surfaces except the saw cuts; the other four sides were slightly convex and of uneven surface. You put it into a vice and started to shape it with files – coarser to start with and then finer to get out the marks of the first. The art of filing itself needs learning; you have to hold the handle of the file with the thumb of your right hand along it, and your four fingers wrapped around it, while the left hand steadies the tip of the file. The motion is produced, not by your arms, which would result in the file being rocked, making a rounded surface, but by keeping your arms and hands still with respect to your trunk, and swinging the body on bended knees, so that the file always stays parallel to the ground.

The task was to produce a right-angled parallelepiped (a solid contained by rectangles) to a high degree of accuracy. This took probably two months of the time that could be spared from academic seriousness. After you had got one of the two larger surfaces reasonably flat by filing, and had got rid of the visible file marks, you moved on to a scraper and a surface plate, a piece of steel about forty centimetres square, and with a perfectly flat surface. On this you spread a kind of greasy, dark blue ink, and in it rubbed your workpiece. Any high spots showed up blue, and with a scraper you removed these, rubbed again, scraped again and on and on until your surface came out uniformly blue. Then, with a micrometer, you tested your piece for uniformity of thickness, and then back to the blue ink and the scraper, until you had two flat planes, parallel to one another to an accuracy of a few hundredths of a millimetre. Then the remaining four sides, to a slightly less demanding standard of flatness, but with right angles as accurate as could be seen with a try-square, and finally you filed a chamfered edge around one of the large faces – 'At forty-five degrees, not forty-four degrees or forty-six degrees,' said the instructor! (He was a retired chief engine room artificer of the Royal Navy, and his skills, patience and abilities as a teacher prepared me for the excellence of these ratings when I met them in the Navy in the years ahead.) When the rectangle was completed, you had to find its centre, by intersecting scribed diagonals on its non-chamfered – to become its lower – face, mark it with a centre punch, and drill a hole through it, and countersink the hole on the bottom face.

Then, as in woodwork, from the flat to the round. You started with a seven centimetre length of brass rod two and a half centimetres in diameter, and set it up in the lathe. Normally, metal turning is done with the aid of a slide rest, adjusted by handles on screw threads which moved the tool in and out, and the rest itself back and forth along the axis of the lathe, but at the beginning we were restricted to a tool rest and hand-held tools. You had two tools: one, a 'graver', made of a piece of round tool steel a centimetre in diameter, ground to a square section at the end and then ground off at an angle to make a diamond-shaped cutting edge; the other was square in section and ground to a half-round cutting edge, so that you could make round grooves.

With these we turned the piece of brass, freehand, into a knob consisting of an almost complete sphere with a short neck broadening out into a shoulder about six millimetres thick, with a stem to fit through the hole in the steel – a typical knob, in fact. This completed, the two pieces were fitted together, the surplus of the brass stem through the hole in the steel cut off, and the end of the stem riveted by a ball-pane hammer, and, voilà, a paperweight!

I have written this lengthy digression, not to give the reader lessons in artisanship, but to explain why I have so often in my life, since Eton, said, 'H.G.C.S., you were wrong. Weighing the worth of what I learned in the School of Mechanics against those things that you felt I was neglecting, I should have spent *more* time there!'

The other big difference between Eton and other schools was in the discipline. When I was caned at Marlborough, my housemaster did it. At Eton corporal punishment was administered by the headmaster with a birch, on a bare bottom, and for grave offences only, reported by one of the masters and put 'on the bill'; by a member of 'Pop', the Eton Society; by a member of one's house 'library', or in college, of the college sixth form. In Chamber there was another level; the Captain of Chamber had the right to beat any of his charges with a siphon – the rubber tube with which one filled one's bathtub. So, if a housemaster adjudged that a boy in his house should be caned, he asked his library to have it done. He could even ask for a 'general tanning'; that every boy in the house should be beaten for an offence which was not traceable to one culprit, but which was sufficiently egregious that the housemaster was not prepared to allow impunity. In my time I think there was only one case of a 'GT', and that may have been apocryphal, but, '*Se non è vero, è ben trovato*.'[3] One of the boys' houses then was J.C. ('Jackie') Chute's. Jackie's wife was annoyed by some unruliness among the lower boys, and caused a notice to be put up on the noticeboard saying: 'Mrs Chute cannot conceive why the lower boys make so much noise.' In the morning this was found to have been edited to read: 'Mrs Chute cannot conceive. Why? The lower boys make so much noise.'[4] No villain could be found, so Jackie (or perhaps his wife) requested his house library to carry out a GT.

'Pop' is a peculiarly Etonian body; there is no reason for its existence, although it performs at least one useful function. Originally founded in the early nineteenth century as a debating society, it soon lost this role and became a self-perpetuating oligarchy. It has some ex officio members – the captains of the school and of the Oppidans, and of the more important athletic activities, as the Boats and cricket. But the rest of the two dozen or so members are elected simply because the sitting members like them and regard them as outstanding contributors to the life – especially the athletic life – of the school. They had (have?) a number of privileges: to wear braid around the edges of their tailcoats; to use fancy, usually double-breasted waistcoats; stand-up wing collars and proper white evening dress bow ties; 'sponge-bag' (fine, black and white houndstooth check) as opposed to striped trousers, and they could carry their umbrellas rolled (which other boys could only do on the occasions of the Eton and Harrow cricket match and Fourth of June). They could, therefore, be recognised by all the boys in the school in the same way

---

[3]If it's not true, it's a good story!

[4]*Obiter dictum*: this incident is also referred to in Nigel Nicholson's *Long Life*.

as a uniformed constabulary. As their authority was visible in their dress they could keep order on public occasions, and reprove individual misconduct wherever observed. And they had the right to summon and beat any boy with a Pop-cane – a particularly vicious type of cane – whangee, which has leaf nodes, and thus a raised ring around the stem, every couple of centimetres or so. All beating was brutal, but the headmaster's birch and the Pop-cane were nothing short of barbaric. I am thankful that I never had to experience either!

A house library and the College sixth form (consisting of the ten academically senior boys in College) had no restraints on whom they chose to beat, nor had the accused any right of appeal to higher authority. So inevitably there was a certain amount of arbitrariness in the proceedings. I can't remember how many times I was beaten nor for what peccadilloes, but one accepted it as part of life, took one's seven strokes (yes, at Eton, different as always, the unit was seven rather than six as at almost every other school) and shrugged it off. Only one beating really got my sense of injustice up; it was in my last half, when I was sixteen if not already seventeen, and I had already taken the examination for special entry to the Royal Navy. I had made friends with several people in Elections above my own, because of common interests.

One was John Waterlow, who made, out of a hypodermic needle with a wire through it, insulated by the annular space being filled with sealing wax, a probe with which he could measure the electric currents in his muscles, and who co-operated with me in demonstrating, at a *conversazione* of the Scientific Society, an electric device for measuring a person's reaction time. (We somehow got hold of the necessary material to show how much a reaction time was lengthened by the ingestion of thirty millilitres of sherry. We had no lack of volunteers for this part!) Another year we demonstrated a form of lie detector. This was an electric circuit, in the form of a 'Wheatstone's Bridge', by which you can detect by the movement of a mirror galvanometer, changes in the electric resistance of the body tissue – in this case between two electrodes, one held in each hand. With our subjects (unless you happened to be privy to something about which they would certainly not tell the truth, like 'Where do you go to smoke cigarettes?') it was not easy to have test lies available, but any question which might prompt a change of emotion, like 'Are you in love with so-and-so?' or 'Did you go to the cinema in Slough last week?' would work. This apparatus was the cause of a good deal of merriment, and some people – usually those who didn't believe it was real – wished they hadn't volunteered.

Others were Neville Temperley, who was a mathematical genius, and Denys Parsons, who made fantastic penny-in-the-slot machines, which achieved nothing but which went through all sorts of amusing antics in the process. Also I was a keen member of the Boy Scouts, and had taken on the job of being an assistant Scoutmaster of a troop in the nearby town of Dorney. Bicycles were not common at Eton, and only a few boys (whose jobs made them necessary) had them. However, someone I knew – I can't remember who he was or what he did to justify a bike – lent me his for the early evenings, twice a week, so that I could go to Dorney without walking for an hour.

Well, one evening, while the sixth formers were having their supper (the standard time for disciplinary proceedings) I heard the summons 'Ritchie wanted' and went downstairs. When I went in, the 'prosecutor' was one John Brown – not a favourite of mine, for no particular reason – until that night. He told me that I was guilty of 'social climbing', associating with people in elections above me, and borrowing a bicycle to the use of which I was not entitled, and would I go outside and take off my gown? Come back in, bend over the chair, and swish, swish, up to the seven times. I couldn't get over the impression that my real crime was just that John Brown didn't like me, and he held the cane hand! Bullying was not prevalent at Eton, and by and large I don't believe that there was much abuse of power. But I still, to this day, think that it is wrong that an eighteen-year old boy should be able to beat another, at most two years his junior, for a totally victimless crime, without what we, in the United States, call 'due process of law' – without the means of appeal, before the punishment, to a master.

I didn't really fit in at Eton; I was not good at games (which were very important) and I was not academically brilliant, which would, to some extent, have compensated for athletic mediocrity. I have already told of feeling that the humanities were very badly taught, and my fun, more and more, began to come from the extra-curricular things. I loved (and learned a great deal from) the School of Mechanics, the Scientific Society and the Boy Scouts. In the Scouts you could earn badges (sewn on to the sleeve of your shirt) for proficiency in all sorts of skill, and we had contacts with a range of competent professionals, who volunteered their time to teach us. I got the reputation of being a 'badge-hunter' – unfairly, because I genuinely enjoyed learning practical skills. I can't remember all the badges I acquired, but they included fireman, first aid, life saving, cook, carpenter (not difficult for one who spent too much time at the School of Mechanics!) sheet metal worker, blacksmith and knots and splices, every one of which has been of more practical use in my life than some vestigial ability to write Greek verses. But it would be churlish and unfair not to acknowledge that Eton did give me an appreciation of books, and some sense of style.

I had some very good friends. Some of these I have already mentioned, but others were David Macindoe, who became lower master and then vice-provost – essentially the business manager of the college – but as I knew him best, was as keen a Boy Scout as I was, and was the leader of the patrol of which I was a member, and Harry Hepburne-Scott, who is now the eleventh Baron Polwarth, and is, alas, the only survivor of my close friends.

The school Natural History Society had a printing press, so that it could print labels for exhibition cases, on special paper which would not turn yellow, and with a special ink which would not fade after long exposure to light. Harry and I, because we had, at some moment, the need to get something printed, persuaded the Natural History Society to allow us to use the press, in return for us printing labels for the society whenever needed. (It was a very inefficient way of getting labels, since replication is the function of printing, and the society needed one copy for the display, and maybe a couple of spares.) With some little help from I can't remember whom, Harry and I taught ourselves the art of printing, from the typesetting in the 'stick' (one metal letter at a time picked out of its compartment in the type case) through the 'justifying' (adjusting the spaces between words so that no spaces are left at the ends of lines), levelling the completed page with mallet and 'planer', making up pages in the 'forme' locked with 'quoins', inking the plate from which the gelatine rollers will transfer the ink to the face of the type, and when the print run is finished, disassembling of the set type and returning each letter to its place in the case. This procedure taught me how difficult good proof-reading is. Before you lock up the type in the forme – when it is still in the 'galley' you pull a galley-proof and read it for correctness.

The jobs Harry and I did were generally small ones for friends, but we did one at least for which we were paid.

One member of our Election, David Simpson, was the son of the rector of a parish, who needed a two-page document, a parish newsletter or something, which Harry and I undertook.

After the job was done and delivered to our customer and had served its purpose, I was distributing the type back into its cases. You start at the end, and so you are working backwards. At the end of one line I picked out e – h – t, and suddenly thought, I've just done that! So I found one of our proofs, and there it was – 'the' at the end of one line, and another as the first word of the next. At least half a dozen people had read that page, and none had spotted the duplication!

One final word about Eton – more specifically about College Chapel. I have never believed in organised religion, and my parents were not churchgoers. I recognise that there is much great wisdom and good teaching in the Old Testament, the New, and the Koran (much of which I have read in Arabic) but I cannot accept the magic with which it is surrounded. But I love liturgy, and especially that of the Church of England – on the high side, with a lot of music, but short of incense.

At Eton we had that. We had a professional choir, and a magnificent organ. We chanted the Psalms, we sang favourite hymns with gusto, the choir sang the anthems, and the organist played voluntaries that did justice to his instrument. When the King – George V – came to chapel (which he did three times during my time) and on the anniversary of his coronation the choir sang Handel's 'Zadok the priest and Nathan the prophet anointed Solomon king. And all the people shouted and said: "*God save the King...*",' and at these four words, every person, except only the King himself, stood up. The emotion was palpable, and I can still feel it as I write, as I can that of the eight hundred or so voices singing Parry's setting of Blake's

'Jerusalem'.

Eton College Chapel brought me as close as I have ever come to being a practising Christian, and the psychological pressure to be confirmed was very strong. My mother, and through her, I, were persuaded that I should be confirmed, and I joined the appropriate preparation classes. There was one snag; I had never been baptised, because at the proper time my father, and his great friend and brother officer who was to have been my godfather, were at the front in France, and didn't get home leave until the war was over, and I suppose the thing was overlooked. So, during the summer holidays in Collieston my two sisters (whose baptism, like mine, had been neglected) and I were baptised as 'those of riper years' by the minister, James Ross, in the dining room of Seaview.

When people ask me (as still sometimes happens) whether I am Roman Catholic, Protestant or what, I answer that I was baptised a Presbyterian and confirmed into the Church of England, but neither of them took.

Part Three

First Career, the Royal Navy

Chapter Nine

Cadet

At Eton I was, to begin with, a professed pacifist (it was not uncommon at the time) and for a year I held out against becoming a member of the Officers' Training Corps. Then, in January 1933, von Papen induced *Reichspräsident* Hindenburg to accept Hitler as Chancellor of a nominally democratic Germany. But in less than a year it became a one-party state, and Hitler consolidated his power by brutality and terrorism. His opponents in the Nazi Party and Socialists and Jews were assassinated or incarcerated in concentration camps. By the middle of 1933 I had begun to listen to Winston Churchill, and to realise that against Hitler and a rearming Germany, pacifism didn't stand a chance.

By the beginning of 1934 my enthusiasm for Eton was waning, and my run-in with John Brown made me begin to feel that I'd better think of leaving. The Great Depression was close to its depth, and I knew that I could not ask my father to pay for a university education; it would be almost two years before I could try for a university scholarship from Eton, and the competition would be fierce, so I was going to have to find some gainful employment somewhere, somehow, and though my father might have taken me on as an articled clerk in Southern, Ritchie and Southern, I knew (and my father probably did, too) that the practice of law was not the right thing for me.

In the late winter of every year we had, at Eton, an exhibition of photographs from *The Times*, and in February 1934 the main subject was the Royal Navy's combined fleet exercises ('war games') in the Atlantic. Each of the Home and Mediterranean Fleets had, at that period, a squadron of battleships, and there was a series of photographs of the Home Fleet's 'R' class battleships[1] steaming at full speed into the teeth of a gale and heavy seas. There was one taken from the bridge of a battleship, 'taking it green' over its bows, and with spray almost blocking out the view of the two forward fifteen-inch gun-turrets. I stood for a long time riveted to this picture, choked with emotion, and suddenly realised that *that* was what I wanted to do. Even as I write now, sixty years later, tears come to my eyes as I see that photograph in my mind's eye.

There was a boy in school called Style (now Sir Godfrey Style, Kt, CBE, DSC), older than I, but whom I knew slightly because his family was a client of my father. He had just left Eton and joined the Navy through the special entry, a scheme planned to give more flexibility in the recruitment of officers than entry at age thirteen through the Royal Naval College, Dartmouth, formally known as HMS *Britannia*. Dartmouth cadets did four years of secondary education with naval sidelines, and in a naval atmosphere, in the RNC, and then two terms of four months each at sea in a training cruiser. Special entry cadets were recruited from public schools between the ages of seventeen and eighteen, and then went to sea in the training cruiser for three terms. So I knew that what I wanted was possible, but I did not think that I would have an easy time getting approval from my parents.

One had to take a written examination, administered by the civil service Commissioners, pass a medical fitness test

---

[1]Super Dreadnoughts of World War I.

and be interviewed by a panel of retired admirals. All of this I could arrange on my own, but the examination required the payment of a fee of five pounds, a sum of money quite out of range of my resources. I waited until the Easter vacation – I had the time – and took the opportunity of lunch with my father one day to ask him for the money and, implicitly, for his blessing.

To my great relief and surprise he said, 'I would never discourage a son of mine from entering one of the armed services of the Crown,' and he gave me a five-pound note. Faced with this fait accompli, and probably having realised anyway that I was never going to follow in her academic footsteps, my mother accepted gracefully – even encouragingly – my plans.

So I filled in all the necessary forms (no parental consent was required – the Navy wasn't going to have any obstacles in the way of enlisting volunteers!) and sent them off with the fee, and in the late spring or early summer I went to London to take the examinations; written, oral and medical. Before the end of the summer half the results were published in *The Times*. Of the nineteen who were accepted for the executive branch, I was number three. We were not alone in the 'entry' for there were also six engineers, fifteen paymasters (later more accurately called supply and secretariat) as well as six for the Royal Canadian Navy, one for the Royal Indian Navy and three for the Chinese Navy (they were the first Chinese I had ever met, and I remember their names – Lin, Liu and Yu). Thus we became subordinate officers of our respective navies, and in due course received orders to join HMS *Frobisher* at HM Dockyard, Chatham, in uniform, on a date early in September 1934. During the summer holidays I acquired from Gieves Ltd, which enjoyed (as it had since Nelson's time) a virtual monopoly of the supply of naval officers' uniforms, all the various items required – a broadcloth suit for 'number ones', a serge one for 'number twos' (worn at sea, and when less than total smartness was required) mess jacket (not unlike the Eton bum-freezer), shirts, starched collars, underwear, engine room overalls (which for some reason were brown) and all the rest.

The family was in Collieston, and so there I dressed up for the first time in my number ones, travelled (overnight) to Chatham, and found HMS *Frobisher*, an oldish cruiser of a not very successful class, modified so that her guns could not be fired, and to accommodate three special entries of about fifty cadets each (we were to spend a year divided into three 'cruises' in *Frobisher*) and two terms from Dartmouth who would spend two cruises – a total of not far short of two hundred and fifty cadets.

We were met on the quayside by a Chief Petty Officer, who, when we were all assembled, got us fallen in in two ranks, and then taught us to turn right, turn left, about turn and to salute, with the admonition that as soon as we reached the top of the gangway, we should face aft and salute the quarterdeck, as we should do every time we came on to the quarterdeck.

Before he marched us up the gangway, he said, 'Gentlemen,' – though *very* subordinate, we were officers, and as such entitled to the presumption that we were also gentlemen – 'gentlemen, when we are all on board, you will be issued your hammock, two blankets and two pillows. You will be shown how to sling your hammock, in which you will sleep every night you are on board, and how to lash it up for stowage in the morning. Tomorrow you will be shown your way about the ship. The next day we will go to sea, and the day after we will be in the Bay of Biscay, where you will learn that, in the Royal Navy, you get six square meals a day.'

'*Six,* Chief Petty Officer?' queried a voice from the ranks.

'Yes, gentlemen, three down and three up!'

The first night in a hammock takes a bit of getting used to, but when you get to sea you quickly realise that (a) you could not get all those cadets into the available space in any other form of sleeping quarters, and (b) that in rough weather nothing beats a hammock for comfort – the ship rolls around you.

The next year, save only two two-week periods of leave between cruises, was spent in learning to be a seaman and an embryo officer. We were available for work all the time, though in principle Wednesdays and Saturdays were 'make-and-mends' – afternoons off – and Sundays had a routine of their own, including Sunday Divisions – a parade in our best uniforms – and divine service. We were divided into watches, and 'quarters' which were our fighting stations, in *Frobisher*'s case, *imaginary* fighting stations, and began to combine academic learning with instructor officers ('schoolies') in naval history, navigation and pilotage, including spherical trigonometry, ship construction and stability, mathematics, communications – semaphore and the Morse code – with work as junior watch-keeping officers on the bridge, and as seamen.

Every morning began with scrubbing the decks (they were of teak wood) with 'hard scrubbers' – brooms with very short, stiff bristles – and salt water from fire hoses. Only in very cold weather did you wear sea boots for this job; bare feet were the norm, as they were for most of the day-to-day tasks around the ship. Bathing in the sea in Collieston and at Hackley had pretty well prepared me for this, but some of my mates took a while to get used to it; not that there was any obligation not to wear boots, other than your own pride.

Frobisher's main armament was seven and a half inch guns, and on these we learned gun drill and, along with it, the need for gun drill to require absolute accuracy in the use of words and instant reaction to them. It was, after all, the superb drill of Nelson's gun crews, who could fire three shots in the time the French and Spanish took to fire one, that was the second vital element in the victory of Trafalgar: the first being Nelson's revolutionary tactics and delegation of authority to his captains.

The ammunition for these guns had to be loaded in separate parts, the projectile and the cordite propellant, which was ignited by a 'tube' (in looks very like the brass case of a rifle cartridge) which went into an opening (the vent) in the breech-block. Tubes could be fired in two ways; locally, by percussion, just like a rifle, or electrically from the gunnery director tower high up in the ship, so that the ship could fire a broadside of all its guns simultaneously. The first thing you did in gun drill, after you had checked all the mechanical parts and movements of the gun, was to check the firing mechanisms. These were the words uttered by the gunner's mate who played the part of officer of the quarters:

'At the order "By percussion fire a tube", two [number two of the gun's crew, whose roles all had numbers] will unmask the vent, insert a tube, trip the tube retainer and close the vent, reporting as he does so, "By percussion – ready". On hearing two's report the gunlayer will see his range clear for at least one hundred yards and fire the gun by pressing his mechanical firing lever, reporting as he does so "Gun fired". On hearing the gunlayer's report, two will unmask the vent, thereby ejecting the tube, which is caught by three in a tube-catcher or, for drill purposes, in his cap. Three will then double smartly away to the officer of the quarters, show him the base of the tube, and report "Tube fired" or "Tube not fired" as the case may be.'

Once the percussion tube had been fired you went on to test electrical firing, and on all the way through the routine of firing, dealing with misfires, and all other contingencies.

A misfire invoked the order 'Still! Misfire – carry on.' ('Still!' was a very important order, it meant what it said: 'Stop everything, until you get another order.') Because a misfired gun could have some smouldering going on inside the breech, it could go off on its own, and so: 'The gunlayer will train the gun on to a safe bearing, and the officer of the quarters will count fifteen minutes by a reliable watch or clock...' Such is tradition that, in drills for guns of smaller calibre, with integral cartridges of projectile and propellant, a misfire still called for a wait of five seconds by a reliable watch or clock.

A defect in the drill book gave the opportunity to make fun of the gunner's mate, which, if not used too often, meant you could virtually stop the drill at the percussion tube stage. Three simply reported 'Tube *not* fired' and the drill book didn't make provision for this, and, since the gunner's mate was programmed to follow the script, he had to go back and start all over again. 'And, please, gentlemen, no playing silly buggers this time.' And no matter how hard we tried, we never got an explanation of what to do if the tube had not fired.

When we were in harbour, we learned how to row a boat, sail a boat and drive a powerboat, and how to lay out a kedge anchor to change the direction in which the anchored ship was heading, or to haul it clear of a hazard, and we got shore leave – not much of it nor very long; we had to be back on board at an hour that didn't cover much opening time of bars!

Our first cruise was to the Mediterranean, where, before I had forgotten all the French grammar learned at school, we visited some places where people actually *spoke* it, and I began to acquire my first working foreign language. We also went to Haifa, and from there we were all taken for a brief visit to Jerusalem. We stayed overnight in a monastery, and had a dinner that I believed was goat, stewed in olive oil;

anyway, it was incredibly rich and greasy. When we got back on board in Haifa, I started to get diarrhoea, and was out of my hammock many times. At an early hour I was in the heads, and didn't feel confident enough to go back to my hammock, so I looked out of the scuttle (porthole to non-naval people) and watched the dawn come up over Mount Carmel. It was a beautiful sight; the water was still, and like a black mirror except where a boat, rowed by two men, standing up facing forward and pushing their oars, left a silver wake. Mount Carmel itself was a silhouette, uniplanar and dark grey, and the sky behind it was a lighter grey, getting lighter slowly as I watched. Suddenly the grey of the sky became tinged with pink, the day dawned and in a very few minutes the flat planes became solids, and the magic broke.

Alas, my diarrhoea didn't get any better, and since the ship's doctors began to worry, I was shipped up to Jerusalem in an ambulance, and admitted to the government hospital. It must have been originally a monastery or a convent: its walls were three feet thick, its floors were scrubbed wood, its beds were narrow, but its care was warm and competent.

My room, however, had one big drawback; the windows weren't closed (for cool and ventilation) and right across the very narrow street was the Russian Orthodox cathedral. Its belfry was almost level with my window, and the bells (one of which was cracked) pealed every hour, except perhaps for a short gap during the early hours. I was very sick by this time, however, and really couldn't sort out what was happening around me, except that I waited every time for the cracked bell.

Luckily, I recovered sufficiently for me to leave the hospital and get back to the ship before it sailed from Haifa, being driven down the steep and winding road at terrifying speed in a Chevrolet sedan by a Palestinian, who kept himself steady by propping the tarboosh on his head against the roof of the car, leaving his luckless passenger to hold on for dear life in the back seat. Back in *Frobisher*, I spent a day or two in a cot in the sickbay, but was fit again for our next port of call.

Before the end of the cruise we had the prize essay competition. The given subject was 'Something I've seen or done during this cruise'. I wrote the story of my dawn over Mount Carmel – and won the prize! Thus I acquired (bound in blue leather) my first of many biographies of my lifetime hero, Lord Nelson. I still have the manuscript of my essay, and (though I don't deny that it was worthy of the prize) it is an interesting commentary on my education – I was almost ashamed of my emotional reaction to beauty: as I have grown older, I have got over that!

The spring cruise was to the West Indies, and in a very exciting way it didn't go according to plan. We sailed from Chatham on 11th January, 1935, in a strong gale and as it was getting dark. On the way to the open sea we had a minor collision with a battlecruiser, luckily with no more damage than a broken ensign staff on the other ship.

It was very cold as we steamed down the channel, and still blowing hard. As we reached the open Atlantic the weather got worse and (as I wrote to my mother) all the new, and some of the old, cadets were seasick ('three down and three up!') and did not let up until the 16th, when the wind dropped and it got warmer. The relative calm was welcome, because in the morning one of the engineer officers caught his hand in a boiler feed water pump. He had to have the second, and the top joint of his third finger amputated. While this operation was being done, the ship was stopped and four cutters (thirty-two-foot open boats, with oars) were lowered, already manned, and we rowed round the ship. This turned out to be a double lesson in seamanship; first in lowering and then rehoisting a boat at sea. The second was more serious; the boat is lowered and hoisted on 'falls' – blocks and tackles. You have to 'snatch' the boat out of the water as soon as the falls are hooked on, because it is rising and falling on the swell. The hauling parts of the falls are manned by a hundred men, who, on the order 'Hoist away!', run away with them to get the boat clear of the sea with as little delay as possible. Alas, one of the sailors in my boat (who had been warned not half a minute before) broke one of the cardinal rules of seamanship and tried to steady himself by holding on to one of the moving parts of the falls, and before he could react, his hand was between the rope and the block. He didn't lose any bones but the flesh of his hand was a real mess. So the sickbay had two hands to repair that day. But the best was yet to come.

On 21st January the weather was again very bad. Soon after 7 a.m. it was announced that we were altering course thirty-five degrees to starboard, lighting up the six of the ship's eight boilers not in use, and going to respond to the SOS of a tanker, *Valverda*, which was on fire. We worked up to full power, which should have given us a speed of twenty-seven knots, but since we were head-on to the weather we made only twenty-four. Green water was breaking over the ship, several of the boats were damaged, and a speedboat privately owned by the Engineer Commander was reduced to splinters. Lockers and hawser reels bolted to the deck broke loose, and some were washed overboard; and for the first time I heard the noise that is typical of any ship hitting rough weather unexpectedly – the continuous smashing of large amounts of crockery from the mess decks.

It was a very uncomfortable night, but early the next morning the *Valverda* radioed that she could see the beam of our searchlight, which was pointed vertically up. At 7.08 a.m. we sighted her, and by 8.40 we were close. The fire was out by this time. It had been in the engine room, and had killed one of the engineers and seriously burned another. But the crew had prevented the fire from reaching the cargo, which was white spirit – 'mineral turpentine' – and so pretty volatile. If this had caught fire nothing could have saved the ship, and the crew would not have had much chance of survival in boats in the heavy weather.

Frobisher set about trying to get *Valverda* in tow, and during the afternoon our ship was connected to her by one hundred and fifty fathoms of steel wire rope six and a half inches in circumference (ours) and one hundred and twenty fathoms of chain anchor cable, *Valverda*'s. Unfortunately, *Valverda* had lost all power, and so could not steer, and her rudder was not centred. As we started to try to move her, she just obstinately turned to starboard, until she was at right angles to *Frobisher*, so the ship was trying to tow against the whole of her lateral resistance, and after ten minutes of pulling, the towline parted. This left us with well over a quarter of a mile of steel hanging from our stern. We coupled this to our after capstan, with a wire rope connecting it to the forward capstan, and a giant block and tackle manned by all the ship's company not on duty – over five hundred men. But no way could we move it, and we had no choice but to let it go.

By this time we had been joined by HMS *Guardian*, a new minelayer with special facilities for towing. She got *Valverda* in tow with two of *Guardian*'s steel wires and sixty fathoms of *Valverda's* chain cable. But it was no good; *Valverda* just turned to starboard again and the tow parted at her end.

We (of course I mean *Frobisher*'s Captain) had radioed to ask for salvage tugs, but not one was available, so it was decided not to make any further attempts to tow until the weather got better – we were in the weather zone known as the 'Cancer Variables', on the fringe of the Sargasso Sea, so we were entitled to hope that we would get calmer seas soon. We were running low on fuel, however, and also of fresh food, so the fleet oiler *Orange Leaf* was sent out to us, and we started to be issued with lime juice to provide our vitamin C. On the 25th the weather changed and the sea was quite calm. We sent over a boat with an engineer, an electrical officer, and a number of artificers, and our workshops made a few replacement parts for *Valverda*'s steering gear. *Guardian* had to leave us about midday, but before she went she transferred two hawsers of piano wire steel, four and a half inches in circumference, stronger than those we had to let go.

We did get *Valverda* back in tow again with our wire and fifty fathoms of the chain cable, but she was still unsteerable, and though we avoided parting the tow again, we made precious little progress in the right direction. By the morning of the 27th, however, she had managed to repair her steering, and by midday our vessel was towing her at 6.9 knots with no difficulty.

During the next night *Orange Leaf* joined us, and stood by to refuel us if we needed it. In the event we didn't and we towed *Valverda*, through one more North Atlantic storm, into Bermuda dockyard on 3rd February. We had been at sea for twenty-two days – the longest time out of sight of land for any ship of the Royal Navy since World War I.

After a few days in Bermuda, where we were royally entertained by many Bermudian families, we picked up the threads of what could be salvaged of our cruise. I think our first call was in Barbados, where the weather and the welcome were so warm that it was difficult to remember it was February. Before we left, we lowered four cutters, provisioned and equipped for a short ocean passage, and each with an officer in command and a crew from the lucky ones among us – I not one of them, alas – and they set sail for St Lucia, one hundred and twenty miles to the west. What better way can there have been to learn seamanship, in its broadest definition, than navigating an open sailing boat on an overnight passage in the open ocean?

St Lucia marked a small milestone in my life; for two shillings and sixpence (not a princely sum, but still two and a half days' pay) I bought my first driving licence. I don't suppose it would have been recognised in any other place, but it did enable a group of us to rent a ramshackle car and drive around the island.

The rest of the cruise is a memory of swimming in lovely warm water, lush, green islands with gentle, unhurried people, and the clearest water I've ever seen. We anchored off Beef Island, Tortola, in the British Virgin Islands, uninhabited and with lovely sandy beaches, and a bay ideal for rowing and sailing races, and for swimming in the nude. The ship was anchored in twenty fathoms (one hundred and twenty feet) of water and from the surface you could see the anchor on the bottom quite plainly.

I had not yet been in the Navy for six months, but I had learned and experienced a very great deal – including one of my most frightening experiences, being sent up, in a gale, to the top of the foremast to read the wind speed on the anemometer. But we got our reward. In accordance with the law of the sea at that time we were entitled to be paid 'salvage' for *Valverda*, the full value of the salvaged vessel to be divided in accordance with a scale (the Captain, of course getting the lion's share) which awarded me £7 12s 11d. As cadets we were paid one shilling per day, so this was almost twenty-two weeks' pay!

The third cruise was to the great naval base of Scapa Flow in the Orkney Islands, then to Trondheim and Oslo in Norway and Copenhagen in Denmark. Pay of a shilling a day (even if supplemented by the generosity of one's family – the salvage money had not yet arrived) didn't permit much gallivanting ashore, but my fellow Old Etonian, Francis Meynell, and I did visit the Tivoli Gardens, and walk around part of the city. As we were walking back to the ship, a large, black, chauffeur-driven car pulled up alongside us, and the chauffeur got out and opened the kerbside door. The passengers were a middle-aged, well-dressed couple, who asked us, 'Are you enjoying yourselves in our country? Where have you been, and what have you seen?' We answered, and they said they hoped we would enjoy the rest of our visit to Denmark. The chauffeur closed the door, got back in the car and drove off.

Several other people who were walking in the street had watched this incident, and as the car receded three or four of them came up to ask if we knew who they were. 'No,' we said. 'Those were Their Majesties, the King and Queen!'

From Scandinavia we returned to Spithead, the roadstead between Portsmouth and the Isle of Wight, where almost every ship of the Navy in British waters assembled for a Royal Review of his Navy by King George V, to mark the twenty-fifth anniversary of his accession to the throne. So we spent some hectic days painting the ship and generally sprucing it up to a standard worthy of a Review by the King.

This was the summer of 1935: Hindenburg was dead, and Hitler had succeeded him as head of the German government, and changed the name of the office to Führer und Kanzler, Leader and Chancellor. He set about making himself the unchallenged ruler of Germany, purging rivals by assassination and concentration camp, and some – all too few to start with – began to see the writing on the wall. So behind the ceremonial of the twenty-one-gun royal salutes and the King and Queen's passing, in the Royal Yacht *Victoria and Albert*, between the cheering sailors of the long lines of the anchored warships, 'dressed overall' with flags, was a more serious purpose – a quiet rehearsal of the mobilisation of the fleet for war. Not that we were conscious of it at the time; the pageantry, the fireworks and searchlight displays in the evening, and the emotion of seeing, not far away, our King, who had himself once commanded a ship of the Royal Navy, dazzled our vision.

After this it was a bit of a let-down to have to spend one's time in the 'passing-out' examinations – so-called because they were the hurdle which had to be crossed to pass out of the training cruiser, and be eligible for appointment to a ship of the fleet as a midshipman. However, I managed to hold on to the third place I got on 'passing-in', and a couple of weeks later I received my official appointment to HMS *Queen Elizabeth*, a fifty-inch gun battleship.

Chapter Ten
Midshipman

I went to Collieston for my leave, and on 9th September I took the sixteen-hour train journey from Aberdeen to Plymouth, arriving at four thirty in the morning, cold, tired and hungry. We (there were three other new midshipmen, one, George Ogilvie, from Dartmouth,[1] the other two good friends from *Frobisher*, Christopher Bax and Francis Meynell) were not due on board until six in the evening, so I spent the day somehow in Plymouth. The ship was in Devonport Dockyard being refitted, fuelled and provisioned, ostensibly for a new commission. A 'commission' was normally a period of two and a half years, at the end of which the ship was paid off – the old ship's company left and was replaced almost one hundred per cent by a new one from the captain down. When we arrived on board most of the old ship's company were still there, and no one knew whether or not the ship would recommission. It was not until a week later that we learned that she would return to her old station, the Mediterranean, as the flagship of Admiral Sir William Fisher, Commander-in-Chief of the Mediterranean Fleet. The old crew would stay, so that there would be no need to 'work up'; to get everyone trained and drilled in running and fighting the ship.

---

[1]The Royal Naval College at high school level.

This decision and the hesitation and uncertainty which preceded it were the result of the international situation. The League of Nations was trying to prevent Italy from going to war to take over Abyssinia (we call it Ethiopia now) by offering a so-called peace plan which would give part of Abyssinia to Italy as a colony, and compensate for that by giving Abyssinia access to the sea by ceding to it a double corridor, carved out of British and French Somalilands. How arrogant we were, and how high-handed we were prepared to be; but how ineffectual when push came to shove. And of course our total lack of resolve was not unnoticed by the Dictators! No one, other than the politicians, really believed that Italy would give in to the League of Nations by accepting *any* peace plan, when Mussolini wanted not only a new colony but a victorious war, and was justifying Italy's actions by the allegation that Abyssinia was a disunited, barbarous country that turned a blind eye to slavery, and so should be expelled from the League of Nations, and civilised by force of Italian arms, as Britain and France had been by Roman!

Once on board, we became members of the gunroom, the mess for the midshipmen, with one commissioned officer, the sub lieutenant of the gunroom, (Peter Norton, later Hill-Norton, to distinguish him from another Peter Norton) as our boss, and to be responsible to the Captain for the behaviour and progress of the midshipmen. In *QE* I learned one lesson that has served me well all my life. Ships had different cultures, and this applied especially to the way in which they treated their midshipmen; we were legally 'subordinate officers' and in *QE* we were treated as, and expected to behave like, officers. In many ships, however, the accent was on the 'subordinate' – jokingly, midshipmen used to be referred to as 'the lowest form of animal life in the Navy' – and they were treated as if they were still schoolboys. The results were startlingly different; we were trusted and were always worthy of that trust. In ships of the other culture midshipmen were often in trouble, getting their leave stopped, and sometimes even caned. Moral: treat people as sensible and reliable, and they will be sensible and reliable; treat them as irresponsible half-wits, and that's what you will get.

We still had only hammocks to sleep in, though once in warmer climates (in harbour at any rate) many of us slept on deck, preferably in a sheltered corner, under an awning. Each one of us had a sea-chest – a mahogany case with three drawers, and a brass handle at each end, and so designed as to be stackable – in which to store our clothes, and we had a share of a Royal Marine bandsman as our servant, to help us keep our uniforms in smart condition, and to polish our shoes. We had our own bathroom, and our own pantry next door to the gunroom itself, presided over by a Petty Officer Steward and two stewards, all three of whom were, as in all ships of the Mediterranean station, Maltese. The PO steward was our 'messman', paid by the Service, and beyond that an independent businessman with whom the mess signed a contract to provide for our feeding. The Navy allowed us one shilling and three pence per head per day for our victuals, to which we added out of our pockets an additional nine pence, for a total of two shillings. For this, the messman entered into a contract with a committee representing the mess to provide a specified level of food: porridge or dry cereal, bacon or sausages and eggs, toast, butter and marmalade for breakfast, as an example. Dinner was to be of four courses every night, except for the weekly guest night when it was five – soup, fish, main course, sweet and savoury – and there were to be little hors d'oeuvres with drinks before dinner. The messman could buy many of the staple foods from the Navy's victualling organisation, 'the Pusser', or from whatever might be available in the port we happened to be in. For the latter, he had, of course, to go ashore, so he would also buy things we wanted, a driver's licence, for example, and at a pinch he would do it on credit. Two shillings a day and a demanding mess committee didn't leave much margin for profit, but most messmen managed to make, if not small fortunes, then at least substantial savings over and above their pay.

If the mess got dissatisfied with the messman, the committee would take him to task, and had as a last resort the ability to cancel the contract, though I cannot recall a case of this drastic course ever having to be taken. I do, however, remember one meeting with a messman (not in *QE*, but later, in a battleship of the Home Fleet). We were all sitting round the gunroom table, with the messman in the dock, as it were, at one end. We voiced a string of complaints, and Midshipman Bailey suddenly added:

'And another thing, messman, the porridge you give us for breakfast tastes like shit.'

Quick as a flash, he received the riposte: 'There, Mr Bailey, sir, you have the advantage of me; I've never compared the two.'

Game and set to the messman, for the meeting dissolved itself in a gale of laughter!

We had a bar, to manage which we elected one of our number as wine caterer, stocked with duty-free booze supplied by one of the two traditional naval wine merchants, Saccone and Speed, or Stokes and Harvey. 'Duty-free' meant that a bottle of whisky cost three shillings, and gin two shillings and sixpence. Gin, or 'pink gin' (flavoured and tinted with a few drops of Angostura bitters), both diluted with water, were the standard naval drinks, and the gin was not the usual London, but Coates's Plymouth gin. I couldn't (and can't) stand the taste of either of them, so I have no idea what the difference in flavour is (or was, for I haven't seen a bottle of Plymouth gin for decades, and have no idea whether it is still on the market). It was the rule that spirits had to be served in units of a 'six-out', that is six out of a quarter-pint, or five-sixths of an ounce. You had to sign for your drinks on a little white chit, made out by the steward who served them. (One of our stewards was called Lorenzo – 'Wentzu' in the Maltese – and he had a little idiosyncrasy which still amuses me; Maltese men very often have Italian Christian names, and Giuseppe was usually shortened to 'Gius', so that when you ordered a tomato juice from Wentzu, you signed a chit that read: '*1 Tom G.*')

It was part of the duty of the gunroom wine caterer to keep a running daily record of each member's wine bill, which was submitted to the Captain once a month, so that he could see whether any of his officers were in danger of becoming alcoholics. For the same reason, you couldn't stand anyone else a drink: you went through the motions of inviting, but each drinker signed his own chit.

After the dockyard's refitting work was done, and a lot of preparatory checks and trials, including a 'tilt test' of all the ship's guns – fifteen-inch, six-inch and four-inch anti-aircraft weapons – tests of the two-pounder pom-poms (heavy anti- aircraft machine-guns), and loading all sorts of necessities from ammunition, through two thousand tons of lubricating oil to the admiral's car, the ship sailed on 28th September for Gibraltar. Normally we would have been sailing at economical speed – about twelve knots – but the League of Nations (in practice Britain and France) was losing patience with Italy, which was clearly determined to go to war to acquire Abyssinia as a colony, and there was some urgency in our getting to the eastern Mediterranean, so we cruised at seventeen knots, later increased to twenty. We stopped in Gibraltar for four hours, and then sailed for Malta.

The day before we arrived in Malta, Italian troops

crossed the frontier of Abyssinia, and war officially began. Italy was duly declared by the Council of the League of Nations to be the aggressor, and as such to be subjected to sanctions by all other members of the League – sanctions that were of as little practical use then as they have proved to be in modern times!

We stopped in Malta for four days, and then sailed on eastward. However, the sense of urgency was not yet so great as to prevent us stopping for half an hour in mid-Mediterranean for the ship's company to swim in the most beautiful dark blue water, two miles deep, before arriving on 8th October in Alexandria. On the 12th Admiral Sir William Fisher hoisted his flag in *QE* (as the ship was invariably known) and she became the flagship of the Mediterranean Fleet.

Alexandria was to be our principal base for most of the next year, though when Italy completed its conquest of Abyssinia in early May, we spent increasing periods based on Malta. Alexandria was a very exotic place for people like me who had never been outside the United Kingdom until I joined the Navy, and it was for some time a lonely place, in the sense that there were few places to go and things to do for eighteen-year-olds earning five shillings a day. So we spent most of our leisure time on board, or sailing the ship's boats in the harbour, which has a huge protected area and is blessed with a good sailing breeze almost all the time.

But I was lucky. The borough engineer of Burnley, Basil Mackenzie, and his wife were friends of my parents, and their daughter Mary was a friend of mine. One day in the ship's mail I received a letter posted in Alexandria from Billie Mackenzie and his wife, saying that he was Basil's brother, and inviting me to dinner at their home. The Mackenzies quickly became friends, and their hospitality extended to many of my fellow midshipmen. Billie was a partner in a firm of Alexandria cotton merchants, Peel and

Company, and though a wealthy man was totally unpretentious, and still spoke with a marked Scots accent. May, his wife, was one of ten survivors of twelve children of an expatriate British Smyrna merchant and his Greek wife. When that city (which had been in Turkish possession since the fifteenth century, though it had a large Greek and Armenian population, and was coveted and briefly occupied by Greece) became definitively Turkish after World War I, the Greek and Armenian populations, and the comparatively few other non-Turkish people fled, or were deported. May, her mother, one of her brothers and Zoë, her youngest sister (later married to a member of the royal family of Egypt, and one of the most beautiful women I have ever known) lived in Alexandria.

Alexandria, before Gamal Abdel Nasser 'purified' it, was a cosmopolitan and polyglot city, and had had a substantial Greek population since it was founded by Alexander the Great. Egypt adhered to *jus sanguinis*, so that its Greek, Armenian, Italian and other 'foreign' residents were not citizens, though most of them had lived there for generations. To get a job as a telephone operator you had to be able to speak Arabic, French (which was the lingua franca of educated people of any national origin) Italian, Greek and Armenian – and there was no shortage of qualified candidates! Billie and May had Egyptian house servants, with whom they communicated in not very good Arabic, and May had a personal maid who had come with her from Smyrna, with whom she spoke Greek, and their social life was carried on in English and French.

The first invitation to dinner led to others to the cinema, to dinner at The Union Bar, a superb restaurant in a very plain and unadorned ambience, and to afternoons at their cabin at Sidi Bishr, a beautiful bathing beach west of Alexandria, and time ashore became very enjoyable. As you will read later in the book, the Mackenzies became even closer friends after the outbreak of World War II.

Life, of course, was not all beer and skittles. A British fleet of four battleships, eight cruisers, a battlecruiser, an aircraft carrier, two depot ships, two destroyer flotillas of eight destroyers each, and a few smaller ships was based on Alexandria, for the essential purpose of protecting the eastern Mediterranean, and especially the northern approaches to the Suez Canal, but it had no influence on the Italian adventure in Abyssinia. Italy just thumbed its nose at the League of Nations, which had mustered no weapons but ludicrous economic sanctions (Britain had recognised that oil sanctions were economic sanctions like any other, but never got up the political will to impose them on Italy) and verbal condemnation, high moral in tone but worse than useless – worse, because Italy's success in flouting the League simply encouraged other nations to prefer belligerence to negotiation.

I recorded in my midshipman's journal (an obligatory chore, which was marked as an exam at the end of one's midshipman's time) for 1st March, 1936, that the Abyssinian army of Ras (Prince) Kassas had been wiped out, and that '*Alexandria is bedecked with Italian flags in celebration of "la vittoria".*' War dragged on, however, until May, when the Emperor Haile Selassie left the country and was taken on board a British warship from Djibouti to Haifa, and thence to Britain, where he was given sanctuary.

During the previous few days my journal recorded (24th February) that '*uneasiness is being caused by persistent rumours that Germany and Italy are negotiating for a joint repudiation of Locarno...*' (the 1925 treaty of mutual guarantee between Germany, Great Britain, Belgium, France and Italy) '*and the formation of an entente to counter the Franco-Soviet one*'. An entry two days later, on 26th February records that the Patriotic Young Officers' Front in Japan had carried out a *coup d'état*, murdering the Prime Minister and a number of other senior government figures and occupying all the main government offices except the Admiralty and the War Office. The insurrection collapsed after two days – the Navy remained loyal – but the shift to a more militaristic line in Japanese policy was one of its consequences. On 24th March the sirens of the Krupp works in Essen led the sounding of the whistles of factories, trains and ships all over Germany to mark the beginning of a one-minute silence in which everything stopped, save only ships and aircraft and '*Germany united in silent self-communion to show that all Germany is ready to follow the Führer to salvation*'. And then, in Morocco, on 18th July the revolt which developed into the Spanish Civil War broke out.

These growing threats of war (which the British government and public seemed scarcely to notice) were the background of our daily routine, of gunnery and air spotting exercises, the running of mine protection paravanes, manoeuvres of groups of ships at sea, and the hundred and one other activities, including sports, sailing and rowing races to encourage teamwork, and where all could take pride in the success of a shipmate and enhance the sense of being a ship's *company.* All this helped us towards battle-readiness, and all the time we needed to remember that battle was what we were in the Navy for.

One element of our preparedness about which the Navy had serious worries was anti-aircraft protection. This was before the days of radar, and long before electronic calculation, so we were essentially dependent on eyes, ears and judgement. To hit an aircraft with a projectile from a gun, you had to aim for its future position, and of course you had to start from its present position, and be able to estimate its speed. I played a little part in two of the attempts to do these better than just the almost instinctive aim-off needed to shoot a flying bird or a running rabbit. Someone in the Navy's back rooms invented a 'sound locator', which consisted of two sound receptors, like old-fashioned ear trumpets, on a swivel mounting, and connected to the operator's ears by a sort of stethoscope. *QE*, and within *QE*, I got the job of trying out and evaluating this device. (You can sense the direction of a sound you hear because if the source is to the right of you, the sound reaches your right ear before your left, and your brain can calculate what angle that delay indicates. It is almost impossible to tell from which direction a continuous, uniform sound comes from – try to find where an electronic peep is!)

The sound locator had the effect of greatly enlarging the distance between your ears, and thus the delay between one side and the other; so by turning the instrument until the noise sounded right ahead, it was pointing to the source with a high degree of accuracy, but only horizontally. To get the altitude as well, you had a second pair of receptors on a vertical plane connected to a second pair of ears. This person either needed to lie on his side, or make, without having to think about it, the conversion that 'right equals up, left, down'. Two of us did get to the stage where we could point very accurately to a plane. But this was only finding present position, and no help in finding future. I thought a great deal about this problem, which at first seemed to require combining an estimate of the speed of the plane and its distance away. Then, suddenly, I realised that speed and distance represented angular velocity, which in turn could be combined with the speed of the gun's projectile to give the required aim-off. I couldn't think of any way to do this, and nor could any of the other officers in the ship that I consulted. It wasn't until sometime during World War II that I learned what the solution was: a constrained gyroscope requires a force to change the orientation of its axis, and that force is proportional to the rate of change of the orientation of the axis, and this principle was indeed used, with electronic calculation, to aim anti-aircraft guns.

My other essay into the science of anti-aircraft fire control came a little later. At close range where you can use machine-guns firing over one hundred rounds a minute, and the shells have 'tracers' so that you can follow their flight, you can correct your aim as if you were using a fire hose, so you may get direct hits. But it is almost impossible actually to hit an aircraft with a shell fired from a four-inch gun (the standard size) which may manage one round every five seconds with a well-drilled crew, so you have to explode the shell close to the aircraft, so that it flies through a cloud of steel fragments. This has to be done by a time-fuse in the nose of the shell to burst it at the moment it is calculated to be nearest to its target. The fuse had to be set before it was loaded, and the gun fired at a moment calculated from the distance, height and speed of the plane. A great deal of effort and practice went into the attempt to perfect this procedure, based on the analysis of actual firings, and imaginary ones at real aircraft. I designed a plotting table to carry out this analysis, and Ordnance Artificer Nicholls made it. Its use did help us to modify our procedures for setting the fuse timings, and we got some respectable results in theoretical exercises, but I greatly doubt that the outcome of World War II was much affected!

Chapter Eleven

Apprenticeship

In 1931, when the Great Depression was beginning to bite hard, the British government decided that one of the budgetary economies it would make would be to reduce the pay of the Royal Navy. This decision was handled with incredible lack of feeling and common sense; there was no preparation, no advanced warning, just one pay day the sailors received their reduced pay on their caps (traditionally, a sailor removed and held out his cap for his pay, in cash in a paper bag, to be deposited on it). The Home Fleet, or a large part of it, was assembled in Invergordon, in northern Scotland, when this bombshell fell. The unbelievable happened, and out of sheer frustration the Fleet mutinied. It didn't last long; the ringleaders were punished, but an inquiry was set up to review what had happened, and to recommend how better to organise the Navy to prevent a recurrence.

One of the outcomes of this review was the divisional system. The whole of a ship's company was divided into divisions: three (Fo'c'sle,[1] Maintop and Quarterdeck) for seamen, Stokers for those who worked in the engine room (though *stoking* as such, the shovelling of coal into furnaces, was long gone), and the one that I was part of, Communications, for signalmen and telegraphists (radio

---

[1]Forecastle.

operators). Each division had its own divisional officer who was responsible for every service aspect of his men's lives, and was available for private advice, counselling and help on problems arising from family life. As may be imagined, when a commission lasted two and a half years, normally without any home leave during it, life could become difficult for wife and children left alone, and often lonely. Part of a sailor's pay could be remitted direct to his family or to a savings account, and one of the divisional officer's duties was to advise a man how much he should remit in his own particular circumstances, and it says a lot for the sense of the great majority of sailors that family break-ups were rarer than the average in civilian life (maybe helped by the truth of the adage: 'What the eye doesn't see, the heart doesn't grieve over', but also by the fact that most naval wives took pride in the Navy, and accepted the price that had to be paid).

While this was not the most time-consuming part of our work, it was very important. A sailor signed on in those days for twelve years initially, after which he could renew his engagement 'to complete time for pension', a further ten years. During that time he could get promoted (in the seaman branch, for example, from the entry rate of Ordinary Seaman to Able Seaman, Leading Seaman, Petty Officer, Chief Petty Officer, and, for a few, Warrant Officer). Each step required the spending of some time in the lower rate, the passing of an examination, and the recommendation of the divisional officer, whose help, advice and encouragement were part of his duties. Along the way, a rating could acquire three good conduct badges (manifested by chevron stripes on the sleeve) after three, eight and eleven years of 'good conduct' (some minor peccadilloes didn't count) and finally at fifteen years ('fifteen years of undiscovered crime') a long service and good conduct medal, which carried a pay increase along with it. There was no central system to keep a tally of any man's progress in any of these regards, and it was up to the divisional officer to make sure that all his men put in, in due season, their requests to the Captain 'To be awarded second good conduct badge', 'To go through for leading seaman' or whatever. And the Captain looked to him for certification that the request was a proper one, and that the conditions were met. Likewise, any rating 'up on a charge' before the Captain (or the Commander, as court of first instance) had his divisional officer as his defence counsel.

To assist the divisional officer in all this, he had the services of a Regulating Petty Officer to keep the records and to help with the paperwork. And in any ship with midshipmen, each divisional officer had a midshipman as assistant, so that we learned, by watching and doing – by apprenticeship – what the Invergordon mutiny had brought home to the Navy, that care for your men was your first duty, to the point that at the time to go ashore, the men went in the early boats, and only then the officers. It also helped greatly to let you get to know your sailors as people, as individuals, and not just a 'name, rank and number' – and how very rewarding that was. I have always felt that ninety-nine per cent, if not ninety-nine point nine per cent of people are fundamentally decent and honest, and that to be treated as such reinforces nature, and I never ceased to wonder at how the Navy could take in men with very little education, often from desperately poor families, whose fathers worked long hours down the coal mines or in the cotton mills, and enable them to become responsible and brave, able to trust and be trusted. This is what I most loved about the Navy, and have tried to carry over into my later life in business.

Apprenticeship also covered other aspects of becoming an officer. We kept watch alongside a commissioned officer, at sea and in harbour. We served as 'doggy' to the Admiral, the Captain or the Commander, dogging their footsteps and running errands, or looking up references in the Sailing Directions ('Pilots') which gave in words information about tidal streams, tricky turns in a channel, or what a bit of coastline looked like, which the chart could not show vividly enough. I was on the bridge as the Admiral's doggy one day, and the Admiral told me to make a flag signal to another ship: 'Manoeuvre well executed'.

I turned to voice pipe to the signalman, who was on the deck below the bridge and said: 'Hoist pennants two, three – duff george.'

The Admiral waited until the signal was hoisted, and then called me over. 'Snotty,' – a generic term for a midshipman, nothing personal! – 'never do what you just did. I know that HMS so-and-so's identification is pennants two, three and every Tom Fool knows DG means "damn good". And there will be a lot of other brief signals that you know by heart. But at some point your memory will be fallible, and you just get it wrong. Accurate signalling is of utmost importance in battle, so remember that you have a signalman who has a Signal Manual in which to look up everything. You tell him the message that I wish sent, and then you make sure that he looks it up before he hoists the flags.'

That is a lesson which has many applications in life, and I try always to remember Admiral Fisher's lesson, and not trust my memory if I have the means of going to the book.

A battleship carried a number of boats. Those that were oar or sail powered were carried as 'sea boats' at davits, from which they could be lowered and 'slipped' (let drop, fully manned) into the sea. The big powered boats were hoisted inboard on the main derrick (of steel tube, hinged to the bottom of the main mast, and supported by a wire rope 'topping lift' almost at the masthead) and stowed in chocks between the funnel and the mainmast. *QE* carried three of her own, a launch and two picket boats, and, if the Admiral was on board, his 'barge' – a picket boat, distinguished from the ship's by being painted green.

All the Admiral's boats, even his small sailing skiff, were green, and this last was one that the junior section of midshipmen – Christopher Bax, Francis Meynell, George Ogilvie and I – got to know well. We were given the task of designing and making a suit of sails, complete with spars. We produced a 'sliding gunter' rig, to give the equivalent of a Bermuda, but which could be stowed inside the boat. When finished the little skiff sailed pretty well, and four midshipmen had learned to sew with a sailmaker's needle and palm, and to sew 'belly' into flat canvas and to do the woodwork necessary to make the spars, and the splicing of wire and hemp rope to make the rigging.

Each of the three powered boats was the responsibility of one of the midshipmen, in rotation, with a back-up so that you were only available for duty twenty-four hours a day, but not seven days a week. Early in my journal I declared my preference for the launch – forty-five feet long, broad in the beam and open so that it could carry over one hundred liberty men ashore, driven by a petrol engine, and steered by a tiller from the very stern. I took this over for the first time in Malta on our passage out, and though I had a lot of trouble from dirty petrol, my launch was, in my eyes, better than a picket boat. A few days after arrival in Alexandria, however, I took over one of the picket boats, and it soon displaced the launch in my affections.

The picket boat was steam driven, with a water tube boiler and a double-expansion piston engine. Both it and the launch were about the same length, but the picket boat was much narrower. It had a small cabin for passengers abaft the engine room, and an open cockpit abaft the cabin with seats around, and some standing room. Just aft of the funnel (which had a polished brass bell top) were the wheel and the engine room telegraph, protected by a weather shield about four feet high, and forward there was another cabin and open passenger space, so its capacity for carrying people was much less than the launch's. It was, however, much faster and more powerful, to the point that it could tow the anchored ship, given reasonable calm, around its anchor to a different heading. Not only did we drive the picket boat, but we were also required to learn about and to operate the engine room, from keeping the right oil fuel and steam pressures and boiler water level, and the right vacuum in the condenser receiver, and obey the commands of the engine room telegraph, for ahead or astern, and for the revolutions per minute appropriate to the required speed. Our training had some resemblance to the system of Mr Wackford Squeers of Dotheboys Hall: 'C-l-e-a-n, clean, verb active, to make bright, to scour. W-i-n, win, d-e-r, der, winder, a casement. When the boy knows this out of book, he goes and does it.' Only *our* teachers knew how to spell! Anyway, I fairly quickly became a more than competent boat handler, which provided the basis for one of the last reports I received during my career: 'Fully qualified to handle any size of ship in any weather.' But I'm jumping ahead.

Towards the end of March, Admiral Fisher handed over his command to Admiral Sir Dudley Pound, who had been Admiral Fisher's chief of staff for a number of months (and who was to become First Sea Lord and chief of the naval staff in June 1939, and hold that office until his death in late 1943). Admiral Pound hoisted his flag (the symbolic moment of the transfer of the command) in HMS *Barham*, another battleship of the *QE* class, and we, with Admiral Fisher on board, sailed for Malta and Devonport, where the ship was at last to be paid off after the postponement in September of the previous year. Admiral Fisher left us to become Commander-in-Chief, Portsmouth.

I was sorry I would not be serving under him in *QE* again; he was, as any admiral must be to any midshipman, an awesome figure, but when you got the chance to talk to him, he was kind, human and obviously very professional. One evening at sea, he invited another midshipman and me to dinner, and he greeted us at the door of his cabin with the words: 'Well, this evening you are going to be subjected to ordeal by dinner.' He then put us both completely at ease, and it turned out to be a very interesting and pleasant evening.

On 30th March the ship arrived alongside in Devonport, and within two hours the job of provisioning the ship began, and drafts of our crew began to leave the ship and be replaced by new ones from the depot. The recomissioning process didn't have much useful for midshipmen to do, so we were lucky and got a month's leave, until 3rd May. On our return we had a week's course at the Devonport Gunnery School, a mixture of drills on various types and calibres of guns, learning about various fire control instruments and so-called 'field training' – learning how to be soldiers. This last was a necessary skill for peacetime, when a ship might be called upon to land a military force to help the civil power, of whatever country it happened to be in, in emergencies – earthquakes, riots, and other disasters made by man or nature. Once off the parade ground, we went on leave again until Sunday evening. George Ogilvie and I went to London, and drove back in a six-year-old Triumph seven horsepower car. I recorded that we made very good time, though where the car came from, or how it got back to where it belonged I have no idea! London to Plymouth was a long (and dreary) drive in those days, so we cannot have had much time in London!

After another weekend leave (known as a 'Friday while', short for Friday while – in its old sense of 'until' – Monday) we sailed for Malta, with a very brief stop in Gibraltar, and had a busy time on passage and after arrival in Malta with all the gunnery and other exercises needed to get us into fighting trim.

Soon we were back in Alexandria again, where our normal routine was enlivened by the entertainment of King Farouk of Egypt on board to witness a number of exercises, some of them quite spectacular. *QE* was leading the rest of the fleet in line at about twelve knots, and the cruiser *Galatea* steamed past, thirty feet away from us, at twenty-five knots. When you have eight thousand tons of steel passing that close, you say a quiet prayer that the helmsman doesn't get a sudden twitch! The next exercise was even more scary; the second ship in line, our sister ship *Valiant*, changed places with *QE*, and fourteen destroyers steamed through the (moving) gap, not twice a destroyer's length, between us, at twenty-five knots. Then all the battleships and the battlecruiser did some ballet dancing turns, some together and some in succession. All the larger ships dropped a lifebuoy simultaneously, stopped, and lowered a sea boat to pick it up. *QE* fuelled a destroyer alongside at twelve knots, the destroyers carried out a mock depth charge attack on a calcium flare to represent a submarine, and then did a torpedo attack with real torpedoes, without warheads, and set to run deep so as to pass under the ship. The show ended with target shoots at a towed target, first by *Barham* with her fifteen-inch guns, with *QE* on her quarter, for a better view – and less noise – and then by four cruisers with a concentration shoot with eight eight-inch guns each. It was, all in all, a very impressive demonstration of the naval might of the time.

During most of the day, King Farouk was on deck with Admiral Pound where he had a good view of what was going on, and at some time during the day I had to go with a message to the Admiral. Nothing much was going on at the moment I was there, so the Admiral presented me to the monarch. Farouk (who had only very recently succeeded his father, Fuad, and had not yet been totally corrupted by his mother and his valet) was a very handsome, slim, engaging sixteen-year old, and our few words were pleasant and unaffected. Sadly, it didn't last. He had come to the throne with a great deal of goodwill and popularity and, I believe, a genuine desire to do well for his country, but he squandered it all.

Chapter Twelve

Malta

The winding down of Italy's campaign to take over Ethiopia was succeeded by the intensification of the civil war in Spain, and this shifted the centre of gravity of the role of the Mediterranean Fleet to the west, and our base to Malta. Before we left Alexandria, however, the fleet held a regatta, which involved almost every boat in every ship, and every branch of the service. I rowed in the subordinate officers' gig race (a gig was a rowing and sailing boat, not used as a sea boat, and of a lighter construction than cutters and whalers)[1] and in my journal I ascribed an abysmal performance to our youth, and lack of opportunity for training. Not many others of *QE*'s crew did much better than us, however, so we had company in our misery!

The evenings before the regatta were enlivened by three concerts; entertainments is a better word. The first two were put on by the ship's company (that is, excluding the officers) in which I was involved as a backstage helper, doing make-up. We had a crew of over one thousand men, but even so, it was extraordinary how much talent there was: singing, dancing, comic monologues, and all the rest of the repertory of the English music halls. So that all the watchkeepers could have a chance to see the show, and so

---

[1]The whaler was a 27 foot oared boat, double-ended, and the standard 'sea boat' in destroyers.

as not to overcrowd the limited space available, this affair was repeated on two successive nights. The following night was the turn of the officers. The admiral's staff did a series of individual turns and the ship's officers put on a ballet. This was the idea of Peter Norton (now a Lieutenant, and no longer our Sub Lieutenant of the gunroom) who was also the author, choreographer, ballet master and producer. The music was from records, and ran the gamut from the Grand March from *Tannhaüser*, through Chopin, from *Les Sylphides*, to 'Bugle Call Rag'. It was a simple story, not very close to life (as many ballets) of a midshipman who forgot to call the commander, and so got into deep trouble. But it was regatta time, and when the stroke oar of one of the ship's crews got sick at the last moment, he took over and stroked his crew to victory, and his ship to the grand prize of the 'Cock'. I was a member of the corps de ballet, who danced the roles of (said the programme) 'Quarterdeck staff, rowers, etc.'. Ballet then had not the appeal and acceptability that it has since acquired, and was indeed regarded as an entertainment for aesthetes, so it was a brave choice, and very successful. It was the only time that I have ever danced in a ballet, but it did open my eyes to the possibilities of the medium, and gives me the opportunity to boast to my unsuspecting friends that 'I once danced in a ballet.'

When we recommissioned in Devonport, Peter Norton was succeeded as our Sub Lieutenant by Otto (real name, Richard) Jenner-Fust, a descendant of Dr Jenner who originated vaccination against smallpox. Otto was a wonderful man to have in the job. He was very amusing, a natural leader, a teller of tales of the highest order, and though not academic (and so not good at examinations) he was a fine practical seaman. I got to know him very well, because we became 'run-ashore' buddies. In Malta I had got to know Meriel, daughter of a retired naval commander who had settled in Malta with his blind wife and his daughter. Malta was a favourite retirement spot for naval officers; there was a lot of naval activity and atmosphere, the climate was good and a pension went much further than in Britain. Otto had acquired as his girlfriend Tanya Mifsud, a beautiful, voluptuous young member of one of the Maltese aristocratic families, and the four of us went, perhaps once a week or once a fortnight, to dance at the Sliema Club, of which serving officers were honorary members. We would go somewhere for dinner beforehand, or, more often, to some little bar for supper, often a naval favourite (with origins in the China Station), a 'cheesy-hammy-eggy topside', or some other simple meal that wouldn't overstrain our resources. These same resources were, however, sufficient for us to hire a car occasionally so that we could throw our net more widely.

There was not, then, anything like the freedom between young people of the two sexes that has since become the norm, so Meriel and I had a totally chaste, platonic relationship. Meriel was, I suppose, technically a member of the 'fishing fleet' of young women brought by their parents to Malta in the hope of catching, from among the large number of naval officers who were there, an eligible husband. Her parents would not have appreciated a relationship with a midshipman, nineteen years old, no private means and an income of five shillings a day. So while I drove the car and Meriel sat beside me in the front, a hand would come over my shoulder and turn the rear-view mirror to the side, and sounds of heavy necking would ensue from the back seat. Meriel and I never commented on this to each other, and I never asked Otto what he had been up to, and the foursome remained intact.

I was a friend of Meriel's father, too. His wife's blindness restricted the sort of social life they could have together, and he seemed to enjoy the company of a serving officer, however much younger, and often invited me to dine with him at the Union Club in Valletta. He was very fond of marrowbones, and used to invite me whenever *QE* was in harbour, and marrowbones were on the menu at the club. I was invited to their house, too, and got to know Meriel's mother. She had been blind before they came to Malta, so she had never seen it, but from verbal descriptions she had come to know it well, and I found it fascinating to talk with her about where Meriel and I had been, and to realise that she could visualise the scene exactly.

Malta was a very pleasant place in which to be based. There were many things to do and see in the tiny (28 kilometres by 13.5 kilometres) island, with harbours, creeks and inlets all round the north and east coasts, from St Paul's Bay, where the saint was shipwrecked on his journey to Rome, to the mighty Grand Harbour, where a squadron of battleships could moor, with two flotillas of destroyers in the neighbouring Sliema Creek. The standard way of getting around Grand Harbour itself was in the Maltese cousin of the Venetian gondola, the dghaissa (roughly pronounced dye-sa) propelled by two oarsmen, standing up and facing the way they were going, with seats for six or even eight in the back. These boats were very picturesque: they had stem and stern posts projecting a metre above the level of the hull, which were very handy to hold the boat when it was alongside a landing place, and they were painted in bright primary colours, with varnished woodwork.

Valletta, the capital, was (I write 'was' because three-quarters of the city was destroyed in the siege between June 1940 and November 1942, and though some of the buildings of the Knights of St John of Jerusalem have been restored, buildings catering to the tourist industry have changed the face of the city) a place of old buildings and narrow streets, and there were shops where you could buy anything, and innumerable bars where sailors could get drinks. Milk was delivered on the hoof, as little herds of goats were driven through the streets, to be milked into containers left on the doorsteps. It was said that Maltese goats would eat anything, even tin cans. I have seen them eat old newspapers and cigarette butts, but closer observation showed that, whatever it looked like, the goat would eat the label off a can and then painstakingly lick off all the glue, before abandoning the can. Goats were one traffic hazard, but another was the platoons of priests or monks walking in double file. Malta seemed to have a higher proportion of clerics in its population than anywhere else, and there used to be a joke that the compensation you had to pay for a fatality as a result of a traffic accident was thirty pounds for a goat, twenty pounds for a person, and only fifteen pounds for a priest.

Looming over Grand Harbour are the fortresses of St Elmo and Castel St Angelo, and the Grand Master's palace, the Auberge de Castille. Valletta itself is virtually cut off from its suburb, Floriana, and the rest of the island, because the Knights above all needed defence against the Ottoman Turks. Maltese rock has an interesting property; it is soft enough to be cut with a saw, but it weathers (after several years) to be as hard as concrete. So the Knights simply sawed away the isthmus that connected Valletta to the rest, and left a valley perhaps fifty metres wide with cliffs seventy-five metres high on either side, though they never quite got down to sea level to make Valletta a complete island.

In 1940 Malta faced a worse enemy than the Turks – the air power of Italy and Germany. During the siege the Maltese had reason to be grateful for their rock: during nine hundred days there were over three thousand air raid alerts, and forty-five tons of bombs were dropped per square kilometre – a ton for every two hundred square metres – but because almost everyone slept, and lived most of the time, in catacombs and caves, less than fifteen hundred people were killed by these air attacks!

Further afield a group of us would sail one of the ship's boats to St Paul's Bay to picnic and swim; Francis Meynell and I went often to Tigne, a little rocky inlet which is a perfect swimming place; or you could take a bus or a rented car to Mdina, the old fortified capital city of the Romans, the Normans and then the Arabs, with almost as many churches as inhabitants, and its neighbour Rabat, in the centre of the island. And one weekend a dozen or more officers from the ship, led by the First Lieutenant (the most senior executive officer below the Captain and Commander) sailed, in several boats, to Comino, an island of under three square kilometres between Malta and its smaller sister island, Gozo, for a weekend of camping.

Comino had sixty-seven inhabitants, who lived there tax- and rent-free, tilled the soil and split the profits fifty-fifty with Captain Cutajar, the owner. We had expected to be met as we landed by the First Lieutenant, but he was nowhere to be found, until we'd all been swimming for about half an hour, and he appeared – from attending the first wedding ever held on the island in living memory. He roped in Sub Lieutenant Crabbe, Francis Meynell and me to go and help at the reception, at which we handed round beer, cakes, sticky sweets and banana, orange and strawberry liqueurs, and were rewarded by an invitation to visit the future home of the couple and admire the wedding presents, which were almost entirely of practical use.

After a good cold lunch, brought from the ship, and being deprived of our intended siesta by the flies, Francis and I sailed the skiff, the one for which we had designed and made the sails, over to Gozo for a swim. After supper most of our party went up to the Comino Bar, which they drank out of beer! I am not, and was not then, a great beer drinker, so I went swimming in the moonlight instead, and so to bed.

The next morning Francis and I (Old Etonians seemed to stick together!) walked up to the five hundred-year-old castle on the highest point of the island. Most of the houses had been built of stones recycled from the castle, and particularly from the original stairs, so we had to climb a very rickety wooden ladder to the top. We were not fifty metres from the edge of the cliff, in which at sea level there is a cave vertically below the castle, and we convinced ourselves that there must be an interconnection between the two. We could find no trace of this from the castle end, so we decided to look from below. We first collected enough rope to climb down but, looking over the edge at the sea below, wisdom got the better of valour, and we abandoned that idea. We went back to the beach, Francis tied a flashlight to his head with a handkerchief and a couple of ties (who could have brought ties on a camping expedition?) and we swam the quarter of a mile from our landing beach and into the cave. It was about fifty metres from the entrance to a white sandy beach with a large chamber beyond it. We tried hard to find a hole leading upwards, but our flashlight was just too feeble. So we lashed it to my head this time and swam back to our camp. We had lunch, and then set off to sail back to Grand Harbour and *QE*.

Chapter Thirteen

Spanish Civil War

We were now spending more and more of our time at sea. The Spanish Civil War was becoming increasingly violent, as the government side, which had started as socialist, became more communist and anarchist, and though it was more numerous it was much less well equipped than the 'rebel' army, and a less-disciplined military force – the Navy, the majority of which was with the government, for example, was being run by the Sailors' Soviet, since most of the officers had been murdered. The rebels, under General Francisco Franco, had the army and the air force, of which General Franco's brother was the head, were largely professional, and enjoyed the support of the Church and the wealthy. This war was too tempting a small-scale try-out for the big-power supporters of the opposing sides. The USSR openly and actively, and France more timidly, supported the government, while Germany and Italy did the same for fellow fascist Franco. By mid-August Franco's forces controlled Morocco, the coast from Gibraltar west to the Portuguese border and north to La Coruña, and along the French border, and the Balearic Islands of Ibiza and Mallorca. The whole east coast south from Barcelona was in government hands, as was a small enclave around Madrid, and Menorca and Formentera. The government was, however, losing ground, and its troops were becoming more barbarous in their ways of dealing with their enemies, and anyone they suspected of supporting the other side. Each side accused the other of atrocities against civilians, and I picked up in two ports, one of each faction, a copy of a pamphlet with a title something like: 'Atrocities committed by the fascist rebels [*or* communist gangs] against workers and peasants [*or* priests and nuns]'. The fact that, apart from the terms used to identify villains and victims, and a few place names, the texts were identical, made one less inclined to believe either, though alas we, and other ships of the fleet, became, not eyewitnesses but recipients of enough hard news to know that it was a very dirty war.

We were hardly back from Comino when we learned that we were to leave for a round trip of the centres of fighting on the east coast of Spain and the Straits of Gibraltar, which was the scene of considerable naval activity. The Spanish navy was doing its best to interdict reinforcements and supplies for Franco from Morocco, and bombarding Ceuta, the principal port and naval base of Franco in Africa.

But Malta was scarcely below the horizon astern when an emergency occurred. One of *QE*'s boy seamen, Boy Parry, developed pneumonia. The destroyer HMS *Wolsey* was in company with us, and the Commander-in-Chief decided, on medical advice, that Boy Parry's life would be in danger if he could not be got into a hospital quickly. The sea was fairly rough, so *QE* stopped across the sea, and *Wolsey* came up to within one hundred metres of our ship, in the comparative calm under our lee, at right angles to us. I was in charge of the cutter, which was lowered and slipped with the patient in a cot, and with our principal medical officer and a sickbay Petty Officer on board. I took the boat alongside *Wolsey* (which had no medical officer of her own) but a few feet away, so that the cot could be hoisted aboard the destroyer by her torpedo davit. I then got right alongside so that the PMO and the sickbay PO could board, and waited just clear until the PMO had finished his briefing of *Wolsey*'s people on the care that Parry needed until he got to hospital. I then went back alongside, picked up the PMO, and returned to the ship. This was the sort of thing we had practised many times, but the first time I'd done it in earnest and in a really rough sea. I came back on board with a new respect for a boat with oars for this kind of a job: it had no speed, of course, but the precision with which a trained crew can manoeuvre a boat was an order of magnitude better than any powerboat at that time.

After two days at sea we anchored in Palma de Mallorca – in Franco's hands – and found ourselves in the company of HMS *Galatea*, flagship of the Rear Admiral (Destroyers) and an Italian cruiser and destroyer, and the following day a French cruiser, *Colbert*, joined the party. Following the traditional courtesy of the sea in time of peace the Rear Admiral (Destroyers), the French admiral from *Colbert* and the Captains of all the ships there paid calls on the Commander-in-Chief, who duly returned their calls.

We – officers and ratings – got three hours' leave to go ashore. It was not much time to see a lot, but enough to begin to appreciate what war can mean to civilians. Every car carried a notice '*Requisado por artillería*', '*...por medicos*', '*...por aviación*', and the streets were full of fascist militiamen. There was no rice or sugar on the island, and flour was running short, but the people were friendly, and the town was clean. But about 10 p.m. we heard bursts of machine-gun fire, and were told the next day that the noise was 'communists being executed'. This, however, did not prevent a large group of ratings and about twenty officers attending a bullfight the next afternoon.

I hated the actual fight, but the pageantry was interesting, and when the fascist commanders entered their VIP boxes, the whole audience leapt to its feet, with arms outstretched in the fascist salute, and shouting '*Viva!*' at the top of its voice. We had all seen this sort of thing on Movietone News at the cinema, but to see it live, in colour in the bright sun, and right alongside you, really conveyed the sense of fear that comes from a fanatical crowd. War seemed a step nearer – as indeed it was. Nevertheless, that evening the Captains of the two Italian ships dined with the Admiral and watched a movie afterwards on *QE*'s quarter-deck with all the rest of us. The camaraderie between seafarers was stronger than political differences!

After the movie was over *QE* sailed for Barcelona, with nineteen refugees, mostly British subjects who had been living in Mallorca. We arrived the following morning and anchored outside the harbour, to join two other British, two Italian, and one each French and German warships. After only seven hours in Barcelona, we sailed for Valencia, where our stay was even briefer. We went on to Alicante, where we didn't even anchor, just stopped while my cutter's crew and I went over to the destroyer HMS *Gipsy*, and brought the British consul from Alicante and the Captain of the depot ship, HMS *Woolwich* to *QE* for a conference with the Commander-in-Chief. As soon as the meeting was over, and the Admiral had been briefed on the situation in Alicante, the cutter took them back to *Gipsy*, and we sailed for Malaga.

There we anchored outside the harbour, inside which was most of the government's fleet: the battleships *Jaime Primero* and *Cervantes*, three cruisers and some smaller craft. I confided to my journal that the Spanish ships badly needed a coat of paint and a scrub, and that as they had no steam up they could only serve as floating gun batteries. In the late afternoon, however, we sounded the 'alarm to arms' and all our anti-aircraft guns were manned and readied, while the rest of the ship's company was sent below armour.

Nothing untoward occurred, but in the early evening we sailed eight miles north-east along the coast and anchored for the night, before sailing for Gibraltar in the morning, with the anti-aircraft guns manned in watches until we anchored in Gibraltar Bay.

During the few hours since we left Malaga the situation had become critical: a large number of the troops had refused to fight the Nationalists (as Franco's forces were now called) and were threatening to loot the city and then depart. Both the Anarchists, and the Loyalists in the ships, took grave exception to this and promised to retaliate by firing on the troops, starting a civil war within a civil war.

QE sailed from Gibraltar in the evening for Malta, and with the intention of visiting Melilla in Morocco on the way. But in the middle of the night we altered course for Malaga again, since the situation there was worsening rapidly, and the lives of non-Spanish residents were in danger. We anchored in the company of two or three other British warships, and an American destroyer, USS *Hatfield*.

The Rear Admiral in command of the first battle squadron, who was in Malaga in the cruiser *Shropshire*, the Captain of the *Worcester* and the British consul all came on board in one of our picket boats, and conferred with the Commander-in-Chief about arrangements for the evacuation of British residents. During the afternoon a considerable number of refugees were embarked by *Worcester*, which entered the harbour to do so, and transferred them by sea boat to *Shropshire* which took them to Gibraltar.

Meanwhile the Commander-in-Chief had asked the admiral commanding Gibraltar to come to Malaga in a destroyer to be on top of the situation there as it might develop.

By the time he arrived, the wind had risen to gale force and the picket boat had had to be hoisted in, so *QE* weighed anchor and made a lee for my cutter to ferry him from his destroyer, *Anthony*, and later back again. We then sailed on for Malta. By the next day two thousand reinforcements for the government troops in Malaga arrived, with new military and civil governors, to fire their predecessors and stabilise the situation there. But the principal result was that all the Spanish warships in Malaga raised steam and sailed for Oran in Morocco, where they surrendered to Franco's forces!

By mid-November it seemed that the fall of Madrid could not be long delayed, and the British minister, Mr George Ogilvie-Forbes, of an old Aberdeenshire Roman Catholic family, and his staff left the city, and transferred what was left of the Legation to Valencia. Many warm tributes were paid to Mr Ogilvie-Forbes for his courage, ingenuity and kindness in helping those, Spanish as well as British subjects, who were in need of help. (How could I guess then that twenty-five years later I would be married to a lady who had been one of Sir George Ogilvie-Forbes's secretaries when he was the British ambassador to Cuba?)

In the event, however, Franco failed to press his advantage. He could have taken Madrid before the month of November was out, but, because he wished to spare the historic city as much as possible, and also knowing that his largely Moroccan soldiers would soon be reinforced by Germans and Italians, he hesitated, and the focus of the war moved northwards.

While these incidents were not my last brush with the Spanish Civil War – I met it again the following year off the Basque coast in the north of Spain, when I was serving in HMS *Resolution* – most of the east coast was in Nationalist hands, and all foreign residents who wished to leave had been evacuated.

Chapter Fourteen

The Aegean, Greece and Admiral's Inspection

Though we midshipmen were working hands most of the time, we were also in the middle of our naval education. We spent an average of maybe six or seven hours a week with the 'Schoolies' – the instructor officers – following on from what we learned in studying the theoretical bases of our profession, including more spherical trigonometry, ballistics, calculus, the mechanics of a ship's movement through water, the electronics (though the word was not then in use) of radio communications, and naval history. The ship, too, continued its education.

After a very short visit to Tribuki on the island of Skyros, for the purpose of visiting the tomb of the poet Rupert Brooke – that 'corner of a foreign field that is for ever England' – we went on to Moudhros, a vast and splendid natural harbour in the island of Lemnos, in the northern Aegean, not far from the coast of Turkey. There we spent ten days doing every conceivable kind of drill and exercise, from letting go a second anchor, and then weighing it (hoisting it back up again) by hand – these anchors must have weighed all of three tons, so it was no easy task – to sending a diver (complete with all his gear, air pump and all) to the flagship and then firing a rocket!

My main task was to lay out a kedge anchor (smaller

than the main bower-anchors) in the first cutter. This involved two planks across two of the thwarts of the boat, to which was secured a reel containing a steel wire rope two and a half inches in circumference. Next, a sufficient length of this wire was coiled around the outside of the boat to allow the anchor to reach the seabed when slipped. Then the anchor itself was lowered from a davit in the ship and allowed to rest against the stern of the cutter cushioned by a 'shot mat'. The anchor was slung in this position by a loop of wire rope, in which a slip was incorporated, secured to the after keel sling plate in the bottom of the boat. Finally the end of the wire outside the boat was shackled to the anchor. We rowed it round to the stern of the ship, and there let it go, and passed the rest of the wire rope up to the ship, where, without mechanical help, it was weighed by the manpower on deck only. As soon as it was secured in the ship, it was again lowered and slung as before on the stern of the cutter. This was done in ten minutes and fifty seconds: I was in charge of all that happened in the boat: I was nineteen.

Since all work and no play makes Jack a dull boy, we had sailing races, water polo matches and even time to go ashore. And one evening the ship's company invited the gunroom and warrant officers to tombola (as sailors called what is better known as bingo) on the quarterdeck. They probably regretted inviting the warrant officers, because one of them, Sergeant Major Crees, Royal Marines, beat odds of ten thousand to one, and walked off with a large share of the prize money by winning two consecutive 'houses'!

Even when all the doings in Moudhros were over, and we sailed for an overnight passage to Phaleron Bay, Athens, we had a mock air attack from fighters and torpedo bombers from the aircraft carrier HMS *Glorious*, and two 'night encounter' exercises with HMS *Repulse*, in which

QE's illumination of the 'enemy' was, I recorded with pride, particularly successful.

Between two intensive periods of exercises, our small squadron, *Glorious, QE* and *Repulse*, made an official visit to Greece. We entered the bay and anchored in line abreast, and *QE* fired the twenty-one-gun salute to our host country. The official calls started soon afterwards, beginning with the British consul's on the Commander-in-Chief, followed by the Captain of the Port of Athens, and the Captains of *Glorious* and *Repulse*. At 11 a.m. the Commander-in-Chief left to pay his official calls, and to have lunch with King George II of Greece (officially of the Hellenes). The President of the Council of Greece gave an official dinner in the evening for the Admiral and his senior staff officers, and the next morning the Greek minister of marine and the British minister to Greece (whose son, John Waterlow, was my great friend at Eton) returned the Admiral's calls, and each duly got his seventeen-gun salute on departure. I imagine that both had to return later for the official lunch on board given by the Admiral.

The next day, Saturday 17th October, however, was the big day. The King of the Hellenes (who had the rank of Admiral of the Fleet in the British Navy) arrived on board at 12.45 p.m., and took the salute of the whole ship's company as it marched past him on the quarterdeck. Lunch on board followed and King George II then transferred to *Glorious*, and finally, in mid-afternoon, he returned ashore.

All Saturday's ceremonial I missed, however, since Christopher Bax and I had got leave from 11 a.m. until the next evening. We stayed in the Hotel Grande Bretagne, then, as now, one of the great hotels of the world, for the price of five shillings – one day's pay, and the equivalent of one and a quarter US dollars – for a double room and continental breakfast. We walked around the city in what remained of the morning, and spent the afternoon at the

Acropolis, which we had virtually to ourselves. Fifty-four years later, Billie and I went on a ship-borne tour of 'the classic sites of ancient civilisations'. We started from Athens, and stayed in the same Grande Bretagne. Our double room, smaller than I remembered Christopher Bax's and my five-shilling room, cost fifty dollars a day. And the Acropolis was as crowded as the first day of the post-Christmas Day sale at Harrods!

Nothing that one can write or say can do justice to the Acropolis, the ravages of time, the Turks and industrial pollution notwithstanding. The sheer work of building it, without any mechanical assistance, overwhelms the mind. The pyramids of Gizeh are of enormously greater volume, but they are after all built of (admittedly huge) blocks of stone, all of the same shape: the temples on the Acropolis, and especially, but by no means only, the Parthenon are of such beauty and such perfection of shape that cannot but excite wonder. What may look like straight lines are often very delicate curves, to offset the optical illusions which straight lines can produce. How did Phidias, the sculptor who supervised the whole project, know how much of a curve to give a cornice to make it appear straight, considering that only very precise measurements can even detect it? And how did he get it executed?

The next day Christopher and I joined forces with two other junior officers from *QE*, and went on a tour to Cape Sounion and Marathon. Cape Sounion is a high rocky headland, the very tip of the Attic peninsula, several hundred feet above sea level, on which stands the surviving twelve white marble columns of a famous, and most beautiful, temple of Poseidon. Its position, its height and its whiteness make it very visible from the sea, and it is (as is only suitable for a temple to the god of the sea) a notable navigation mark to mariners. It is defaced, alas, by having Lord Byron's name, carved by himself, on one of its columns. The Greeks, however, presumably pardon (or had pardoned) the vandalism in the light of his contribution to the liberation of Greece from the Ottoman Empire, for the carving was covered by a protective glass in a wooden frame.

At the foot of the cliff is a spring of fresh water, not five metres from the edge of the sea, where the local fishing boats get their drinking water. Here, in the clear blue water, the four of us had a swim before going to the Sounion Rest House for a very good lunch, and then driving on to Marathon. As everyone who knows about the modern athletic marathon is aware, Marathon lies 26 miles, 385 yards from Athens, and is the distance run by Pheidippides to take the news of the Greeks' victory over the Persians to the city. At the time of the battle in 491 or 490 BC, the narrow plain between the mountains and the sea on which Marathon stands was grassy, but is now all wooded, except at the south end where there is a mound, about ten metres high, under which are buried the 129 Athenians who died in the battle. The bottleneck of the plain and the discipline and tactics of the Greek phalanx allowed the Greek army, outnumbered many times by the Persians' fifty thousand men, to destroy one-seventh of Darius's army and rout the rest. The Athenian victory saved Greece and probably all of Europe from being overrun by invaders from Asia.

Those two days were very emotional, and the next day would have been a big let-down, if we hadn't all been very busy. Starting in the morning all the boats on the boat deck (one higher than the quarterdeck) were lowered into the water, and the crutches in which they normally rested were removed to leave a clear space for the dance which the ship was to give in the evening. The quarterdeck and boat deck guard rails all had their canvas screens rigged, hundreds of potted plants were brought on board to decorate, and the fighting ship was transformed into a ballroom.

All the midshipmen were kept busy that evening. The dance was to start at 10 p.m., and at 9.45 *QE*'s picket boats, those of *Glorious* and *Repulse* and the Admiral's two barges were inshore to start bringing the guests on board. Two of us were stationed at the bottom of the gangway ladders to give people a hand getting out of the boats, and others were guides to cloakrooms and toilet facilities, but by about 11 p.m. we were free to join the dance. I danced a lot with a Greek girl who, though she spoke no English did speak French, and who knew Alexandria, where we discovered we had mutual acquaintances, so that, as I wrote rather pompously at the time '*I was provided with a subject for conversation and a medium for it, and thus with a solution of the really difficult problem of small talk at a cosmopolitan dance.*' Music was provided by a joint Royal Marine band from the three ships in company, as well as *QE*'s own amateur dance band.

Then back to training for war: on Trafalgar Day, 21st October, the squadron left Phaleron Bay for the overnight passage to Suda Bay, in Crete. This, like Moudhros, is a very large bay, at the head of which is Khaniá, one of the principal cities of Crete. The three ships anchored, *QE* fired the national salute of twenty-one guns, and almost at once the formal calls, both ways, began; two of these, of the general officer commanding the Khaniá garrison and the acting governor of Crete, called for thirteen- and fifteen-gun salutes respectively. Obviously, one of the things that we were learning along the way was the formal, indeed formalised protocol – who calls on whom first, and who gets how many guns, and so on – which oils the contacts between one navy and another.

In Suda Bay, *QE* was to undergo the ordeal of an inspection by the Commander-in-Chief, so we spent the whole of our first full day there, and from 5.40 a.m. the following day, giving the ship its final clean-up before the

Admiral's eagle eye was upon us.

There is a tale – perhaps apocryphal – about a battleship awaiting an Admiral's inspection. The Commander, as the ship's executive officer, had the responsibility for having everything ready. All the sailors had had haircuts; the depth of the 'duffel bags' at the lower ends of their black neck scarves was checked for uniformity by ruler; all medal ribbons were horizontal; the bilges in the bottom of the ship were all red lead painted under the bilge boards; and the copper tot measures for the rum ration were polished to brilliance. All brass work was shining, and all cordage on deck was appropriately coiled. The Marine band was ready on the quarterdeck, and at the head of the gangway the Bosun's Mates were standing by with their calls[1] to pipe the Admiral over the side. The Captain was standing a little apart, while the Commander had a last look round, watching the flagship through his telescope every half-minute or so. At last he saw the Admiral step on to the gangway ladder and go down into his barge. All officers were dressed in frock coats, and these had pockets in their tails.

When the barge was about halfway from the flagship, the Commander reached into one of his tail pockets, pulled out a potato and, to the Captain's horror, rolled it out of sight under the tail of the fifteen-inch gun turret. He called the Commander over and said, 'Commander, what the devil did you do that for?'

'Sir if we don't let this bastard find *something* wrong we're going to have the hell of a time.'[2]

---

[1]Whistles.

[2]I have used this principle much in my life. I call it 'the policy of the potato', and use it to give someone, who I know will not agree with the whole of a proposal I am making, something to find. Often he will let what's really important to me go by unargued once he finds whatever it is I know he dislikes.

Our inspection lasted four days. On the Saturday the Admiral inspected the engine room department, and then the fifteen-inch gun turrets (not manned – he was looking at the condition of the hardware) and the Fleet Accounting Officer inspected our accounting department. On Sunday it was the turn of the ship's company; everyone fell in as Divisions, and the Admiral walked round and inspected all of us, stopping every now and again to talk with an individual. When he was finished, we all marched aft for prayers on the quarterdeck, while the Admiral inspected the mess decks, and the separate messes for officers and Petty Officers. The next two days we were inspected at action stations, doing gun drills and such, and then he gave us a series of general drills, much as we had done for ourselves in Moudhros. I struck lucky, and was given the same exercise as there – lay out a kedge anchor. My cutter's crew benefited from the previous experience, and all went well. We were to let the anchor go two hundred yards from the ship, and before we did so the Admiral came alongside in his barge to see whether he approved of the way we had things in the boat rigged – thank heaven, he did! And if he found anything wrong in his four days of (to use a sailor's expression) 'looking for fly shit in pepper', we didn't hear about it.

So we left Suda Bay for Malta with our morale high, and a sense of relief. On our first full day at sea, in very bad weather, we carried out a full-calibre fifteen-inch gunnery practice, with *Repulse* as our 'target', with a six° throw-off. This, of course, didn't tell you whether you had got your direction right, but the 'target' could observe whether you had the range, which was the difficult part of aiming big guns. No sooner was this over than we began a full-power

---

what's really important to me go by unargued once he finds whatever it is I know he dislikes.

trial, and achieved eighty thousand horse power, five thousand horse power over designed power – not bad for a ship nearly twenty years old. All four of us (by now) senior midshipmen were employed reading the torsion meters on the propeller shafts, so we were the sources of the original data for calculating the horse power achieved.

Our return to Malta brought a big bonus to us midshipmen. The Admiral went ashore to live at Admiralty House, and his staff transferred to the historic Auberge de Castille (now the offices of the Prime Minister of Malta). This left cabins unoccupied, and the senior ones among us were able to move in and, until the Admiral came back to his flagship, enjoy a standard of comfort degrees above a hammock and a sea-chest.

We soon became busy again, for in November a squadron of the Turkish fleet was to visit Malta. The battlecruiser *Yavuz Sultan Selim* was the flagship of this squadron, accompanied by four destroyers and four submarines with their depot ship *Erkin*. *Yavuz* – the other two names were almost always dropped – was to berth between two buoys, and my first cutter and I got the task of securing her bows. This was normally done by 'catting' an anchor, that is supporting it from the deck, and unshackling the chain cable which can then be coupled to the mooring ring of the buoy. Oddly, *Yavuz* had no means of catting her anchor, and so had to rely on four parts of heavy wire rope. I wasn't looking forward to having to moor a visiting foreign ship – the honour of the Royal Navy was at stake – but I need not have worried; my cutter's crew and I had now worked together long enough to take on most jobs!

As soon as the formal calls were over, a calling party from *QE*'s wardroom and gunroom went over to *Yavuz* to make arrangements for the entertainment of our guests. We were plied with many-hued cigarettes, sweet wine, chocolates and lots of Turkish coffee by about a dozen charming men, many of whom spoke tolerable English. The first major event was to be that evening; a gala performance at the Royal Opera House. This, an eighteenth-century building, was destroyed during World War II, but it was a little gem. The market for opera in Malta was not large, and so we had to make do with third-rate Italian companies who couldn't get better engagements in Italy or Sicily. That evening the opera was *La Bohème*, and one hundred and thirty officers and over one hundred ratings from both fleets attended.

At the time, prima donnas did not dress in costume, but wore, as if it had been a concert performance, their best evening dresses. Our Mimi was tall and fat, and dressed ('upholstered' describes it better) in white satin, very décolleté, her neck draped in necklaces and her hands covered with rings. These hands were a sight in themselves, looking like nothing so much as small hams with five veal sausages pendent from each. The tenor, in contrast, was plump and short, so that even his elevator shoes, which raised him a good two inches, scarcely brought the top of his head to the level of Mimi's chin. This was my first opera, but I knew that this art form required a certain level of suspension of belief. However, when we came to the aria '*Che gelida manina*' (I knew that the accepted translation of his words was 'Your tiny hand is frozen...') and our shorty Rodolfo held up the bejewelled ham, visibly dripping sweat, it was just too much for me, and it put me off opera for twenty years.

The next night the gunroom entertained a baker's dozen of Turkish junior officers to dinner. Otto Jenner-Fust made a very good speech after dinner, before the toasts, and was answered in excellent English by a Turkish Sub Lieutenant, who ended with the words: 'We are taught at school that the English are terrible people: now we are very surprised!'

They sang Turkish songs to us, and we replied in kind, though I hope I am right in remembering that we didn't include any of the typical gunroom ballads! Rowing and sailing races, tea parties, cocktail parties, the ceremony of Beating the Retreat and visits to each other's ships kept us busy for the rest of the visit.

Interpolation

In the summer of 1936 King Edward VIII chartered the yacht *Nahlin,* which he and his party joined at Sibenik, on the Dalmatian coast, and left for a holiday at 'destinations unknown'. Two destroyers of the Mediterranean Fleet escorted the *Nahlin*, and some of their people must have become aware that the King's principal guest was his mistress, Wallis Simpson, but no word of this seems to have leaked out, except to the American, French and German press. How the conspiracy of silence in Britain was maintained has always puzzled me, but this, of course, was long before the days of press leaks and paparazzi. As Prince of Wales, Edward VIII enjoyed great and general popularity, not only in Britain but in the parts of the Commonwealth (the Empire, as it was then) to which he paid official visits, and especially in the Navy; he had been educated at the Royal Naval Colleges at Osborne and Dartmouth, and so was one of our own. His palpable sympathy for the plight of unemployed people during the Depression – especially demonstrated on visits to the worst-hit areas of the country, like south Wales – and his charm and unroyal informality enhanced his reputation, and few monarchs can have ascended the throne with a larger store of goodwill.

We now know that he had another side to him, that he could be boorish, and even downright rude in situations that bored him, as contemporary photographs, never published at the time, make all too clear. But none of this was public knowledge in Britain, and nor was his considerable sympathy for Hitler.

There must have been an increasing number of people who were aware of what was daily news in the American press, but a sense of loyalty to the Crown and reluctance to give full credence to what I for one described in my journal as a '*reprehensible and altogether indecent campaign of publicity and scandal*' kept the story out of the UK press. And after all, if *The Times* didn't have the story, it couldn't be true! On 3rd December, 1936, I wrote, indignantly, that the press in the USA had gone so far as to suggest that the King was contemplating a marriage which would be incompatible with the dignity of the throne.

It was one week later, on 11th December, that the King executed his instrument of abdication, and late in the evening of the 12th he broadcast a message to the nation. Rereading it now it seems typical of what we know his true character to have been – shallow and utterly selfish – but at the time I described it as moving and dignified, and wrote that '*the Country and Empire have lost a faithful champion and true friend*'. It was a terrible shock to the Navy – *his* Navy – and it took some days for the full enormity of the situation to sink in: that we had been kept in ignorance by the press and the government. We felt let down; worse, we felt betrayed by him, and by institutions, the government and the press, which we felt we had a right to trust. It was perhaps best summed up by a Petty Officer friend of mine, the coxswain of my picket boat who said, 'Who could ever have thought that our King, who was an Admiral of the Fleet in our Navy, could give that up to become third mate of an American destroyer?'

It was bitter at the time, but we have since come to realise that Wallis Simpson did us a great favour; Edward Windsor would have been, during the war, at best lukewarm, and, at worst, as an admirer of Hitler, a virtual fifth column.

Chapter Fifteen

Engineering and Destroyer Time

We were being trained to be executive officers, for what is now, I think, called the 'seaman branch'. The running of ships and then command was our end, and none of the 'specialist' branches; engineers, paymasters and others, could aspire to command, but clearly you cannot run a ship unless you have a more than superficial knowledge of how it works, in the mechanical sense. In battle you may have to override the professional advice of an engineer officer, and you can't do this unless you have a basic understanding of the consequences.

So, in late December Bax, Meynell, Ogilvie and I started an engineering course. We began by making a sketch of all the machinery spaces throughout the ship and recording the function, size, capacity and so on of all the auxiliary machinery. Then we understudied various engineer officers and took part in preparing for sea – warming through the turbines so that both rotor and casing could expand to the size they would have under steam, 'flashing up' boilers, working up vacuum in the condensers, starting the circulators which cooled them and the air pumps which created the vacuum.

Once at sea, we stood watch with the engine room people, and got, among other tasks, to man the main steam valves to the turbines. The demand for steam from the turbines had to be matched by what the boilers were producing, which in turn controlled how much fuel was burned, how many sprayers were in use, and at what pressure the fuel was supplied to them. Too little air with the fuel produced black smoke, too much, white, so there were observation windows in the funnels watched by an observer who told the boiler rooms what was happening, to allow the air pressure in the boiler room (which is always above that of the outside) to be adjusted to keep a clear funnel. Once back in harbour we worked on closing down the boilers which were not needed, closing down boilers at their main stop valves, and cooling them by injecting cold feed water so that the residual heat of the boiler and furnace didn't generate more steam and blow the safety valve. Climbing on to the top of a boiler to close the stop valve is still the hottest job that I know of!

The rest of my time in *QE*, until I rejoined later in the year, I spent in the roles of stoker, stoker Petty Officer or understudy to the engineer officer of the watch.

Our next spell was 'destroyer time'. Christopher and I were appointed to a new destroyer, *Hasty*, of the second destroyer flotilla. In this ship we had the great luxury of a cabin to ourselves, though since I (for some reason) got the bunk, Christopher had to sling a hammock in the passage outside.

Life in a destroyer was very different from that in a battleship. We were members of the wardroom mess, where all the officers, including the Captain (a total of nine, counting the two of us) lived and had their meals, so we had much closer contact with all of them, and opportunities to ask questions and discuss problems in a relaxed, social atmosphere. We kept watch at sea as understudies, and in harbour, on our own, and at sea we would often be given the job, normally done by the officer of the watch, of station-keeping – adjusting the course and speed to keep the ship at the right distance in the right direction (astern, abeam or on the quarter – forty-five degrees from the course on which the unit is steaming) from the next ship ahead.

At first, I found this very difficult. When you find you are dropping back, you increase speed; it doesn't seem to make much difference at first; you increase a bit more, and suddenly find you've overshot; you decrease speed, but again there's a delay in getting the result you want, and you find your ship acting almost as if it were connected to the ship ahead by a rubber band, bouncing around the place you want to be. But with a bit of practice you learn to allow for momentum, and if you get really good at it, you don't vary your station by more than a few yards. Bad weather makes it all a lot more difficult, and we had a lot!

The British doctrine of naval war in 1937 was that there would be only one main fleet action, which would effectively leave the fleet of the loser sidelined. The role of the destroyers would be threefold: anti-submarine protection of a battle fleet ('screening'), searching for the enemy fleet, and torpedo attacks on the enemy's capital ships. The French and Italian navies built large ships, almost light cruisers, as destroyers; the British much smaller, but in larger numbers. Though this was never, I think, officially stated as policy, British destroyers were considered expendable. Their offensive armament consisted of eight twenty-one-inch torpedoes, in two sets of launching tubes, and all eight would normally be fired, at right angles to the ship's course, one after the other while the ship was turning, so as to cover a wider target area. No reload torpedoes could be carried in such small ships, so the destroyer was a one-shot weapon. To fight its way through an enemy screen to the capital ships, and out again after an attack, they had four 4.7-inch guns, and in those days before we had any real experience of air attack, anti-aircraft armament of a few World War I machine-guns – what the sailors would have called 'farting against thunder'!

It was newspaper photographs of combined fleet exercises that crystallised my desire to join the Navy, and in *Hasty* we took part in those of the late winter of 1937. They began in the western Mediterranean, where the weather was bad, but not as bad as when (after a brief stop in Gibraltar for fuel) we got into the Atlantic: so bad indeed that we could not maintain the speed of the fleet without risking severe damage, and the destroyers were ordered to act independently. We carried out, none the less, search, shadowing, screening and torpedo attack exercises, and learned many lessons. Radar did not exist then so the only contact with an enemy was visual, and in retiring after an attack a smoke screen provided pretty good cover, but any sudden reduction of visibility, like a rain squall, made it all too easy for you to fail to sight the 'enemy', or to lose him if you were shadowing. Despite the weather, and middle watches (midnight to 4 a.m.) it was very interesting, almost fun; and when the exercises were completed, after nearly three weeks, all the ships taking part met in Gibraltar, and we had the opportunity of seeing again old friends and swapping bad weather stories!

On the return we visited the city of Tunis, and had a fascinating time. Tunisia was then a French protectorate, and we were given wonderful hospitality by the French officials, the British consul-general, a (British) major of the Egyptian police, retired to Tunis, and many others. The consul-general and his wife gave a delightful party in their home, which had been one of the Bey's palaces, given by him to Britain for this purpose. Christopher Bax and I tried to find the ruins of Carthage, but the sign '*Aux ruines*' was equivocal, and we went downhill instead of up, and after lunch decided it was too hot to climb back up, so contented ourselves with a swim at Plage Amilcar. On the way back we walked through a very lovely Arab village, Sidi Bou Saeed, which more than made up for missing the '*ruines*'.

Eventually *Hasty* worked its way back to Malta, where, on 11th April, I woke up with a headache and a slight fever, and in the evening was admitted to the Royal Naval Hospital, Bighi, and diagnosed as having hepatitis. This is a nasty disease, sometimes known as jaundice (one of its symptoms) which causes an inflammation of the liver. Starting with the whites of your eyes, your whole body turns yellow, but this is not the worst symptom: you really do get a jaundiced outlook on life! At my worst, I felt like jumping out of the window; but luckily it has its built-in safety mechanism. However jaundiced you feel, and however desirable an end to life seems, you just don't have the will-power to get out of bed and walk to the window. But it illustrates vividly the well-known apophthegm and amphibiology 'Is life worth living? It depends on the liver.' There is no specific treatment but rest and a very dull diet. It exemplifies the cynic's view of the practice of medicine, that the doctor's job is to keep the patient amused, while nature effects a cure. Well, I wasn't very amused, but after three or four weeks they let me out of the hospital, not fully recovered, and 'found unfit for further service on the Mediterranean station'. So I joined HMS *Barham* for passage to the UK. There I was transferred to the Royal Naval Hospital, Haslar, was 'surveyed' (such was the term) and had my blood and other things tested, found fit, and so was able to rejoin my old ship, *QE*.

Chapter Sixteen

Last Months as Midshipman

The day before *Barham* reached Portsmouth had been the coronation of King George VI and Queen Elizabeth, and one of the celebrations of this event was to be a naval review by the King in Spithead, the anchorage between Portsmouth and the Isle of Wight. The ships of seventeen foreign navies were to attend, and the first arrivals were already in Portsmouth when *Barham* arrived. So when I returned on board *QE* (still flagship of the Mediterranean Fleet) she was in the midst of preparations for the review. A stage was built for VIP guests, brass work was polished, we practised illuminating the ship with light bulbs all round its silhouette, and 'manning ship'; having a single line of sailors facing outboard round every level of the ship, ready to 'off caps' and cheer the King as the royal yacht *Victoria and Albert* passed us in his review.

My job that day, under Lieutenant Commander Tothill, was to be in charge of the guests. Many members of foreign royal families and other dignitaries attended, and were on board the larger British ships present. Our greatest guests were Prince and Princess Chichibu of Japan, and it fell to me to receive them at the bottom of the gangway, and offer my white-gloved hand to help them out of the boat. While the sea was not rough, it had enough movement that the boats rose and fell a little when alongside the gangway. The Prince ignored my proffered hand and stepped nimbly out of the boat. The Princess, a very pretty, tiny young woman in her twenties, dressed as if for a garden party, including high-heeled shoes, likewise shunned my hand (members of the Japanese imperial family, to this day, do not touch commoners – if they can help it) but she was less agile than her husband, and tripped as she tried to step from the boat to the gangway. If she had not been so light, and I had not been able to grab her arm, nothing could have stopped her falling into the sea. However, she recovered her footing, gave me a slightly nervous smile, and went on up the ladder. I often wonder what would have been my fate if I had not succeeded, and allowed a daughter-in-law of the emperor of Japan to get a ducking – or worse!

The review was a very impressive occasion, and the following day the King visited *QE*. The Captains of all the ships of the Mediterranean Fleet were presented to His Majesty, the ship's company marched past him and then, as he left, gave him three cheers. And the day after that the paying-off pendant was hoisted at *QE*'s masthead, a red cross on a narrow white ground, and a white tail a yard long for every week the ship had been in commission. We had had a splendid finish to our service in a very happy and efficient ship: I had been eighteen when we joined, and was now a few days short of my twentieth birthday, and I had grown up. A few days later all midshipmen went on leave for two months!

For the last four months of our midshipmen's time our gang of four – Bax, Meynell, Ogilvie and I – was appointed to a Home Fleet battleship, HMS *Resolution* (the name, my father told me, referred not to Hamlet's 'native hue of resolution', but to the Resolution of Parliament that abolished the monarchy, and established Cromwell's Commonwealth. *Reso*, as she was known, was of the class of battleship previous to the *QE*'s – older, slower, similarly armed, and, for the gunroom mess, more comfortable.

At the end of their sea time, midshipmen were required to pass a series of examinations, and in our early days in *Reso*, the ship's officers gave us mock exams, which allowed us to identify and correct weak spots. But these had to be fitted in between serious duty, for we sailed in mid-August to patrol off the north coast of Spain, where the last of the Loyalist government was holding out. Franco's forces were slowly but surely strangling the ground forces, Italian and German aircraft were bombing the coastal cities – Guernica, target of the most notorious attack, recorded by Picasso in his most famous painting, had been almost totally destroyed in April, and Gijón and Santander were virtually the only ports left to the Loyalists. The population was becoming dependent on imported food, much of which was being supplied by British ships, small and scruffy, but with entrepreneurial and brave Captains, of whom the best known was 'Potato' Jones, who, and whose successive cargoes of potatoes, seemed to have charmed lives. These ships had to run a blockade of Nationalist warships, and our job was to warn them of the dangers of trying to enter (and then having to leave) north Spanish ports, and to ensure that no British-flag merchant ships were interfered with outside the three-mile limit, in international waters. I imagine that the logic of using a battleship for this task was that *Reso* outgunned and was far more heavily armoured than any Spanish ship that might feel like arguing.

We were based at St Jean de Luz, in French Basque country, halfway between Biarritz and the Spanish frontier. It is a lovely little fishing port (anyone who knows La Côte Basque restaurant in New York can see a vivid mural painting of it on the west wall) against a background of Pyrenees. Its two harbours were too small for battleships, so we had to anchor off the port, and put up with the perpetual Atlantic swell. Biarritz was in easy reach, and

Francis, Christopher and I went there one afternoon to see what the high life (in French, *le 'eeg leaf*) in that Mecca of fashion was like. The swimming was great, but as crowded as Blackpool at the height of its season: we were under twenty-one, so could not get into the baccarat or roulette rooms of the Casino Bellevue. The boule room was deserted except for three dejected croupiers, so we settled for tea at the Hôtel du Palais Impérial, a building as magnificent (and as dated) as its name, and not really up to snuff at '*le thé de fiv o'cloque Anglais*'. But St Jean de Luz made up for the afternoon's relative disappointment, for it boasted (I hope it still boasts) a simple but excellent restaurant, La Taverne Basque, where three midshipmen could eat a sumptuous meal and drink a bottle of wine very cheaply.

The next day was Sunday, and after Sunday Divisions and stand-up church, we got to bathe over the side, to be met, when we came out of the sea, with the news that we were to sail in the early afternoon. A British merchant ship, SS *Millbank*, was going to attempt to get into Santander to evacuate disabled soldiers. We arrived off the port early next morning, where *Millbank* also was waiting, and two Nationalist warships, the cruiser *Almirante Cervera* and the minelayer *Jupiter*, were cruising around, watching. It was not until the next day that *Millbank*, which dared not enter the harbour because of heavy fighting in and around the city, lay off the port and embarked a large number of refugees who came out to her in small boats. By the Wednesday a British destroyer, HMS *Keith*, lay off Santander and embarked some British refugees, the Basque government and a number of Nationalist hostages who had been held by the Basques. This was just in time, because during the morning the Loyalist police and the shock troops mutinied, and compelled the government to surrender the city to the main Nationalist army (three of the five divisions of which were Italian regulars) with the sole condition that no women or children should be shot.

Virtually the only large port on the north coast of Spain left to the Loyalists was Gijón and our patrols therefore moved to the west. We watched air raids on Gijón which, if not as totally devastating as the destruction of Guernica in the spring, were an unpleasant foretaste of what was to come in Britain in three years' time. Our role was much the same as it had been off Santander, always with the same overriding restriction: Britain was not a belligerent, and nor (officially at any rate) were Italy, Germany and Russia, though the first two of these three were using the Spanish Civil War as a proving ground for a coming conflict. This status required absolute propriety in our actions, especially if we were in territorial waters, and it also called for great care in avoiding even the semblance of a hostile act, though, just in case, we spent a lot of time at action stations, especially if warships or aircraft of other nations were close. We nearly had an incident which could have led to problems. The Germans were trying out their dive-bombers, Stukas, and the techniques of their use, and one afternoon, after a raid on Gijón, a damned silly Stuka pilot decided to show off, and carry out a mock bombing run on *Reso*. He started fairly high and started to dive, at sixty degrees below the horizontal, straight at us. All our anti-aircraft guns were trained on this plane, but luckily, seconds before the Captain would have ordered 'Open fire', the pilot pulled up and turned away. Of course, he had almost certainly dropped his bombs on Gijón, but a lot of adrenaline was secreted by many of *Reso*'s ship's company!

In early October *Reso* was on patrol off Gijón for the last time, and after less than an hour in the patrol area we received a radio message from the British ship *Dover Abbey* that she was under fire from a Nationalist warship six miles offshore. We lit up six more boilers and rushed to the scene of the supposed incident, but saw no signs of *Dover Abbey*. We did meet another British ship, *Bramhill*, and from what she told us we asked *Almirante Cervera*, who was rarely out of sight, for news of *Dover Abbey*, and were told that *Dover Abbey* and another ship, *Yorkbrook*, had been captured inside the three-mile limit and were being towed to Santander, so there was nothing we could do. Two days later we left the patrol area, but before we left our Admiral sent a signal to *Almirante Cervera*: 'I expect to leave for England soon. Rear Admiral Calvert in HMS *Southampton* takes my place. All in *Resolution* wish you goodbye and good luck. I hope we shall meet one day in the future.'

To my mind, the words 'and good luck' got perilously close to the boundary between inter-naval courtesy, and an expression of political partisanship! *Almirante Cervera* replied: 'Thank you for all your good wishes. I pay you my respectful salute, and I wish you a most happy return to your country.'

On the way home, we stopped in La Pallice for a day, and the boats were hoisted out on the main derrick, worked by midshipmen, the classes for promotion to Petty Officer, and leading seaman. For four hoists we switched jobs; I did the first one as main derrick officer, and the last one as stand-in for the commissioned shipwright. What I had to do in this role, and how or when I'd ever learned the necessary skills, has vanished from my memory! We then went on to Quiberon Bay in Brittany, where we met *Southampton*, and formally handed over to her the north Spain patrol. From there we sailed, by stages (and exercising all the way) to our home port, Sheerness, near Chatham.

In between ship's duties, we, the four senior midshipmen, finished our examination papers, and on Sunday, 14th November, knowing that my log had only a couple of weeks to run, I started the entry with an illuminated capital – a red 'T' entwined with the Navy's foul anchor badge and a laurel wreath. The next Sunday had a dolphin peering through a 'D', and weekdays had plain red capitals occupying three lines. This was my farewell flourish to the rank of midshipman (and to HMS *Resolution)* for on 1st January, 1938 I was promoted to the rank of Acting Sub Lieutenant, backdated four months by reason of my exam results, so that my seniority was of 1st September, 1937.

I have written at (perhaps too) great length about my naval sea training. But I want to do full justice to the quality of that learning. I joined HMS *Frobisher* as a schoolboy of seventeen; I left HMS *Resolution* as a young man of twenty, having learned discipline, initiative, loyalty (up, down and sideways); to think, and to act on the results of thought, and to be a *seaman*; and having started to learn to be a fighting naval officer (it would take World War II to complete that lesson). It was a superb foundation for life, both in the Service and in the civilian world – and it was *fun*!

Chapter Seventeen

Courses

If times had been normal, we would have gone from *Reso* to the Royal Naval College at Greenwich, housed in the old Royal Palace and Royal Hospital (for sailors), for four months of university-level education in naval history, warfare, advanced mathematics and physics, but the shadow of the coming war dictated that our training be cut short, so that we could become available to the fleet earlier. We went, therefore, straight to the technical schools at Portsmouth, for courses in gunnery, torpedo, navigation and communications, and, as a poor substitute for Greenwich, a short 'war course'. This included two things I remember vividly.

One was an exercise taken from real life: a cruiser was on the South Atlantic Station, in the River Plate, and was required to get to Malta 'with utmost dispatch'. We were given the ship's fuel capacity, her consumption per hour at various speeds (and as you would expect, the faster, the higher the consumption per mile), the various ports at which she could refuel on the way, with the rate of loading of fuel at each. The problem: how does HMS *Imaginary* get from the River Plate to Malta in the least possible time?

In today's world, you could solve this on a computer in fifteen minutes, but we had to use our imagination and calculate each possible leg manually. One tended to try to do as many legs as possible at full speed, or as close as one could. We were in groups of three, and my group had got a pretty good solution, but we were troubled by the slow pumping rate at one intermediate stop, and suddenly asked ourselves how slowly we would have to go to cut out that port. And behold, doing one longer hop at a lower speed, instead of two at full speed, with a longish fuelling stop in between you achieved a shorter time. We had done better than the real ship, and the 'staff solution'. The staff were none too happy, and checked and double-checked our arithmetic before, reluctantly, accepting that we were right.

The other glorious moment was the final words of a lecture by the Commander-in-Chief, Portsmouth, Admiral of the Fleet, the Earl of Cork and Orrery, known, from the colour of his hair and his family name, as Ginger Boyle. As Admiral of the Fleet, he wore on his sleeves four gold stripes of normal width and one three times that width. He was not a tall man, so the gold reached almost to his elbows. His hair was now liberally tinged with grey, while his bushy eyebrows were still flaming ginger. His subject was 'The Offensive Spirit' and was essentially a disquisition on von Clausewitz's principles of war, with the emphasis on the fact that defence can't win a battle, only attack can. Therefore we must all have the spirit of the offensive; always be looking how to attack the enemy. He normally wore a monocle, grasped under one bristling eyebrow, which gave him a real look of the offensive spirit. But to be able to read his lecture notes he wore pince-nez, which didn't sit horizontally on his nose, with one side higher than the other, which made him look like a very popular English comic cinema actor of the time, who specialised in roles of a bumbling, ridiculous schoolmaster. Both his aids to sight were hung on black silk cords around his neck. He spoke from behind a lectern, so that his arms were not visible, until the end of his prepared lecture. Then he wrinkled his nose to eject the pince-nez, jammed the monocle into his eye with a fierce gesture, grasped the collar of his jacket high up on his neck so that the whole area of the gold braid was suddenly visible, glared around the room at us and said, 'So… if you don't want to fight… get out! Good morning.'

The gunnery school at Whale Island taught what its name implies, but also a lot of military style drill and marching. On Whale Island you moved at the double whenever you went from one place to another, and smartness in movement was always required, and there were a lot of gunner's mates to observe and demand compliance with the spirit as well as the letter of the rules.

I acquired, from over the doorway of the ammunition section, a saying which, with the first word adapted, I have used in many circumstances: 'Ammunition is perfectly safe until you forget it is dangerous.' Substitute 'electricity', 'gasoline', 'machine tools' or 'mountaineering' and you have an adage for all seasons. And we had fun too. One of the desiderata of marching 'in file' – in line, one behind the other – was that you should 'keep locked up in file', so that, if you all turned right or left together, you were in the correct spacing for marching abreast. The group, fifteen or twenty of us, of which I was a member, made the ability to do this a trademark. We could get so locked up that our arms swung up practically into the armpit of the chap in front and the front foot of the man behind you came further forward than your back foot. It took a lot of practice, but we achieved a standard worthy of the Radio City Music Hall Rockettes, and we stood out among other sections, which didn't hurt when you came to be marked on your drilling skills. The climax of drill was battalion drill. The parade ground at Whale Island was about an acre of flat asphalt, with a grassy slope up at one end, making a kind of acropolis from which the battalion commander could see the whole of his battalion – four companies of four platoons each – and manoeuvre them as the instructor ordered. The other end was a grassy slope down to the railway tracks on which the heavy stuff, fifteen-inch guns, one-ton shells, and so on could be moved around the school. The role of the battalion commander was taken by a Gunner's Mate or Sub Lieutenant in training. One day, a Sub Lieutenant was up there, with a Chief Gunner's Mate beside him to observe. He had got the whole battalion marching away from him, towards the slope down to the railway, and got so nervous that he couldn't think what command to give, until the Chief Gunner's Mate (one of the requirements for this rating is a stentorian voice) roared out: 'Well, say something, even if it's only "Goodbye".'

There was a fifteen-inch gun turret, or at least the inside works of one, in which we did turret drill. These guns weighed, if my memory isn't failing, one hundred tons each, and a shell weighed one ton. With things of this size everything was operated by hydraulics. The gun was loaded by means of a gun-loading cage, a contraption of three storeys, which was itself loaded in the magazine in the depths of the ship. The lowest level took the shell, and the other two a half-charge of cordite (it looks like uncooked spaghetti, contained in a silk bag) each. At the right moment the cage came hurtling up from the magazine and stopped in line with the open breech of the gun, and the hydraulic rammer went into the rear of the cage and shoved the shell into the gun so hard that the rifling of the barrel bit into the copper ring at the back of the shell. When the gun was fired, the shell would spin on its axis, and this gyroscopic action would stop the shell tumbling in flight. The half-charges meanwhile were held in the upper two compartments of the cage by trapdoors. When the rammer was withdrawn, one of the gun's crew pulled a lever on the cage which allowed the half-charges to drop down one level, so that the first could then be rammed into the gun.

For drill purposes, of course, all these pieces of ammunition were imaginary, so you couldn't see if there was a half-charge there to be rammed in. Thus if the man on the rammer operated it before the lever on the cage had been pulled, he would have been ramming nothing. The Gunner's Mate who was our turret drill instructor had a stock phrase for drawing attention to this failure if it happened. 'Still!' he would yell. 'What d'you think you're loading into that gun? A load of raspberries?'

So when we came to do our turret drill examination, we bought half a dozen cans of raspberries, and surreptitiously loaded them into the cage. When the imaginary shell had been loaded, and the rammer withdrawn, the lever was pulled and the cans rolled on to the loading tray, the man on the rammer pushed them slowly into the breach. 'Still!' roared the instructor. 'What are you loading into that gun?'

In unison, and at the tops of our voices, we answered, 'A load of raspberries!' extracted them, and gave them to him to take home to his wife. We all got one hundred per cent for that test!

Our courses were squeezed into eight months, and in September 1938 we became no longer 'acting' but full-fledged Sub Lieutenants. I was appointed to HMS *Royal Oak*, an R class battleship of the Home Fleet, whose home port was Devonport, next-door neighbour to Sir Francis Drake's Plymouth, the port out of which sailed the fleet that defeated the Spanish Armada, and I became Sub Lieutenant of the gunroom.

Later in the year, or early the next, I learned that I had come top, not only of our class, but of the three classes that had been through the examinations for the rank of Lieutenant in the year. For this I won the Ronald Megaw Memorial Prize (given by his family in memory of a naval officer who died tragically young) which consisted of a sword and forty pounds' worth of books or instruments.

The sword was made by Wilkinson, the greatest of all sword-makers (outside Japan and perhaps Toledo) and has my name and the occasion chased into the steel of the blade. The money I spent on a pair of Barr and Stroud binoculars – standard in the Navy – and, on my father's advice, a six-volume edition of Boswell's *Life of Samuel Johnson*. It is a custom in the United States to hang, in your office or in your study at home, your 'sheepskin', the certificate of your being admitted a lawyer or a doctor, or becoming a Master of Business Administration, or of whatever other educational achievement you are proud of. In a country in which much importance is attached to being a college graduate as a minimum, and preferably the possessor of an advanced degree, I am, in this respect, naked. If I need to impress in an application for something, I write down 'Eton College', trusting that the reader will not know that Eton is not a college in the American sense, but only a high school. If anyone asks me what that sword hanging on the library wall is, I tell them it's my sheepskin, and if necessary, I draw it to convince the doubter! On most occasions, however, when people ask me where I went to 'school' (meaning university) I just tell them I'm a high school drop-out, and leave them to wonder whether I'm joking.

Chapter Eighteen

HMS *Royal Oak*

My time in *Royal Oak* was, or so it seems in retrospect, rather humdrum except for four things. The first concerns the game of poker. I became a member of a seven-person poker school; we used to play after dinner, usually at sea (because, in harbour, too few people would be available). At sea, too, one or two of the school would be on watch, so we were often six or five. The Navy required a captain to keep an eye on the behaviour of his officers, and in two specifics at any rate this was done by 'the book'. You could not buy a drink from your mess bar for cash, nor, in theory, could you accept a drink paid for by a mess mate: every drink had to be recorded in the gunroom (or wardroom) wine book, which the captain saw, and initialled, every month. Likewise, you could not play cards for cash, but only on credit, recorded in the card book, also seen once a month by the captain. By these means he could tell whether any of his officers were boozing too much, or getting themselves into dangerous debt. In our school we had a five-shilling-limit rule, that any player who in the course of the evening got more than five shillings down had to drop out. We did, however, every now and again decide, by common consent, to play for the evening with no limit. One such evening was my downfall. We didn't play with straights or flushes, so fours were the highest hands. I was dealt two queens, so I threw in three cards and drew three. I got two more queens and an ace, so only four kings could beat me. There were only four players from a very early stage in the game, and as the Surgeon Commander and I started raising our bets, two very soon dropped out. The two of us still in went on upping the stakes, until I had five pounds – almost half a month's pay – riding on my confidence.

'I'll see you!' said the quack (for so we called every surgeon officer) and I, slowly and triumphantly, laid out my four queens. Half the wardroom was watching by now, and applauded as my opponent laid out four kings! Since that moment I have never again played cards for money, and have been very leery of betting on anything!

The third was a five-day visit in the spring to Brest, to call on the French navy. Each side seemed to wish to outdo the hospitality of the other, and the succession of functions was interrupted only by football matches and other sporting events. The French navy had a number of 'Star' class sharpies, the principal sailing boat of the Olympic Games, and a wonderful boat to race. I was the crew of one of our teams, and the helmsman was a junior Lieutenant in the ship. We got to practise (neither of us had ever sailed a Star before) for a couple of hours one afternoon, and the race was to start at nine in the morning of the last full day of the visit. The previous day was one of almost non-stop eating and drinking: in the morning the gunroom wine committee, of which I was a member, went ashore to stock up with French wines. We tasted goodness knows how many reds and whites, of which the wine merchant (to whom we had been recommended by our hosts) gave us sips. But when it came to the champagnes, a bottle once opened cannot be kept for future sipping, and he didn't have any half-bottles. We were four on the committee, and we tried three bottles, which we had to buy. We weren't about to waste any, so by the time we got back on board for lunch, we had each drunk three-quarters of a bottle. We had guests from some of the French ships for lunch, which of course was not a dry affair. In the late afternoon our hosts offered a '*vin d'honneur*', which was followed by dinner in one or another of the French ships.

After dinner, three of our hosts invited three of us to a nightclub, at which we were joined by six young women with whom we danced. The tune that was most popular in France then was '*Je t'attendrai*', and occasionally one still hears it, mostly on the canned music of a French restaurant, and it always brings back the romantic memory of that evening. We drank – mostly champagne – and danced, talked naval shop to our hosts and had supper, and it was 4 a.m. before they took us back to our ships. I'm sure that I have never before or since drunk so much in one day, but it was all spread out so much in time, and interspersed with so many meals, that (while I won't deny that we were perhaps exaggeratedly cheerful) no one was the worse for drink: not then, anyway.

We had to be in our Star before 8 a.m., so I arranged to be called at 6.30, and had breakfast with lots of coffee. I met my helmsman, who hadn't got back on board in time to get any sleep at all, and had had even more to drink the night before. However, we hoisted our sails and sailed around, getting the feel of the boat until we were ready to get into position for the start. It was a day of very light wind so there was not much need for the sitting out to windward which was normally needed to keep a Star upright enough to sail. The wind slackened more and more as the race went on, and all the boats were pretty well bunched up until we were on the last leg to the finish line, dead into the wind. I suddenly noticed that not only was the wind slackening, but that it was changing direction too, and I suggested to the helmsman that if we went about on to the starboard tack the shift of wind would favour us. No other boat followed us and, as they stayed on the port tack, it became clear that we had got well into the lead, and it was too late for the others to copy us. We finally got to the finish line, and just drifted across in what had virtually become a flat calm. No other boat finished, but our triumph was marred by my helmsman's stomach; for no sooner had the finish gun gone off than he was violently sick over the side. I have sailed many races in my life, but only one in which the winning helmsman had not been to bed, and got rid of his hangover in the very moment of victory.

Royal Oak did not have a qualified French interpreter, and as my French was as good or better than that of others, I was the ship's official interpreter, and I had learned, from a vocabulary that we had on board, a large number of naval technical terms, so that the Royal Navy kept its end up in our serious discussions with our hosts. It wasn't all a drinking party, because we were all too conscious that only a miracle could prevent our two countries getting into a war with Germany.

Queen Maud, wife of King Haakon VII of Norway, was a member of the British royal family, and on 20th November, 1938, while on a visit to her cousins, she died at Windsor Castle. *Royal Oak* was assigned the sad task of transporting her body back to Norway, and we went to Portsmouth to receive it there. King Haakon and his son Olaf, the Crown Prince, were to join the ship to accompany the Queen's body back to her country.

It was to be a couple of days before they could arrive, so our ship's company (or three-quarters of it) got an unexpected overnight leave at short notice. For this every sailor required a leave pass, about the size of a postcard, which required an officer's signature, and I happened to be the officer of the day. So I had the job of signing over seven hundred and fifty little pieces of paper between breakfast and noon. Until then, my signature had been legible as *J.D. Ritchie*. By noon, it was a single squiggle with a flourish over the top which had formed itself out of the crossing of the '*J*' and the '*t*' and the dots over the two '*i*'s, and it has remained that way until today. And my hand ached for days!

Eventually, the Queen's body was brought on board with appropriately solemn ceremony, and laid on a bier in the flat outside the Captain's cabin, draped with the Norwegian flag. Four officers, with reversed swords, or four ratings with reversed rifles kept watch at the four corners of the bier for the duration of the passage to Oslo, and one evening the King himself (in his uniform of Admiral of the Fleet in the British Navy) and the Crown Prince stood the guard themselves, with the Captain and the Commander of *Royal Oak*.

One evening on the way over the King entertained all *Royal Oak*'s officers and spoke with all of us individually. When the voyage was over, he gave every member of the ship's company a little silver dish with his monogram, H VII, on it. I have managed through countless moves not to lose mine, and still look at it with warm memories of a sad occasion and a gracious monarch.

In due course we arrived in Oslo, and (again with solemn ceremony) Queen Maud's body was carried ashore by our people, and passed over to the Norwegians, led by the King, at the bottom of the gangway. I was in command of the honour guard on our quarterdeck, where we gave the last British salute to the dead Queen.

This story has a funny little footnote. When I was working in Shell Argentina, we had on our staff a young Norwegian called Hjornevik, who had migrated from Norway to Argentina in search of a better life at the end of World War II. One day, after a cocktail party in our house we invited, as was our custom, a small group of friends to stay on for 'breakfast'; yes, cocktail parties in Buenos Aires started about 9 p.m., and didn't break up until 2 or 3 a.m.

and scrambled eggs and bacon at 4 a.m. was often the only way finally to say 'goodbye'. At one of these Hjornevik and his wife were with us, and we got to talking about Norway and I told him the story. His eyes almost popped out of his head, and he said that he had then been in the Norwegian Naval Academy, and he had been a member of the Norwegian honour guard at the foot of the gangway. We had been for those few minutes within fifteen feet of each other, and had to come halfway round the world to meet!

I have left the second of my four things out of chronological order, because it was of much greater impact than the others. While we were on our courses it wasn't all work and gun drill, and we all had some social life. At a party one evening I met a very attractive young woman, Phyllis Round. We saw a lot of each other and became very close. In mid-March the ship was in Plymouth, and we got a few days' leave. Phyllis's father had just died, and she asked me to take this chance to go to Portsmouth (she worked and lived in Southsea, which is essentially part of Portsmouth) to help her get used to the idea. I went there on Friday, 17th March, and on the next day Hitler sent his *Wehrmacht* to back up his proclamation of Germany's annexation of what remained of Czechoslovakia, breaking the pledge he had made to Britain and France in the Munich Pact, at the time that these two countries had acquiesced in the German takeover of the Sudetenland. Over the weekend we agreed that war was now inevitable, and we decided to get married. On the Monday we got a special marriage licence, and on the Wednesday we were married.

All naval officers were required to inform their commanding officers if they married, and this I duly did. The Captain of *Royal Oak*, aware that no engagement had been announced in *The Times*, and having had no other advance notice, was quite sure that it must be a shotgun wedding, though he couldn't quite bring himself to ask me outright if I'd got the girl pregnant – he couldn't imagine any other reason for so hasty a decision – and my story didn't sound convincing to him. Every commanding officer was required to write, at the end of an officer's service under his command, a confidential report on him, and to hand to the officer a 'flimsy', a *very* flimsy piece of paper, six inches by four inches, recording that the officer had served 'in HMS — under my command, from — to — during which time he has conducted himself…' in words which were required to be in general agreement with the confidential report. This was usually abbreviated to 'To my satisfaction' (though there had been a time when the first words were 'With sobriety and…' the omission of which implied a lack of sobriety). The stuffy old Captain of *Royal Oak*, however, wrote (unfairly) 'A promising young officer who has recently let his private affairs come between him and the Service.'

Chapter Nineteen

HM *MA/SB 3*

I might have protested at this appraisal, but just before my twenty-second birthday I was appointed to the command of HM *Motor Anti-Submarine Boat No. 3*, abbreviated to *MA/SB* (pronounced *Masbee*) *3*. The vessel was still in the final stages of construction at the yard of Hubert Scott-Paine's British Power Boats at Hythe, near Southampton, and it was standard practice for the captain and a few key ratings to be sent to a new ship for the last couple of weeks at the builders, to learn their way around, to criticise details of layout with practical seamen's eyes, and to be with the ship for the acceptance trials, before she was commissioned as one of His (in those days) Majesty's ships. I had realised during my sea training that my standard of seamanship was above average, and I loved driving boats, so this appointment was heaven-sent. She was only sixty feet long, but, powered by two World War I vintage Napier Lion aircraft engines, of five hundred horse power each, modified for marine use, she would do twenty-eight knots; she was my *command,* and I would get two shillings a day 'command money' over and above my pay. And, while in theory there was room for me to live on board, we Captains were allowed to live ashore, and be paid a subsistence allowance for so doing. So Phyllis and I rented a modest one-storey house for a rent of twenty-one shillings a week, next to a cemetery, which was a very pleasant park, in

Weymouth.

We were to be a flotilla of eight boats, armed with depth charges and equipped with sonar,[1] fitted in a streamlined pod at the lower end of a retractable stem which passed through a watertight gland in the boat's keel, lowered about six feet to operate and raised to allow the boat to draw less water. We were attached to HMS *Osprey*, the anti-submarine warfare school at Portland, where our senior officer, Commander Falcon-Steward, an anti-submarine (A/S) specialist, had his office.

I was the sole officer, and my crew of seven consisted of the coxswain, Petty Officer Meatcher, A/S trained; telegraphist Henderson; able seamen Monks and Coombes, and a third – the A/S operator – and a leading stoker and stoker in the engine room. The names of these last three I can no longer dredge up out of my memory.

We spent the next two months in intensive training, individual and as a unit, searching for and making mock attacks on real submarines in Weymouth Bay. And we kept up normal naval routine, including Sunday Divisions. King's Regulations and Admiralty Instructions, *KR & AI* for short, was the Navy's Bible, and it required that, in the absence of a chaplain, the commanding officer (of a ship, or in our case, of the flotilla) should read divine service after Sunday Divisions, for which officers wore frock coats and swords and white gloves, and the sailors their 'number ones'. This was a formal parade, and was inspected by the commanding officer. 3rd September, 1939, was a Sunday and, since Hitler had invaded Poland on the 1st, we were all on tenterhooks. Commander Falcon-Steward had inspected Divisions, and read a brief divine service during which we sang a hymn.

The parade had been dismissed, and we were all stand-

---

[1]This is the modern word for what was at the time called Asdic.

ing around on the quay when the BBC announced that the Prime Minister, Neville Chamberlain, would address the nation at 11 a.m. He recounted the ultimatum that Britain had issued to Germany and went on: 'I have to tell you that no answer has been received, and accordingly a state of war now exists between us and Germany. God save the King.' His voice was ineffably sad: he had totally misjudged Hitler, and he was horrified that the war he had tried so hard to head off was now upon us.

We were not surprised, of course, but we all kept silent or spoke very quietly and sombrely as we tried to imagine what was happening to us. This mood was broken however by the arrival of a sailor on a bicycle with a bunch of signals, one for the senior officer and one for each boat. The message was short and to the point:

> To all ships from Admiralty. Commence hostilities against Germany forthwith.

I found myself wondering, Where do we start? Where is the nearest German? How do you commence hostilities? Petty Officer Meatcher, who was one of those people with a gift for breaking the ice, usually with a laugh, came up to me and said, 'We don't want no Victoria Crosses, do we, sir?' Very different from the bellicosity with which the young men of a generation earlier had greeted the outbreak of World War I!

I put the signal and my white gloves into the pocket in the tail of my frock coat, and later left a supposedly mothproof tin trunk with all my dress uniforms at the home of Home Kidston, the senior of the Captains of the flotilla, and later Commander Falcon-Steward's successor as senior officer. When I recovered them from him after the war, the moths had had a feast on my uniforms: only the gold braid was spared, my white gloves were yellow, and the signal crumbled into dust.

Top: Collieston Harbour entrance: calm.
Middle: Collieston Harbour entrance: storm.
Bottom: Making speldings.

Top: Jock (right) in his first command.
Middle: What three successive Ritchie owners have turned the old bakery into.
Bottom: Burnley, 'The Weaver's Triangle', before the Great Depression (by permission of Lancashire County Library, Burnley Division).

Top: HMS *Lancaster.*
Middle: Lancaster preparing to lower a whaler to take her doctor to HMS *Rockingham.*
Bottom: Passing a tow to *Rockingham.*

Top: Rockingham's people manhandling the tow, as *Lancaster* steams very slowly past her bow.
Middle: Captain (left) and Number One on the bridge: 'Should we sink her in case she becomes a hazard to navigation?'
Bottom: No need! Two minutes later *Rockingham* sank by the stern.

Chapter Twenty

Commence Hostilities...

As luck would have it, the questions I was worrying about on Sunday were answered on Monday. With HMS *Kelly*, commanded by then Captain Lord Louis Mountbatten, we were engaged in an anti-submarine patrol off Portland. Lord Louis's biographer, Richard Hough, writes briefly, 'Even before she delivered the Duke and Duchess of Windsor to Portsmouth [on 12th September] the *Kelly* had been in action, an anti-submarine exercise turning into the real thing, when the ship's "Asdic" [sonar] caught a "ping" and the *Kelly* released a pattern of depth charges.'

What actually happened was this: *MA/SB 3* was about a mile and a half from *Kelly*, when one of my crew yelled, 'Torpedo tracks!' And, sure enough, all those of us who were on deck saw the tracks coming towards us, headed past us towards *Kelly*. We called her by light signal and said: 'Torpedoes coming at you.' Dickie (as Mountbatten was known in the Navy) was on the bridge, and though he didn't see the tracks, he immediately turned towards us, to offer the smallest possible target, and the torpedoes passed harmlessly by. Meanwhile we had also turned towards the direction from which they had come and started a search. In a few minutes we had a contact, which sounded genuine; it had 'Doppler', the difference in frequency between its echo and the background echo from the water which indicated relative movement. So we did what we had been trained to do; we carried out a depth charge attack on our target. As we closed in, I had a terrible worry about whether I needed permission, and if so from whom, before I could expend three depth charges (in peacetime – yesterday morning – you had needed official approval to fire one revolver bullet) but I remembered the 'All ships' signal, and that had indubitably said 'Commence hostilities', so we did, and dropped our pattern of depth charges. Our contact was a very convincing one, and the torpedo tracks spelled U-boat, but the waters off Portland Bill had notorious tide races which could easily give echoes as hard as a submarine, so we may have attacked a false contact. Anyway, we didn't succeed, and hours of subsequent searching couldn't find anything.

The next morning Dickie sent for me, and asked about the incident. Neither he nor anyone else on *Kelly*'s bridge had seen the tracks, but when he asked his whole ship's company the following morning, members of one gun's crew said that, yes, they *had* seen tracks. Asked why they hadn't reported them, they said they had thought they must have been 'practice torpedoes fired at *Kelly* by that motor torpedo boat that was in company'. They had some reason for mistaking what kind of boat we were, because British Power Boats also built MTBs on a hull design identical to ours, and one day into the war it was scarcely surprising that it might be difficult to believe that, this time, torpedoes could be in earnest.

After the excitement of that first day we settled into a routine of defensive anti-submarine patrols, stepped up whenever a big ship came into Portland Harbour, without incident. This lasted about six months, until in the late winter of 1939 to 1940, during the so-called 'Phoney War', *MA/SB 2* (whose Captain was Lieutenant Charles Lapage) and *MA/SB 3* were ordered to the Mediterranean station. The boats themselves were loaded into a freighter, and the crews travelled across France by train, and from Marseilles to Alexandria by ship, so we arrived first, and were there to receive our boats, which had made the trip unscathed. We became part of the Alexandria Local Defence Force, and spent most of our time, day on, day off, at short notice, prepared to engage any suspected submarine, with spells of patrol along with the other A/S equipped ships of the force. As in Portland, Charles and I slept ashore on the nights we were not the duty boat, and received a subsistence allowance to make this financially possible. During the day we were berthed at the jetty of the Egyptian coastguard, which was in the process of becoming the Royal Egyptian Navy, and they helped us with chores, like refuelling out of two hundred-litre drums of 87 octane aviation fuel. We got to know the officers of the two ships that occupied the other side of the jetty, and with some of them I became close friends. The more senior officers of this group had been educated in seafaring in England, in HMS *Worcester*, which, despite its designation, was a training ship, not for the Navy, but for the Merchant Marine. My closest friend was Ezz-el-Din Atif, who was not in either of the two ships, but was attached to the office, at Ras-el-Tin fort, of the Rear Admiral, Alexandria, who was the commander of the base, and to whom we reported.

Atif (he always goes by this name, even to his closest family) has remained a friend to this day;[1] he is a charming man (though now stricken by Alzheimer's disease, he has not lost his charm) and he was a superb naval officer. General Mohammed Neguib (now alas almost forgotten as the first President of Egypt after the deposition of King Farouk) appointed Atif as Commander-In-Chief of the Egyptian navy, but Nasser, becoming the power behind the President, cancelled the appointment on the grounds that

---

[1] Alas, he died a couple of months after this was written.

Atif was too pro-British, and that the junior officers didn't like him! Thus are talents wasted!

A month after the outbreak of war, Phyllis had become pregnant, and hated the idea of having her child without my being close at hand. So we got permission from the Admiralty for her to join me in Alexandria, at our own expense and risk. Phyllis organised the channel crossing and the train journey from Calais across France to Marseilles, and her passage from Marseilles to Alexandria in the Egyptian passenger and cargo ship *Misr*. We just had enough savings to pull this off! It was barely a month before the German invasion of the Low Countries and France, and that all this was possible for a mere civilian really shows how 'phoney' the war appeared at the time. One fellow passenger in *Misr* was Sheila, the wife, also pregnant, of a commander in the Special Branch of the RNVR, Guy Rudderforth, who was working in intelligence in Alexandria. Another was a major in the Egyptian police, Ramzi Bey, who took the two women under his solicitous care, and whom I was to meet almost ten years later in Suez. In due course Sheila and Phyllis became godmothers to each other's respective offspring.

When she arrived in Egypt we arranged to be paying guests of the Masters, an English couple who were long-time residents of Alexandria. Then one day when we were guests of the Mackenzies at their cabin at Sidi Bishr Beach. Phyllis's pregnancy barely showed, but she asked May Mackenzie some question about the Anglo-Swiss Hospital, where we were arranging for the baby to be born. When May recovered from her surprise, she insisted that we should move into their house and stay until the baby was at least some weeks old, and they could help us find suitable housing. In due course, on 11th July, 1940, Jeanie was born in the Anglo-Swiss. *MA/SB 3* was on duty that day, and it was not until the late afternoon that I was able to get to a telephone and ask the hospital how Phyllis was. 'Oh, as well as can be expected' was the conventional reply. So I asked when the baby was expected, and in some surprise the nurse told me that Jeanie had been born several hours before. May's brother-in-law, Ihsan Hasan Mohsen (nicknamed Sonny, from the final syllables of his three names) arranged for us to rent, for two pounds (just five per cent over two pounds in sterling) from the sequestrator of Italian property – the Italians now being enemy aliens – a very pleasant apartment in a nice suburb west of Alexandria, on the tramway which communicated with the city. For another two pounds we hired Abduh, a Nubian house servant, and, for double his wages, Araxi Tchakarian, a polyglot Armenian nanny for Jeanie. In this household we lived, comfortably, well within our means, for almost a year. And May Mackenzie became Jeanie's godmother.

The war was no longer phoney, and we had occasional air raids by Italian planes out of Libya, the occasional ship damaged in action came into Alexandria for repairs, and the MA/SBs were called out more often to investigate suspicious noises and sightings, all false alarms. I could still spend many evenings at home, because one of my Egyptian officer friends lent me a very ancient motorcycle – so old that its kick-start pedal was worn to a sharp point. But it ran, and could get me to my ship within ten minutes of a telephone call.

On 13th September the Italian army in Libya, two hundred thousand men under General Graziani, invaded Egypt, but was halted and held at Sidi Barrani, a small port three hundred and fifty kilometres west of Alexandria, by the harassment of barely one-tenth of its number of British troops. By December General Wavell's British forces had been reinforced by units of the Indian, Australian and New Zealand armies, and on the 9th he launched an attack on the Italians, and rapidly drove them out of Egypt, and later out of Cyrenaica.[2] Wavell soon overran the port of Salum on the border of Egypt and Libya, which became the supply base for the thrusts into Libya. This base needed anti-submarine and anti-aircraft protection, and the two MA/SBs were immediately sent there – not that our anti-aircraft weaponry, two pairs of .303-inch Lewis guns, were much help – but we did try!

Salum's dock facilities were simple; one jetty and, until the army added more, one crane. But since they were the only forward supply point for Wavell's army, they were busy from dawn to dusk. We had to go alongside the jetty to fuel with a handpump out of drums, and to draw our food supplies from the Royal Army Service Corps. Petty Officer Meatcher quickly made friends with the sergeant in charge of unloading the supply ships. Meatcher noticed that any broken case or carton of tinned food was left to one side, because, said the sergeant, they were no use to him; all the contents would spill out of the truck. So our victualling store rapidly acquired a supply of buckshee broken cases of sardines and butter. We carried enough ship's biscuit to last us for weeks, and, since bread was unobtainable, we lived for well over a month on a diet of biscuit, butter and sardines; and without risk of scurvy too, because one of the Egyptian ships came into port, and Mahmud Hamdi, who was a good friend, was her executive officer, and through his good offices we got half a dozen crates of oranges.

We were working watch on, watch off all the time because, except for the brief time we spent alongside the jetty every few days, we were on patrol round the clock. The coxswain and I shared the bridge between us, and each of us had to spend an hour or so on our paperwork every day. So one's four hours off had to be divided between eating (biscuit, butter, sardines and oranges three times a

---

[2]The eastern half of Libya.

day, seven days a week, except when the coxswain had pity on us and gave us corned beef or baked beans for a change), a 'bath' once each day, standing in a bucket and washing down with a flannel, and then clean underclothes (except for these five minutes or so we remained dressed all the time, even in bed) and any administrative work that had to be done, before getting to sleep for the remaining two and a half hours. And this didn't allow for the time that we were all at action stations, which was at least once a day for some air raid or submarine alarm. It was difficult to keep track of the days of the week, though the time of day was easily identified by the air raids, for almost every day, at first and last lights, Italian bombers came over and attacked the army's supply operation. It was very ineffectual, for we didn't see one successful hit on the ships, the jetty or the supply dumps on shore, though we were straddled one evening by a stick of bombs. We saw the first explosion about one hundred metres to one side of us, then the second closer, the third not fifteen metres away, all in a straight line towards us. Waiting for the fourth was awful (it illustrated vividly the truth that war is ninety-nine per cent being bored to death, one per cent scared to death!) but it fell over, though close enough to shake us up.

Before the war Mussolini had boasted that 'eight million Italian bayonets' would earn Italy its rightful place in the sun, and its fair share of colonies. The British army was taking thousands of prisoners as it drove the Italians west, and these caused a logistical problem of their own: they had to be moved to the rear, fed and guarded until they could be shipped out of the theatre to India or South Africa. One day, while the boat was alongside the jetty, fuelling and having some engine maintenance, I walked up to the top of the escarpment (whence the desert rolled virtually flat to the south) where was the road that led west to the front and east to Alexandria. It was a busy scene of columns of troops and trucks of supplies, many being loaded at Salum, others having come up from the rear. Suddenly I saw a familiar face, my old fag master from Eton, Peter Blundell, in the uniform of a captain in the Guards. I was sorely tempted to point out to him that since he was only a captain in the Army, while I held the equivalent rank in the *Senior* Service, he was now my junior! We chatted for a few minutes, and then he had to move on.

Then I met a naval medical officer that I knew, and we talked as we watched a column of Italian prisoners of war marching. (Marching? I've rarely seen men in uniform moving at such a dispirited shamble!) There must have been three thousand of them, led by an open-bed Australian truck in the back of which sat one Aussie with a rifle, with another such bringing up the rear. As this procession slowly passed us, my doctor friend suddenly said, 'Look, eight million Italian bayonets!'

The next line the Italians held was at Bardiyah, the first Libyan port west of the Egyptian border, under the command of General Bergonzoli. This colourful officer had a bright red beard and was known in Italian as 'Barba Elettrica' and to the British as 'Electric Whiskers'. Bardiyah fell to a British attack on 5th January, and General Bergonzoli escaped to the west in a truck with a small escort. His next line of resistance would be Tobruk, and the British forces wanted, if possible, to prevent him reaching there. So *MA/SB 3* was given the task of going along the coast, as fast as possible, to try to capture him.

We set off at full speed, but could not keep very close to the shore because the chart showed shallowish water with hidden rocks for about a quarter of a mile offshore. After an hour or more past Bardiyah, we spotted a lone Bedouin with a flock of goats, and were able to get close inshore near him. I had learned a few words of Arabic, including those for 'Italian', 'truck' and 'what time?' from my coastguard friends, so I landed in our little dinghy, and asked him if he had seen an Italian truck going that way, and when. He said yes, about an hour ago (this last with the aid of pointing at my wristwatch). I gave him a few Egyptian piastres, and went back on board. We reckoned that an hour's head start would be difficult to catch up, but in another hour (it was lunchtime) we saw smoke rising from over the sand dunes just inshore. So I turned inshore, going slowly to avoid the sharp peaked rocks we could see under the surface. Coombes and Monks were both fine swimmers, and they were detailed as our landing party. They chose their own rig and weapons. Both took revolvers, with the appropriate khaki webbing belt and holster and a steel helmet as their only clothing, and Monks added a hand grenade. I took the boat as close as I dared to the shore, though I lost our sonar dome on a pinnacle rock that we hadn't seen, and the landing party half waded, half swam with the revolvers held up in the air to the flat rock, fifty centimetres above the water, which was the shore. They scrambled up the sand dunes, while we 'covered' them by spraying Lewis gunfire left and right of the smoke plume. Obviously neither had ever been a soldier because, once at the top of the dunes, they started running along the skyline as perfect targets, and then turned downhill, inland and out of our sight. In the meantime, I had anchored where I reckoned we could swing without our propellers being damaged.

In a few minutes, or perhaps half an hour, our two came into view, escorting eight men with their hands up. When they came within earshot, we learned that the general and some others had escaped westward in the truck, leaving a gazelle partially roasted over their fire. The problem now was how to get our prisoners on board. We decided that our dinghy would be very difficult to use against the rocky wall, especially as the afternoon breeze was causing not inconsiderable waves to break on it. So PO Meatcher, also a good swimmer, said he'd swim ashore with a line and a Mae West life jacket, leaving enough line ashore so that they wouldn't lose the end, while we could haul them back to the boat, one at a time. We got all this set up, and the three of them, with much difficulty, got a very reluctant Italian into the Mae West. They could lead him to the water, but they couldn't make him get into it – until AB Monks lost his patience.

His prisoner was standing, with his feet slightly apart, literally shivering on the brink. Suddenly Monks pointed his revolver between the prisoner's feet, yelled, 'Joomp, you fuckin' Eyetie, *joomp!*' and pulled the trigger. The 'Eyetie' *joomped* indeed – almost halfway to the ship, it seemed. We hauled him over, got him to our ladder, and manhandled him inboard. The Mae West was hauled back to the shore, and the rest of the prisoners, seeing that the first hadn't come to any harm, submitted, and it only took time to get them and our own people back on board.

It was still early January; the days were short, and once the sun set the temperature dropped like a stone. It was after dark when we got everyone back, and our own three out of their shivers, dried and dressed. Buried somewhere in *KR & AI*[3] was, I knew, a provision allowing the captain to issue an extra tot of rum to any ratings that had been exposed to unusually cold weather, provided that he entered into the ship's log his reasons for doing so. I got out the book, read the Regulations, and, quite clearly, naked sailors who had been working like Meatcher, Coombes and Monks, and turned blue in the process, were qualified. So I authorised the tots, Meatcher entered them in his victualling account, and I made the appropriate record in the log, little dreaming how those three-eighths of a pint were to haunt me. But that's another story.

---

[3]See p.211.

We got under way to return to Salum, and the sailors' warm hearts got working. Only a few hours ago our prisoners had been 'fucking Eyeties', who needed shots between their ankles to get them to do what they were told. Now, they suddenly became 'poor shiverin' bastards', to be wrapped up in blankets while their clothes were taken down to the engine room to dry, and plied with mugs of hot, strong, sweet tea heavily laced with condensed milk, and made comfortable in the crew's mess deck, where we wrote down their names, ranks and numbers. Thus we discovered that one of our eight was an officer, and accordingly he was put into my quarters. When we were clear of the offshore rocks, I went down and spoke with him. On Italy's entry into the war, I had bought myself a 'Teach Yourself Italian' book, and could communicate on a very simple level, though not enough to interrogate a prisoner sensibly, so our conversation was limited to his asking me (slowly and loudly), 'Noi, prigioneri – India o Sud Africa?' making clear that his preference would be the latter. I had never realised (what I suppose many of the Italians knew) that this would be their choice, and so I couldn't help him.

As soon as I had reported to the senior naval officer in Salum, and we had handed over our captives to the military police, we sailed for Alexandria to have our sonar dome replaced, and have a captured Italian 20 mm automatic gun fitted by the Alexandria Tramways workshops.

Then we turned straight round and came back. By now Tobruk was under attack, and bombardment from the sea was provided by the recently formed 'Inshore Squadron'; three ancient gunboats, *Aphis, Gnat* and *Ladybird*, and the monitor, HMS *Terror* (essentially a shallow-draught hull armed with a twin fifteen-inch gun turret). We were part of the inshore squadron's anti-submarine screen, and during night bombardments, we 'created a diversion'. While the fifteen-inch guns were being fired, we, closer inshore and off to one side, loosed off 'thunderflashes' and fired streams of 20 mm tracer shells from our newly installed Italian 20 mm automatic gun. We didn't need to economise ammunition, because there were hundreds of cases of it lying all over the desert to be picked up. It was quite fun, but whether of any military value I doubt. The Italians should have found little difficulty in distinguishing between the noise and the flash of fifteen-inch guns and our Guy Fawkes Day fireworks – we really were, in the old naval expression, farting against thunder! Tobruk fell on 22nd January, and the British army pressed on westwards, while we returned to Salum and to anti-submarine defence of the supply ports.

Not for long, however. On 10th January, Admiral Cunningham's Force H in the Mediterranean was involved in an operation designed to escort a convoy of four large merchant ships from the west, three bound to Greece, and the fourth to Malta. One of the ships in Force H was the aircraft carrier, HMS *Illustrious*, which provided air cover. By this time the British had pretty well got the measure of the Italian Royal Air Force, but on this day a new element entered the battle, in the shape of Stuka dive-bombers of the *Luftwaffe*, making their debut into the Mediterranean. They concentrated on *Illustrious*, and damaged her badly in a wave of attacks. On fire, having her aircraft lifts damaged and her steering crippled, *Illustrious* managed to reach Malta, where, in spite of continued attacks from the *Luftwaffe*, the dockyard managed to get her seaworthy, and on 25th January she arrived in Alexandria. But to be made battle-worthy again, she would have to go through the Suez Canal to get to the United States for complete repair. Meanwhile, HMS *Formidable*, another aircraft carrier, was waiting in the Red Sea to join Admiral Cunningham. The Germans, therefore, adopted the obvious ploy; they tried to close the

Suez Canal by air-dropped mines. The first mines were dropped on 30th January, and the canal was closed. At first these mines were thought to be magnetic, but it was soon discovered they were acoustic – they were exploded by a ship's propeller noise, and they had a nasty trick. It was not necessarily the first ship to pass over a mine that exploded it, but any from the first to the thirteenth. The sinking of quite a small ship could effectively block the canal, so it was not possible just to have thirteen sacrificial lambs to lead the big ship, and anyway, there could be more mines ahead. The banks of the canal were therefore lined with soldiers, about two hundred metres apart, to spot where the mines fell, and then either divers went down and attached a line to it so that it could be towed to the bank, or attached a demolition charge to blow it up.

But this was all unknown to us. We were somewhere off the Western Desert in the latter part of February, when I suddenly got orders to go to Alexandria, and then to Port Said, where I was to report to the Staff Officer, Operations. When I went in to see him, during the afternoon of 27th February, he told me about the need to get and keep the Suez Canal open for *Formidable* to get north and *Illustrious* south, with a deadline of 5th March. He related the story of the mining, and what was known about the mines, including the delay mechanism, and that there was one mine left, at kilometre a hundred and twenty-something, south of the Bitter Lakes. It was believed that the volume of propeller noise was the trigger, and for normal ships the speed limit of about six knots kept this volume low until the ship was close over the mine. A MA/SB, however, could safely ignore the speed limit without creating a dangerous wash, and at full speed her propeller noise should explode a mine well before the boat was over it.

So our orders were to sail early the next morning at full speed to the site of the mine, which would be marked by a red flag on the bank. Then we were to run over it at full speed, and when half a mile beyond, turn round and do the same on the opposite course, and keep at it until the mine exploded. Whether he really believed this information or not I shall never know, but he had it wrong: the mine exploded at the moment the propeller noise had reached a peak and just started to decline, and this happened to us on our second run. I was standing with my right foot on a step in front of me, with my left leg braced, and I was recording the time at which we had reversed course in my navigator's notebook balanced on my right knee. As we came up to the red flag there was one hell of a bang, and the boat was blown up into the air. My left leg bent the wrong way, and my foot came up, and, as it were, looked me in the face. I pushed it back where it belonged without feeling any pain, and I clambered out of the conning tower, through the hatch which was sixty centimetres by forty centimetres and down the short ladder to the deck. The stern of the boat was sinking, and three or four of the crew were up in the bows, so I walked up there to join them and assess the situation. Before I arrived I realised that I couldn't stand any longer, and collapsed in a heap on the deck. The coxswain told me that we were all still alive, though the stoker in the engine room had had the bad luck to be standing with both his knees braced, leaning over an engine, and had broken both of his knees, while AB Coombes had a nasty wound on his cheek. He had been lying on deck, sunbathing, using his steel helmet as a combined pillow and sun shade for his face. One of our boxes of Italian 20 mm ammunition, of wood with steel-bound corners, had been blown into the air and had come down on his steel helmet, and, as it tipped over, one corner caught his cheekbone. Without his helmet, his head would have been crushed!

There is a gentle current in the Suez Canal, from south

to north, so we were drifting slowly north. We had to get into the bank, so we joined all our heaving lines together, and Coombes, his cheek dressed with adhesive tape, and the best of our swimmers, swam to the side with the line. Several soldiers had seen what happened and were gathered on the bank to help, so when Coombes got to the shore, they took his line and turned it round a convenient post. Thus tethered, the boat slowly drifted on the current into the shallow water. The stern was now under water, but the bows still held a big bubble of air which kept us afloat until Coombes, joined by Monks, and the soldiers managed to pull the boat right to the bank so that those who could still walk could land. The stoker and I waited on the deck (as being more comfortable than the rocky bank) for the military ambulance which the soldiers told us was coming. When it arrived the two of us were carried ashore by our shipmates and gently accommodated into the bunks of the ambulance. The stoker was put into the bottom bed on one side, and I on the one above him. I was now in pain, and was lying there with my eyes closed when I heard a third person being loaded in.

'Who's that?' I asked.

'Able Seaman Coombes, sir.'

'I thought you were all right,' I said.

'No, sir, from where that foockin' box dropped on my cheek, sir, I've got a foockin' 'eadache.'

Just before the army medical people closed the doors of the ambulance, Petty Officer Meatcham stuck his head in and said, 'You can leave the boat to me, sir. I'll do whatever we can.' That was the last time I spoke with him, and I will never forget that loyalty.

Chapter Twenty-One

Canvas Hospital

The destination of our ambulance was a tent hospital at Geneifa, about thirty kilometres north of Suez, on the banks of the Great Bitter Lake, which formed part of the canal waterway. It consisted of a rough circle of fencing, topped by barbed wire (to keep light-fingered Egyptians out, and Italian prisoners of war in) on a flat plain of sand. I was put into a bed in the officers' ward, and was soon being looked after by a doctor. I was taken to the X-ray tent, where my knee was duly X-rayed, and then back to bed again, and my leg was put into a plaster cast from ankle to thigh. Finally, I was given a painkiller-cum-sleeping injection and knew nothing until the next morning. The ward sister, complete with cap and cape, and accompanied by a nurse, less splendidly dressed, made my bed between them, and told me the medical officer would soon be in to see me. When he came – it seemed like a wait of hours – he told me that my knee was fractured and dislocated, the tibial condyle was partially cracked off the main bone, and the strings holding my knee together were stretched, but, as far as they could tell, not ruptured.

'There is no surgery to repair this kind of damage; we can't operate on the knee joint, but you should be able to walk on crutches in a month or six weeks, and in another month or so walk with a stick. The cast will have to be changed periodically, because your muscles will shrink from disuse. Meanwhile, we'll do our best to keep you comfortable.'

I had a horrible vision of this being the end of my naval career (well, it was, but not for another seven years!) and was pretty miserable at the prospect.

The hospital was surreal. It consisted of tents, large enough to hold twenty-four beds, twelve along each side, with a canvas 'door' at either end, and a canvas curtain all round the rest of the perimeter, which could be hitched up during nice weather for ventilation, and lowered at night and during sandstorms; not that it (nor few other things for that matter!) could keep out the sand during a khamsin. This is a hot, dry wind that blows over two thousand kilometres of sand, until it arrives in Lower Egypt as a yellowish-grey cloud that cuts visibility down to fifty metres, pits the glass of a windscreen and will sandblast the paint off a car. It gets under bedclothes, into food and drink, and between your skin and your underclothes. The floor of the tent was canvas, and at one end (or perhaps both) there were primitive toilet facilities.

Our diet was extraordinary. We had, for lunch and dinner twelve times a week, chicken (which one of the wags in our ward said must have been driven from the Nile valley on the hoof, so tough were their muscles). The other two slots, Wednesday lunch and Sunday dinner, were filled by duck, every bit as tough as the chicken. The head cook was said to know that in hot climates, people needed lots of salt to make up for what was sweated out: we were in a desert, therefore the climate was presumably hot – never mind that at night, the temperature got down close to freezing! So, if he didn't actually make his soup with water from the Great Bitter Lake, as we alleged, it certainly tasted like it. And for at least a dozen years afterwards, I simply could not eat chicken in any form!

Once a day, towards the end of the morning, the matron

made her rounds. Two nurses held open the door flaps, and the ward sister (senior nurse) met her at the entrance. Dressed in white and scarlet, with starched cuffs and a cap so crisp that it must have been starched too, she appeared in the doorway, leaned to one side and then the other to look down the rows of beds. In a deep voice, and a strong Scots accent, she would say, 'Sister, number nine bed on this side is out of line!' and then walk down between the beds and check that all were made with proper hospital corners to the blankets. Never did she say a word to a patient, and, as far as we could hear, she didn't ask the sister about the state of health of any of us! If the beds were in order, then presumably we were all doing fine.

The evenings were enlivened (and we were deprived of sleep) by one of the Italian officers in the tent just the other side of the dividing wire. He had a voice good enough to have been a professional opera singer, and soon after dark he would burst into song, and for hours we would get all the well-known tenor arias, with pauses just long enough to fall asleep before he started up again. One day the colonel in charge of the hospital was doing his rounds, and unlike the matron he did talk to us. Someone complained about the singing, and he said he was aware of the problem, but they couldn't do anything about it. So one of us suggested, 'Sir, couldn't you just let him escape?'

Luckily I did not have to spend all my hospital time there, though before I escaped it was consoling to be lying in bed and watch *Formidable* sail through the lake to restore air cover to Force H.

May Mackenzie, who must have entertained every senior officer of all three services and so had some chips to cash, pulled some strings, and arranged for me to be transferred from Geneifa to the Military General Hospital in Alexandria, where she and her sister Zoë, and of course Phyllis, could come and visit me; Zoë, who knew my taste in desserts, used to bring in chocolate mousse covered in whipped cream to enliven the military menu. I was, I suppose, about another month in hospital until I was let out, still with the heavy plaster cast, and walking on crutches. I soon got pretty expert on these, to the point that I could go up to the top deck (where one could smoke) of the Ramleh Tramway between the city and home. I could do almost anything for myself, except put on and lace up my left shoe, which Abduh would do for me. I suppose that my state brought home the war to him; he was very solicitous for my comfort and well-being, and I think a little disappointed that I wouldn't let him bathe and dress me completely, to the point that it was almost embarr-assing. But he was totally genuine in his caring, whereas Araxi's nose was a little out of joint that she didn't get to do up my shoes!

During this time there occurred a bureaucratic interruption of otherwise peaceful days. A letter came from the base supply officer in Alexandria, observing that the victualling accounts for *MA/SB 3* for the month of January showed the issue, on the 6th of the month, of ten tots of rum, when the ship had only seven ratings entitled to draw their grog, and would I please explain. I wrote back, quoting *KR & AI*, and said that the circumstances had been duly recorded in the log. *Answer: would I please send the log to them?* I apologised, but explained that the log (which covered three months, to the victualling accounts' one) had been destroyed when the ship was mined on 28th February.

The response was curt: '*Without proper documentation, your explanation is not acceptable; please expedite transmittal of your ship's log.*' I wrote back that the log had been destroyed by enemy action, but there was no way of convincing them, and it was not until two years later that the base supply officer in Alexandria gave up the pursuit!

I used to go back to the hospital about once a week to be

monitored and to have my cast changed a couple of times, as my muscles slowly atrophied and shrank. While the cast was off, my knee was X-rayed and the doctors made noises which, if not encouraging, were at least comforting. We lived a very quiet and peaceful life, with occasional visits from or to May and Zoë, until, on 30th May, just after my cast had been finally removed, I got a telephone call about noon saying that we must be packed and ready to leave the next morning, and that a car would be sent for us, to take us to Suez for passage to the UK. We spent until three in the morning packing our clothes and few household possessions, and paying off Araxi and Abduh, both of whom were in tears; Abduh because, oh, well, it was the will of Allah, and Araxi because, where would she find another job?

In Suez we embarked in RMS *Otranto,* a passenger liner just becoming a troopship, which took us, with a call into Mombasa, as far as Durban, where we transferred to RMS *Empress of Canada,* of the Canadian–Pacific Line. There were, for most of the voyage, very few passengers in either ship, and we were accommodated in two adjoining first-class cabins, so Jeanie had one to herself. The *Empress of Canada* had not yet wound down from peacetime conditions, so there were plenty of stewards, and a more or less peacetime menu in the dining saloon (except that every evening there was a fish course for dinner, with a fancy name: sole bonne femme, saumon grillé aux fines herbes, turbot poché and so on, which, when ordered, turned out to be the same coarse-grained, tasteless fish as the night before, and the night before that. But we were on the way home, and it was a small gripe! We called at Cape Town, where we were allowed ashore for a few hours, and Trinidad, disembarking a few familiar and embarking a few fresh faces, and taking on fuel and stores (but no change of fish!) before we arrived in Halifax, Nova Scotia. From the docks Halifax looked a very flat, dull place, due, they told us, to the fact that in World War I an ammunition ship had blown up in the harbour and flattened a large part of the city, which had been hurriedly rebuilt, and, because of the Depression, never properly renewed.

There we waited the best part of a week, not having the least idea why, until one morning we got the news that we would be embarking part of the Fifth Canadian Division, which started to arrive almost at once. Jeanie had to give up her cabin, into which two officers moved, meals had to be in two sittings, and the space we had enjoyed for six weeks suddenly became crowded with men in khaki. Once we sailed there was little for them to do, so we got into long conversations. Many of them had come from the middle provinces and had never seen the ocean before, so were totally unprepared for the North Atlantic. They were very curious about Britain, and were grateful to find a seasoning of people other than fellow soldiers to share the voyage with them. We sailed alone until about halfway across, and then joined up with several other fast passenger ships to be escorted as a convoy the rest of the way to the Clyde, where we arrived at the end of July.

Chapter Twenty-Two

Unfit for Sea

We went to stay with my parents in Burnley, and after a day or two I was admitted to Queen Mary's Hospital in Roehampton, which was dedicated to the rehabilitation of the wounded and injured. I wasn't kept there long, because all the rehabilitation that would be any use to me I could do myself; exercise, and later ride a bicycle. But those few days made me appreciate my good fortune. We, some twenty officers, were in one big ward, and across the aisle from me was a Captain, RN, who had been injured by a shell fired from one of the German long-range guns at Cap Gris Nez, across the channel at Dover Castle. During the day he walked a little, rather stiff-legged, but at night, to go to bed he took off his jacket and sat down on his bed, and took off two pairs of braces, one which held up his trousers, and the other which held his prosthetic legs. The shell had severed his own below the knee, so he swung his body and his stump thighs around and lay down on the bed, leaving the legs standing there like those of Ozymandias. He was, however, extraordinarily cheerful.

The same could not be said of some of those, mostly from the Royal Air Force, who had been burned about the face, one with no ears, though he still had his hearing. There was a group of volunteers, young women – some married with husbands away, some unmarried – who went out to the pub or the cinema with the disfigured patients. I made friends with one of the young plastic surgeons on the hospital staff, who told me that lost legs were not difficult to accept, but arms – even one, or as little as a missing hand – were a much greater trauma, and worst of all were faces. If one could hardly bear to look at oneself in the mirror, it was difficult to imagine that anyone else could look without repugnance. But the volunteers, by going out with these men, by looking at them without showing any distress, with warmth, by kissing them, and by holding a 'hand' that wasn't there were a vital part of the rehabilitation.

Later, Phyllis and Jeanie went to stay with Phyllis's grandfather in Newport, Isle of Wight, while I went into the Royal Naval Hospital, Haslar (in Portsmouth Harbour), to be 'surveyed'. They found me unfit for service at sea, and not yet fit for any service even ashore. I was sent on more sick leave, and joined my family in the Isle of Wight, where Jeanie discovered a taste for cheese. She used to sit – she was not yet mobile – on a blanket in the middle of the lawn, playing with her toys. One day Phyllis went out and found her eating a very old and dry piece of cheese. No one had been near her and there was no other explanation of how she had got it except to suppose that a bird had dropped it. From this incident she developed her first multi-word communication. 'Peace!' she demanded. We never decided whether she meant 'Piece' or 'Please', but it didn't matter, the next two words were clear enough. 'Peace what, Jeanie?' someone would ask her.

'Peace more!'

'Peace more what, Jeanie?'

'Peace more sheese!'

Sick leave lasted until late September, by which time I was able to walk pretty well, though with a stick, and I was appointed to a shore establishment, HMS *Northney,* in Hayling Island, as First Lieutenant: the administrative officer. This was only 1941, and the United States was not yet in the war, but we were engaged in training people for handling landing craft against the moment, which would come one day, when we would have to invade Europe. Landing craft were still very much embryonic, and we received various designs with which to experiment in mock landings. We were also hosts to a fascinating small group of people, whose mission was to cross the Channel in a fast motor boat under cover of darkness and rendezvous with members of the burgeoning resistance in France, to take them communications equipment, and occasionally to bring back a handful of escaped prisoners of war. This was nerve-racking business, and after two or three trips the people needed a complete break for a few days. They stayed at *Northney* where they had their meals, and went to their houses nearby to sleep. Often the first night at home was one long party, where they calmed their nerves with whisky. I was talking with the leader of this group at breakfast one morning, and asked him how things were.

'Oh, fine,' he said, 'until we had a big party last night. Towards the end there were only three of us left, and someone thought of a new game. One of us left the room, and the other two had to guess who'd gone. Then we decided it really *was* time to go to bed.'

HMS *Northney* had been a Butlin's holiday camp, and so consisted in large part of family-size chalets, built of wood. We needed other, larger, buildings as lecture rooms and for training on the experimental equipment, and mostly these were Nissen huts – prefabricated, but needing a concrete foundation and connections for drains, water and electricity. The bureaucracy which could authorise such things was the various departments of HM Dockyard, Portsmouth, the Superintending Electrical Engineer, Civil Engineer, and so on. Once these bodies had given their technical blessings, the project required the final approval of the Commander-in-Chief for the expenditure of so many pounds, which he certified as being appropriate expenditure for advancing the war effort.

During my tenure we had one such project, and we were gathering the approvals of the electricians, plumbers, concreters, drainage experts, all of which came in the form of attachments to the docket. It was a time-consuming process, but one day I was in with the Captain when my assistant, a Lieutenant in the WRNS, knocked at the door of the Captain's office, and came in, very excited. 'Sir, we've got the Superintending Civil Engineer's signature on the docket. Now all we need is the C-in-C's approval for an erection.'

The Captain looked at her over his glasses and said, 'Young lady; when we need the C-in-C's approval for that, you can say that we've lost the war!'

Chapter Twenty-Three

Second Command – HM *Steam Gunboat No. 4*

Towards the end of the year a medical board decided that I was again fit for sea service, and in January 1942 I was appointed to command HM *Steam Gunboat No. 4,* still in the final stages of construction at the yard of Yarrow and Co. at Scotstoun on the Clyde, downstream from Glasgow. These SGBs were an experimental design, and a flotilla of nine boats was ordered. Nos. 1 and 2 were damaged in an air raid in their builder's yard and abandoned, so No. 4 was in fact the second. At two hundred tons and over one hundred and forty feet long, they were almost twice the length and over four times the displacement of the standard motor torpedo boats and motor gunboats, were built of steel instead of wood, and powered by steam turbines instead of petrol engines. Although called 'gunboats', they carried two eighteen-inch torpedoes, as well as a two-pounder (fully automatic) pom-pom and a Rolls-Royce semi-automatic two-pounder. And we had an – albeit primitive – radar. At almost thirty-five knots SGBs were, however, slower than the smaller MTBs and MGBs.

Since she was not yet completed, *SGB 4* was not in commission, and would not be until her acceptance trials were completed. I reported to Yarrow's yard, and found that the First Lieutenant to be, Lieutenant John Erskine-

Hill, RNVR,[1] was already there, and had, with the coxswain, been providing the seafarer's input for several weeks, while the engine room ratings had been learning their way around the machinery. The ship was not yet liveable, so I found lodgings with a very nice working-class family in Scotstoun, and was soon joined there by the third of our officers, Sub Lieutenant Peter Hood, RNVR, who became a superb naval officer and the finest navigator of any small ship that it was ever my privilege to know.[2] The family was delighted to have us, not only for the money we brought in, but because we had service ration books, which provided much more generous amounts of food than civilians got, and of course we let the lady of the house buy all that we were entitled to and spread it out equally, and since Peter and I normally had some kind of lunch at the yard, and went out to dinner a couple of times a week, the family did well. But when we ate in, we had splendid breakfasts, ample high teas and light suppers before bedtime, in the proper Scottish pattern of meals.

In two or three weeks the trials were completed, and HM *SGB 4* hoisted her commissioning pennant and the white ensign, and I accepted her from Yarrow as part of the Royal Navy. We loaded stores, ammunition and victuals, the crew – there were thirty-four of us in the ship's company – had settled in, and we sailed for the south coast,

---

[1] Royal Naval Volunteer Reserve.

[2] When we were operating off the French coast, one of our marks was a lighted buoy off Berck-sur-Mer. This was radio controlled so that the Germans could have it lit only when they needed it. The radio antenna was on a separate floating platform a small distance from the buoy itself. One night *SGB 4* was to do a sweep north from Berck buoy. It was a dark, rainy night; Peter was in the chart room, I was on the bridge. Peter called up the voice pipe 'We should be at the Berck buoy in thirty seconds' and at that very moment we passed between the buoy and its radio antenna!

where we were to be based. During the first few weeks, we 'worked up' – trained to become a fighting unit, each man knowing his job, and knowing how to work as part of a team, of people in each ship, and of ships in the slowly growing flotilla.

For this we were based in Portland, and by chance my sister Id was living in next-door Weymouth with her eighteen-month-old son, Patrick. Her husband, Sam Haighton, who, despite having three of the vertebrae of his spine fused together, had managed to join the RNVR, had been appointed First Lieutenant of a motor launch, based in Portland, and had just been reported 'missing in action' in the daring raid of 28th March, 1942, on the French port of St Nazaire, near the mouth of the Loire, the only dry dock west of the Straits of Dover that could take the bigger German warships. I almost wrote 'the *ill-fated* raid'; losses of men and ships were very heavy: only five of the landing party and three of fifteen coastal craft came back, not including Sam's motor launch, but the objective was achieved. The ex-American destroyer HMS *Campbeltown*,[3] her bows packed with explosives, rammed the dock gates at high speed, and exploded the next morning, with three dozen German officers on board. The dry dock was out of action for the rest of the war.

On 1st April Id had just got the news that Sam was missing, and had six weeks of anxious waiting before she heard that he was a prisoner of war. One evening I managed to borrow a car and go over to see her. She made dinner for us, and afterwards we got to talking about what was the best thing to do in an air raid warning, and both agreed that, all things considered, the best policy was to do

---

[3]One of the fifty acquired by Britain in the Churchill–Roosevelt deal – long before Lend-Lease – in exchange for base rights in Bermuda and British colonies in the Caribbean.

nothing. Soon after this, the sirens sounded and I rushed back to Portland, and a real air raid began. One of the bombers flew over our heads, within range of our pom-poms, and we opened fire on it; alas, without effect! The next morning I got a message through HMS *Osprey,* the anti-submarine school, that Id's house had been hit by a bomb, but that she and Patrick were unhurt and were staying in a hotel. I borrowed the car again and went over to see her, and what remained of the house, and to hear the story. Across the road from the house was Weymouth Beach, on which were built a number of concrete blockhouses with machine-guns. These were manned by a detachment of the Welsh Guards, in the charge of Sergeant Harry Campfield, who had become friendly with Id and Patrick as they walked along the front and on the beach. Just after I left, he had come over to Id's and insisted that she got Patrick out of bed and over to the refuge of a blockhouse – through the doorway of which they were virtually blown as the bomb hit the house. It entered through the side wall and exploded on the ground floor; if Id had acted on our joint advice of the night before, she could not have survived.

I went back to the ship and rounded up half a dozen of my sailors, and a few shovels and crowbars, to help Id find whatever possessions she could in the rubble. We worked, sifting through bricks and plaster and broken woodwork, and found quite a lot of stuff, including most of Id's jewellery. But the most interesting thing was to see that Patrick would have been unscathed. He was sleeping in a cot with high sides and sturdy posts. On what was left of the upper floor was the cot, standing upright with the bedclothes just as Patrick had been pulled out of them, and with not a scrap of plaster or even dust on them. A section of the ceiling, not heavy enough to crush the cot, but strong enough not to be penetrated by the slates off the roof, had fallen on to the cot, and been supported by it, as the upper floor of the house fell to the ground floor.

We soon left Portland for Newhaven – in happier times the English terminal for the ferries to Dieppe – from where we started operating. The flotilla grew slowly as the later boats were completed, but the first four of us were No. 3, commanded by George Pennell, senior officer of the flotilla, No. 4 (me), No. 7, Ronnie Barnet (a French naval officer, René Louis Bardet, one of quite a group who, before de Gaulle had got the Free French organised, had determined to keep up the fight, and been taken into the RN under assumed 'English' names, and Canadian identity papers to justify French as first language) and No. 8, Ian 'Griff' Griffiths. Our mission was to interfere with the enemy convoys off the French coast, roughly in the area between the mouths of the Somme and the Seine.

As more coastal craft were becoming available, it was the British objective to harry German traffic every night that the weather allowed. As the SGBs could operate in worse weather than the smaller boats, we were able to go to sea on more nights, so we were busy. In his foreword to his book *The Battle of the Narrow Seas*, Peter Scott, who became senior officer of SGBs in the late summer of 1942, wrote: 'strain, discomfort and boredom... are the three predominant factors in modern warfare', and we spent many nights at sea without incident. The Royal Air Force had not yet achieved the superiority in the air that came later, and we had to try to be north of the centre line of the Channel between dawn and dusk, to avoid attack from cannon-firing ME 109s, which limited the number of hours we could spend on patrol.

The Commandos had only recently been formed, and in 1942 they started to raid the enemy coasts, mainly, at first, to destroy radar stations. They were men picked for courage and the ability to take action on their own, in the light of the situation as they found it. Nelson would have understood; they were trained to do the soldierly equivalent of the last sentence of his orders to his fleet before the Battle of Trafalgar: 'in case signals cannot be seen... NO CAPTAIN CAN DO WRONG IF HE LAYS HIS SHIP ALONGSIDE THAT OF AN ENEMY' (Nelson's capitals). The Commandos were carried to their targets in landing craft, escorted by ships of coastal forces, usually motor launches, and often some of the SGBs were in a covering force, further offshore, as happened on 5th June. The Commandos had raided some targets at Boulogne but had not been able to withdraw quite as early as planned, so that at sunrise they were still on the French side of the Channel, where they were attacked by six Messerschmitt 109s. We, Griff and I, hurried to get in to give closer support, and our and the motor launches' gunfire finally drove them off. We were supposed to have had fighter cover, but the Commandos' lateness had delayed our aircraft. One of the MLs in particular, No. 137, was damaged and had essentially stopped, and took terrible punishment for almost ten minutes as the German planes were able to attack her from a low altitude, in the face of no more than small arms fire. I said, to no one in particular, 'Where are those bloody Spitfires?' to be answered by John Erskine-Hill (who was never at a loss for a tension-breaking comeback), 'Oh, they've gone to get their medals.'[4]

As the Messerschmitts turned away, our own fighters came in from the west, and we were able to pick up the pieces uninterrupted. Griff took ML 137 in tow, while I went alongside her and took off the casualties. The worst wounded were her Captain and Coxswain, who had been

---

[4]There was a certain amount of (basically good-natured) inter-service rivalry about decorations – it seemed to us in the Navy that the Air Force got more than its fair share!

on the bridge and so the most exposed. Both had been hit by cannon shells; the coxswain's leg had been almost severed, and the Captain had been hit right on the diaphragm, so that he was badly wounded, and his guts were exposed. My crew did yeoman work at first aid; it was a beautiful morning, so only the walking casualties were taken below, and we were able to make the rest comfortable (what a misuse of the word!) on deck. I left Griff towing the damaged motor launch as fast as her condition permitted, while we went off at full speed for harbour. As soon as I could I went down to see how bad things were. My chaps had done a good job of stopping the coxswain's bleeding, but the Captain was in terrible pain. We did what we could to tuck his guts back in and bandage them, but he kept screaming in agony, 'Let me die! Let me die!'

Among our medical stores we had a supply of morphine syringes, to which only I had access. The instructions on the package said to give no more than two every four hours, so I gave him two, which seemed to have little effect. Fifteen minutes or so later, he was still obviously in no less pain, so I thought, *What the hell, he's not going to survive that lot*, and gave him two more, and later another two. The package had said that five syringes could be fatal, but he finally calmed down, and was obviously still alive when we got alongside and the ambulance men took him away.[5]

Our next, alas inconclusive, action was in early June, when three of us engaged a German T class torpedo boat (six hundred tons, with six torpedoes, two 104 mm and two 37 mm guns, and a speed of thirty-four knots, so they outgunned us, but *they* broke off the action). Then, on 18th

---

[5]I was sure I had killed him, but had no qualms about it. Imagine my surprise, therefore, when several months later I ran into him in the office of the staff officer, operations, in Portsmouth. He had no memory of the incident at all.

June, Griff, Ronnie Barnet and I, supported by the Hunt class destroyer *Albrighton*, attacked an escorted merchant ship in the Baie de la Seine. Two of us got off four torpedoes, and one of Ronnie's, which failed to run at its proper depth, nevertheless sank the target. But we were in a brisk fire fight with the escorts; Ronnie's boat, *SGB* 7, was sunk, and Ronnie and most of his crew were taken prisoner.[6]

At the very end of June or in early July I got word that I was to get a new appointment, and that Lieutenant Ron Ashby, RNVR, would relieve me on 11th July at noon. He joined the ship a couple of days ahead, and on the 9th July Peter Hood, our navigator, was sick, so Ron took over that job for the night's operation. Griff and I were to patrol off the coast of France north and south of Étaples, where intelligence suggested there would be a southbound convoy. It was a dark night, with no moon, and a steady, fine drizzle. The sea was almost glassy calm, so it was not easy to tell where sea ended and sky began. I was in the lead, and about 2 a.m. we were steaming north, at about twelve knots, when I saw, on our port bow against a lighter bit of sky, a dark shape on opposite course, about two hundred yards away. We identified it as a German R boat, a diesel-powered wooden minesweeper, somewhat smaller than us. We opened fire at once, and before she was abeam I saw two more, each on a course closer to us than the first, so they were evidently in quarter-line (echelon) formation, quite normal for minesweeping. Griff opened fire about five seconds after we did, and as soon as I saw his fire hitting, I shifted target two to the right, leaving the second

[6]Ronnie, despite many attempts to escape, remained a prisoner for the rest of the war. His captors never seemed to realise that he was French, which was just as well, since he had been condemned to death by Vichy as a traitor!

boat to Griff. Almost at once I saw two more, on courses closer still to us. We engaged No. 5 in his line and (as I wrote at the time) '*fairly plastered him*', and I decided to turn round the tail of the enemy line and engage them from a parallel course on their other side. Not to waste time, I rang for full speed. The sky ahead was inky black, and the flashes from our pom-pom made it even more difficult to see; we were increasing speed and I was just about to put the wheel to port, when I saw No. 6 only about thirty-five yards ahead. We were closing one another at a relative speed of over twenty-five knots, so it was only a matter of seconds before he hit us on our port bow, and his stem-head came sixteen feet into our hull. We were all thrown on our faces, except for Able Seaman Ross, our nineteen-year-old pom-pom gunner, who had a seat that cradled him, and we suffered our only casualty of the action – poor Ron Ashby broke a tooth as his face slammed into the rudder indicator. As the water rushed into the mess deck, our ship started to heel to about thirty degrees before we started to right ourselves. The R boat, meanwhile, started to break round alongside us, and half the planking from her side was ripped off, leaving her inside with all its lights on visible to us, like one of those drawings of a cruise ship with its side cut away, to show what it's like inside. AB Ross meanwhile used up all his ready-use ammunition on the R boat's bridge and superstructure. We had to tell him to cease fire, because his shells were bursting uncomfortably close to our bridge – bits of shrapnel were whistling over our heads! During all this, the R boat didn't fire, that we were aware of, one single shot.

Finally the two boats broke apart, the R boat's lights went out and she disappeared from sight. *SGB 4* by this time was out of control, and the bows were so close to the surface that waves were breaking over us. I stopped the engines and suddenly all was quiet, until inimitable John suddenly said, in the darkness, 'Has anyone got a nasty taste in his mouth?'

While John got busy on what damage control was possible, we began to move as much ammunition, stores and people as possible aft, to try to get the bows up and the stern down. I had a reputation for being a damage control fanatic, and in every dockyard we were in I collected softwood plugs of various sizes, they were fine for plugging small holes in steel plating made by gunfire. John shored up the bulkheads either side of the flooded compartment, and came up to the bridge to report.

'What's the damage like?' I asked him.

'Sir,' he answered, 'we haven't got any plug that big!' and then went on to give me his best impression of what we had suffered, though of course he couldn't see anything below the water. It was not until we got into dry dock a couple of days later that we knew the hole was eighteen feet long at deck level, and twenty-two feet high, and reached within ten inches of our keel. What we could see was that, where our plating had crumpled it had gripped the enemy's wooden side planking, so we had hard evidence of his damage. I tried to get some way on the ship as soon as possible, but to begin with the rudder had so little grip on the water that she would not steer. I tried to get the French coast behind us, it was brightly lit by then, but even by using the engines I could not stop the ship swinging ninety degrees before she would respond and swing ninety degrees the other way. As we got more weight moved from forward to aft, however, the rudder had more water to operate in, and we managed to reduce the amount of yaw.

Griff, meanwhile, had slowed down, knowing that I was in the dark somewhere ahead of him, and not wanting to get tangled up with whatever I was doing, had managed to finish off the first R boat and was engaging another at very short range, when he saw minesweeping floats 'whooshing along' (his words) close by, and to avoid getting his propellers mixed up with wire rope turned away and lost contact. His telegraphist tried to contact me, and when he could get no reply, Griff got worried, and started to look for me. Soon, however, to his relief, his telegraphist heard me radio Dover, and then I signalled that I was on a course of 321° at eight knots. I said '321°' because that was the course from where we were (as best we knew) to the Bullock Bank light buoy, which I wanted to find, and I wanted Griff to know it. When he made contact he made me a very rude signal by light, ridiculing the idea that a ship yawing ninety degrees either way could state its course so nicely; and when daylight came and he could see our damage, he made an even ruder signal – something to do with virginity! We gradually got better at steering, and I was able to increase our engine speed until we were making good twelve knots, thanks to the still calm sea. If the weather had turned the least nasty, the only way we could have got home would have been stern first. Griff kept some distance ahead to do the navigation so that we could follow him, until we were within a quarter of a mile of Newhaven, when he came alongside and we made fast, bows to stern, and he towed us in. Poor Ron Ashby duly assumed the command at noon, and had to accept my apologies for passing on a ship that was going to need many days in dock before it would be seagoing again.

A few weeks later the *London Gazette* announced that Griff and I had both been awarded the Distinguished Service Cross for this action. As soon as she heard the news, Griff's wife went out, bought half a yard of DSC ribbon and made up a bow which she sewed on to his pyjama jacket. The action had taken place on the day before my daughter Jeanie's second birthday, and when, decades later, I mentioned this fact, she asked for what I had earned my decoration. I told her the story, and her only comment was: 'You mean you got the DSC for just getting your ship all smashed up?' Alas no man is a hero to his valet – or his daughter!

Chapter Twenty-Four

On the Beach Again

The appointment which the Admiralty had in mind for me was as senior officer of a flotilla of MTBs, of the hard-chine (planing, as opposed to displacement) seventy-foot design, built in the United States. My knee was standing up pretty well to the SGB in any kind of weather, but I was worried that the pounding of a hard-chine ship might be too much for me to be able to operate efficiently, and the doctors agreed. So I got another shore job, at HMS *King Alfred,* in Brighton. This establishment occupied the Brighton municipal public baths and swimming pool, and was where ratings who showed promise were trained to become officers. The selection process included tests of education in the obvious areas – literacy, numeracy and the ability to think logically – and an interview with a panel presided over by a retired Rear Admiral. This may have served to screen out candidates who clearly were not possessed of what the Navy called OLQ – officer-like qualities – which had in theory been done by the commanding officers of the ships that recommended the candidates in the first place.

The men accepted were of all branches of the Navy, from cooks to sickbay attendants, and from even more varied civilian occupations. One hundred of them made up a division, and there were five or six divisions at *King Alfred* at a time, each with a divisional officer, of whom I became one. Our duties were akin to those of a tutor at Eton. We did teach general subjects such as seamanship and boat-handling, but mostly our job was as guide, counsellor and friend, while specialists taught the more specific skills like navigation, gunnery and communications. We followed the progress of our cadet ratings, and tried to get as many of our hundred to qualify as officers, who were desperately needed in the fleet. The selection process obviously worked pretty well, because rarely did more than five out of the hundred fail the final 'passing-out' examinations. The weakest link in the selection was, sad to say, the admiral's interview panels. We got their reports on all our men, along with the rest of their histories; some suggested a glimpse of a personality, but what was I to make of 'Tall, bald-headed man; needs watching'? We had a division for twelve weeks, and then the successful ones got their commissions as acting Sub Lieutenants, changed their uniforms and had another few weeks of practical training before being appointed to ships.

I met a number of men from my division later on during my naval service, and at least two afterwards; one a canon of the Church of England, at an old Collegers' dinner at Eton, and another the energy correspondent of the *Christian Science Monitor* newspaper in Boston; it was flattering that I had made an impression on both. The Navy was a lot stickier than the other services in not accelerating promotion of regular officers during the war, but abiding strictly to the peacetime rules, for example a Lieutenant was promoted to Lieutenant Commander only with eight years' seniority. For wartime-only officers, however, this system didn't work, because men who entered as Sub Lieutenants might be a lot older than their regular counterparts, or have valuable skills which justified a higher rank. But it was still a little galling, two years later, to meet a man whom I had last seen as an Acting Sub Lieutenant of one day's seniority, but was now a Lieutenant Commander whom I had to salute and call 'sir'. It was not until nearly the end of the war that the Navy introduced the rank of (believe it or not!) Quasi-Permanent Acting Lieutenant Commander that put some of us whose careers were the Navy on the same footing as a bunch of johnny-come-latelys who had got their two and a half stripes after only two years of seniority with two.[1]

I only did three and a half months at *KA*, that is, I saw one division through, and I was moved on to a new job, on the staff of the Rear Admiral, Coastal Forces, Piers K. Kekewich, who had been Captain of *Frobisher* during part of my time in her as a cadet. His offices were in a block of flats in Hampstead, north of Swiss Cottage and west of the Finchley Road, called (I think) Wentworth Court. I was Assistant Staff Officer, Operations, a misnomer of a job, because the RACF had only a second-hand interest in operations (which were the responsibility of the senior officers of the operational bases). Our field was essentially the translation of operational experience into the design of *matériel*, and I don't remember getting much satisfaction (though a little fun!) out of my job. One of the senior members of the staff was Captain (Special Branch) Lord Reith, who had been the first General Manager (from 1922) and then (until 1938) Director-General of the BBC, who must have been taking a sort of sabbatical between ministerial appointments. What he did I was never quite sure, but he was an amusing colleague, and put up, very good-humouredly, with some rather childish pranks from the rest of us – like having the back of his chair labelled 'Lord Reith slept here'.

The office had no catering facilities, so we had to bring in something from home, or go out for lunch, usually at

---

[1]Two and a half stripes on the sleeve of a Lieutenant Commander; two on a Lieutenant's.

one particular pub that made very good cheese sandwiches, which, with a half-pint of bitter, made a very satisfying meal. Two of us had to be on duty every night, and had to go out, one at a time, to dinner. It was either another cheese sandwich or, if you were lucky and the pub hadn't already sold the day's quota, a sausage, or find a restaurant. This wasn't easy: the city was blacked out, so there were no illuminated signs or lighted windows to attract one; you just had to walk along the Finchley Road and hear enough voices to suggest a restaurant, or try to find one you thought you had identified from the bus in the morning. The results could be surprising.

One evening I opened a door that sounded promising and indeed found myself in a restaurant. I sat down at a table, and a middle-aged waitress came up and said something in a language I couldn't identify, never mind understand. I asked the other customers if anyone spoke English, and drew a blank, but a thought suddenly lit up the waitress's face, she said something and disappeared into the kitchen, and came out with the chef, who at least spoke some (very bad) French, and from whom I was able to order, from his very limited, wartime menu, something to eat.

The area was part of a predominantly Jewish district, and London was host to many tens of thousands of refugees from Hitler, and from some of the faces and the sounds of the language – I didn't recognise one word – I guessed that my fellow diners were probably Jewish refugees from somewhere in central Europe. Anyway, they didn't show any resentment of my presence, and when I paid my bill and left, I was sent on my way with smiles and friendly gestures. How I wished I had been able to talk with them, for refugees were people one read about in the newspapers and for whose plight one felt a lot of sympathy and anger, but whom one never (knowingly) met, except for those naval people who had left their countries and joined in the war under their own flags, but operationally as part of the British Navy.

I held this job for a little under three months, before I was transferred to HMS *Bee* in Weymouth, where my experience and skills could be of much more use than polishing the seat of a chair in London. *Bee* was the 'working up' base for all newly commissioned coastal forces craft: motor launches, motor torpedo boats and motor gunboats. It was our job to teach individuals in the crews the necessary professional skills: gunnery, torpedoes, communications, navigation and pilotage, radar, engine care and maintenance, and then the boats as whole units, tactics, and the other skills of fighting. The training activity as a whole was the responsibility of the Training Commander, Roland Swinley, with a Lieutenant Commander RNVR, whose name I cannot now recall (TO 1), and me (TO 2) as training officers, and later, when I persuaded Swinley to ask for him, Peter Hood for navigation, reporting to him.

When individual skills were at a satisfactory level, we arranged tactical exercises, always at night, since that was when the boats would be operating, in the form of war games, with two opposing forces. Sometimes we could get the services of a trawler from Portland to represent a merchant ship, and it and an escort of motor gunboats would go to sea early and get out of sight before beginning its imaginary course as the enemy. Then the attacking force would get its 'intelligence briefing', sketchy and often inaccurate as in real life, and set off to attack. Swinley, the two TOs and Peter would be distributed among the two forces to observe and record who did what, and in the morning the two TOs would put together an analysis of the 'action', and in the afternoon Swinley would present this to the assembled officers of the boats involved, with his comments and observations, and there was a general discussion of lessons learned, with recommendations for how things could be done better. Our analyses began to command respect, to the extent that Lieutenant Commander (later Sir) Peter Scott, the artist and founder of the World Wildlife Fund, who became senior officer of the SGB flotilla in March of 1943, began to write to me a series of letters, one after each noteworthy action, for analysis and comment by *Bee*'s people, as individuals and not officially, so that we could all write frankly. Peter clearly found this correspondence useful because he kept it up as long as he was in the job: several of his letters to me are quoted in his biography by Elspeth Huxley.[2]

I had done a lot of seagoing while at *Bee,* and was getting more confident that I could go to sea again, so when my next routine medical survey came due, I determined to be found fit again. Many naval medical officers were Irish: Trinity College, Dublin turned out more doctors (and very good ones) than the Irish market could absorb, so many joined the British fighting services. Moreover, their lives tended not to be very busy; except, of course, in action. The joke had it that Naval 'quacks' (always so-called, to their faces) had only three diagnoses: CDA (caught disease ashore), PUO (pyrexia of unknown origin) and RTH (refer to hospital). In a ship they saw any patients in the morning, and so by lunchtime the day was over. This was useful to the rest of the wardroom, as the quack was often roped in to do chores, like keeping the wine accounts, for which others might not easily find the time. It also meant that he could give himself the luxury of a gin or two at lunchtime. I knew slightly the Surgeon Captain who would probably carry out my survey; he was Irish, with a strong Irish accent, and would only have two gins at lunchtime if he'd decided not to have three. So I wangled an appointment

---

[2]Faber and Faber, 1993.

with him for after lunch. He had me haul up my trouser leg, and he felt my knee and found the limits of its movement. Then he looked at the X-rays, taken that morning, and compared them with others from earlier surveys. While he was busy at that, I dropped my left trouser leg, and hauled up the right one. He swivelled his chair around and gave a desultory palpation of the wrong knee, and said, 'It looks pretty good to me; how d'ye feel yerself? Do you t'ink ye're fit fer sea?'

I said: 'Yes, sir!'

'That's foine; I'll report you fit.'

Whether my little deception worked, or he just thought, If this silly bugger wants to get back to the fightin', whoy sh'd I be stoppin' him? I never knew. But I determined that only in absolute *extremis* would I ever have another survey. And in early October, 1943, I was sent on a four-day course at the Damage Control School followed by a two-week gunnery refresher course at the Gunnery School, both in Portsmouth.

Chapter Twenty-Five

HMS *Mackay*

These two courses turned out to be in preparation for my appointment, on 12th October, 1943, to HMS *Mackay*, as First Lieutenant of the flotilla leader of the Captain (D) of the 16th Destroyer Flotilla, Captain S.V. Jephson, who was also Senior Officer of the Harwich Escort Force. I didn't serve under him for long, for five weeks later he was relieved by Captain R.F. Jessel, who proudly claimed to be the only Jewish Destroyer Captain in the Service. 'So, as well as your normal duties, you'll have to take church for me on Sundays' was his greeting to me. *Mackay* was a leader laid down in the last months of World War I, and completed in mid-1919 (a leader is distinguished from a destroyer mainly by having extra cabins and office space to accommodate the Captain (D)'s staff, the flotilla gunnery, torpedo, engineer and so on officers). The flotilla consisted of a number of 'V' and 'W' destroyers of World War I vintage, and some modern, but slower and less powerful Hunt class, as well as some smaller ships, including a sloop commanded by Nicholas Monsarrat (author of *The Cruel Sea*, a wonderful novel of life in an escort ship during World War II). Our roles were the defence of the southern North Sea, and escorting convoys down the east coast of Britain.

Before my time in her, in mid-February 1943, *Mackay* had taken part in one of the worst-botched actions of the war – the attempt to stop the German battlecruisers *Scharnhorst* and *Gneisenau,* and the heavy cruiser *Prinz Eugen*, from getting back home from refuge in Brest. The botching was not on the part of the ships of the Navy involved, where there was much gallantry and initiative, but resulted from the total failure of co-ordination between the three commands of the Royal Air Force, and between the RAF and the Navy, and finally by the Army's failure to cancel a signal exercise for the artillery along the Channel, which was supposed to begin with the news that *Scharnhorst* and *Gneisenau* had broken out of Brest. When a signal announcing the real thing arrived in the signal office, without the prefix 'Exercise Only', the officer to whom it was delivered thought it was a mistake, and added the prefix!

There was public outrage in Britain: *The Times* said that 'Nothing more mortifying to the pride of our sea power has happened since the seventeenth century'. But it was a Pyrrhic victory for the *Kriegsmarine*: Grand Admiral Räder described it as a tactical victory but a strategic defeat. Hitler had wanted the three ships in Norway, because he was sure that there would soon be a combined British and Russian attack on Germany's northern flank, and if the ships couldn't get there, he wanted their guns removed and taken to Norway. And from Britain's point of view, the ships were much less of a threat in Kiel than in Brest, with access to the open Atlantic. In fact, *Gneisenau* was crippled in Kiel two weeks later, *Prinz Eugen* was torpedoed by a submarine, HMS *Trident*; *Scharnhorst* escaped to Norway, for the purpose of attacking the Allied convoys to Russia, but was sunk in her first serious sortie, the day after Christmas.

The 'Channel dash' of the German big ships is the scene of an amusing tale from *Mackay*: we had in our ship's company Able Seaman Burgess, formerly Bourgeois of the French navy. His English was not very good, but he was always able to communicate with the Chief Gunner's Mate. His action station was in one of the magazines, passing ammunition from the storage racks to the hoist up to the gun. That day, *Mackay* was on a gunnery exercise, and Burgess's job was to pass up practice shells with no explosive in them. He'd taken part in dozens of such exercises during his career, so he knew the routine; first, on the same course as the target (towed by a tug) fire six salvoes, turn to opposite course and fire six more. He was in the magazine and, on the first run, duly passed up his six rounds. Then he felt the ship increase speed, and turn, and continue to turn both ways.

He thought, *These British are pretty incompetent at getting round to the other side of the target*; but couldn't do anything about it. The ship was obviously going at full speed, and the weather was getting worse, but the second practice run never seemed to happen. After a while someone brought mugs of cocoa and corned beef sandwiches down to the magazine crew. He ate, still puzzled.

Then, some time later, came the 'open fire' bell again, and he reached for a practice round, but one of his mates yelled, 'No, not those, *those*!' pointing to the live ammunition – and he went on passing up rounds long after the six he'd expected.

Huh! Not only incompetent, but extravagant, he thought, but mentally shrugged his shoulders. Eventually the 'ceasefire' gong rang, and after another wait a second mug of cocoa and sandwich for each was delivered. He wasn't wearing a watch, and completely lost track of time, but finally the ship slowed down, got into calmer water, and action stations were stood down. So Burgess found his friend, the Chief Gunner's Mate, and asked about the strange exercise.

'*Exercise*?' said the CGM. 'That was no exercise; we just carried out a torpedo attack on the *Gneisenau*!'

This was a digression from my story, but I have always

felt sorry for AB Burgess, missing all the excitement, and have wondered how he would tell the tale to his grandchildren.

We spent a lot of time at night at 'Action stations, relaxed'. At each station two men were on watch, and the remainder were there but able to rest and sleep. As second in command of the ship, my action station was as far from the bridge as feasible, at the after conning position beside X-gun (near the stern of the ship, on a deck raised above the main upper deck) where there were duplicate steering, engine room telegraphs and a binnacle, so that if the bridge was wiped out, I might still be available to drive the ship. I didn't keep watch so I could sleep all night if not called. The bridge offered comparative shelter, but X-gun deck had no protection from the weather. I had an inflatable beach mattress, and I got our shipwright to make for me a shelter, canvas on a wooden frame, eighteen inches high, eighteen inches wide and about four feet six inches long, into which I could thread myself, leaving exposed only my lower legs (on which I had a pair of US bomber pilot's boots, the gift of a grateful airman rescued from the 'drink' after ditching on his way back from a one thousand-bomber raid). I slept in my little shelter fully dressed, with a balaclava helmet and gloves to keep head and hands warm, with my steel helmet ready for use on the top. Once I was in there the men on watch assumed that I was asleep, and chattered away as if they were alone. So I got to hear some intimate conversations, and some very amusing. British sailors of fifty years ago used to lard their conversations with swear words (perhaps they still do) and to convey the full flavour of these without the epithets is not possible. So here goes.

The Admiralty frequently sent out Admiralty Fleet Orders (AFOs), usually on matters concerning the Service, but from time to time in a noticeboard edition, for general information. Naval ships in wartime often found themselves in parts of the ocean where peacetime sailing – usually direct from one port to another – would not take them; and several of the officers and men would have binoculars when on duty. So, by way of an AFO, the National Birdwatching Society asked for the help of naval people in recording sightings of unusual birds. A couple of nights later, I overheard one sailor saying to the other:

'I'm the fuckin' bastard they should 'ave asked about birds.'

'Why, Lofty, you don't know nothin' about fuckin' birds!'

'Yes, I do: there is only three kinds of birds – shitehawks,[1] arse-up ducks and fuckin' sparrers!'

Another gem was this tale of a romance of a sailor with three good conduct badges, and therefore known as 'Stripey'.

'What d'you do last night, Stripey?'

'Ooh! I went a-fucking-shore, and I goes to this fucking pub, and I meets this fucking party,[2] so I buys 'er a fucking port and fucking brandy, and then we 'as another, and maybe a fucking third one, and we decides to go for a fucking walk on the fucking common. We finds a fucking place with some fucking bushes, and I takes off my fucking macin-fucking-tosh, and we sits down. Soon I slips me fucking 'and up 'er fucking skirt, and I slides 'er fucking panties down…'

And so on for a blow-by-blow description of a seduction. His mate listened open-mouthed, and when Stripey paused he said, 'And what d'you do then, Stripey?'

To which the latter rather sheepishly replied, 'I lay wiv 'er!'

---

[1] Seagulls.

[2] To a sailor, every girl was a 'party'.

Of course action stations were not always relaxed. We did anti E boat patrols, anti-submarine sweeps, we watched the German bombers on their way to London – always out of the range of our anti-aircraft guns – and we escorted convoys along the mineswept channels, a mile wide, and marked by a line of buoys down the centre line. So very rarely did we get a full night's sleep, and when we weren't at action stations I took my turn at watch-keeping on the bridge.

In harbour there were all the manifold duties of the ship's executive officer to carry out, from the organisation structure, through planning training, to seeing defaulters as a court of first instance, to pass on to the Captain the serious cases. I must have done these things well, because when the Captain of one of the Hunt class destroyers went sick, I was appointed by Captain (D) as her temporary commanding officer. I had never handled a destroyer before, so I was very nervous when I had to leave harbour the first time, but my background in picket boats, *MA/SB 3* and *SGB 4* served me well, and by the time the proper Captain came out of hospital and back to his ship, I was able to hand it over without a scratch. And when I left *Mackay*, the last words of my flimsy were the magic ones: 'Recommended for the command of a destroyer.'

I must not leave *Mackay*, however, without bringing in to the story someone who became a very close friend, who is indeed godfather to my younger daughter. Selwyn Chidgey – he didn't like the name Selwyn, so he was always just 'Chidge' – is Australian. He was an infant prodigy violinist who played his first public concert at the age of twelve, and he continued with the violin until 'the jive got me', and he switched to the saxophone. At fifteen he ran his own jazz band, until (he says), he got more sense at seventeen and switched to playing in other people's bands. He carried his 'bubble-gun' around with him, and could sometimes be persuaded to play in the wardroom of an evening. He was – I hope still is – a superb musician, and could play 'Popeye the Sailor Man' so as to make his saxophone literally talk. He had a fund of stories, and a gift for telling them, that made him the best messmate anyone could want, and he was a fine officer too. He was Number Two to my Number One in *Mackay,* and when I got my own command, I wangled Chidge's appointment as my Number One.

Chapter Twenty-Six

HMS *Lancaster*

As the war continued to take its toll of experienced officers, and at the same time the number of ships increased, there had to be a certain devaluation in the qualifications for jobs. In peacetime captains of destroyers had been Lieutenant Commanders with a few years of seniority, and some would be Commanders. But now, increasingly, Lieutenants were beginning to slip in. So, after only a few months in *Mackay*, I was sent on an anti-submarine course, had some leave, and on 28th April, 1944, was appointed to HMS *Lancaster,* one of the ships of the Rosyth Escort Force, 'in command'. I was twenty-six, and had got my most responsible job ever – captain of a destroyer in wartime. *Lancaster* was of the Town class, one of fifty surplus American World War I destroyers that had been laid up in the United States in care and maintenance status, transferred to the Royal Navy (under the Churchill–Roosevelt destroyers for bases deal) in September 1940 when Britain was in desperate need of ships to protect Atlantic convoys. In the US navy they had all been named after officers and men who had distinguished themselves in action. When transferred to the white ensign, they were given names of towns common to the US and Britain. *Lancaster* had been USS *Philip.* Her keel was laid down in 1917, by the Bath Iron Works in Maine, so my ship and I were born in the same year! The Rosyth Escort Force was so-called because it was based in Rosyth, on the north side of the Firth of Forth, just west of the Forth railway bridge, and its job was to escort convoys of merchant ships down the east coast, to the Thames estuary, where more modern escorts took over ships going down the English Channel.

While Rosyth was our base, my family came to live near Inverkeithing, not far away, in a private hotel called Dhuloch. This was an old wealthy family's house, in several acres of grounds, with many old trees, but not much else in the way of landscaping – gardeners were very scarce in wartime Britain. The two owners were both fond of the bottle, and by dinner time they were obviously to some degree (though not unpleasantly) under the influence, but this didn't interfere with the cooking and service, though rations were not conducive to any standard of meal above the basic. There was no central heating in the building, but the public rooms and all the bedrooms had fireplaces, and the guests were perfectly at liberty to cut their own firewood from dead trees to keep their rooms as warm as they liked, as long as they contributed to keeping the public rooms supplied with fuel.

There were about a dozen guests in all, including the father of *Lancaster's* Number Two, Douglas Paffard, a retired but wartime serving Captain in the Navy. Captain Paffard was one of a regular four who played bridge almost every evening, and another was the widow of an executive of the Indian Railways. She was hard of hearing and, when necessary, used an old-fashioned ear trumpet. She made this do double duty, using it as an ashtray, flicking into it the ash from the cigarettes she chain-smoked, so that by the end of the evening there was quite a lot of ash in it. The four players were always at odds with one another over whose bid was silly, or who played the hand wrong – indeed, this acrimonious discussion was often continued over breakfast the next day. One evening, however, Captain

Paffard was more than usually upset with the widow, who had been his partner. He was being vociferous about it, but she had her ear trumpet on the table, and couldn't hear everything. 'What did you say?' she asked, and as Captain Paffard leaned towards her she put the trumpet to her ear, just as he shouted 'I said you are a stupid old woman!' with such vigour that he got a blast of ash in his face!

Phyllis was pregnant with our second child, and Jeanie was four, and very inquisitive about things around her. Phyllis always did a lot of knitting, and Jeanie was familiar with the procedure that first one sleeve was knitted, then the other, then the back and then the front, each piece being put away into a drawer until all were ready to be assembled into a finished garment. We had told Jeanie, so that she could get used to the idea of a sibling, that Mummy was making another baby. She watched Phyllis one day put a finished sleeve into a drawer, and peered curiously in as if looking for something. Then, very suspiciously, she asked, 'Mummy, this baby you're making; where are the pieces?'

The Towns had four funnels (one to each boiler), and were known as 'four-stackers', or to British sailors, 'packets of Woodbines'.[1] They were flush-decked (with no raised fo'c'sle, though there was a raised superstructure roughly from number one funnel to number three). They were fast – thirty-five knots – and narrow gutted, three hundred and eleven feet long, and just over thirty feet wide. The dead wood under the stern was not all cut away, so they had a lot of directional stability and a correspondingly wide turning circle: one thousand yards at twelve knots. But they might have been designed by Henry Ford: they were very

---

[1]Woodbines were the cheapest of British cigarettes, short and thin, and sold in paper packs of five, with one quarter of the length showing. With the middle one out, the rest was not a bad icon for a Town.

simple mechanically and so had a degree of reliability surprising for their age. They rolled like nobody's business, they were said to be able to heel to over ninety degrees and still have a righting moment, though no one I knew ever quite put this to the test. They were very wet when steaming into the sea, but good sea boats none the less. Most ships are difficult to steer when going astern, especially in any wind, because the propellers tend to hold the stern in place while a raised fo'c'sle acts as a sail and blows the bows downwind, so that the stern turns up into the wind, but the four-stackers were much easier in this regard. Despite this, they had a reputation for being hard to handle, and most captains got tug assistance when leaving and entering harbour.

Even before Chidge joined, I had a very good group of officers. The engineer officer was 'Chiefie' Davies, who in peacetime had been chief engineer in cargo ships belonging to penny-pinching owners in Cardiff, in which he had acquired a sixth sense for machinery that was what he called 'gettin' ripe', needing maintenance very soon: ideal for a twenty-six-year-old ship. The quack was Donald Kerr, a graduate of the Edinburgh school of medicine, born in England of a Scots family, and who owned and played a set of bagpipes. Our midshipman, Gannon, claimed to be the only bearded, bald-headed midshipman in the Service. All these were reserve officers, and only Lieutenant Douglas Paffard, the number two, was a regular. And when my request that Chidge should be transferred to us was granted, the ship really came alive. He was exceptional at getting along with the ship's company, and very soon enjoyed general respect, despite what some stuffy people (from other ships) regarded as unseemly informality. As First Lieutenant, responsible for all the day-to-day work of the ship, his contact with the ship's company was through the Chief Bosun's Mate, known as 'the buffer'. A traditionalist naval officer, on receiving a report from the buffer, would acknowledge with the words: 'Very good, Chief Bosun's Mate.' Chidge's version was 'Good-oh, Buffs', which used to cause an occasional raised eyebrow.

As well as this support, I had one other person who made my life easier, Able Seaman Rudolph, my sailor servant. This may sound a very menial job, but it was in fact very popular, because, while he had to take care of me, keep my shoes cleaned, send my shirts to the laundry, make up my bunk and so on, he didn't have to be involved in any of the routine chores of the ship, so he could often be in a warm cabin while his mates were working out in the wind and the rain.

After a couple of weeks of experience, I had got the hang of handling *Lancaster,* and never had to resort to help from a tug. The southern end of our convoy route was Sheerness, on the Isle of Sheppey where the River Medway joins the Thames estuary. There, as often as not, we berthed alongside another destroyer already moored at a buoy. As long as the wind wasn't too strong, I had found that, with our directional stability, I could bring *Lancaster* alongside the other ship only a couple of feet away so the eye of the mooring wire could be just handed across.

One day we were coming alongside and a sailor in the other ship called out, 'Chuck us a heavin' line, mate.' (This was the normal way of passing a wire: you threw across a line with which the crew of the other ship hauled it over.)

I could hear the pride with which our sailor answered, 'We don't use no heavin' lines aboard this packet, mate!'

The port of Rosyth was not very spacious: destroyers were berthed in 'destroyer pens' formed of jetties at right angles to the dock wall, with space for four destroyers, two on each side, between them. We came in bows first, so had to leave stern first, and either get a tug to turn the ship, which my pride wouldn't accept, or turn on the screws (one engine ahead, the other astern) in the small space of open water inside the breakwater, and then turn out into the open Firth. Because of their underwater shape, four-stackers took a long time to turn this way, and one day on the bridge I said, to no one in particular, 'It'd be a damn'd sight easier to get out of here stern first than doing all this push me pull you!'

I think it must have been Chidge who asked, 'Then why don't you?'

'Next time, I will, dammit', I said.

By this time we had started to have Doc Kerr on the fo'c'sle playing his bagpipes as we left harbour, and in accordance with tradition all the seamen were standing smartly in line on deck. The next time we sailed, I made good on my threat, and went out of the harbour stern first, turning by rudder only, and when the ship was pointed more or less in the right direction, went ahead to pass under the Forth Bridge towards the open sea.

The Admiral Commanding, Rosyth, had a house on the top of a cliff, looking over the dockyard and south to the Forth Bridge. One day, soon after I'd adopted the stern first exit, we returned to Rosyth and found a signal summoning me to see the Admiral at nine o'clock the next morning. He asked me to sit down in his office, and said, 'I notice that you have a somewhat unconventional way of leaving harbour. Why?'

So I explained to him the steering characteristics of the four-stackers, and therefore why I found my method easier, and that it avoided the use of a tug.

'Oh,' he said, 'If you think it's the more seamanlike way to do it, well, you're the Captain of the ship, and who am I to interfere? By the way, I love the bagpipes: have a cup of coffee!'

He went on to demonstrate his enjoyment of our bagpipes by coming out into his garden to wave to us as we left harbour, even, one morning, in his pyjamas!

I was not at that time aware of the Hawthorne experiments at the light bulb factory of the Western Electric Company, in Cicero, Illinois, in 1927. A group of mostly women workers were segregated in a work area separate from the main factory floor, and their productivity recorded as their working conditions were changed. The experiments began with measuring the effect of increased lighting. Productivity rose. Then lighting was reduced to a level below the starting point. Productivity rose again. The lighting level was lowered yet again, and still productivity rose. Over a year many other changes were tried, and almost every one caused improved productivity, though pay and hours of work were not changed. This was the beginning of the study of behavioural science, and showed what beneficial effects the mere fact of showing an interest can bring about – if you feel that people notice you are different, you will *be* different. For *Lancaster*'s ship's company, no tugs, no heaving lines, bagpipes on the fo'c'sle, leaving harbour stern first, and 'Good-oh, Buffs' set it apart from other ships. It was a lesson that was of great use to me in my next career.

The passage took two days and two nights; our routine was for two destroyers and some other, less powerful, escorts to meet the convoy in mid-morning at the junction of the Firth of Forth and North Sea swept[2] channels, and shepherd them south, picking up more ships from the coal and steel ports of north-east England: Blyth; Tynemouth and South Shields for the Tyne; Hartlepool and Middlesborough for the Tees. The dangerous part of the trip was the second night, when we were in the narrow southern triangle of the North Sea, not far from the German-controlled ports of Belgium and Holland. So the

[2]Swept, and kept clear of mines.

escort was strengthened during day two by a third destroyer out of Immingham Dock, in the estuary of the Humber. We escorted the flock as far as the Thames estuary, which was the destination of the largest number of the ships, and spent the night in Sheerness (thus named, naval lore had it, because nobody would go there except out of sheer necessity). Mid-morning the next day we helped the north bound convoy assemble, and headed back up the North Sea, and on the second evening, every other trip, it was our turn to go into Immingham, to go south again next morning.

In the last hour or two of the passage to Sheerness when I was busy on the bridge, Rudolph used to sit in the wardroom pantry, which had a serving hatch giving on to the wardroom itself, and listen to what plans were being made for the evening that involved me. Then, as we separated from the convoy at the mouth of the Thames and were on our own going into Sheerness, I would become aware of Rudolph, lurking discreetly at the back of the bridge waiting for me to have a quiet moment, when he would sidle up and tell me, 'You're going ashore this afternoon, sir, with the First Lieutenant and the Doctor, and going to the cinema to see that new film of Rita Hayworth's, and then having dinner at the Bull in Sittingbourne. But first, sir, the Captain of the Port wants to see you. It looks like it's going to rain, sir, so I've laid out my raincoat for you; *ours* is getting a bit shabby.'

Another bit of Rudolph's initiative came one day on the way out of Sheerness. Midshipman Gannon had some rich friends somewhere near Rosyth, and in the pheasant-shooting season they invited him to a shoot. He came back on board with a brace of pheasants the day before we sailed south. At dinner in the wardroom we discussed how long the birds should be left hanging before they were cooked. Gannon urged tradition – hang them by the feet until they dropped off. I protested that I liked to eat birds before they had putrefied, and there were other opinions everywhere in between. Eventually we agreed that we would have them for lunch on the first day out of Sheerness north bound, giving them four days to mature. I was busy getting the convoy organised until long after lunch time, but finally I went below to my cabin and called down to Rudolph to bring up my lunch. My cabin was at upper deck level, and had a door opening aft a little way from the hatch that came up from the wardroom. I was sitting at my little desk table, very hungry from having been maybe five hours on the bridge, when I became aware of a terrible stink approaching along the upper deck. I called out, 'Is that you, Rudolph? And is that stink my lunch?'

'Yes, sir. Shall I ditch it? I've got some corned beef standing by.'

So my serving of pheasant was duly ditched and Rudolph brought up my corned beef.

'Good God, Rudolph,' I asked him, 'did they eat that stinking mess?'

'No, sir; there was only two of them that did. The midshipman, sir, he had to, seeing as he'd shot them, and he was the one that wanted them high. And the Engineer Officer, sir, he's got such a bad cold that he couldn't smell nothing, sir, and he didn't know *what* he was eating.'

Back in Rosyth we had a post-mortem on the pheasants, which we agreed should not have got to that state in four days, until we discovered where they had been hung – against the bulkhead of the wardroom pantry, on the other side of which was a very hot boiler room.

It was coming out of Immingham one day that I put *Lancaster*'s stability to the test. There was a strong northerly gale blowing, and with a tailwind the convoy had made much better speed than we had calculated from the last position report we had. So when we got out to the swept channel it was several miles ahead of us, and we had to increase speed to catch up. The gale had caused a long swell from the north, and we found ourselves going just faster than the swell. These are the conditions in which it is all too easy to 'broach-to', to find yourself riding down one swell, so the stern is higher than the bows, and driving the bows into the slope of the swell ahead. This causes the bows to be slowed down at the same moment as the stern is lifted, and has less grip on the water. A little tendency for the stern to swing one way can suddenly deprive the ship of the effect of its rudder, and to swing right round until it is at right angles to the swell, and listing very dangerously downwind, to the point of capsizing.

Luckily I realised very quickly what was happening, and was able to stop the swing and reduce the ship's speed so that we didn't get near capsizing. But all over the ship was the noise of breaking crockery, and I hit the gyro compass repeater with the side of my face and broke a tooth! And the roll indicator indicated a list of forty degrees.

Immingham was the home of a 'plot', a large-scale chart of the operational area with all the intelligence from ships, from shore radar and from radio messages laid out on it. It was manned around the clock, mainly by WRNS[3] officers and ratings, whom we used to meet, off duty, in the Officers' Club, for a drink and maybe some dancing in the evening we spent in port. Two of *Lancaster*'s officers used to show off their skills on these occasions. Chidge would offer to give the saxophonist in the club's dance band a spell, and for an hour or more he would play his 'bubble-gun' (Chidgese for an alto sax, as 'grunt iron' was for a tenor). It was a bit unfair, because Chidge was just so much better a player that the dancers never wanted to let him go.

Chiefie Davis had a more esoteric skill. To men, at any

---

[3]Women's Royal Naval Service.

rate, he was not attractive; his face was sallow, grey and shiny with oily secretion. His head was the same colour, and his hair was black and sparse, and lay in oily strands across his scalp. He would sit in a chair at a table with a glass of beer, and though he didn't stir from it, he was never without female company. Chidge and Chiefie and I sat down together one evening, and Chidge asked him how he did it without ever taking the initiative. 'They tell me I've got animal magnetism,' he said, and, pointing out a group of three or four girls the other side of the room, asked us which we'd like to come and join us. We suggested the blonde in the orange dress, and without Chiefie saying a word, or making any facial gestures, in a few minutes the blonde in the orange dress came over to join, not us, but just Chiefie.

The convoys were part of London's lifeline, for they brought all the coal for its electric power stations, and when the flow of newly built Liberty ships from America really got going, we might have fifty or more ships in one convoy. In two columns within the southbound half a mile wide lane of the swept channel, the convoy could be two or three miles long, and longer in bad weather or if station-keeping in the merchant ships was not up to scratch, so our escorting could not be very close. We had little fighting to do: at this stage of the war the MGBs from Felixstowe, Ramsgate and Dover were usually able to deal with the E boats closer to their homes, and the few that ventured into our waters usually turned away if we fired star shells to illuminate them.

More dangerous, if unintentionally, was Hitler's boasted secret weapon, the flying bomb, the V1. Of eight thousand launched in the summer of 1944, two thousand were erratic, and our convoy route was right under their flight track – all were aimed at London. Their hot exhaust gases were easy to see on a clear night, and their noise, just like a very loud single-cylinder motorbike, was easy to hear. If they flew close enough, we, escorts and merchant ships both, tried to shoot them down, and actually got a few, but one more than usually errant one gave me a very long scare. We saw it coming in from the south-east, flying low on a course to pass astern of the convoy. But at just the wrong moment it turned parallel to our course, and started to fly, at masthead height, right up between the two columns of ships, the whole length of the convoy. Its engine might stop at any moment (and when that happened the V1 dived and exploded on impact) but a much bigger danger was that some trigger-happy gunner in any of fifty ships might open fire, and others join in and spray the other column of ships with explosive shells. Luckily, discipline held, and the V1 flew harmlessly on, and turned again to head back for the Dutch coast.

The V1s had something more personal against us too. Douglas Paffard seemed to attract them, to the point that people hesitated to go ashore with him. One night when we were in Sheerness he was going to see some family friends that lived not far away, but a longish walk from the bus stop nearest to their house. Douglas had just bought a new uniform suit and was wearing it. Earlier rain had stopped, but the ditch alongside the road was full of water, and, as Douglas was walking along, a flying bomb came into earshot, headed straight for him. When it was about forty-five degrees above him, its engine stopped and it dived downwards. The only cover was the ditch, so Douglas had to jump in and lie down in the muddy water. The bomb exploded fifty yards from him, and he wasn't hurt, but oh, his poor new uniform!

In early June 1944 we were all becoming aware that the Allied invasion of *Festung Europa* was not far off, but the actual date was a matter of speculation. On about the third or fourth day of the month we were all in the wardroom after dinner, due to sail the next morning, and inevitably talk turned to when D-Day would be. I must have been in a relaxed mood because I said, 'I know when it is.'

Everyone jumped down my throat with words like 'Oh! Come off it! Of course you don't know!'

'I do, and I'll tell you when we go to sea tomorrow.' That evening, on the bridge, a couple of the officers reminded me of my promise, and I said that it was a very auspicious date, my birthday – tomorrow, 6th June. Not ready to have my bluff called yet, I said, 'Okay, let's get the telegraphist to rig up a loudspeaker on the bridge for first light tomorrow, and we'll listen to the seven o'clock BBC news, and you all be up here!'

Duly at seven the BBC relayed General Eisenhower's announcement that the invasion had indeed started – and I got some very queer looks, until Chidge burst out laughing, and said, 'You Pommie bluffer – you almost had me fooled. But happy birthday anyway, *sir*!'

Looking back, it was, of course, a very silly prank. If we had had to go into harbour with engine trouble or for any reason on the evening of the 5th, and someone who had gone ashore had said, 'Our skipper says that tomorrow's D-Day' and this had got to the ears of the intelligence services, I would have had a very rough time talking my way out.

A few weeks before D-Day the number of brand-new Liberty ships in our convoys increased dramatically. It was well known that these ships were prefabricated, and a ship could be completed within a week. I had a theory that, not only the ships were prefabricated, but that the whole thing was programmed by Critical Path Analysis, so that the cargo of tanks, guns and ammunition were delivered and loaded into the cargo holds before they were welded to the rest of the ship, and the captains also were prefabricated and delivered to the ship just as it was launched. This was based on evidence that at any rate some of the captains were very inexperienced. There was indeed a case of two ships that, on their way from the Thames estuary to a port in the English Channel, failed to turn right in the Straits of Dover, and instead turned left, right into Boulogne and the arms of the Germans. These convoys were now of much more importance as the bearers of back-up supplies for Operation Overlord than for the supply of coal to London. It was humdrum work but never boring, for the long lines of ships, many with their first experience of convoys and the art of station-keeping, kept the sheepdogs busy. But when your grandchildren ask 'What did you do on D-Day, Granddaddy?' you hurriedly change the subject.

During my last weeks in *Lancaster*, on 28th September, 1944, we were escorting a convoy just off the Firth of Forth, when at 4.45 a.m. we received a radio signal from HMS *Rockingham* (another Town class destroyer) saying she had been mined about forty miles south-east of Aberdeen, followed ten minutes later by another saying 'Help urgently needed'. I turned over the job of senior officer of the convoy's escort to the next most senior Captain, of HMS *Leicester City,* and just after 5 a.m. set course for *Rockingham*'s reported position, which we calculated was inside one of our minefields. Since we ourselves might well be in some danger, I sent all our people to action stations. We made preparations to take her in tow, and to pick up and receive survivors if she sank, and put *Lancaster* into a state of maximum watertight integrity. When, about 6 a.m., we reckoned we were about ten miles away, we asked *Rockingham* to fire tracer shells vertically: we spotted them and fired three bursts ourselves to acknowledge visual contact. We plotted her position by radar, and confirmed that she was in the north-east corner of the minefield, and she signalled that she could neither steam nor steer, and was at anchor. The sea was rough, and the wind was strong from the west, so I asked that

Rockingham slip her cable, and drift to the east out of the minefield: we calculated she was drifting at about two knots. I laid a buoy about a mile clear of the minefield to give ourselves a reference point as we drifted and manoeuvred around. *Rockingham*'s Captain said his ship did not appear to be in immediate danger, but he had ten casualties who were 'all ready in the whaler', which presumably he was going to drop to come over to us for medical help, and one of his engine room crew was missing. Doc Kerr, however, advised that all the casualties should be kept below decks until he could get over there. At 9.17 a.m. *Rockingham* was due south of my buoy, but the wind and sea had worsened, so I went round to windward of her and at 9.40 we dropped our whaler to take Doc over.

As soon as the boat was back and hoisted (with the assistance of oil poured on troubled waters!) we started to try to pass a tow. We fired our first line – first of three increasingly thicker and stronger – at 10.11, but it parted, and it was 10.50 a.m. before the third of our lines, of coir rope, because it floats, was hoisted up to the 'bullring' at *Rockingham*'s bows. She had little steam, and no power to help haul the tow inboard; everything had to be done manually. Both ships were lying across the wind, with our stern close to her bows, but we were drifting at different speeds, and the coir line had a sharp nip around the bullring, and eventually parted at 11.30 a.m. This left us with the whole of the tow, two thirty-five-fathom lengths of 'extra-special high-tensile flexible' steel wire rope with fifteen fathoms of double eight-inch circumference hemp rope as a spring between them – one hundred and seventy metres in total – hanging from our stern bullring, and it was two hours before we were able to recover it, and another forty-five minutes before we were able to pass it again; this time successfully. *Rockingham* shackled our tow to her chain cable, and veered a length of it so that its weight would act as a shock absorber.

By this time we had been joined by HMS *Vanity* (a British World War I destroyer) and three trawlers, HMTs *Strephon, Robert Stroud* and *Harry Melling.* The wind and weather had worsened again during this time, and it took me half an hour to tow *Rockingham* round to the course we needed to steer to go through the gap in the minefield. As the weather continued to worsen, the tow began to come 'bar-taut' out of the water, until *Rockingham* had veered two hundred metres of chain, and even then I couldn't make better speed than four and a half knots. By 3.15 p.m. *Rockingham* reported that the after bulkhead of her engine room was in a parlous state, though her Captain thought she could last through the night. Nevertheless I ordered the three trawlers to keep station close astern of her. All seemed to be going well, until at 4.30 p.m. a squall of hurricane force hit us, and the tow parted in *Rockingham*'s chain cable, and we were left with the tow and a length of cable hanging from our stern. I ordered *Vanity* to try to get *Rockingham* in tow, while we recovered our tow, and I suggested to her Captain that he ought to disembark all casualties and surplus ship's company, and that if she were got in tow again all should leave. He told me that this would mean stopping the pumps that were keeping the ship afloat, so I suggested that only the very minimum should remain on board.

As a start, *Harry Melling* went alongside and took off all the casualties, except one who was too injured to be thrown across to the trawler – the only available method of transfer! At 7.15 p.m. *Vanity* abandoned his efforts to pass a tow, and told me he thought *Rockingham*'s ship's company were too tired for another attempt, but her Captain said they were willing to try, so I started to move into position when *Robert Stroud* succeeded in passing a tow, and *Strephon* took off forty-five officers and ratings. In half an hour, however,

Robert Stroud's tow parted, and all our efforts were now concentrated on saving men. The seas were too heavy by now for the trawlers to get alongside, so *Vanity* went in, and I stood by to try if she failed. She didn't, and at 8.20 p.m. reported 'all left'. I told the rest of the ships to get clear to the northward, while we stood by to sink *Rockingham* if it seemed she might become a derelict and a hazard to navigation. Douglas Paffard came up to the bridge, and asked me for 'Permission to sink her by gunfire, sir.'

'No,' I said, 'torpedo.[4] Only one fish, and don't bloody well miss!'

She didn't need our help: at 8.38 p.m. *Rockingham* lifted her bows out of the water, and slid stern first into the cold grey sea.

In my letter of proceedings to my senior officer I wrote: '*All HMS* Lancaster*'s ship's company were on deck from 5 a.m. until 8.30 p.m. and working hard from 5 a.m. to 6 p.m. and 7.30 to 8 p.m. with only alfresco meals, hurriedly eaten as opportunity offered, a few men at a time.*'

I singled out a few for special mention, among them Petty Officer Telegraphist Evans who was in the radio room without a break of more than ten minutes from 5 a.m. on the 27th until 1 p.m. on the 28th. These were men who were far from well paid, many of them conscripted into the Navy, but they never let down their mates, nor did their officers let them down. It was this spirit that made the Navy such a joy to serve in. It was a special day for Chidge too. Like many distinguished sailors, from Nelson to King George V, he never got over seasickness in bad weather. But on this day he was in charge of everything that we did, worked more hours than anyone and just never had the time to be seasick! It's an ill wind...

---

[4] Gunfire makes holes above the waterline: one torpedo would make a big hole below.

I got a little personal bonus from this affair. I knew I was not going to be much longer in *Lancaster,* and the family needed somewhere to live. The Captain of *Rockingham* had a house in Hayling Island, near Portsmouth, and he offered to rent it to us for as long as he didn't need it himself. It was a cedar house with a thatched roof, very warm and comfortable, as well as attractive, and we were delighted. And in nearby Emsworth Hospital our second daughter, Sarah, was born on 7th January, 1945, while I was 'in command' of a ship whose only movement was to swing with the tide. And Chidge became her godfather – but I anticipate.

Chapter Twenty-Seven

Hunt Class

In late November 1944, I left *Lancaster,* on being appointed to the command of HMS *Wensleydale,* an escort destroyer of the Hunt class, smaller and less fast than a four-stacker, but almost twenty-five years younger, and with more modern armament and radar. I must have had some leave and probably a refresher course of some kind over Christmas, for I joined the ship on 27th December. She was moored to a buoy in the Medway, and her only movement in the two weeks I commanded her was to swing one hundred and eighty with every turn of the tide, because in the interval between my appointment and joining her, she had been mined, and had a great big hole in her side. This was going to require several weeks in dock to repair, during which a captain would not really be necessary. So I asked my senior officer, Captain (D), 21st Destroyer Flotilla, for permission to go up to the Admiralty to ask for an active appointment, particularly as on 1st January, 1945 I had been promoted to two and a half stripes, even if only Quasi-Permanent Acting Lieutenant Commander – who but a British civil servant could have invented such a rank?

The Admiralty was sympathetic, and on 13th January I left *Wensleydale* for passage to the Mediterranean to become Captain of another Hunt, HMS *Catterick*. Before I left I went to the Royal Naval College at Greenwich for a tactical course, and so was close to London. By happy chance

Chidge had also left *Lancaster* to go back home to Australia after serving three years in UK waters, and we had to leave London on the same day, he to Liverpool and I for Plymouth, to join our respective ships for Australia and Alexandria. Not only Chidge was in London, but also AB Rudolph, and Chidge's servant from *Lancaster,* AB Derby. So we invited them both for a drink and lunch with us in a pub, for us all to say goodbye to one another. After lunch, Chidge and I still had a couple of hours before we had to catch our trains, so we decided to have our hair cut at Trumper's, the *ne plus ultra* of gentlemen's hairdressers in Mayfair. Neither Chidge nor I was blessed with much hair, so it should not have taken long. But in front of each chair, beside the mirror, there was a list of all the services on offer, with prices. Chidge said he'd never get back to Trumper's again, so he was going to have the works: cut, shampoo, scalp massage and so on, finishing with a singe, while I had cut and shampoo.

There were two barbers, it was early afternoon and no new customers appeared. Sitting rather disconsolately to one side at her professional chair was a faded middle-aged blonde manicurist. I had never had a manicure, so out of a mixture of curiosity and feeling sorry for her, I decided to have one. She was just finishing one hand, and the other was dangling in the bowl of soapy water, softening up, while the barber ran the singeing taper over Chidge's hair, when there was an almighty bang as the whole front of the shop was blown in by the explosion of a V2 ballistic missile almost overhead. These travelled at supersonic speeds, so you couldn't hear them coming. If you heard the bang, you'd survived!

Chidge's instinctive reaction was to cover his face by pulling up the barber's sheet that was tied round his neck; I was psychologically trapped by my hand in the soapy water, and could do nothing! The whole floor of the shop was deep in broken glass, and the twisted metal frames of the windows were half fallen into the room. But miraculously nobody was even scratched, and we quickly came to our senses. One of the barbers found five brooms and we set to work to sweep up the glass and push the broken frames as much out of the way as we could. Londoners had had four years of air raids by then, and were getting blasé to the point that you got back to routine as soon as you could. So Chidge's barber was soon back at him with the taper, and the manicurist sat down to work on my other hand. She got hold of it, with a nail file in her other hand, and approached my nails. But she was shaking so badly that I said: 'If you go on like this, I'm afraid you'll saw my finger off!'

She was very relieved, and I had no choice but to make do with one manicured hand. And I've never had that other half: I have an uneasy feeling that if I ever tried it, I'd be the target of another ballistic missile, and I remain probably the only man who has had to live his life through with only half a manicure.

As soon as I arrived in Alexandria, I reported to Captain Blackman of HMS *Blenheim,* our Senior Officer, and then went to board *Catterick*. I was received at the gangway by the First Lieutenant, Lieutenant G.L. Weston, RN, and three Bosun's Mates who 'piped me over the side' with due ceremony.

As the piping ended the First Lieutenant greeted me. 'Welcome aboard, sir. Do you play bridge?' His disappointment at my negative answer was very evident; my predecessor had been a bridge player, and there were three others, but by not being available to make a fourth, my stock, with my Number One at any rate, dropped like a stone.

I have no continuous memory of what *Catterick* did between my arrival, and our departure, in early summer, for the UK to recommission – in part, at any rate. So my narrative has perforce to be a series of vignettes, not even in a chronological sequence for the accuracy of which I can vouch, though I can in the main separate between before and after VE day. The evening of VE day itself we spent in Alexandria. We were berthed alongside a depot ship, with another destroyer and two submarines. The wardroom officers of this ship invited all the officers of the ships berthed alongside to a celebratory dinner. We toasted the Allied victory in free-flowing champagne, had an excellent dinner, and then sat down in little groups for after-dinner drinks. The mood before and during dinner had been gay and upbeat, but after dinner someone in the group that I was in said, 'What a shame that so-and-so [someone many of us had known] didn't live to see this day.'

And one by one we began to recall those friends who had given their lives in the good fight, and we became increasingly pensive and sombre, and many of us were close to tears recalling that victory had been won at great cost. It was not the kind of celebration that anyone would have expected, and not what the next day's newspapers would have reported.

To begin with, while the war was still on, our mission in the Aegean was to harry the Germans in the islands, shut off their supplies and prevent them from moving around, while ourselves providing transport and support for the various commando-type British forces operating in the area, and for the Greek force, the Sacred Brigade, which was working to provide a Greek presence in the Dodecanese. The Germans had a military headquarters in Rhodes, the principal island, but their main forces were based in the islands of Leros (developed as a naval base by the Italians) and Cos, while we had a forward base – little more than a place where we could moor in sheltered waters – in Symi. These and other Aegean islands had been colonised from Greece in the eleventh century BC, and

Greek was the language of the people, despite the fact that the Turks took them over in the sixteenth century. In 1912 they were seized from the Turks by Italy, and now, since Italy had joined the Allies, were under German control. So there were several parties interested in the outcome, including Britain, which was trying to win its war against Germany. One could sense, however, that the war here was winding down, and that the Germans were short of supplies and low in morale. The opposition we faced – we, the Navy – reminded me of the background noise to the burial of Sir John Moore after Coruña: 'the distant and random gun that the foe was sullenly firing'. For the raiding military, of course, opposition was more serious, though casualties were thankfully light.

We usually spent two or three weeks at a time in the Aegean, with a break of a couple of days in Alexandria, and often gave passage to a few army officers going to join one of the British units or returning to Alexandria for leave or medical treatment. Preparing to leave harbour occupied all the executive officers and the engineer officer, so the medical officer, Surgeon Lieutenant Douglas Stuart Ferguson Robertson RNVR (whose parents clearly wanted no doubt about his Scottishness!) had the task of greeting our passengers, and finding somewhere for them to sleep and to stow their gear. Doc (to which monosyllable his rank and name were reduced) had an impish sense of humour, which tended towards the practical. He had been a guest (or victim, he would say) of the army for his transport from the UK to Alexandria, and had taken a violent dislike to the bureaucracy this process involved, and by extension to all army officers. So he would pick on one of our passengers, and demand to see his Movement Order.

'What, no Movement Order? Then I'm afraid we may have to take all your gear ashore again. You know you can't travel without a Movement Order.' He would finally allow himself to be satisfied by the production of a copy of a message from someone saying 'You will take passage in HMS *Catterick* on such and such a date', though not before he had pointed out that *Catterick* had not had a copy of the message, and that therefore the poor man couldn't expect much from us.

The toughest ordeal of all was reserved for the not-very-senior officer who joined us at Symi for the return trip to Alexandria, and started his conversation with Doc by complaining that the magazines in the wardroom hadn't been changed since three weeks earlier!

The trip up our operating area was usually very pleasant, since German air power in the eastern Mediterranean, and serious naval power too, had almost ceased to exist, and we kept having to remind ourselves that there was still a war on. We often went, as our first port of call, to Chios or Lesbos (more and more often called Mytilini, after its principal city, to de-emphasise the reputed sexual mores of its women!) to disembark some of our military passengers, and to buy fresh food, especially fruit. The prevailing wind was out of the north, so we were steaming up wind, and forty miles away from Chios one could smell the scent of orange blossom, growing stronger as we got closer. The people of the islands were very friendly and hospitable; they found us a pleasant change from the Italians, their theoretical political overlords, and even more from the Germans, until very recently the unsubtle occupying power. Lesbos, one of 'the isles of Greece, where burning Sappho loved and sang', made it very easy to understand how it got its reputation: the women were beautiful, animated and charming, the men dour and dull. But in both islands our ship's company had some very pleasant breaks between operations.

But operations we did have: Greece itself had largely been cleared of Germans by mid-October 1944, and the

Aegean islands were slowly being liberated one by one by the Sacred Brigade and the small British forces, leaving only Rhodes, Cos, Leros and some small islands in enemy hands. The Allied forces operated largely by stealth, moving around in caiques, the fishing and cargo boats of the Aegean, to make sharp commando attacks. We would take a raiding party on board and rendezvous with one or two caiques (with crews of local people) at night in a bay or other shelter, as close to the target area as possible while still out of sight of the enemy. Dozens, if not hundreds of caiques fished around the islands, and were unmolested by the Germans, because they had virtually no offensive naval vessels left, and anyway they needed the fish. If the military's target was protected by a gun battery (or was the battery itself) we provided supporting gunfire, and stood by to protect the caiques as they were withdrawing. I believe that *Catterick* probably fired the last shots in anger of the war in the Mediterranean, for on the night of 4th or 5th May we bombarded a battery of howitzers which threatened the Sacred Brigade's landing and withdrawal. How successful we were we never knew, but the battery was not able (or had not the will) to interfere seriously.

Preparing for one of our operations which called for a more than usually active participation from us, including the availability of our medical help, produced a reaction from Doc which almost caused me to burst a blood vessel. In addition to his dislike of army officers as suppliers of transport, he disliked their ignorance of manners on board ship.

'They will come into the wardroom with their caps on, and salute below decks [naval officers did neither] and on the way in they don't look where they're going, and trip over the door coaming.'

Furthermore, Doc had a strong aversion to Irish doctors, alleging that Trinity College, Dublin, produced more doctors than Ireland itself could employ, resulting in a serious oversupply of doctors in the market, to his economic prejudice. In early afternoon Doc and I were sitting in the wardroom, chatting idly, when the Bosun's Mate from the gangway knocked on the open door and said, 'Sir, there's an army officer come on board to see either the Captain or the Medical Officer.'

'Well,' I said, 'here we both are; ask him to come in.'

There appeared an officer in battledress, with his cap on, who in one movement did an exaggeratedly smart salute, tripped on the coaming and fell flat on his face. He picked himself up and said, 'Good afternoon. Me name's Dogan, and Oi've come to talk about the medical arrangements for tonoight.'

I scuttled out to avoid catching Doc's eye and bursting into laughter, and left Doc to his own devices. Professional duty presumably prevailed over Doc's delight at our guest's discomfiture, because I got a message the next day from Captain Dogan thanking *Catterick* for Surgeon Lieutenant Robertson's invaluable co-operation!

We had a number of suitable spots from which to raid Cos and Leros, but Rhodes itself was more difficult. However, Turkey had come into the war on the side of the Allies in February, and I was ordered to negotiate with the local officials to get approval for our forces to use the Bay of Marmaris, on the Turkish coast just opposite Rhodes. This beautiful bay (now a popular tourist resort) is almost landlocked, and the entrance is a curve such that movement inside the bay is invisible from the outside. I took *Catterick* into the bay, anchored and went ashore in one of our boats. I knew that the Turkish word for governor was '*mudir*' (that was the extent of my language skill in Turkey) but my use of the word induced a soldier from the dock to escort me, and a signalman I'd brought with me to keep communication with the ship, to the local government offices, shabby and in need of repair. After some delay I was taken to the local boss-man, not a 'governor', but equivalent to the mayor of the town, I suppose. He spoke a little French and he had a subordinate whose French, though not as good as mine, was still good enough for us to be able to converse, hesitatingly. Coffee was produced, and we exchanged rather laboured pleasantries for a quarter of an hour – I assumed (correctly) that the formalities would be close to those in Egypt, which I had learned back in 1940 from my friends in the Egyptian navy. I said how much we welcomed Turkey as our ally, and that we looked forward to co-operating against our common enemy. I explained what help we were asking of our ally; to allow us to use their bay as a base from which to mount attacks against the Germans in Rhodes, without asking for any active help. The *mudir* was clearly hesitant to authorise anything that might produce a German reaction, and said he would have to telegraph his superior before he could agree, and that we should meet again the following morning.

All through our conversation I had noticed that he kept scratching his wrists and pulling his hands out of sight into his sleeves, and I saw that they were covered in a red rash. As we shook hands before I left, I commiserated with him on his rash and offered to bring our ship's medical officer with me tomorrow to see if he could help, at least to ease the irritation. Back on board I talked to Doc, who said that if it was psoriasis, it was probably incurable, but that if it was anything else he could probably, at the very least, take some ointment that would help in reducing the irritation and perhaps curing any secondary infection from the scratching.

So the next morning we went back, and started by Doc examining the rash and applying some antibiotic cream (the very word 'antibiotic' caused a minor sensation – clearly all those in the office had heard of such things, but they were not available in Turkey) and an analgesic ointment, of which he had brought a supply to leave with the mudir. Then, after the obligatory coffee, and my doing my best not to show any urgency, we got back to business. I had discovered the *mudir*'s name, but not knowing the Turkish polite form, I confined myself to '*Votre Excellence*', which seemed to go down well. He told me that his superiors had authorised him to co-operate with us, subject to certain conditions – essentially that I would guarantee that there would be no hostile German reactions. I could not of course give any such *absolute* guarantee, but I told him that our best intelligence was that the Germans no longer had the means to attack the Turkish coast, and that in the event of any hostile action our guns would be available to defend Marmaris. In an hour or so of his vacillating and my gently reminding him of the duty of an ally, and of Turkey's splendid military past, he finally agreed, and sealed the deal by presenting me and Doc with a large jar of honey and a wine-size bottle of local eau de Cologne, both perfumed with a mixture of roses and orange blossom.

When, a couple of nights later, we had a detachment of the Sacred Brigade on board, I ceded my cabin to the commanding brigadier (I could use my so-called 'sea cabin', a bunk in a little cubby hole off the chart room, just below the bridge). There was a voice pipe direct from my cabin to the bridge, and I was on the bridge before dawn (I always was, because if there were to be any hostile action, this was the most likely time) when gradually we all became aware of the perfume of roses and oranges, growing stronger every moment: it was the brigadier completing his morning toilet by swilling himself in *my* eau de Cologne!

We got to know the brigadier quite well: his battledress uniform was always beautifully pressed and his boots polished, and he looked (and smelled) every inch the parade ground soldier. But his people told us that he was a very fierce warrior, of great bravery, much imagination in planning, and determination in executing his operations. His hatred of the Germans was palpable, and he clearly felt that Greece was defiled by their presence, which he and his brigade had a sacred mission to end.

The commander of the British special force to which we were closest was also a great character, Colonel Ian R. Baird, after whom his unit was called 'Bairforce'. He came from a county infantry regiment, and thus was by no means in the 'aristocracy' of army officers (the Guards, the Hussars, the Rifle Brigade) but he sounded as though he had been sent by central casting to play an Indian army colonel. He had a fine war record, and was doing a superb job in harrying and demoralising the German forces in the area, and it was not until after VE day that we came to see just how demoralised they were. We were not privy to his plans or his operations, except in so far as was needed for us to do our part, but from the reactions of the people he commanded the morning after, in fighting he yielded nothing to the Greek brigadier.

We used to have him on board to dinner as often as we could, and he kept us amused all evening. His manner of speech was a caricature of the Indian army colonel: he spoke in short, staccato bursts, punctuated by 'What?' and his sentences ended with 'What, what?' as a full stop. He would say what he had to say at full length, and then, in case someone had missed the point, he would repeat his gist in telegraphese.

After VE day, he became the Deputy Military Governor of the Dodecanese, based in Rhodes, in the Castello, which had been remodelled in full dictator style for Mussolini. The officers' mess had as a dining table a solid piece of granite, ten centimetres thick and six metres by two and a half metres in area, and here Colonel Baird invited me to dinner one evening. Many of the staff officers had abandoned their battledress uniforms, and the majority of them turned out to be from cavalry regiments, and so could be recognised by the little triangles of chain mail on their shoulders. In a silence halfway through dinner, Baird suddenly turned to me and said, 'D'ye know, I once knew a cavalry officer, what? [*pause*] who was so stupid, what? [*pause*] that even his brother officers noticed it, what, what? [*longer pause*] Cavalry officer – so stupid – brother officers noticed – what?'

The other character in the senior people around us was SNODEC (Senior Naval Officer, Dodecanese), a retired Naval Captain whose speech was very similar to Baird's, to the point that, when one of them had dinner on board with us, he would often amuse us by imitating the other ('Lend me one of your naval caps, what? And I'll give you an impersonation of SNODEC, what, what?') almost by being himself.

My favourite recollection of SNODEC was his taking the official surrender of the German forces in Leros. We took him there in *Catterick* and were greeted at the dock by a German colonel, dressed in his best uniform, wearing a sword, and with an escort of half a dozen soldiers, whose uniforms had all seen better days, and who all looked hungry. The colonel immediately took charge – he spoke a few words of English – and led us round the end of a row of warehouses or workshops to a large parade ground, surrounded by similar buildings. There, formed up on three sides of a square, were, presumably, the whole of the rest of the force, at least a thousand men. In the middle of the fourth side was a dais with two steps leading up to it, and a podium on it. As SNODEC saw this he said to me, 'This damn'd fella thinks I'm going to make a speech; I'm not going to say a damn'd word!'

I said, 'Sir, I don't think you're going to be able to avoid it; he's obviously got it all planned.'

Inexorably the colonel led us to the dais, and, grumbling under his breath, SNODEC was manoeuvred on to it. The colonel then called all his troops to attention (the *Wehrmacht* would not have been proud of the smartness of their drill), proceeded to draw his sword and, holding it horizontal with his right hand on the hilt, his left holding the tip, formally offered it to SNODEC, saying in carefully rehearsed English, 'I hereby give you, sir, my sword [with the 'W' pronounced, as in 'sward'] and formally surrender to you all the forces under my command.'

SNODEC was very reluctant to take the sword – he looked as though he thought it might bite him – and hurriedly passed it to me, saying, 'Here, you take this damn thing!'

But the colonel hadn't done with him yet, and steered him to the podium. Still grumbling, SNODEC said he wasn't going to speak, until I persuaded him that the German had planned his surrender, we had no alternative plan, and he would have to bring the ceremony to an end. So suddenly he grasped the lapels of his jacket, high up so that his four gold stripes were visible, leaned forward, glared around all three sides of the assembled troops, and made his speech: 'I've only got one thing to say to you fellas [*pause*] and that is [*longer pause, then very emphatically*] I'm damn glad we've beaten you! Good morning.'

I have always treasured this speech as the perfect one for accepting a surrender, though this is scarcely an occasion that presents itself to many of us!

I wrote that it was not until after VE day that we really appreciated how low the German morale had got. We had acquired from the military government, on permanent loan while we were in Rhodes, a Volkswagen (military version), complete with German driver.[1] One afternoon Colonel Baird invited two of us to go with him, in our vehicle, on a visit to the German headquarters outside a town in the hills behind the city of Rhodes, ten kilometres away, over a pretty awful road. (Baird's comment: 'Bumped, banged and buggered about, what?') The two of us who were naval officers were dressed in tropical rig: white shirt, white shorts and white shoes, with only epaulettes on the shoulders of the shirt and our uniform caps to show our service and rank. We arrived at the place where we had to leave the car and set out, escorted by a German officer, to walk to the garrison buildings. We had first to cross a grassy square, and by the time we got to the other side, my stockings were covered in black specks: fleas! We brushed them off as soon as we arrived at a building, and were met by a horrible stench: what had been the mess hall, a large room twenty metres square, had half its floor area covered in piles of human excrement, buzzing with flies. The troops had got too demoralised to bother to dig latrines in the (admittedly stony) ground, and the officers no longer had the authority or will to make them. In a corner we found a pile of hundreds of empty champagne bottles, all from Reims or Épernay, with labels saying '*Cuvée spéciale pour le Wehrmacht*'. Alas, there were no full ones we could have claimed as spoils of war! I did pick up, however, a German machine rifle which I subsequently traded with King Farouk of Egypt (an ardent collector of guns of all sorts) for a Jaeger le Coultre watch, with his monogram and the date in Arabic engraved on the back. I still have it, and it still goes!

Roughly on the site where the Colossus of Rhodes, one

---

[1] About the same time, I bought, for six bottles of South African brandy, a British motorbike, captured by the Germans in 1941, and 'liberated' by the unit that I bought it from.

of the wonders of the ancient world, once stood is the modern cathedral, which incorporated an abbey. On the cathedral tower was one of the things I abominate, a stopped clock, which I itched to get going. I asked Chiefie if he would join me, and the two of us went and found the abbot (he, and all the priests and monks were Italian and Roman Catholic). With my few words of Italian, eked out by some Latin remembered from Eton, we offered to see if we could get the clock going again, and the delighted abbot led us to the tower and showed us the steps up to the mechanism of the clock.

It didn't take long to diagnose the trouble. It was a clockwork clock, driven by weights on a chain; an ingenious endless chain with a ratcheted sprocket by which the driving weight could be wound up without taking the weight off the movement. The chain was just ordinary bicycle chain, but out of it had been cut enough length to make chains for, we estimated, three bicycles. Well, there was no way in which we could get any more chain, so we had to shorten what was there and join the two ends.

Chiefie went back to the ship to get the tools we needed, and while he was away I had a primitive and fragmentary conversation with the abbot. Once we had the tools it was a matter of minutes to join the chain, wind up the weight, apply some oil, set the hands to the right time and give the pendulum a swing to start the clock. And, behold, it ticked! When we got back to ground level a few of the monks had joined the abbot, and all were watching the hands move again. With a wide smile, the abbot shook our hands, and then invited us to kneel. With some reluctance (and Protestant trepidation!) we both knelt. Since my left knee would only bend about seventy degrees, I was pretty unstable, and I hoped that, whatever the abbot had in mind wouldn't take long. It didn't; he laid his hands on my head and in a proper ecclesiastical voice said: '*In nomine patris, filii et spiritui sancti, cento giorni de indulgenza,*' and then repeated the process with Chiefie, waved us to our feet and said goodbye.

When we were out of earshot, Chiefie asked me what that was all about.

'He gave us a hundred days' indulgence, so I suppose we can do what we like for the next hundred days without it being sin,' I told him. When we got back on board and told the story in the wardroom, Chiefie began to think of all the things he might do. 'It's a pity my mother-in-law is so far away...' he began to say, when a Roman Catholic spoilsport explained what 'indulgence' meant – that after death we would have to serve a term, perhaps as short as a thousand years, in Purgatory, and our hundred days would be time off for good behaviour, reducing our thousand years to 999 and 265 days. To which Chiefie's reaction was: 'Let's go back up there and cut that bloody chain again!'

Before I had joined her, *Catterick* had spent some time off Crete, including landing an armed platoon and getting into a fire-fight with some Germans, supplying and supporting the Cretan guerrillas who operated out of the mountains behind Khaniá, under the leadership of a remarkable man, Christo Vadouvás. So there was some excited anticipation of meeting old friends when, some time after VE day, we were ordered to Suda Bay to support the army's occupation force, which was greatly outnumbered by the surrendered German troops. While they were in occupation of Crete, the Germans were the victims of much hit-and-run warfare (ambush by night was the Cretan's favourite tactic) and the reprisals were ruthless.

Christo carried in his belt a hunting knife which was his weapon. One day he was showing us the row of notches filed across the back of the blade, and said each was a dead German. One of us made (interrogatively) the gesture of drawing the side of the hand across the throat, but Christo said 'No', grabbed one of his friends from behind with his arm around his neck, and made a gesture of stabbing downwards behind the collarbone into the jugular vein – with a broad smile on his face!

There were several hundred German troops as prisoners of war in Khaniá, and less than a hundred of our own to guard them. Christo's people were determined not to allow more Germans than they could help leave Crete alive. So while the terms of surrender deprived the Germans of all their heavy weapons and most of their vehicles, they were allowed to keep a small quantity of small arms and ammunition to protect themselves against the guerrillas – in at least two cases that I knew of, in vain.

Catterick had acquired from the British army, as in Rhodes on permanent loan while we were based there, an American Ford open car. It had only two of its original three gears left – first and top – but its V8 engine was in good shape, and it gave us the means of getting around. One evening we had been to dinner[2] with Christo and his wife, and four or five of his friends. After dinner we invited the men (women's place was strictly in the kitchen; at dinner Christo's wife sat in the same room, but at a little table all by her self, and served the wine at Christo's call of '*Oino!*') to come back on board for a glass of brandy. Christo and one of his friends were in our car, which I was driving, and the rest of the Cretans were in an ex-German truck of their own. On the dark road we passed a group of three Germans: Christo and his friend exchanged some excited words, and then urged us go full speed to the ship. As soon as we got to the gangway, our two jumped out and into the truck, and roared off into the night. The next day we met Christo somewhere, and with pride he showed us

---

[2]We had supplies of rice in the ship: Christo had sheep. So we exchanged a bag of rice for fresh lamb.

the knife. A bright, fresh notch was filed in its back.

It was, probably still is, the custom in Khaniá on a Sunday afternoon for there to be a band playing in the stand in the centre of the square, while the people, in groups of two or three or four, arms linked, strolled around. One Sunday a number of our ship's company were sitting in bars or cafes around the square, when a German pick-up truck drove into the street that formed one side of the square. Apparently without a word being said, and without the band pausing in its music, the people coalesced into a crowd that blocked the street, so the pick-up had to stop and was quickly surrounded. Two or three men, in very old British battledress, stripped of all insignia, suddenly appeared out of doorways, ran to the truck, dragged out the driver, stabbed him to death and left him in a pool of blood in the street. The crowd, as if nothing had happened, resumed its slow circumambulation, while the band played on. Someone must have raised an alarm, because in a few minutes a group of British military police arrived in a Jeep and took charge. One of them, with an interpreter, started asking the people around about what had happened, and the next day they asked me if they could come on board and interrogate our men who had been there. They told us that not one Cretan admitted having seen anything, and it was only from our men that they got the story. The murdered man had been the local head of the Gestapo, and the killing had clearly been planned on the basis of accurate intelligence of the man's plans for the afternoon.

Later, I was chatting with one of our ratings who had been very close to the scene. Pretty gruesome, he thought it was, but 'the bastard deserved it!'

'For what he'd done to them?' I asked.

'Well that, too. But I meant, knowin' what he'd done, for bein' so fuckin' stoopid as to go into town alone.'

In the next few weeks the military occupation forces had

got things under control, and most of the prisoners of war had been evacuated, so the need for destroyers evaporated, and at the end of June we left for the UK, where we were to pay off about half the ship's company and get new people, and modernise some of our radar and other equipment, prior to having a three-week refit in South Africa and then being transferred to the Japanese theatre. In early August, before we sailed for Gibraltar as our first port of call, I was entrusted with an envelope (of the level of secrecy we referred to as 'destroy before opening') which I was to deliver personally, in Casablanca, to the senior British political official in Morocco, with whom a rendezvous had been arranged for 13th August, our planned day of arrival. There, also, we were to be joined by another Hunt class destroyer, the name of which I have completely forgotten.

In the early morning of the 12th, we were making our landfall off Cape Trafalgar when the telegraphist called very excitedly up the voice pipe: 'Sir, somebody keeps making V-J, V-J, V-J, on the radio!' So we asked him to get one of his 'oppos' (naval abbreviation for 'opposite numbers', one of his mates) to rig a speaker on the bridge, and find a BBC station. He did, and in a few minutes we heard the news that Japan had signed its unconditional surrender – *the war was over!* Although it was still very early, I told the officer of the watch to go and call the First Lieutenant, and to send Bosun's Mates right round the ship with the news. Even from the bridge, we could hear the hum of excitement, a drawn-out, collective sigh of relief.

VE day was for me one that ended in sadness: VJ day was a horror! We arrived in Gibraltar about breakfast-time, and we needed fuel and water before sailing in the evening for Casablanca and the addressee of my 'TOP SECRET' envelope. So I went in search of the Staff Officer, Operations, while Chiefie went to arrange fuel. I couldn't find anyone in the Admiral's offices, except one duty WRNS officer, who told me nobody would be in that day, though they would all be at a party in the wardroom about eleven. Chiefie hadn't had much more luck than I. The regular workforce in Gibraltar dockyard was Spanish, who came in for the working day and went back home in the evening. But today, in case someone in Gibraltar decided he didn't like people from the one remaining Fascist state, they were not allowed to cross the border, but he did find someone who said that, if we would provide the labour to handle and connect the hoses, he would find the keys and get the valves opened.

Meanwhile I found the wardroom, and managed to buttonhole the Staff Officer, Operations, before he'd had too many gins. I was feeling very out of place: I, and I alone, it seemed, was sober, and everyone else was determined to get royally drunk to celebrate. I told him that my orders were to sail that evening for Casablanca, to deliver my envelope. He said, 'Oh, don't be silly, you can't sail today. Stay and celebrate with us.'

Finally, when I persuaded him to read my orders from the Admiralty, he agreed to give me orders to sail that afternoon (without which I couldn't leave) but said I couldn't count on much help from Gibraltar Command. Naval etiquette demands that when you arrive in a new command, you pay a call on the commanding officer to report your presence, so I sought out the Admiral and did my duty. He too, tried to persuade me to stay and join their celebrations, but he accepted the hierarchy of my orders, and wished me luck.

Soon after I got back to the ship, and we had lunch, Chiefie's people had manhandled the fuelling hoses and filled our tanks, so we started to get ready for sea. We had closed down our boilers, so had to raise steam again. Part of the routine for this was to open various valves in the boiler room. Many of the smaller ones were opened and closed from the upper deck, by inserting the triangular end of a large T-shaped key into a round brass deck plate which could be rotated to open or close the valve by a system of rods and gearing; this avoided the necessity of a man having to climb into a very crowded and hot space on top of the boiler. The valve itself was screwed into the boiler, and held firm by a short, open hexagonal spanner which held the valve body, and was itself held by a stud through its handle screwed into a plate welded to the boiler. We had changed a large proportion of our engine room people while in the UK, so we had many inexperienced men. One of the valves that had to be opened this way was that for saturated steam to auxiliaries – such things as pumps, dynamos and so on.

The stoker who went to do this job (which he had not done before in this ship) was a big strong man. He unscrewed and unscrewed and when he came to some resistance; he just applied a little more strength, and went on unscrewing, not realising that, in Devonport Dockyard, the retaining spanner had not been fully secured. So, with a sudden explosion, the whole valve came out of the boiler, and flooded the boiler room with saturated steam. Only one man was very badly hurt; the others were close enough to the doors to escape with no more than first-degree scalds on exposed skin. The boiler was shut down in very short order, and the injured stoker got out. Our own first-aid team and medical officer did yeoman service with anaesthetics and burn dressings, but it took us what seemed like hours to get an ambulance – all the drivers were either drinking or already drunk – in which we sent the stoker to the hospital. Our doctor went with him, and had difficulty in finding a sober colleague to take over, but finally found medical and nursing help fit to look after the injured man. He stayed to help until the hospital staff had done everything urgent before he came back on board, fuming about the gross failure of professional duty on the part of everyone ashore in Gibraltar.

On board, meanwhile, we had had to allow the boiler room to cool down enough to get the valve back into place and properly secured, and only then (it was now around sunset) could we start to raise steam again. It was almost 10 p.m. by the time we were ready to sail. The harbour at Gibraltar is protected by two breakwaters rooted on the land, and a third, an island, which partly covers the gap between the others, leaving two not very wide gaps for ships to pass through. All the ends have navigation lights on them, of different colours, so that a ship can see the opening at night. Outside the breakwaters there is a strongish current flowing across the gap, so you have to be sure that you can get clear without the current pushing you sideways into the end of a breakwater. We were moored alongside the western breakwater, so we had to get away from the wall, steam east and then turn sharply to port through the opening.

People ashore and in other ships in the harbour were playing with searchlights, waving the beams about in the air, and firing off rockets and letting off flares in an impromptu firework display. I had just let go our lines – there was no one on shore to do it for us, so we had to rig two ropes, just round the bollards and with both ends inboard. This way the ship was held and we could let go our wires, and get our men back on board. I was lucky in that the wind was blowing us away from the breakwater, which gave me a little open water in which to manoeuvre. I had picked out the two lights between which we had to go, when someone saw us moving, and soon every searchlight in Gibraltar was focused on us, and all of us on the bridge were virtually blinded and the coxswain on the wheel could see nothing through the glass window of the wheelhouse. I started the ship swinging while I tried to see my navigation lights through the dazzle. I saw one, and rang for full speed head, while conning the ship by giving wheel orders to the coxswain. It was a risk – if we had hit the breakwater at full speed it would have made a nasty mess of our bows! But, for the first time that day I was lucky; we went between the breakwaters at close to twenty knots, so the current didn't affect us much. The searchlights followed us for several miles, but then got bored and went back to waving: I mentally shook the dust of Gibraltar from off my feet, and indeed, I have never been back there since.

My envelope was duly received and signed for when we arrived in Casablanca the next morning, but we had no excuse to tarry; indeed we had reason to go on, because our accompanying ship was there and waiting for us. Its Captain was a Lieutenant, senior to me in that rank, but junior to me as Acting Lieutenant Commander. For a week or two – probably until the end of August – I was senior officer, I led and he kept station on me astern. Then on 1st September, he became a real Lieutenant Commander, and we changed places in line, as acting is junior to real!

We steamed down the west coast of Africa, calling at Dakar, where we participated in the victory parade of the French navy based there; Freetown, where it rained twenty inches in the little over twenty-four hours we were in port; Pointe Noire in Congo; Walvis Bay in what was South West Africa, and is now Namibia, then Cape Town, and our destination, the dockyard of Durban.

Our refit, which was designed to fit us for war against the Japanese in the Indian Ocean by upgrading our armament, as well as overhauling the engines, boilers and the rest of what made us go, was due to last three weeks. But the workers at the dockyard soon realised that we might well be their last job, and spun everything out so that it lasted over four months. The ship soon became uninhabitable, and most of us moved out to accommodation in Durban, though we had one officer and a small guard party camping out on board every night. The Durban Club generously made all the officers of both ships honorary members, so that we could live there. Many of us did so for a while, until we were invited to the homes of friends we made, or moved to hotels which were less stuffy than the Durban Club – most of the people who lived there fell into the category of pompous old buffers, and were not good company for young officers, just beginning to enjoy peacetime. There was a little to do on board in the way of bureaucratic routine (and watching what the dockyard was doing), so many of us spent the mornings on board, going ashore for lunch, and coming back or not as circumstances (and one's sense of duty) dictated.

In wartime Britain, and to some extent in the Navy, there were foods which we had almost forgotten: unstinted butter and milk, cream (and ice cream made from it!) abundant meat, oranges, grapefruit, bananas. In South Africa we wanted for nothing. A short tram ride from the ship there was a milk bar where one could get the most delicious milk shakes, thick and creamy, and loaded with calories (and – a word we didn't know then – cholesterol). Very often, indeed almost every day, a group of us used to go there for a mid-morning snack, sometimes going back for lunch, and a third visit in mid-afternoon. At that time my weight was, and had been since I left Eton, nine stone seven, and nothing that I did or ate ever changed me by more than a pound or two; until the milk bar, and a recipe someone had given me for breakfast (two half-pint tankards, one full of orange juice, the other of cream) brought me up seven pounds, to ten stone.

South Africa, or to be precise, Natal, was like the words of the hymn: 'Where every prospect pleases, and only man is vile'. Apartheid was in full force; every dockyard worker had a black helper, who did all of the hard work – and much of the skilled too – while the 'skilled man' looked on, without ever uttering a word of civility. It offended me to the root of my being, and all the very generous hospitality we received came with a sour taste. And nobody could see that, sooner or later, the majority of the people would defeat the privileged minority. The worst were the Afrikaners, many of whom were little above the 'natives' in skill, but even those of British origin were blinded by the economic advantages they enjoyed on the back of the 'natives'.

Two incidents illustrate these attitudes. One day there was a British warship in port, which had some Chinese among its ship's company. I was on a tram in Durban, and at one stop a man in the uniform of a Petty Officer cook, wearing the ribbons of his campaign medals, his long service and good conduct medal, and an award for gallantry in action, the Distinguished Service Medal. He sat down, and the conductor came to take his fare, took one look at his Chinese face, and said, 'Hey, you! You get off!' and insisted until the puzzled Petty Officer did get off at the next stop.

I asked the conductor 'Why?' and got the answer: 'He's a native, and natives aren't allowed on our trams.' I pointed out that he was a member of the British Navy, and moreover had been decorated for gallantry in the war that had saved us all from dictatorship.

'I don't care: he's a native, and he doesn't get on this tram!'

At this, I lost my temper, and said, 'If he's not good enough to be on this tram, then neither am I.' And in a quixotic but useless gesture, I got off. The conductor was an Afrikaner, but what saddened me was that evidently not one other passenger, Afrikaner or British, shared my feelings. The other, not strictly an 'incident', was in the small ads column of a newspaper: 'For sale: large quantity of galvanised steel plates. Suitable for feeding animals or natives.' How lucky the South Africans are that Mandela was the leader of their revolution, rather than the kind of hate-filled firebrand who might have come along a few years later!

While our refits were going on, both ships were the victims of robbery. The other had a number of rifles stolen from the rack to which they were chained, itself in a locked compartment. The Durban police, to whom the theft was reported, were very concerned about firearms getting into wrong hands, and the Navy was always concerned about loss of His Majesty's property. The police buzzed around the ship taking fingerprints and looking for other clues, but they found out nothing, except that the steel hinges of the door had been cut by flame, and then welded together again.

If the Navy was worried about the theft of rifles, it came close to paranoia when our loss was discovered. For we had been robbed of several gallons of rum! The normal storage space for rum had to be left open for access during the refit, so we moved it all to one of the magazines, which were in the very bowels of the ship, and were not going to need to be opened for work. The loss was only discovered when the refit was nearing its end, and we started to re-embark the ammunition that had been removed to shore storage at the beginning of the job. At first there were no signs of tampering with access to the magazines, but finally we found that the round hatch from the upper deck, through which ammunition came up to the guns, had been cut from the deck, and then re-welded into place, and repainted so that it was only by seeing two beads of welding in some spots round the hatch that we saw the trick. Each Captain was then obliged to form and preside over a Board of Inquiry into the circumstances of the theft from the other's ship, and make the required formal reports to the Commander-in-Chief of the South Africa station. In neither case was it possible to ascribe any blame to anyone, so we both came out unscathed! But the incidents left a nasty taste in the mouth.

Of course, by the time these two ships were ready for service again, the need for more destroyers was gone. So, soon after the beginning of 1946, our companion received orders to return to the UK, and we, to Malta. Before we sailed from Durban I was invited by the South African Broadcasting Company to be interviewed on radio. It was my first experience of this ordeal, but it went off quite well, and I was able to hear a recording of my voice in the evening. Neither tape recorders, nor their predecessors, wire recorders, were available to the market at that time, so I had never heard my own voice, and that in itself was a surprise. Also, we gave a party to as many as possible of the South Africans who had befriended us, and given hospitality to our ship's company. It was gratifying to see how many people had been kind to us, but disturbing that there was scarcely an Afrikaner among them – a shadow of coming events that were a nasty surprise to Britain. As we sailed, there was a large gathering to wave us goodbye, another sign that *Cattericks* had been welcome in Durban – and two or three of our men had found themselves South African wives.

It was, of course, summer in the southern hemisphere, and as we steamed north to the tropic of Capricorn and beyond to the Equator, the weather was unremittingly hot, and by the time we entered the Red Sea I had lost all the seven pounds that I had got from South African milk shakes and ice cream! But the voyage was uneventful, though one stretch of it kept me awake for the longest consecutive period I have ever undergone. From some distance south of Sharm al-Sheikh, the strait that is the southern entrance to the Gulf of Suez, and for most of the length of the gulf itself, there are navigational dangers; rocks and shoals which demand the Captain's presence on the bridge all the time – or at least allow him little time to go below; enough to lie down for a quarter of an hour, but not long enough to go to sleep. When making the passage by night, the weight on the Captain's shoulders is heavier, and we did it by night, arriving to anchor in Suez roads at breakfast time. Have a bath, change your clothes and eat breakfast, and the Suez Canal pilot is on board, wanting to get going. No ship may go through the canal without a pilot: a ship going too fast can erode the banks, and the effect of lateral pressure on a ship's hull going round a curve can affect the steering – not much for a ship the size of a destroyer, but seriously for a big ship – and this is what the pilot is for: his knowledge and experience. But, though you must legally allow the pilot to con the ship, you, the Captain, are the one with the responsibility for its safety, so you stay on the bridge all the time. The passage takes almost twenty hours, so you arrive in Port Said in the late evening. You drop the pilot, and get clear of Port Said and the hazards off the mouth of the canal, and only then, after being awake, save a few catnaps, for forty hours, can you put on your pyjamas and turn in. And it does not seem long before the officer of the watch is calling you as the ship approaches the Great Pass into Alexandria.

In a short stay in Alexandria we embarked fuel, water and victuals, and got some sad news. We were ordered to proceed to Malta, there to pay off the ship and turn it over to the Royal Hellenic Navy. *Catterick* became His Hellenic Majesty's Ship *Hastings,* called after a retired British officer who joined the Greek navy in the war of independence against Turkey, in which he served with great success, destroying a much stronger Turkish force in the Battle of Salona in 1827.

I was not in effective command for the handover to Greece, because soon after we arrived in Malta I developed a high fever and swollen glands. When a couple of days in bed in my cabin didn't improve things, our medical officer packed me off to the Naval Hospital. In the then state of medical science they could not make a definitive diagnosis, though from the behaviour of my temperature (low in the evening, so you had hopes, and then high again next morning) they guessed I probably had what was then called glandular fever (now, mononucleosis). But certainty required the Paul Bonnell test, which called for the killing of a sheep, and they liked to have a few cases before the sacrifice, to economise on sheep.

However, *Paul Bonnell* and a sheep did eventually confirm mononucleosis, and after a couple of weeks in hospital, I was replaced in my command, and 'invalided home'.

Chapter Twenty-Eight

HMS *Hornet* – ACXE

I flew from Malta to the UK in a converted Dakota (DC-3) troop transport – not much converted at that! The seats were canvas mounted on steel tube framework, and far from comfortable. But to get home and to see my now sixteen-month old younger daughter was a great joy. The family was living with Phyllis's mother, Grandma Round, in a house which she and we had acquired jointly, in Horndean (ten miles north of Portsmouth) where Jeanie went on the bus every day to a local school. This house, though really too small, turned out to be not too inconvenient, since I was soon (on 24th April) appointed as 'Trials Officer' of the Admiralty Craft Experimental Establishment (AXCE), part of HMS *Hornet,* the base of Coastal Forces in Haslar Creek, off Portsmouth Harbour.

This job brought me back to one of my first loves, the world of MTBs, MGBs and MLs. The 'trials' in my job title were the evaluations of captured German craft and equipment, and of new ideas that were emerging from the design teams in the Admiralty. I became a member of an Admiralty committee, comprised of representatives of the Admiralty itself, the Department of Naval Construction, the Admiralty Engineering Laboratory and me, which considered and commented on burgeoning ideas about small craft. My role was described by a member of the committee one day as: 'Our professional cack-handed[1] sailor.' Besides providing input of ideas at early stages of concept and design, I, with a little team at *Hornet*, tried them out at sea: would they corrode when exposed to salt water, and would they break in clumsy sailors' hands? And, for me especially interesting, what could we learn from captured German *matériel*? So I spent my time between meetings in London in civilian clothes, and sea trials in, all too often, rough-weather gear. The things that were passed to us ranged from the Heath Robinson[2] to those, like gas turbine propulsion for ships, which changed the face of the Navy.

The first category included a typewriter for radio operators which automatically converted the struck key into its Morse Code equivalent, so that in theory a touch-typist could get out more words in a shorter period of time, and a paper 'hard copy'. Unfortunately, whereas a Morse key is always in one place, and is operated by wrist movements while the forearm can be resting flat on a table, almost proof against any kind of rolling, pitching or bumping, touch-typing needs two hands, and movement of the forearm as well as the wrist, and if the ship is falling, the hands tend to rise into the air. When we found this fault, the design boffins came up with a 'cure', a padded bar horizontally across the mid forearms to hold them in place. We tried it out, honestly, in bad weather, with a very expert telegraphist, and Morse beat it hands down!

Little more successful was a design for a one-man miniature motor torpedo boat to be dropped by aircraft, and piloted to torpedo range of its target by its (suicide mission?) crew. Presuming success, no one managed to work out any reasonable means of recovering the crew –

---

[1]Naval term for one whose fingers are all thumbs!

[2]American, 'Rube Goldberg'.

much less the boat itself.

The German craft, however, were much more interesting, and a more fertile field for usable ideas. We had hydrofoils, which were almost all too underpowered to climb out of the water quickly, but which allowed research on the mechanics and economics of the concept. But the Admiralty's interest in these waned fairly soon, and their development was taken over by potential civilian users, for the high-speed passenger traffic which is now so familiar. We had one version of the Kriegsmarine's 1945 programme E boats, of which only a few had been built, and three survived. We got one, the United States got one and the USSR the third. We also got an R boat, a minesweeper of the type that rammed *SGB 4*. In the Royal (as opposed to the US) Navy, engineer and executive officers followed, from almost the beginning of their careers, different paths. Executive cadets and midshipmen received a fair smattering of engineering education, but the engineers were visibly second-class citizens – no engineer officer could ever get to command a ship. This had the inevitable effect that engineering input to design was overshadowed by the executive. It was a long time, for example, before captains accepted that steam power was superior to sail, and the sort of fleet mobility enjoyed by the US Navy (put so brilliantly to use after Pearl Harbor, and making possible the defeat of Japan's Imperial Navy) was never achieved by the Royal Navy. The Kriegsmarine, on the other hand, went to the opposite extreme: engineering considerations predominated.

Both E and R boats had diesel engines, whereas we relied on Packard petrol engines of 1,300 horse power, and most of our boats had three of them. All our faster, smaller boats – seventy to seventy-three feet long – were hard-chine design, and had speeds of forty knots, or just under. The 1945 E boat had three supercharged Mercedes-Benz

V20-cylinder, high-speed diesels of 3,300 horse power each, for a total of almost ten thousand horse power in a ship only one hundred and twenty feet long, with a displacement (that is a non-planing) hull. Any small, fast ship has a tendency to 'squat' at high speed, as its bow lifts out of the water. This increases the resistance, and limits speed.

The Germans had developed an ingenious way of ameliorating this problem by 'effect rudders': two rudders which turned with the main, steering rudder, but could also be turned relative to it. This, by means of the venturi effect, created a higher water pressure under the stern, and so lifted it, and levelled the running angle of the hull. These rudders were well named, because the effect of using them was to increase the boat's speed by three or four knots, to almost forty-five. The engine controls were simplicity itself; each had a lever, of stainless steel, fifteen centimetres long with five positions: stop, in the middle, start ahead and astern at the limits, and run ahead and astern halfway back to stop. It was started by compressed air on five cylinders turning the engine, and as soon as it fired you moved the control to the 'run' position, and all twenty cylinders were operating. The exhausts were under the water, so the engines were almost soundless. But there were disadvantages; the engine wouldn't start unless it was warm, so in home bases hot-water lines were connected to the boat so that the engines were always warm. As a back-up, there was a small auxiliary diesel that ran the electricity generator, and the cooling water of this could be circulated through one of the main engines, and when it was hot it could warm the other two. But this process took over two hours, very different from the instant start of a petrol engine. Moreover, to save weight, the engines' cooling jackets were made of thin aluminium, so you had to use distilled water to cool. Well, at sea it is almost impossible to keep every grain of salt out of water so the water jackets kept developing pinholes from corrosion. These we patched with sharpened matchsticks, or chewing gum, which gave these engineering marvels a surreal look. They had a practical disadvantage, too. Slow speed, on only one engine, was thirteen knots, and the boat jumped as the engine started, so manoeuvring in a confined space was tricky.

The seamen, in comparison, got a raw deal. Our boats had power steering, with a wheel like a car's. The E boat had a wheel like that of a clipper ship, made of wood, brass-bound, a metre in diameter and with twelve spokes; it had no power assistance, and took no less than forty-four turns to turn the rudder from hard over one way to hard over the other, and at high speed it was all one man could do to move it! The way of fighting these craft was to approach the target at very slow speed, to avoid detection, get into torpedo-firing range, fire the torpedoes and turn and run away as fast as you could. I would have hated to be an E boat captain and have to have the wheel turned twenty-two times by hand, while a little steel throttle control in the engine room could get me up to forty-five knots very quickly. The bridge of the E boat was very wet; it sacrificed visibility and some comfort for a low silhouette, and whereas we had a trunk in the centre of the bridge through which the captain could see the chart in the chart room below him, with all available intelligence and his own course plotted on it, the German chart table was not big enough to take a chart except folded, and to see it he had to turn to his extreme right.

Putting the E boat through the series of trials that the Admiralty asked for gave me a great respect for its basic design: after all, it would not have needed much modification to power the steering, and give the captain a drier bridge and a better view of his chart, and the engines corrosion-proof cooling water jackets. All of which led me to be so rash as to say, in one of our committee meetings in the Admiralty, that I thought the German boats were better sea boats than ours.

'Okay,' said the Chairman, 'take your boat right round the British Isles and let's evaluate its performance.'

It was after the autumnal equinox, so we couldn't count on good weather, but off we set; east in the Channel and then north up the North Sea. We were going 'widdershins',[3] which every Scot knows is 'wanchancy'[4] – we should have gone the other way. We had a breakdown of some sort in the engine room, which forced us to go into Peterhead for a day to get the necessary repairs done, and when we came out in late afternoon there was a north-westerly gale blowing, but the sea was not too bad to begin with, while we were more or less in the lee of the land. The darkness of the night was, for several hours, lightened by the most magnificent display of the aurora borealis I have ever been privileged to see. The cloudless sky to our north was illuminated by great sheets of light, sometimes blue, sometimes green, but mostly a beautiful violet, never still, sometimes almost fading away, moving through the sky as though someone was waving a giant floodlight across it. At its brightest you could almost read by it.

But once we rounded Duncansby Head and entered the Pentland Firth we were exposed to the full force of the gale, and the seas became very heavy. But the E boat behaved as I had predicted; it kept going at fifteen knots and, though rolling and pitching heavily, was never in danger. Its poor crew, on the other hand, were having a tough time. Our little galley was not designed for long voyages – after all, E boats, like our MTBs, were designed for operations

---

[3]In a direction opposite to the apparent movement of the sun.

[4]Unlucky.

during the hours of darkness and to be home in time for breakfast – and it could not cope with preparing hot food in weather like this. Somehow we managed to boil water to make 'kye', hot cocoa, whitened with condensed milk. But for solid food we had to rely on baked beans, eaten with a spoon right out of the can. Not until we reached Stornoway in the Outer Hebrides the following day could we use the galley. The bridge gave very poor protection against spray, and until we reached the lee of the Outer Hebrides the next day I could not leave it, and, wet weather gear notwithstanding, I was soaked to the skin. The helmsman, who shared the bridge with me, at least had only a four-hour trick, and then was able to get his clothes dried in the engine room and get some rest in his bunk. The crew must have been asking themselves the same question as I was – 'What in God's name are we doing this for?' – but no one complained. In three or four more days of generally improving weather we were back in *Hornet* and the availability of hot baths and food, and we had proved my point – the German boats *were* better sea boats than ours, though as fighting machines ours were immensely superior. A marriage of the two would have produced splendid offspring.

Chapter Twenty-Nine

Gatric, and so on

Jet engines had brought about a quantum leap in the performance of aircraft, and the Admiralty was anxious to see if the gas turbine could be practical in ships. The firm of Metropolitan-Vickers undertook the design of a marine propulsion unit based upon its aircraft engine, and code-named 'Gatric'. It was installed in place of the centre one of three Packard 1,350 horse power engines in *MGB 2009*, a displacement hull of 115 tons, 117 feet long, and handed over to us for trials.

I was involved with the project well before the engine was fitted, and I paid several visits to Metropolitan-Vickers in Manchester to learn about it and the main problem of taking an aircraft jet engine to sea: in the air it did not have to turn a propeller, but just produce a high speed stream of gas, and of its very nature it revolves very fast. A marine engine needs to turn a screw at perhaps one-tenth of the revolutions per minute of a jet engine, so a large reduction gear is essential; then there is the problem of reversing the screw to go astern, and to act as a brake. The physical layout had to provide for a huge intake airflow, uncontaminated by salt spray, and the exhaust of a much larger volume of the products of combustion made a great deal of noise, much of it above audio frequency, and thus unhearable, but with worrying implications for possible effect on the human ear. Except for the last (which was left to see if the crew really suffered more than ordinary headaches!) these problems were worked out, and *2009* was handed over to us for its trials. We left harbour and manoeuvred on our outer Packards, and only started the gas turbine in open waters. Whereas a piston engine or a steam turbine needs time to warm up and accelerate to its full speed, a jet engine can go almost at once from start to full speed. Gatric's power was greater than a Packard's, and drove a larger screw, and the acceleration it imparted to our 117 tons was exhilarating!

We took to sea with us a number of civilian experts, from Metropolitan-Vickers people to boffins of various kinds from the Admiralty, and hundreds of pounds of measuring instruments, and in a few weeks and many runs over the measured mile we established beyond any doubt that gas turbine propulsion was practical for ships, and none of us seemed to suffer from the exhaust noise.

Many months of further trials, for example to find out the probable life of the engine in service, and to establish maintenance routines, had still to be done, but the Admiralty was already sure that we were on to a good thing, which could be marketable to other navies. So it invited the naval attachés of all our wartime allies to a demonstration. They spent the whole morning at sea with us as we put Gatric through its paces, and then we invited them for a drink in *Hornet*'s wardroom followed by lunch. I found myself taking care of the naval attaché of the USSR, a genial Captain whose English was fairly rudimentary, but enough to tell me that he was a destroyer captain at heart, so we got on pretty well. Gin was the traditional wardroom before-lunch drink, so we offered him a gin, which he swallowed at a gulp. I asked him if he liked gin, 'Yes, gin very good – but not like vodka!' he answered. Would he try a whisky? He did, again it was 'very good – but not like vodka!' He tried sherry, and brandy, neither of which lived up to vodka, of which he must have been used to largish quantities, since in fifteen or twenty minutes he drank four different drinks with no apparent effect.

He was accompanied, and closely watched and listened to, by a young and junior officer – one stripe to the Captain's four – who was a nasty, smarmy person, and presumably the Captain's political watchdog, who spoke excellent and fluent English. I took an instant and deep dislike to this little twerp, which stood me in good stead later. It started with an invitation for my wife and me to attend a reception at the Russian embassy in London to celebrate the thirtieth anniversary of the Great October Revolution – in November, because the Russian calendar in 1917 was 'old style'. It was not customary for naval officers to wear uniform at such affairs so I went in civilian clothes. We arrived at the splendid Soviet embassy in Kensington Palace Gardens and, after a minute scrutiny of our invitation card and its being checked against a list of names, were ushered into a room full of people, most of whom looked like caricatures of pro-Communist intellectuals – long hair, loose jackets and Oscar Wilde neckwear – though I did recognise Ernest Bevin, the foreign secretary. A waiter came by with a tray of soft drinks and things to nibble, who informed us (it was barely fifteen minutes after the time of our invitation, though perhaps arrival times had been staggered) that 'Vodka – finish. Champagne – finish. Caviar – finish.'

We were ruefully accepting a glass of sweet liquid of indeterminate origin, when a functionary came up to us and said, 'You in the wrong room; please come with me. This room for intellectuals only. Military people over here.' In this next room there was a good sprinkling of Russian officers in uniform, one of whom soon attached himself to us, and though caviar, champagne and vodka were 'finish' here too, there was available some sweetish white wine. We started conversation with the Russian officer in the hackneyed way: 'How long have you been in London?'

'Five months.'

'And do you like London?'

'*Not* like Leningrad!'

'Oh! Why?'

'In Leningrad, we heff streets sixty metres wide, ent since the end of the war, we heff built six hundred t'ousand housink units, ent...' and so on, for several minutes, giving, obviously by rote, the whole propaganda spiel for the achievements of the glorious Russian Revolution that we were celebrating. End of conversation!

I looked around for my fellow destroyer lover, the naval attaché, but didn't find him, but we were soon spotted by his nasty little watchdog, who smarmed over, asked us to call him Yevgeny, and started to exercise his phoney charm on us, and expressed a fervent wish to see me again. We left as soon as we decently could.

That was 7th November: in mid-December I received a Christmas card from Yevgeny, with a warm invitation to visit his flat the next time I was in London, which I just ignored. But in January came a very effusive letter from him, again inviting me to his flat, where I would meet some of his friends: '*I know some very nice girls, and we can have some drinks and all have a lot of fun.*' This was when the Russians were still our gallant allies from the war, and before the Iron Curtain, so if Yevgeny had been a nicer person, I might well have accepted, because we were not then aware of the technique of concealed cameras recording compromising situations as a means of recruiting informants. I wrote, declining (politely) but he wouldn't take no for an answer, and for the next few months pestered me with invitations, until I left the Navy, and HMS *Hornet* ceased to be my address. When we finally began to understand the method, I looked back in a cold sweat at the possibility of too much vodka in his flat, followed by seduction by a very nice Russian girl, the production of the photographs and 'an offer I couldn't refuse'. Thank heaven he wasn't a nice man!

But I digress from Gatric, which was truly an epoch-maker in marine propulsion, thanks in large part to the faith of Commander (E) C.M. Hall, the brilliant innovator who had been head of the Admiralty Engineering Laboratory, and was now head of the Gas Turbine Section of the Engineer-in-Chief's department. Our trials showed beyond doubt that gas turbines could become standard marine propulsion. *MGB 2009* was the first gas turbine engined ship, albeit with petrol-engined back-up: the first ship solely powered by gas turbines was another old friend, HM (no longer 'Steam') Gunboat *Grey Goose,* once *SGB 8.*

The R boat was of less interest: its diesel engines were run-of-the-mill, but it had Voith-Schneider propellers. These are ingenious, if mechanically complex, and difficult to maintain. The engine drives a steel ring, two metres in diameter (two of each in the R boat) in the ship's bottom on graphite bearings. Through this there project downwards a number of vertical blades, the inclination of which to the fore-and-aft line of the ship is controlled by a linkage to a central *Steuerpunkt*, steering point, which alters the angle of each blade, so that the one that is travelling in the direction of the ship is edge-on to the water. The one opposite is at right angles, and those in between are at varying angles so that each has some component of thrust in the desired direction. The beauty of this is that by moving the *Steuerpunkt*, you can have the thrust ahead, astern or sideways in seconds. So, if you want to turn quickly you direct the whole thrust at right angles to the ship, and you turn on the proverbial sixpence. Doing the trials of this system was fun, because the handling capability of the ship was so unlike anything conventional, when you depended on a rudder to turn and engines going one ahead, the other astern, for turning in tight spaces. With Voith-Schneider you could do all this, with the engines going at full speed, though the way the boat listed when you turned hard was quite scary!

The Navy did not push its interest in Voith-Schneider very far, but the system was, for a time at any rate, used for tugs and ferries where the ability to manoeuvre easily, quickly and decisively in limited sea room was of sufficient value to outweigh the problems of maintenance: a two-metre hole in the ship's bottom in which a large steel thing has to rotate, without leaking. Nevertheless, the R boat was not without personal benefit: we had all the German instruction manuals, which, with the aid of a dictionary and an intelligent engine room artificer, enabled us to keep it running, and from which I got my favourite German word: *Kraftstoffinspritzzubringenpumpe* (fuel injection booster pump). And the German crew had left on board a pair of German naval binoculars, made by Carl Zeiss and so really good. I still have them, and they live close to the big window in our house in Collieston, to keep a watch on the neighbours!

Chapter Thirty

Transition

ACXE was full of interest up to my last moment in the job, but that last moment was coming ever closer. The Admiralty announced that it was going to have a physical examination carried out on all serving officers. The acronym for this was PULHEEMS, each letter standing for some part of the body, and we were to be put through it over a period of months. I knew this was a test I was not going to pass, and, since the object of the programme was to weed out officers of questionable fitness, in part as a means of cutting down numbers, that I would be put on the retired list. I was married with two children, no private means and negligible savings, and I knew that since whatever pension I got from the Navy would not be a living wage, I had to find a job quickly. The moment was not propitious: I had no civilian experience, and the very real qualifications acquired in a Naval career were not always evident to potential employers, and ex-service officers were ten a penny in the job market.

The first lead came from my last Captain but one, Tom Pakenham of *Hornet.* He knew people who were developing a hotel in Kenya, out in the bush, so that visitors could live cheek by jowl with the wildlife – the hotel that finally became the celebrated Treetops. He must have sold me well, because I was a strong candidate for the job of manager of this hotel. I was not sure I wanted it, because it would not have been the best of circumstance in which to bring up a family, and because my South African experiences made me chary of becoming the European boss of a crew largely made up of 'natives', but beggars can't be choosers, so I did my best to keep the opportunity open. The next possibility too came through Captain Pakenham, and was more interesting. It was to become the director of the Institute for Muslim Education in Mombasa. The fact that I spoke a few words of Arabic was one of my attractions, because the population of coastal Kenya was largely Muslim,[1] but more important was that the purpose of the institute (still in the setting-up stage) was to train men as officers for merchant ships, for which I had all the requisite knowledge, and a reputation for being good at training.

I started an active search, too, and wrote to everyone I knew who might be able to introduce me to companies who could be interested. I answered a newspaper advertisement from the BBC for announcers, and was provisionally accepted. Through Uncle Douglas I got a message from British Petroleum that it would offer me a job in its fifty per cent subsidiary, the Kuwait Petroleum Company. A naval friend arranged for me to meet a retired Rear Admiral who was Manager of Estates and Personnel for British Aluminium, who was getting ready to retire, and wanted to find a successor – preferably a naval officer. The 'estates' in his title were huge land holdings in the west of Scotland, where BA generated large quantities of hydroelectricity for the smelting of alumina, and which the company wanted to conserve as catchment areas. This job was in the bag, but one of the orthopaedic specialists that I was seeing as part of my medical last ditch effort to stay in the Navy advised very strongly against it. 'Your knee is full

[1] I prefer this spelling, as being closer to the Arabic.

of arthritis, and it isn't going to get better. There's probably no worse climate for you than the damp cold of western Scotland. Try to find yourself a job out of this country, somewhere warm and dry!'

In the event it was Guy Rudderforth who found me my opening. He had been, before the war, the head of the Marine Lubricants Department of the Shell Group, and when demobilised he went back there. One night, between two meetings at the Admiralty, Guy and Sheila invited me to stay the night with them, and Guy, hearing of my problem, undertook to get me an interview with Shell. Within a few days I was invited to London to meet a triumvirate of senior personnel people in Shell, Messrs Ayling, Blair and Lovely. This meeting was followed by others, until one day they told me that, since I didn't have a university degree in the liberal arts, I was of no interest to Shell's marketing people, (I have always thought that this was a total non sequitur!) However, Personnel itself would like to consider me, and if it hadn't an opening, then Materials (the procurement organisation) almost surely would.

I had a series of interviews with the top personnel people, and finally the head man, Duncan Mackintosh, made me an offer: Shell would hire me in August 1948 for overseas service. My salary would be, initially, six hundred and fifty pounds per year, rising to eight hundred pounds when I was posted to an operating company out of the UK – and I shouldn't expect to spend much of my career in the UK office. It says a lot for the supply and demand situation in the market for ex-officers at the time that Shell could offer so little, and for my urgency that I accepted.

I left *Hornet* in mid-July, to be 'invalided out' as Lieutenant Commander (retired) at the end of September. This was the end of the life I had wanted since February 1934, and had lived since September that year, and it was a trauma, made the more bitter by the 'flimsies' I had received from my last two Captains. Tom Pakenham wrote, in March 1948, that I had conducted myself: 'to my entire satisfaction. A talented officer who has proved himself a capable seaman and administrator in charge of the Experimental Section. If his "gammy" leg prevents him pursuing a naval career, his departure will be a serious loss to the Navy.'

In August, Peter Carey said 'very much indeed to my satisfaction. If he had been remaining in the Service there are no limits to the heights he might have attained. The Service has lost a unique officer.'

Part Four

Royal Dutch/Shell Group

Chapter Thirty-One

Egypt – Suez

But it was no good looking back: I had to earn a living. So on 3rd August I presented myself at Shell's offices in St Helen's Court in the City of London. I had possessed one civilian suit, and had bought another, ready-made and cheap, during my leave, but was otherwise totally unprepared for business life. But Shell made me welcome, and with a dozen other newcomers put me through an 'induction' (now we'd call it 'orientation') course. I also had a 'welcome' interview with Duncan Mackintosh himself. He said that from my record it was clear that I had a good grasp of people management and training, but I would have to get accustomed to the big difference between the Services and commerce and industry.

'When you're fighting a war,' he said, 'you don't have to think about costs, whereas we must have them in the forefront of our minds all the time. In the Navy, you could just go ahead regardless of costs.'

I should have had the courage to say, then, what I thought, but I was new that morning and didn't want to start by disagreeing with the boss. I should have dared to say, 'Of course we had to think of costs all the time; how much fuel have we left? Or ammunition? And in the last analysis, our costs were counted, not in currency, but in ships and men's lives – and one surely takes those into account!'

I was destined for the industrial relations side of personnel, and spent two weeks with the ministry of labour in London, learning about trade unions, safety and welfare. It seemed my first posting was likely to be to Venezuela, then the fastest-growing oil production part of the Shell Group, and one where personnel problems loomed large, so I arranged to start Spanish lessons at the Berlitz School as long as I was in London. This was not long, because I was sent to spend a couple of weeks at the Stanlow oil refinery in Cheshire, to learn the basics of turning crude oil into usable products, and to go through a course of 'Training within Industry' which was a product of the joint British–American productivity study. This was an excellent introduction to management at the first level. It took three areas, job relations, job methods and job training, broke them all down into 'bite-size' pieces, and taught them by discussion with a trained leader, and with practical examples. At the end of the course you got three cards, playing card size, with a summary of what you'd learned on one side, and on the other three snappy instructions. I kept my three cards for over forty years: I threw them away only when we moved to Florida five years ago, and I used to refer to them every now and again to remind myself of the very basics of my trade. I still remember the headlines of the three points on the 'job relations' card: 'Get the facts'; 'Weigh and decide'; 'Take action': sound advice for almost any decision-maker!

Next I went to spend a week with a branch of the Transport and General Workers' Union in North Wales. This was fascinating, not only for having the opportunity to see labour problems from the inside, but also for getting to know the secretary of the branch. My first morning was the occasion of the branch's weekly meeting, and Mr Jones, the secretary, introduced me to his colleagues and requested them, as a courtesy to me, to agree to conduct their business in English rather than the customary Welsh. I was impressed with the seriousness with which the meeting tackled its business, the union's genuine concern for the success of (and pride in) the enterprise, and the total absence of extremism and dogmatism.

But the real joy was Mr Jones himself. Before the war, he had been a typical Welsh socialist, pacifist and fiercely conscious of the class struggle. He gave up a lot of his time to entertain and educate me, and we became good friends. We talked about running meetings, and the importance of the rules of order, and he told me of the most difficult meeting of his life.

'I was Chairman of the Pacifist Alliance of North Wales, but the Spanish Civil War got under my skin, and suddenly I decided that pacifism would get nowhere against determined fascists. So I joined the International Brigade to go and fight against Franco. You should 'ave seen their faces when I announced this as soon as I had called the meeting to order!'

He went and fought in Spain, was taken prisoner and condemned to death, but was saved by the British government's intervention, though he spent many unpleasant months as a prisoner of war. 'But if I 'ad to do it all over again, I would. There are some injustices you 'ave to *fight* against!'

With this basic learning under my belt, I went back to St Helen's Court, and shared a tiny office with another newcomer to the Group, Oliver Sebag-Montefiore, who had an advantage over me; he was a relation of the founder of the English component of the Royal Dutch/Shell Group, and because of that knew his way around, and was very helpful. By then Venezuela had faded as my future, and been replaced by Egypt; so I changed my Berlitz classes from Spanish to Arabic. I spent my time reading relevant files and having interviews with people who could help me understand what I should be facing in Egypt, of which the most urgent was the Egyptian government's recent legislation limiting both the numbers of expatriates who could be employed at various levels of the company, and the extent to which their salaries could exceed those of the nationals. The Group was very worried about the effect this 'Egyptianisation' programme would have on efficiency, since jobs at comparatively low levels (my job, for example, was to be the number three man in the labour department of the oil refinery in Suez) were filled by expatriates. In the event this worry was quite unfounded: as I knew from my acquaintance with the Egyptian navy, people are people, no matter what their nationality, and though considerable numbers of staff were affected, quality never suffered, and in a number of cases was enhanced by the change: very few expatriates learned enough Arabic to discuss with a government official, in his language, any serious business, let alone any conceptual problem.

On 15th May, 1948, Britain's renunciation of its mandate over Palestine came into effect. The previous day, the Jewish Agency declared the independence of the State of Israel, and armies from Egypt, Iraq and Jordan, joined later by Lebanon and Syria, invaded. Fighting was halted for short periods, but it was not until 7th January, 1949 that the United Nations secured a shaky truce. So when, a couple of weeks later, I arrived in Egypt (alone, the family was to follow) the country was seething with anti-Israeli feeling (though this did not – yet – extend to the many Egyptian Jews) and licking the wounds to its military pride. And there was a less intense, but none the less real residue of a feeling that, really, the whole thing was the fault of Britain, the mandatory power. Moreover, the 1936 Treaty of Montreux (of alliance and mutual defence) by which Egypt had become a sovereign state after fifty years of British occupation, but which established the right for Britain to station ten thousand troops in Egypt, was still in force. Such treaties had really gone out of fashion after the end of World War II, and there was a simmering resentment of Britain, and an as yet incoherent surge of Egyptian nationalism.

I had travelled by air, but Phyllis and the girls came by sea, and I went to meet them in Alexandria. The immigration and customs bureaucracies were very slow, and we ran into a surprising problem. We had all had to get visas before we left England, which were duly stamped in the passports – in Phyllis's in the case of the children. Phyllis and Jeanie were quickly approved, but when they came to Sarah Elizabeth, doubts started. 'Is your daughter not Jewish?' asked the official.

'No,' I said, 'we are all Christians.'

'But Sarah and Elizabeth are both Jewish names; are you sure she isn't Jewish?'

'No, she isn't; you agree that her parents and her sister are Christians, so how could she be Jewish?'

'Then why does she have a Jewish name?'

And he took a long time to be convinced that both her names were, despite their Jewish origins, nevertheless common among Christians; after all, weren't the Queen of England and her elder daughter both called Elizabeth? It took fifteen minutes of patient argument (I had learned in my naval days in Alexandria that it was no good trying to hurry any Egyptian official to a decision) and finally reference to two successive higher levels of officialdom before Sarah's Christianity, and therefore admissibility to Egypt, were accepted by a reluctant rubber stamp on her papers.

I lived, for my first weeks in Egypt, as guest in the house of my boss, the Manager of the Labour Department, Donald Hunt (who had become known as 'Willie', because someone in the refinery, upon hearing that Hunt was to join them, said, 'Oh! I know Willie Hunt', and it stuck). He and his wife could not have been kinder, and their house little prepared me for where we were going to have to live, until some new flats, still under construction just outside the refinery gate, were finished. Until then the company rented for us a flat in the city of Suez. In itself, this was a tolerable living space, but its surroundings were awful. We were on the fourth floor of the block (which did at least have a lift, albeit a rickety one) but right across the very narrow street was a mosque, and we were level with the minaret. The muezzin didn't climb the minaret to call the faithful to prayer, but his place was taken by three loudspeakers, the output of an electronic amplifier of very poor quality and very loud volume. Later on, when I had learned more Arabic, I came to appreciate the call to prayer, and indeed to be able to chant it. But for the few weeks we lived there, that distorted, railway station quality call five times a day did not make our surroundings congenial.

It was not the only inconvenience of our neighbourhood. On one side of the mosque there was an apartment building under construction. The laws did not require anything like a certificate of habitability before people could move in, so what happened was that an entrepreneur who had a little money would buy the land, and start building, in reinforced concrete, from the ground up. As soon as the ground floor was completed, he would rent it out to provide funds for the next floor, which would be built over the heads of the ground floor tenants, and so on up to the height of the building. Up the front of the building there was a system of scaffolding, with a zigzag series of ramps sloping up about thirty degrees above the horizontal. There were no mechanical aids to construction: concrete was mixed by shovel at street level, loaded into shallow steel containers which were carried up the ramp on the heads of a steady stream of labourers, to be dumped into the forms at the top. Egyptian workers all lightened their labours by singing – chanting is perhaps a more accurate word – so the noise level was pretty high. And on the other side of the mosque was a cafe, with a blaring radio and high decibel conversation from morning until late at night. One adapts, and in time we were able to sleep through the noise, but it seemed a very long time before the new staff flats at the refinery were completed!

Luckily, we didn't have to spend many of the daylight hours in the flat; I was at work from 6 a.m. to 2 p.m. every day of the week except, Egypt being a Muslim country, Friday, and Phyllis and the children were able to use the facilities, notably the swimming pool, at the staff club at the refinery. Jeanie (who was eight) already knew how to swim, and Sarah very quickly learned and became an expert. There were children of the same ages with whom they made friends, and the expatriate families all managed to be friendly with one another. But once back in the flat in Suez I couldn't help thinking of what I had been – captain of a destroyer and then in charge of a unit helping to develop the naval hardware of the future – and wondering what on earth I was doing in this noisy world, and with a job that didn't seem likely to stretch my abilities.

We were three expatriates in the labour department, responsible for safety, training and welfare. We kept the statistics of accidents at work, and used them to help the operating departments reduce the time lost and the human distress of accidents. When the operators identified areas where things could be done better, we were available to advise on the design of training, on the job or in courses, and in the follow-up to be sure that the effort was producing commensurate results. Lastly, we were the conduit between individuals and the company, and much of our time was spent dealing with employees' personal problems, trying not to be too paternalistic with a workforce whose culture was essentially one of paternalistic expectations. In all these fields, we worked closely with our labour union. The head of this was a pipefitter, Anwar Salama, who, I gradually came to realise, was one of the most extraordinary men I have ever met. His formal education cannot have been very profound or extensive, but his command of English was good, and his powers of reasoning and arguing were superb. He was a great organiser, and had made the union a real force to be reckoned with.[1] It was always pushing to improve the lot – wages, fringe benefits and working conditions – of its members, but deep down Anwar knew that the company had to flourish too. In his discussions he was always patient and polite – '*adab*', good manners, is highly esteemed in Islam and in Arab culture – but he was determined, and it was always a real struggle to get to an agreement with him that was not too prejudicial to the company's efficiency or economic well-being. Not that, in my lowly position, I ever played a substantive role in serious negotiations; that came later. But I was fairly soon handling individual 'claims' (the word was the generic term for any problem a workman had) with the interpretative assistance of one of the Egyptians in the office.

We (Anglo-Egyptian Oilfields, AEO for short, was the company's name) encouraged all our expatriate staff to learn Arabic, and offered two financial bonuses for gaining proficiency, twenty-five Egyptian pounds for level one, and two hundred for level four. The levels were those of the School of Oriental Studies of the American University at Cairo: *one* was conversational skill at daily practical needs: *four* was advanced classical Arabic, which required reading and writing, a thorough knowledge of Arabic grammar, and

---

[1]Anwar Salama eventually became minister of Labour in Gamal Abdel Nasser's government.

the study of some parts of the Koran, the Bible in Arabic, pre-Islamic poetry and modern Arabic literature. Level one was almost a *conditio sine qua non* for continued employment, level four didn't cost the company much money in bonuses.

We had two teachers on the payroll to teach us; one was an *effendi,* an educated, English-speaking, middle-class employee, the other, a sheikh, a graduate of al-Azhar University (founded in 969, so probably the oldest university in the world) who wore the traditional garb of turban and long robe, and spoke only Arabic, in which he was deeply learned. This combination was an excellent one, because the *effendi* could explain grammar and syntax, while the sheikh taught us correct pronunciation, for example to differentiate between *kalb* (dog) and *qalb* (heart), and proper ceremonial manners, which are, in Arabic, extremely important.

I have often said that my mother must have been frightened by a parrot, because I am a born mimic. This gift, combined with understanding of the basic principles of language learned at Eton, and a desire to know what people around me were saying (about me?) quickly made me fairly competent in everyday Arabic, and I soon got my twenty-five pounds. But it was a long time before I could negotiate with Anwar in Arabic.

When I was still in the very early stages, but reckoned I could deal with most of the minor claims that came into the office, an incident one day punctured my illusions. We had a large force of *ghaffirs*, watchmen armed with six-foot staves, who were at the bottom level but one of our job classification. They were recruited in Upper Egypt, from where most of our unskilled men came, and brought with them their own little hierarchy (but not families – they stayed behind in the village): each dozen or so men had a *Rayyis* – a chief – from the same tribe and village, who would accompany and support any man with a claim. One day a *ghaffir* came in to see me: he wanted a loan to repair the roof of his house. In my newly learned Arabic I laid out the rules. It was company policy, I told him, to be prepared to make loans to employees subject to certain conditions: a maximum of one month's pay, to be repaid by payroll deductions over no more than twelve months, for the purpose of dealing with unforeseen eventualities, illness and suchlike, but not for routine maintenance, clothes for the children, or anything for which a provident head of a family would have saved. I asked the *Rayyis* if the need to repair the roof arose from weather damage, or fire, or what.

'Just old age,' said he. So I told the ghaffir that, since this didn't meet the company's conditions, I could not agree to the loan being granted.

He listened to all my speech with apparent understanding, but when I was done, he turned to the *Rayyis* and asked him, 'What did he say?' To which the *Rayyis* just answered, 'He said "No".'

Saying 'No' to requests for loans, petty bureaucratic paperwork, and sitting in at occasional meetings with the union did not make for a high level of job satisfaction, but I had my Arabic lessons, which I greatly enjoyed, and I used to spend time with the heads of the operating departments and in the plants learning what the refinery did, and how it did it; and then, suddenly, I got my big break. The company decided that it would make sense to set up a subsidised canteen to provide meals on the job for all our labour. We employed about one thousand three hundred people not classified as 'staff', of whom eight hundred or so were day workers while the rest worked shifts; oil refining is a continuous process, so a refinery never stops. I was given the job of organising this, and supervising it when it was implemented, so suddenly I had a clear goal and the appropriate authority, and others could deal with *ghaffirs*' claims!

I told Anwar of our plans, and asked for his help and support in making a success of the canteen, and in deciding on the menus we should offer; just one hot dish each day, with rice, bread, salad and a sweet, and promised in return that we would welcome comments and complaints through the union. I told him that the employees would have to bear about half the cost of the meals, which we had calculated to be about five piastres – a little over one shilling sterling, or twenty American cents. Anwar, of course, wanted it to be free, but I had to be very clear that that wouldn't fly, and suggested three and a half piastres with a beef dish twice a week, with the company picking up the rest.

Bargaining is an Egyptian art, and it was not possible to reach agreement during our first meeting. But during my naval service in Alexandria I had accompanied Sonny Mohsen on a couple of shopping expeditions, and had learned some of the principles: patience is all, and you have to be prepared to walk away if the other party isn't moving enough, though you judge that in the end he will. And if, the next day, he is in tears and wringing his hands, you know that both sides are satisfied with the deal. Anwar knew that a meal in the refinery was a genuine benefit to the employees, and that my suggested price was, if not a bargain, at least about what a man would pay for the simplest meal – a loaf of Arab bread[2] alone would cost eight-tenths of a piastre – and finally we agreed on two and a half piastres, but beef only twice a week.

The premises didn't take long to construct: an open space, about seventy metres by thirty metres, just inside the refinery fence, was cleared of what little it had on it, and a

---

[2] 'Pitta' bread – a hollow, flat loaf, partly leavened, and in Egypt, of whole wheat.

roof of thatch (for shade from the sun rather than protection from rain, it hardly ever rains in Suez) built to cover it. At one end was the entrance, where the prospective eater had to give up a ticket, and at the other the kitchen, simple pressure oil burners that would take the eighty-litre aluminium pans in which the food would be prepared, with a serving table in front of it. The remainder of the space was filled with long tables with benches each side.

As soon as the story got around Suez, I was besieged by butchers, bakers and vegetable merchants wanting to grease my palm to get the contracts to supply the food. I told them all that the purchasing would be done by our materials department, to no avail. 'But of course, your honour will have to tell them which merchant to buy from, because you'll be the responsible party.'

I was offered every sort of bribe, never in cash, but mostly in terms of liquor or food. I turned them all down, but they would be back the next day with a better offer. The most persistent of all, a butcher, went so far as to arrive on our doorstep at six o'clock one evening. We had by then moved into the new company flat, which was on the upper floor of the building, so 'doorstep' was in fact the little square of concrete at the top of the steps. I happened to be nearest to the door when he rang the door bell, and found him with a twenty-pound live turkey under one arm, and at his feet a basket with a bottle of whisky (not of any decent brand), a bottle of Greek brandy, several bottles of Egyptian wine (yes, there is such!) and boxes of chocolates, *halawa*,[3] Turkish delight and fruit.

As soon as I opened the door, he started to unload the contents of the basket inside the doorway, and press the case that his meat had no equal on the market. I called

---

[3] Halva, Turkish nougat.

Hassan, our *suffragui*[4] to put them all back in the basket, and while this battle of wills was going on, the turkey, which had been put down on the doorstep, suddenly made a dash into the flat, where Jeanie tried to round it up, and managed to corner it in the bathroom, where it perched on the lavatory seat. Finally Hassan had got all the goodies back into the basket, and the butcher was beginning to accept defeat, so Hassan came to collect the turkey, which expressed its feelings by performing that act which was, above all others, most appropriate to its perch – right into the pot! Hassan got the bird back under the butcher's arm, and we were able to shut the door. The next day the butcher came to see me again and asked me: 'What *do* you want to give me the contract?'

'A Packard,' said I. (Packard then, at any rate in Egypt, occupied the niche that today belongs to Cadillac.) He knew that I was not seriously expecting him to agree, and finally got my point. Ironically, when the meat contract was awarded through Materials Department's procedures, he got it!

For the first couple of weeks, I was on the spot for every meal we served, and Anwar or another member of the union's committee was alongside me, watching for short measure, or stale bread, or tired salad, but gradually we settled down to a steady performance without troubles. It was not long after we had opened that the month of Ramadan came along, when Muslims must fast from dawn – the moment that a black thread can be distinguished from a white – until sunset. During these hours nothing may pass the lips. So we served a couple of dozen meals at lunchtime, to our Copts, Greeks and other non-Muslims, and an *Iftar*, breakfast after sunset, to those shift workers who could get away from their jobs for a few

---

[4]Cook, houseman.

minutes, and in these arrangements it was Anwar who steered me through the religious and traditional requirements of the events. In 1949 Ramadan fell in the summer (the Muslim year is lunar) so the fast was long, the weather hot, but the watermelon in season. The moment of sunset is announced by the firing of a cannon, but of course people know more or less when it's coming, and have a slice of watermelon ready. I spent many evenings of that month in the refinery, and have imprinted in my memory the sound of sunset; the *bang* of the cannon followed instantaneously by the *crruunch* of two hundred and fifty sets of teeth biting into watermelon, combining the slaking of thirst with a shot of energy from the sugar.

Chapter Thirty-Two

More Egypt

Presumably I had been fairly successful in Suez (though we did not receive much feedback from our managers in the culture of that time) because after about nine months there I was transferred to the head office in Cairo as number two in the company-wide Labour Department, under Hugh Feetham, a first-rate mentor and a good friend. In this job I began to get a broader perspective on the work of Shell Egypt and AEO, and to have more responsibility. But notably I began to get to know my Egyptian colleagues, whose friendship and support were to be very important in the coming four years. Alas, Mustafa Zohdi, Mustafa Sidky, Ibrahim el-Fawwal and Selim Attié are dead, and I have lost touch with Yahya Sharara. Selim Attié's children are still friends, and we exchange cards each year with Farid Mahrus and Wagih Qutb[1] (he now spells it 'Kotb' in an effort to make his name more pronounceable to those who don't speak Arabic) and Wagih and I have worked together since we both retired, I from Shell and he from Shell Egypt's reincarnation after it was nationalised by Nasser.

I had one setback. I went down with paratyphoid fever, and was ill to the point of delirium when Hugh Feetham responded to Phyllis's alarm call, and drove me to the Anglo-Egyptian hospital. Until this time paratyphoid

[1] Since I wrote these words, Wagih too has died.

usually kept its victims *hors de combat* for as long as a year, but I was lucky. A drug of the sulphonamide family, effective against typhoid and paratyphoid fevers, had just become available, and I was the first patient whom Dr Hamilton, Shell's outside doctor, had been able to treat with it. In ten days I was able to leave hospital, and in three weeks I was back at work. Before this disease hit I weighed the same as I had almost since I joined the Navy, sixty kilograms. I left the hospital weighing under fifty-five, and I looked like a skeleton. But my metabolism had been completely changed: I used to be able to eat a lot of food without ever putting on an ounce of weight, except in the orgy of cream and ice cream in Durban. But soon, despite eating less, I began putting on weight as fast as a baby, and in a couple of months I was up to almost seventy-seven kilograms. None of my clothes fitted any more; even my shirts were too tight, and I had to renew my whole wardrobe. This cost me more than my hospital bill had cost Shell, and it took years before I got back to stability at around my present sixty-seven.

By the end of this assignment I had passed level three in my Arabic – I was now going to the American University at Cairo for my classes – and was able to discuss matters with the labour and staff unions in their language, though it was a year or more before I could carry on a full negotiation, to the point of a written agreement, with little more than an occasional nudge from Wagih.

Expatriates' contracts of employment were for three years, after which we were entitled to three months' home leave, and I hoped to be in Cairo for the balance of my contract. But it was not to be: I was transferred for my final few months to the oilfield of Râs Ghârib, on the coast of the Gulf of Suez, in the Eastern Desert, two hundred kilometres south of Suez, as head of Personnel and Administration. Râs Ghârib was Egypt's biggest oilfield then, but it was virtually 'drilled up', so the emphasis of our task was efficient production of what we had rather than the drilling of new wells. In the course of my apprenticeship with Shell I had learned in theory about production, but it was an advance in my education to be involved in it.

The so-called road from Suez was paved for the first fifty or so kilometres; the rest was desert, as nature had made it, or, in the worst stretches, heavy crude oil was sprayed on to the sand to make some sort of a stabilised surface. Râs Ghârib crude is heavy, so the lighter fractions are soon evaporated by the sun and wind, and you are left with, essentially, asphalt. This road continued southward along the coast to an older oilfield, Hurghada (correctly, Ghurdaqa; now the site of a Club Med resort) and on to Port Safaga, where it turned inland to Qena in the Nile valley, three hundred and fifty kilometres from Râs Ghârib. These two roads and two small, eighty thousand ton tankers, which shipped out our crude and brought back our water, were our links to the world. Water came in two qualities; that for washing in the oil tanks, and although the oily residue was separated, the smell could not be; drinking water had segregated storage in the ships and was as good as you could get in Suez, perfectly drinkable. Food came in trucks from Qena; meat, in the shape of half animals, overnight (for the coolth) twice a week, to be cut up into marketable sizes in our butcher's shop. Flour, canned foods, fruit and vegetables came more often, and though the journey took eight or ten hours, the quality was as good as you might get in a city. Bread we baked in our bakery, or families made their own.

The oilfield employed not far short of one thousand people (not all men, we had women nurses for the hospital). Most of the workforce came from two tribes around Qena, the Ashraf and the Barahma, traditional rivals, but who generally lived together in peace. Many of them had their families living with them in company-provided housing. Their comparative prosperity and the culture, that children are wealth, kept a high reproductive rate, so hundreds of children lived in Râs Ghârib. We were required by law to maintain schools for them, so we had a dozen schoolteachers. The law was represented by a detachment of the coastguard and a couple of customs officers. It was my job to keep all this population contented, and the administrative side was every bit as time-consuming as the personnel.

Nothing grew, but football fields and a golf course had been created out of sand. The beach was narrow, but the sea was always warm and lovely to swim in. There were clubs for the staff and for the labour, where we showed films and organised other entertainments, and which enabled us to meet socially the families of our colleagues and get to know people we didn't work with very closely. We arranged classes for employees to learn handicrafts, with notable success in kilim carpets. Ninety per cent of the year the wind blew steadily from the north, often strong enough to keep the surface sand in motion, which was ruinous for machinery and the paintwork on cars, and a headache for housekeeping, but on the whole we lived happily in our self-contained community.

Golf was not like St Andrews: the greens of our nine-hole course were rough circles graded more or less smooth with a crude-oil-stabilised track one metre wide from one point on the circumference to the hole in the centre. A string was kept tied to the flag; once your ball was on the green, you used the string to measure its distance from the hole, picked it up and put it down on the oiled track the same distance from the flag. And there was one hole that was my nemesis. It was a short par three; the tee was at the edge of an escarpment twenty metres higher than the hole, and it was straight into the wind, which was blowing uphill to the tee. If there had been no wind a number eight iron would have been fine, but since that rarely happened, you needed a longer club. One day I was playing with Bashir es-Sudani, who was in my department in charge of welfare, and my regular golf companion. The wind was blowing strongly, so I picked a six iron, got too far under the ball and hit it into the sky, where the wind took it and landed it fifty metres behind me! Back at the club, Bashir had a lot of fun at my expense! After that I played the hole with a full swing of my putter, which worked pretty well by keeping under the wind.

Some time before my arrival, the Personnel Department had organised a party for the children of our labour, introducing them to the games that British children played on such occasions. It was all good fun until the last game, musical chairs. The children cottoned on to the game very quickly and were enjoying it until the very end. The last two boys, the contestants for the one remaining chair, happened to be one Ashraf, and one Barahma, who each had a hand on the chair, and tried to keep on the seat side as long as possible, while their fathers, their uncles and their cousins and their neighbours from both tribes began to finger their staves and glare at their tribal rivals.

The man at the gramophone saw the situation and kept the music going until a few senior people got as much between the rivals as possible, and one brave man picked up the chair and carried it away. Bloodshed was avoided by a very small margin: each side claimed that rightful victory had been snatched away from their tribe, while those without tribal allegiance speculated about what would have happened if the music had been stopped and one boy had got into the chair. He would have been really roughed up if the other side had got him, the man with his hand on the music would have been accused of partiality, and staves on both sides would have been swinging indiscriminately. Even when I arrived, these tensions had not been totally relieved, and one of my first tasks was to preside at a *maglis es-sulh* – a conciliation session – between the elders, my qualification for the job being the fact that I spoke passable Arabic, and could not have been partial since I wasn't there. I learned to be very careful not to try to mix cultures!

I became, partly, I think, because of my participation in the *maglis es-sulh*, *persona grata* with the committee of the union and other influential members of the labour force, and was invited to meet them in the office of the union or in the labour club. Hashish was totally illegal in Egypt, but most of what was available entered the country over the coast of the Gulf of Suez, in the little ports which were too small to justify a resident coastguard, so it was not difficult to get. Indeed, it was sometimes difficult *not* to get – as presents. Most of the traffic along the Suez road was AEO vehicles. Between Suez and Râs Ghârib, there were two oases, Ain Sukhna ('Hot Spring') and Za'farana, at each of which there was a coastguard station. The people who manned these relied largely on passing cars and trucks to travel between homes in Suez and their stations, and I rarely drove in either direction without giving a lift to one or more soldiers.

One day I picked up one at Ain Sukhna, who wanted to go to Râs Ghârib, and on to his home further south. We chatted happily on the way, and when we arrived, he pressed into my hand a lump of hashish the size of an egg. I refused, politely, but he insisted: I refused and he insisted, until I said to him that if he went on much longer, somebody would overhear, and reluctantly he put it into his pocket. Despite draconian penalties for possession of hashish, many people in the oilfield would have accepted, clearly did accept, because it was freely available; indeed, the coastguard was recognised as being one of the main sources.

I smoked it at least twice: one of my good friends persuaded me that as qualification for my job I at least be able to recognise its taste and smell, and showed me how to doctor a cigarette. You roll it between your fingers until some of the tobacco comes out at one end. You crumble a little piece of hashish, mix it with the ejected tobacco, and refill the cigarette with the mixture. I smoked one of these and didn't get enough to have any effect, though it spoiled the taste of the cigarette. I had no desire to try again, but the next time I couldn't escape. I was invited to meet the union's committee one evening, 'for a cup of tea'. They were sitting in a circle, and there was a spare chair for me. In the middle there was a 'sheeshah', a hubble-bubble or hookah.

The end of the flexible tube through which the smoke is drawn, bubbling through water, is passed around the circle, where each person in turn fits his own mouthpiece (of amber, porcelain or plastic) to the tube and inhales a long, slow lungful or two, before passing it on to his neighbour. The tobacco is burned on a tiny charcoal fire in an earthenware cup at the top of the water container, and an attendant with a little tongs adds charcoal from a brazier, or a lump of tobacco as needed. If it's available, hashish is added with – or instead of – the tobacco.

This night there was a clear smell of hashish, and I knew what I was in for. I didn't have my own mouthpiece, so I was lent one (scrupulously washed before I used it) and politeness demanded that I join in. Not to have done so would have been an insult to my hosts, and would have cast serious aspersions on my manhood, and reduced my credibility in my job. I dissimulated as much as I could, and took tiny draws, just enough to have some smoke to breathe out, and avoided the desired euphoria – 'seeing yourself as a sultan'- of the addict. I thought the taste was awful, and was never tempted to try again.

Once the school terms were over in Cairo, the family went home and took rooms in a small private hotel in Southsea, while I worked out the last few weeks of my contract. The times were troubled. The Egyptian government of the Wafd party, the standard-bearer of Egyptian nationalism, had, in October, abrogated both the 1936 Treaty of Montreux and the 1889 Agreement which established the British–Egyptian condominium over the Sudan. Demonstrations against Britain degenerated into guerrilla warfare against the British troops, followed by British retaliatory action in the city of Ismailia, which in turn led to the burning of Cairo by mobs on 26th January, 1952. My luck was that I had left Cairo by air the previous day for my three months home leave.

In April I was back in Cairo as number two in the Staff Department, under Kit Bland, for whom I quickly became a regular crew in the races at the Cairo yacht club. We sailed drop-keel one-design 'Nile' class boats, five metres long, with a large sail area for the size. So they were fast, but easily capsized in a sudden change of wind and, as Kit said, the trouble about sailing on the Nile in Cairo was that every time someone in one of the blocks of flats that lined the river opened a window the wind changed. Most businesses in Cairo had working hours of 8 a.m. to 2 p.m., six days a week; if necessary, you went back to the office in late afternoon. The yacht club had races every Wednesday, Saturday and Sunday, starting at 3 p.m., so we used to leave the office at two, buy a sandwich at the club and eat it in the boat before the start. The club owned a number of boats, which members could sail for the day, and many members had their own. Some boats were better than others, but Kit and I built up a pretty good record of wins, provided we could get not too bad a boat; I still have a little silver dish with the initials CYC commemorating a season's success. I eventually bought myself a boat, Number 23, which was known to be slow, but all that I could afford. In a club boat Kit was helmsman and I crewed: in 23, the other way around. We developed a simple way of working together: the helmsman watched the sails, the crew watched the rest of the fleet, and for signs of a shift of wind that suggested a change of tack. The crew talked an unending flow of information; the helmsman kept his mouth shut, and we won lots of races, even in 23.

In the first few months of our work together, Kit and I totally redesigned the salary system for our staff, and got approval for it from our management, and from Central Offices in London, as well as the appreciation of our staff, Egyptian and expatriate.

This working and sailing together made it very difficult for me when our boss, 'Weary' Kendall, General Manager of Personnel, was suddenly transferred to Sarawak, and I was asked to take his place, jumping over the head of Kit, who was next in seniority under Weary. Kit was very generous to me, and showed no sign of resentment; for a time, though, I felt awful. For this sudden big promotion I think there were two reasons: I had now passed the American University's fourth level exam, and was working for their ultimate, advanced classical Arabic, and Kit was close to retirement age anyway. I was able to take part in negotiations in Arabic with any level of government or union, and could read and write correctly, and reasonably fast, a standard which few expatriates, even in the foreign service, attained. Now, alas, I can read and write slowly, with much recourse to a dictionary, and can keep up a conversation with an Egyptian taxi driver in New York, of whom there are many, but, 'Ichabod... the glory is departed.'[2]

---

[2]See 1 Samuel 4:21.

Kit stayed on for a while as head of the Staff Department (and my skipper or crew at the yacht club) and then went on pre-retirement leave. He was visiting the Group's Central Offices in London, then in St Helen's Court in the City. He had just been to the Insurance Department, and was crossing the court to go to Pensions, when he dropped dead, without any previous signs of illness of any kind. He had been a very good friend, and was a remarkable man. One of his arms was slightly withered, but despite this he was a superb craftsman. He made a doll's house to a scale of about one-tenth, complete in every detail, down to a scale replica of itself in the nursery, and in the replica yet another model (just the solid shape) to a scale of one to a thousand! Though I believe he had intended it for a child that he knew, it was eventually presented to King Farouk on the occasion of the birth of his son, Prince Fuad. He also made an exact scale model of the *Spray*, the sailing boat which Captain Slocum found rotten in a field in New England, was given to him, and completely rebuilt by him, and in which he sailed single-handed around the world in the late 1890s. He left detailed records of his rebuilding, from which Kit made his model.

Kit's place as head of the Staff Department was taken by one of our very able young Egyptians, Yahya Sharara (whose father was the Sheikh of Al Azhar University) and Wagih Kotb was head of the Labour Department. Ibrahim Fawwal, head of the Welfare Department, completed my team, and we became a close group of friends as well as colleagues in the office. The company's public affairs were managed by Christopher Wren (yes, a descendant of the designer of St Paul's) who left soon after I took over personnel, and his number two, Christopher Cheshire, came into my group when I was asked to take over that job as well. In addition to the tasks that properly belonged to my office, I used to get involved in assisting the chief representative (Geoffrey Tait), the General Manager of AEO (Bill Lethbridge) and the head of Finance, Frank (later Lord) McFadzean in negotiations with the government on the question of new concessions for oil exploration.

My role was to make sure that we didn't get lost in what the Italians describe as '*Traduttore traditore*' – a translator is a traitor – but that which went down on paper in Arabic was what we had agreed. A group of American companies were negotiating for concessions in the Western Desert at the same time as us, and one day the government's director of mines and oilfields, with whom we negotiated, left us at our side of his desk while he went to talk to his minister. Lying on the desk, upside down to us, was the latest draft of the American company's agreement. While he was out I amused myself by reading what was on the page we could see, which happened to be a summary of the key terms, which I related to our team when we got back to the office. This got me a little spice to my reputation: 'Not only can he read Arabic, but he can read it upside down.'

I had become a member of the top management team of the companies, with Geoffrey Tait, H.M. 'Jonah' Jones, Bill Lethbridge and Frank McFadzean. I had an air-conditioned office, and a company car and driver, Abd-el-Malik. But though my salary did get increased, it was nowhere near the level of the rest of the team: Shell's policy on paying senior people at that time was much like that of the Church of England and the Navy; people have a vocation for it, so we can afford not to be competitive. And the market for senior executives was not developed (outside the United States) and job-hopping was dangerous, and just *not done*! I loved my job, and especially enjoyed the friendships I made with many Egyptians, inside the company and out. I got involved, too, with specifically British community activities, and became a member of the parochial church council of the Anglican cathedral in Cairo.

None of this was risk free, however. In July 1952 a coup by the 'Free Officers', led by Colonel Gamal Abdel Nasser, threw out the monarchy and established a republic. Though Egypt moved slowly in foreign affairs, notably relations with Britain, Abdel Nasser's regime rapidly became an absolutist military government, with a strong security system, led by Colonel Zakariah Mohyi ed-Din. I had learned Arabic: I had been in the British Navy (and still got some letters addressed to 'Lieutenant Commander') and therefore, to a security service still very insecure about who were its friends and who enemies it seemed obvious that I must be a spy. But Egyptians are not made to be security conscious, and there were various people among my friends, who were also close to the military, who kept me advised of the various concerns the Free Officers had about my activities. One day, one of these friends came into my office, and told me he had been asked to find out what was discussed at a 'secret meeting of the leaders of the British community at the cathedral' a few nights ago; the police had taken the numbers of all the cars that had been parked there, and mine was among them. I told him just to go and ask my secretary to show him (and let him copy) the minutes of the meeting. They included such politically dangerous things as accepting the treasurer's report, the programme for the evening gramophone classical music concerts in the close, accepting the bid for the rebuilding of the cathedral organ, and increasing the salary of the minister who was head of our associated Egyptian Anglican congregation.

In the summer of 1953 the Free Officers were getting tired of the restraint exercised by Mohammed Neguib, and the tensions within the revolution were beginning to manifest themselves in anti-foreign and especially anti-British noises, to the point that Shell decided that all the families of expatriate staff should be evacuated to Cyprus until things looked less dangerous. So we were left bachelors and had to find ways of passing the time. We got together with the people of the British embassy, and the British–American Tobacco Company, who were in the same boat as ourselves, and someone hit on the idea of a pentathlon, for a team of four from each. The five sports were to be cricket, tennis, swimming, sailing and golf. The form cricket took was ingenious: each batting side was allowed a limited number of overs, and its four players could be in as many times as needed to complete that number. The other two sides fielded, and were reinforced by three employees of the Gezira Club, one of whom was permanent wicketkeeper. When the allowed number of overs had been bowled, the score was determined by dividing the runs scored by the wickets lost. I hadn't played cricket for years, some competitors had never played golf, or sailed, but each side managed to field a team which could in some degree cope with the games.

In each sport, the winning side got four points, the second two, and the last none, and in the case of a draw the two possibles were divided between the two teams. This kept us, and the increasing number of our non-participating fellows who came to watch, busy for many afternoons that might otherwise have been lonely and sad. The score was honestly kept, and at the end all three teams were equal. The prize was to have been a dinner paid for by the loser, but we all just had to pay our share.

Even the pentathlon didn't absorb all the spare time, so I decided to make a model of my Nile class boat. One could buy balsa wood in dimensions suitable for model aircraft, which would do of course for boats. So I copycatted Kit Bland and his *Spray*, and made every piece of wood in the original on a one-tenth scale, and the same with all the fittings. With the aid of dental drill burrs (of which my dentist gave me a boxful) I made blocks with pulleys in them of boxwood cannibalised from a thicker than usual ruler. The mainsail had a belly to it, though its cloths were not to scale, for the seams would have been too minute for my skill on a sewing machine. Phyllis and the children were back before I got this model finished, so they at least got to see it. An exact scale sailing model won't work, because while lengths are one-tenth of the original, areas, like sails, are one-hundredth, and weights one-thousandth; so to give my model stability I made a streamlined lead weight that fitted on the bottom of the centreboard. This added weight meant that if the hull filled with water, there would be no positive buoyancy, so I planned to fill the open space with ping-pong balls. It was Sunday when the project was finished, and I could not find any shop open where I might buy my ping-pong balls. The breeze, however, was light, and I decided to risk a trial sail at the yacht club, with one of the club sailors in a rowing boat ready to go to the rescue. I set *23 Minor* on a course across the river, close-hauled to the wind. She sailed away perfectly, and had almost reached the middle of the river when a tiny puff of stronger wind turned her over, and she sank. No amount of searching or dragging recovered her. When I told the tale to a couple of my friends on the Monday, they asked if I wasn't terribly disappointed. And I was almost totally honest when I said 'No,' I had had all the fun of making her, and I had seen her sail. And I moved on to make a model, solid this time, for a glass case, of the gas turbine powered MGB *2009*.

Being busy was essential, for suspicions of Lieutenant Commander Ritchie continued with no let-up. I was followed wherever I went, and my telephone was tapped, which were irritants to start with, but gradually became a strain on the nerves. Being Egypt of over four decades ago, however, both had their comic side. My tail was a man wearing a tarboosh in a very old Ford V8, with no top (and, as far as I ever saw, unique in Egypt, so that it was anything but inconspicuous). He clearly knew my routine, because as soon as we left the office, he fell in behind us, and never got separated by more than two other cars. On Wednesdays and Saturdays Abdel Malik drove me to the yacht club, and then went home on a bus, leaving the car for me when the races were over. Tail, meanwhile, parked in a side street right opposite the club, and dozed off, to wake when he heard my car start. So one day I suggested to Abdel Malik that it was a shame that he should waste the day, and the heat of the day at that, doing nothing, and that he should tell Tail, once I'd gone into the club, that the race would last until five or five thirty, and that tea would follow, and keep me there until six at the earliest. Tail was grateful, and disappeared; when post-race tea was over, I'd go to the car, and he would have come back to follow me home. Clearly he trusted us, and we never let him down – though what would have happened to him if he'd come back and found us gone, one can only imagine.

The telephone tap was different. For calls inside Egypt the (very evident) listening-in was sporadic. But calls to London, which I needed to make fairly often, had to go through the operator, and were usually subject to delays measured in tens of minutes, at least. The operator would then call me back, 'Your call to London is just coming through.'

Two people, evidently both of the security apparatus, could be heard, in stage whispers, 'He's just coming on: are you ready?'

'Yes, I'm ready.'

'Okay, start recording.' And then, to the operator: 'You can connect now.'

Of course it wasn't always that I was able to overhear the words, but the switching on and the hum of the recorder were always audible.

These things were petty annoyances, but things got more serious. There were two schools in the Middle East where foreigners could learn Arabic, Shamlan in Lebanon, run by, and mainly for, the British Foreign Service, and my Alma Mater, the American University at Cairo. I knew Shamlan by its products only, but it seemed to me to concentrate too much on literacy at the expense of easy, fluent day-to-day conversation, which I thought was, for business people at any rate, more important than an ability to read *Al Ahram* newspaper rapidly and critically. As the centre of gravity of world oil production moved into the Arab world, Shell began to take the teaching of Arabic to its expatriates very seriously, and Central Offices started to debate which school was the better, and asked for my views. I said that I was biased by my own experience, and so I was asked to pay a visit to Shamlan, and then write a report on my views.

Sounds simple, but one needed an exit visa to leave Egypt. So I applied, and nothing happened, for weeks. We tried all the bureaucrat-hustling techniques, to no avail. One of our employees, and a good friend of mine, Mustafa Sidqi, was the sort of person who was everybody's friend, because he was somehow always able to return a favour. He had come from the military himself, and knew a number of the Free Officers well, and eventually he arranged for me to see Zakariah Mohyi ed-Din himself. He gave me a cup of coffee and listened to me, apparently sympathetically, acknowledging that the teaching of Arabic was one of the roads to international understanding, and a worthy cause, and promised to handle my case personally. Nothing happened, and I began to get worried, so I asked Mustafa to see if he could find out why. After two or three days he came back with disturbing news, which he told me only when we were alone in a car together. Shamlan, his military intelligence friends told him, was a British spy school, and I could only be wanting to go there for very sinister reasons, and he thought that I would only get an exit visa if they could be satisfied that I was leaving for good. I began to get seriously disturbed.

One day I was having early dinner with two of my closest Egyptian friends at an open-air restaurant on the banks of the Nile, called Café des Pigeons, because its only offering was pigeons, split, grilled over a wood fire and served with salad. I told them of my worry over my exit visa problem, and said that perhaps I ought just to resign, and get out right away. They talked me out of this, and the next afternoon they came together to my office and presented me with a beautiful example of Arabic calligraphy. White letters with gold decorations on a black background, it consisted of two of the *hawadith* – the traditional sayings of the Prophet – which translate: *'Arm yourself with patience and with prayer: verily Allah is with the patient.'*

By this time Jonah Jones had succeeded Geoffrey Tait as chief representative, and he and I had become close friends. So I went to see him, and told him of my concerns. We decided that there was no point in making an issue of my visit to Shamlan, but that we should, in plenty of time before the due date, start applying for exit visas (for 'final departure') for the whole family, as the end of my contract was only a few months away. At the same time he told me that my next job should be in marketing, after all, that was where the money came in, that it should not be in the Arab world, and should not be where Shell was the market leader, as in Egypt. Well, it was not easy: my date was getting closer and closer, and I was getting more and more apprehensive. The support of my friends, expressed in calligraphy, did give me the patience I needed. Its gold is now nearly black, and its black, light grey, but it has always hung where I can look up from my desk and read it, and remember the true friendship of Wagih Kotb and Yahya Sharara.

I gave up the idea of trying to go to Shamlan, but about six weeks before my contract was to end in late April, we made reservations for ourselves and our car on a ship from Alexandria to Italy, and I went to see Zakariah Mohyi ed-Din again, and asked him for his help in speeding up our exit visas. I told him, just as I was leaving his office, that I had greatly enjoyed my five years in Egypt, the chance to learn Arabic and to make many Egyptian friends, and was sorry that Shell's plans were for me not to return to Egypt. He promised to do his best – and he did. He asked me to give him details of our travel plans, and on the day we were to leave, a young army Lieutenant and two soldiers with a big car and a pick-up truck arrived at our apartment. The soldiers loaded our luggage into the truck, and we were loaded into the car, and we drove to Cairo Station for the train to Alexandria. The officer commandeered a compartment for us and told the conductor of the train that we were not to be disturbed; at the last moment he ordered one of the soldiers, rifle and all, to board the train with us, and to stay in the corridor outside our door, in case we needed any assistance, and then to make sure we boarded the ship without hindrance, and to keep us company until the ship sailed.

His affiliation must have been known, because we were whisked through all the passport and customs formalities, and ensconced in our cabins under his watchful eye, but without any of the normal baksheesh-seeking. It was all very polite, but what was happening was crystal clear: we were being escorted off Egyptian territory without making contact with anyone!

In fact, I tried to get a visa to visit Egypt several times in the next twenty years, to no avail until Anwar el-Sadat succeeded Abdel Nasser, and Egypt turned away from the USSR.

Chapter Thirty-Three

Marketing

We left the ship in Genoa, and, after a little difficulty in Italian immigration – I failed to respond when I was called, because I didn't recognise 'Reet-key-ay' as my name – we set off to drive across Europe to Calais for the ferry to Dover.

As I have written earlier, my father had died in early March, just before we left Egypt, so my mother was living alone in Brownhill, her house in Burnley. There we all went to stay with her for a couple of weeks while I went to Central Offices to find out what I could about my future assignment, and we could organise somewhere to live for the two months of our home leave. Walking into the sitting room of Brownhill was very poignant. It was the room most closely associated in my mind with my father. His chair, the fire in front of which he sat, his books were all there, but its characteristic faint, pervasive smell of Romeo y Julieta cigars was gone. The awful finality of his death and my loss suddenly hit me.

In London there was a long programme of interviews waiting for me; the heads of all the departments concerned with Egypt, personnel in its various facets, marketing people, and even a couple of managing directors. But nobody could tell me where or what my next job would be. I did learn, though, that I was being sent on a Shell executive course, to widen my knowledge of the oil industry, and of the Shell Group's place in it. This course had the reputation of being a filter for middle management jobs, and how one acquitted oneself in it was regarded as important for one's chances of future promotion. Also it could be a lot of fun! It was divided into three parts, all residential: the first in Shell Lodge in Teddington, the Group's training centre, covered the history, structure, development and management of the Group. The second, in The Hague, dealt with exploration, production and refining; and for the third we were split into two groups to study the operations of a marketing company. One half stayed with Shell Nederland, and the other (luckier?) went to Shell Française, to spend some time in the head office in Paris, and then split into two yet smaller groups, each to a different marketing region: Brittany for my sub-group. All but I in the French group had had experience in marketing, or at least in a marketing company. So I had more to learn, and more of a *tabula rasa* on which to imprint new knowledge. I think I also had more curiosity to question (not always to our hosts, but among ourselves) some things, accepted as givens, but of which the explanations didn't always seem to ring true. I kept being reminded of a cartoon in the *New Yorker*: a tycoon is sitting behind a huge desk, which he thumps as he tells a subordinate, 'I tell you: there ain't no reason. It's just policy.'

We were royally entertained by our hosts, and the last two or three days in Paris for a final wind-up were particularly hectic. The meeting room assigned to us was on the top floor of the office, with a big window along the side, facing south-west. Lunch was preceded by an aperitif, accompanied by at least two wines, and rounded off by a brandy or liqueur. Whether this was a kind of test of our ability to withstand ordeals by lunch, or just exaggerated hospitality, we never knew. But the afternoons were difficult: the speakers all seemed to be dull, the room was hot in the afternoon sun, and lunch was not conducive to rapt attention. Many of us slept, and we were saved from shame by one of the members – from Rhodesia, I think – who had a great gift. He could sleep through all the speaker's words, but if he paused our friend could wake up, ask an apposite question, and go back to sleep before hearing the answer.

The Shell Française people arranged for us the basic sightseeing in Paris, took us to the Lido, and pointed us towards good but not too expensive restaurants where twos or threes of us could dine together after the working day. And, of course, we had resident comedians in the group who kept us amused in our few idle moments. One of these became a special friend, then and later. Walter Bedon was in Shell Italiana's Public Relations Department, and the two of us went to dine in a little restaurant between the Shell office and the hotel where we were all staying. It had nothing Italian about it, except that it had on its menu pizza à la sicilienne. I had never heard of pizza, it had not yet really burst on to the world scene, but at Walter's urging I ordered it, and have never found so good a pizza since.

For these last few days in France some people had invited their wives to join them, and at a party Walter was talking to one of our members and his wife. She asked Walter what sort of things we had been doing in our spare time. He answered that her husband had been one of the most studious of us all.

'He wouldn't come out to nightclubs with us; he and I spent one evening studying the economy of Brittany, because we didn't quite see the relationship between the fishing industry and the sales of diesel fuel. He read the *Petroleum Handbook* from cover to cover, he wrote letters to his family…' and a lot more in the same vein, then smiled innocently and turned to the husband: 'That was all I was supposed to say, George, wasn't it?'

And then there was a New Zealander who asked me

(because my French was reasonably fluent and his non-existent) why every theatre in Paris had on the same show. I expressed puzzlement, and he said, 'Yes; it's called "*Fermeture annuelle*".' Of course, it was August, when every theatre and many restaurants in all of France do indeed have their annual closing!

It was while we were in The Hague on the executive course that I received an invitation to dinner that in the event was a turning point in my life. It was from J.C. 'Fitz' FitzGerald, the manager in London responsible for the Group's marketing companies in the Caribbean, Central and South America, who wanted me to meet (and – unspoken – be vetted by) Julio Iglesias, the President of Shell Cuba, to which I was being offered as a marketing trainee. I passed muster; and after leave was completed, and then a couple of weeks in the London office, learning about Shell Cuba, and taking Spanish lessons at the Berlitz School twice a day, I travelled to New York in the *Queen Mary*, and from New York to Havana in a ship of the United Fruit Line. It was September, and both Jeanie and Sarah were in schools, so the family stayed in England for a few months.

Shell Cuba was as different from Shell Egypt and AEO as could be. It had at that time about eighty employees: in Egypt we had three thousand and more. The President was Cuban, and there were, after my arrival, three expatriates. The office was one floor of a modern building, laid out on an open plan, so that only the President and his secretaries were behind full doors: partial privacy was provided for the rest of the managers by partitions two metres high.

It was a Saturday when the ship arrived, in the early morning, in Havana. I was met by the (expatriate) Operations Manager, Paddy Reilly, who delivered me to a hotel to have a bath and breakfast before he picked me up again to take me to the empty office to begin a briefing on the organisation. Paddy's office door was open, and suddenly we heard the main door open, and rapid, angry footsteps walking quickly along the hard floor of the open hall. In a few seconds a woman, in high heels, a *café au lait* linen skirt over a crinoline (then in full fashion) and a sleeveless Madeira-embroidered linen blouse flashed past Paddy's door. I don't think she even noticed that there were two people besides herself in the office as she went through the door into the President's private quarters, and slammed it behind her. In the split second that she was in sight I had a sudden eerie feeling that that woman was, somehow, going to be important in my life.

'Who on earth was that?' I asked Paddy.

'That was Mrs Sunderland, Julio's secretary,' he answered. 'I'll take you in and introduce you in a few minutes.'

When we went into her office she had cooled down a little, but was clearly still annoyed: every Saturday her hairdresser came to her flat, and had just finished the shampoo when Western Union Cable Company telephoned her to say that there was a coded cable of the kind that only she was allowed to receive, which she could pick up at their office in the Hotel Nacional. She had brought it into the office, with her hair still wet, and was busy with her code books, decoding it.

'Why do these damn things have to come on Saturdays?' she expostulated, greeted me perfunctorily, and showed us the door.

'Whew!' I said to Paddy. 'Is she always like that?'

'No,' he replied, 'she's normally a nice person. And she's very good at her job.'

The next day I met Julio again, and he told me what he expected of me. He wanted me to work with every section head in marketing, to help them in what they needed most at the moment, and to tell him if I ever didn't have enough to do. *'Y tienes que aprender español, carajo'*[1] ('And you've got to learn Spanish, expletive!') I told him I'd like to live with a Spanish-speaking family, and he called in the Personnel Manager and told him to arrange it. The next day I moved out of the hotel, and took up residence with Señor and Señora Moran. They (despite his Irish ancestry) did not speak a word of English, which was ideal. Hunger is a powerful stimulus to learning a language, and very soon I was speaking very little English in the office, except with Billie Sunderland, Paddy Reilly, and the Finance Manager, Michael Lloyd-Hirst.

At first my contributions to Shell Cuba's prosperity were insignificant, but little by little people began to want to discuss things with me and to take notice of my ideas. I travelled all over the island and got to know the agents who handled Shell's business in the provinces outside Havana, and the contractor who built all our new service stations, and gradually metamorphosed from trainee to contributing member of the team, and my Spanish became pretty good.

I have a classification of stages through which you must pass in learning to speak a foreign language. First is taxi driver and domestic help, where grammar doesn't matter: 'Turn right', 'Stop here', 'Number 23 Station Street', 'Please wash shirt'. Next is restaurant, where you need to understand most of the menu, and order from it, specifying 'Well done', 'Not too much salt'. Then comes the ability to talk about your work, in concrete terms. Next, your work in conceptual terms. After that, discuss the problems of your business with a government official, and be able to influence him. Close after that comes make a speech designed to persuade, in public. Finally, the peak is to be able to entertain a well-educated woman, older than

---

[1]This last word is, to most Cuban men, the equivalent of a full stop at the end of every sentence.

yourself, at a cocktail party – talking about *nothing*!

Julio César Iglesias was an ideal man under whom to serve as a trainee. He is an instinctive trader and marketer, and an educated businessman, and Shell Cuba was a very successful company. He is foul-mouthed in the totally innocent way that anyone who saw the movie *La Belle Epoque* will recognise as typically Spanish, so I was able to learn from him those words and phrases that are most difficult for a student of a foreign language to acquire.

During my year with him, he persuaded the Group that a refinery in Cuba – the company to import crude oil instead of refined products – would be profitable. His final meeting with the committee of managing directors of the Group at which the decision yes or no was to be taken was to be in London, in the afternoon. During the morning a number of meetings had been planned for him, as was usual when a chief executive of a subsidiary was in the Central Offices. Julio had travelled via Paris, and on the morning of the meeting Air France went on strike, and in sympathy the traffic controllers prevented all competitor airlines from flying into or out of Orly. So Julio failed to turn up for his morning appointments, and when he had not arrived at 2 p.m. for the big meeting, everyone knew why, and they decided to go on without him. But at five minutes past, in he walked, to everyone's surprise. Asked how he had managed, he said he had chartered a plane. After the meeting, Jimmy Platt, who was the Managing Director with responsibility for Cuba, mildly chided Julio. 'Of course it was an important meeting, but we don't expect people to go quite to the lengths of chartering planes. But go and see my secretary, and she'll arrange for the cost to be refunded to you.'

'Oh, no!' said Julio. 'It didn't cost me anything. There were four American businessmen waiting in Orly, and I invited them to share my charter. They were delighted, and each happily paid over a quarter of the price I had negotiated. So I even made a profit on the deal.' Which is why Shell had picked him as President of Shell Cuba.

Shell's normal way of building a refinery was to design it in house, in detail, and then contract out all the various parts of the job. Julio objected, and said that he would like, subject of course to the technical blessing of Shell's experts, to ask for tenders and award the project, on a turnkey basis, to the lowest bidder. No other president of a subsidiary could have got away with this, but Julio was very valuable; for his success, for his being a one of the very few chief executives, outside the larger European countries, who was a national of the country, and for his very close relationships with the parts of the Cuban government that could expedite or delay the progress of the job. So when he said 'I would like', all those around the table knew that this meant 'I insist'. So they agreed: Bechtel Corporation won the bid, and the refinery was built in less time than the Group engineers had estimated, and at little over half their estimated cost.

The refinery project had some interesting moments. Julio, himself an engineer, took on the task of recruiting the Cuban engineers who would be needed to run the plant. He went through all the résumés of the candidates, and produced his own shortlist from them, and those people he interviewed personally. One of the posts he had to fill was instrument engineer, and five young men duly presented themselves at half-hour intervals. One of these was missing his left hand, and had in its place a device which produced a grip by movement of his elbow, and which could be fitted with tools of various kinds. Julio was taken aback, and said, 'With that handicap, how can you be an instrument engineer, carajo?'

The candidate asked Julio to show him his wristwatch, an Omega in a gold case. 'Are you prepared to trust me?' he asked. 'If so, I'll take your watch to pieces here, and put it back together while you see me do it.'

Julio handed over the watch, the young man took out of his briefcase a set of tools made for his gadget, and reduced the Omega to its components – and then reassembled it, wound it, set it to the right time and handed it back to a very impressed Julio.

Impressed, but not yet totally satisfied. 'But in a refinery, many of the instruments will be high up in the various plants, and you'll have to climb ladders, and work up there.'

The candidate just said, 'Try me, like the watch!'

Julio tried him; he succeeded, and got the job.

Many engineering firms from around the world were interested in becoming subcontractors for such things as roads, tanks and pipework. We had a cable one day advising that a well-known Lebanese contractor would be sending a representative, with an unmistakably Arab and Muslim name, who would be contacting us by telephone. For fun, I asked the telephone operator to put him through to me. When he called, I spoke to him in Arabic (which had not yet seriously started to decline) and got the greatest compliment ever on my proficiency: after we had finished the business part of our conversation, he asked, 'And your honour is an Arab from which country?'

Chapter Thirty-Four

Argentina

After almost exactly a year of being a trainee (and a jack of all trades) under Julio Iglesias, I had presumably passed the test for a career in marketing, and was appointed in late September 1955 to the job of Sales Manager of Shell Argentina. Phyllis, Sarah and I left Havana for Buenos Aires on the first passenger service to operate since the deposition of Perón and his flight to Paraguay. We arrived on 1st October, late at night, and were taken to a hotel almost opposite the offices of Shell Argentina. When we woke the next morning, I tried to order breakfast, and learned one of the big lessons in acquiring Spanish, that common things tend to change their names when you cross a frontier. I succeeded in coffee and toast, and a glass of milk for Sarah, but then I tried to order fruit. I asked for *toronjas*, which in Cuba means grapefruit. The waiter looked puzzled, and I asked him, 'Don't you have *toronjas* here?'

'Yes, we do,' said he, 'but we don't eat them.'

'You don't eat them, why not?' I asked.

'Because they're poisonous!'

So I went on to try various other fruits by their Cuban – usually the correct Spanish – names, and kept drawing blanks. So I tried *plátanos*, bananas in Cuba. The waiter began to run out of patience, and said, '*Plátanos*? Sir, please come with me, over to the window. You see those trees lining the street? Well, those are *plátanos*,' – they were plane trees! – *and we don't eat them!'*

Then Sarah said, in English, 'Well, if we can't get bananas, what can we have?'

The waiter's face burst into a broad smile, and he said, 'Ah, *bananas,* yes, those we do have!'

Argentina is a country with three times the population of Cuba, in an area twenty-five times as large. Both were, or, in Argentina's case, until a couple of weeks before, had been, governed by dictators, Batista in Cuba, Perón in Argentina, but were totally different in their economies. The Cuban peso was stable on a par with the US dollar, and commerce was free of controls. The Argentine peso on the 'free' (in fact, illegal) market was about twenty-five to the dollar when we arrived: a year later it was at eighty, and by 1964 the *official* rate was 178. But Perón's economics, in theory designed to decrease the country's dependence on agriculture and livestock, used as its tools a variety of exchange rates and import and export controls. In general, industries were favoured, and agriculture, cattle-raising in particular, was penalised. And since Perón owed his power to the army and the labour unions, brilliantly (and totally unscrupulously) organised by his charismatic wife, Evita, there was money for weapons, housing and food were ridiculously cheap, and 'welfare' for unionised labour was a lot more generous than the economy could afford.

Cars were prohibitively expensive, even when local manufacture began. Shell Argentina had bought, just pre-Perón, for use by its salesmen, a number of Chevrolet cars. By the time I got there, these cars had run three hundred thousand kilometres but were getting expensive to maintain, and we decided to sell them: we got, in dollars, twice what they had cost new! The head of our Engineering Department was a very low handicap golfer. You could join the municipal golf club in Buenos Aires for three pesos – for life! – but he could not play golf, because he couldn't afford to buy balls, which, being rich man's toys, were scarcely granted any import permits, and so were only obtainable on the black market at sky-high prices, half a dozen costing roughly what a set of clubs would cost in the UK or the USA.

Although it is situated on the eastern fringe of the country, Buenos Aires is the effective centre of everything. Railways and roads radiate from it; the federal government lives there, and so did three million of the total population of twenty million. And of this total one-eighth were foreign born. Indeed there were more people of Italian nationality or children and grandchildren of Italians than all the rest put together. The contrast between the patterns of immigration into Argentina and into the United States is very striking. The historical flow to the latter has been escape from religious persecution or political disenfranchisement. The unspoken contract between these people and their new country was 'Give us political and religious freedom, and we'll take care of ourselves.' That of the immigrants to Argentina was the opposite. 'Give us the opportunity to make a living, and we won't interfere in politics.' Many immigrants started as casual agricultural labour; they worked the summer harvest in Italy or Spain, travelled to Argentina steerage (in the ships that, on the return voyage, carried the agricultural exports) for the southern hemisphere season, went back home, and repeated the cycle until finally they decided to stay, and brought their families.

The Pampas, west of Buenos Aires and reaching almost to the Andes, are one of the largest and most fertile regions of agricultural land in the world. They say you can drive a plough from Buenos Aires to Mendoza in the foothills of the Andes without hitting a stone, and with seldom less than two metres of topsoil under your feet. Cattle can be grazed all year long without the need for shelter, and natural pasture is backed up by easily grown alfalfa. Wheat and other cereals grow abundantly, and Argentina was one of the biggest exporters of wheat in the world. Only two other countries have larger populations of sheep, raised mainly in the poor land of Patagonia at the rate of one sheep per hectare, and chilled beef and frozen lamb are very important exports.

Roads were, in general, poor – little stone was available – but the railway system was extensive and good, though handicapped by having three gauges. Population density outside the big cities was low, and there was no significant pressure of people on the land. Industry was becoming increasingly important in the big cities, Rosario, Córdoba and the suburbs of Buenos Aires, but was inefficient and so required considerable economic protection. This took the form of prohibitive import duties on competing imported products, and very favourable exchange rates for the purchase of raw materials and machine tools from abroad. Cars were made in the country, but not planes; light planes were needed for crop-spraying (and even for getting around the biggest estancias) so that, if you were in the right industry you could buy a plane more cheaply than a saloon car. Many industries were owned and run by the armed forces: the largest steel mill, and most of the smaller ones, were owned by the army, as was one of the lorry factories. Its president was a general, its department heads colonels, the foremen were sergeants and the operatives private – often conscript – soldiers. It made some (pretty unreliable) trucks, which required a subsidy of twice their selling price to be able to compete with the Fords and General Motors, so it tended to have to rely on incestuous sales to the army itself.

As so often happens in extremely nationalist countries, 'El Petróleo' was a highly sensitive political issue, with a national oil company, Yacimientos Petroliferos Fiscales

(YPF) in a dominant position in the industry. The country was self-sufficient in crude oil production and in refining capacity, but exported some crude and imported some products, mainly heavy fuel oil, to balance demand. YPF had over a fifty per cent share of the market, while Esso and Shell had about twenty per cent each, with some smaller players accounting for the rest. Prices were set by the State, and were uniform throughout the country, with no difference allowed for variations in the costs of supplying a little service station in the far north of the country and a big one right outside the refinery gate. A company's revenue was in the form of '*retenciones*', that fraction of the sales price which you were allowed to keep. These were calculated from an average of the costs of all companies in the market, which we were required to report to the National Energy Authority every month, and allowed a large margin for the State. Politicians seldom have any appreciation of the economic truth that prices are made at the margin, and in countries with strict price controls I have found that companies also tend to ignore this fact, and forget the adage that there are lies, damned lies, and averages. Certainly the Shell Argentina that I joined in October 1955 had long since forgotten it.

There were in fact two Shell Group companies: Shell Argentina which did the distribution and marketing, and Diadema Argentina which produced oil in Comodoro Rivadavia in Patagonia, and refined it in a big plant in the Dock Sud industrial suburb of Buenos Aires. One similarity with Shell Cuba was that the chief executive of the two companies together was a national of the country. In that one respect only were the two men similar: Julio was, and at over eighty, still is, an entrepreneur; the late Enrique Puricelli was a Byzantine bureaucrat, who had become top man through the genius the Shell Group had at that time of acting on the Peter Principle, 'discovered' by

Dr Laurence J. Peter, which states that most people get promoted to their level of incompetence. Puricelli had a good range of contacts in business and official circles, and he had been a successful salesman of heavy fuel oil to the very few big industrial customers, where personal contact was everything, but he had no talent for management.

Later on, when I got to know him fairly well, I used to urge him to delegate more to his senior people, but he simply didn't understand what the word meant; that you tell people what results you expect of them, give them the necessary resources and authority, let them get on with it, and judge them by their achievements. What he thought it meant became very clear one day. Two high level bankers from the UK were visiting, and Puricelli had them to a meeting in his office at which 'Dickie' Dijkstra, our treasurer, was present, and invited them to lunch afterwards. That afternoon he said to me, 'You're always asking me to delegate more, but how can I? I told Dijkstra to reserve a table for five at Harrods,[1] and when we got there the table was only for four. I just can't trust people to get things right; how can I delegate?'

In this case, the most likely explanation for the mistake was that Harrods had got it wrong.

But I'm jumping ahead. I should write something about our living conditions. In most countries Shell was still very paternalistic in its relations with its expatriate staff, who were expected to be available for transfer to any part of the world, and never to expect an assignment to the Central Offices in their home countries. Every job had attached to it a range of 'Group basic salaries' (GBS), expressed in sterling. And every individual had his or her own GBS, which would be adjusted within the range depending on seniority and, to some extent, performance. Since freedom

---

[1]Yes, there was a Harrods, with restaurant, in Buenos Aires!

of currency exchange was then more often the exception than the rule, part of one's GBS would be paid into a sterling bank account, so that you could use it for school fees, or to save, without it being exposed to the income tax of the country you worked in. Each operating company then had a system for converting GBS into a local salary, which in theory would give you a standard of living equivalent to what your GBS would give you in the UK. In countries (like Argentina) with rapid inflation this was not easy. People who had lived there for several years could have bought a car, or even a house with pesos worth ten – or fifty – of current ones. No expatriate could embark on buying either, and rents were high. So we paid a percentage of our GBS for housing, and the company rented for us a house suitable to our standing in the company hierarchy. This of course did not always work out very fairly; friendship and 'because thou art importunate' coupled with patience in searching the market could land you a better house, while impatience to get out of a hotel and get your children into a garden might mean you had to settle for second-best.

Local circumstances, too, could affect what local salaries could be, and local management could introduce significant distortions. During my five years in Argentina, for example, local salaries were adjusted to bring them into a supposedly 'correct' relationship with GBSs on 1st February, 1956. In the next four years my GBS increased to 172% of what it had been at the start: the index of the value of my net after-tax take-home pay – my standard of living – had risen early in the period to 110%, and then sank to 88%, so I was getting scarcely half of what the theory should have produced. And, of course, I was not alone: every expatriate was feeling the same pain, resentment was growing. Our Distribution Manager, Bill Stanton, was perhaps the only lucky one. He had come to us from Venezuela, where salaries were very high, and where everyone had to be paid a substantial bonus on leaving. Bill's earnings on his Venezuelan separation payment exceeded his total pay in Argentina. By that time I was one of the two most senior expatriates, so I took the issue to Puricelli. (The percentages I have quoted above are direct from a graph I prepared to show the situation to him, which I still keep – and it still rankles!) His answer was a flat refusal, on the grounds that 'I can't pay my staff more than judges get.'

And, though I was very tempted, I couldn't insult the nation by saying, 'But don't judges have *other* sources of income?'

To begin with I didn't report direct to Puricelli; there was another layer of management between us, in the shape of Macnamara, the General Manager of marketing, whose job was to co-ordinate sales (my responsibility) and Bernard Glover's bailiwick of operations – distribution and engineering. Macnamara, a bachelor, was reputed to be a championship-level bridge player, but as a manager he was hopeless. To begin with, his Spanish was rudimentary, so he could never take up an issue with, for example, his opposite number in YPF. He agonised over the simplest of decisions, and one spent endless hours in his office explaining and arguing, and going over the same ground several times. But he soon began to leave me to get on with things, as long as I observed the formalities of telling him what I was intending that the sales organisation should do, and reporting what it had in fact done.

His heavy and insensitive hand, not to say almost total lack of understanding of the job, was, I am sure, one factor in my developing a bad duodenal ulcer. My doctor, who became a good friend, Juan Jaime O'Farrell, made me stay at home and rest, ten hours a day minimum in bed, for two weeks, followed by two more working half time, on a rigid diet of small, bland meals at three-hour intervals, and a list of prohibitions which began: 'No: smoking, alcohol, tea, coffee… sossidges [*sic*]…' and continued for lines more.

The first major decision I faced concerned a service station in the far north of the country, with a below-average sales volume. YPF was dangling some incentive under the nose of the owner-operator of this station, who was trying to get us to give him a better deal. I got all the relevant individual figures for this bit of business (and I had to keep insisting that averages wouldn't do), and it became very clear that we lost money on every litre we sold there: the real cost of delivering the product a thousand kilometres from our refinery swallowed up all our retención and more, so I said to my group of people, 'Let YPF have it; we'll be better off.' It was heresy, but they couldn't deny the figures, so we went to Macnamara, and then to Puricelli, both of whom argued for not losing a litre of sales volume, and took a lot of convincing that surely we weren't in business to lose money knowingly. But finally and reluctantly they agreed, and we undertook to recover the lost few thousand litres a month by upgrading a station much closer to home.

This gave me the opportunity to start getting figures that were not just averages, over the resistance of Bobby James, Manager of Marketing Service and provider of our information. Bobby was an Anglo-Argentine, who probably owed his job more to his bilingualism than his intellect, was due to retire fairly soon and did not want to be made to disturb the even tenor of his ways in his last months. But the younger people saw that the move made sense, and began to look enthusiastically for other opportunities. As for YPF, they were delighted; they didn't have any financial discipline, and the more volume they sold, the merrier.

The *retenciónes* pricing system applied only to main petroleum products, and we had three other businesses which were very profitable: household and agricultural products, and bitumen. The first included paint solvent, also used for home dry-cleaning, domestic spray insecticide and lubricating oil, and mosquito spirals, made of sawdust, pyrethrin extract, saltpetre and wax. These you stood on a tinplate stand and lit. They burned for several hours and the smoke they gave off not only scared off mosquitoes, but actually killed them, so they made evening entertaining in the garden possible. We made pyrethrin-based insecticides for agriculture too, and two grades of herbicide, sheep-dip soap, and a coloured wax coating for oranges, which increased their shelf-life and greatly enhanced their appearance. Bitumen's big market was for roads, where prices were very competitive and margins low, but preservative paints for fence posts, roofing felt and caulking for boats helped make money.

After a little over six months in my job of Sales Manager, Macnamara left, and I took his place. By this time my team was in pretty good shape, we were getting management information which gave us a basis for setting our goals, and the means to monitor our performance. I kept records of my own of the more important numbers, in a small zipper-closed loose-leaf leather folder, which I still have and has served many other purposes. Each goal was set out in the form of a Z-graph, with the targets in ink and the actuals in pencil. The bottom line showed (in litres or in money) the target month by month: the diagonal slope was the year-to-date cumulative figure, and the top line a moving twelve-month total.

Although the cost of supplying distant service stations was a constant preoccupation, we began to be inquisitive about other things, and people began coming up with all sorts of ideas, like getting back-haul loads of industrial alcohol from the wine-growing regions of the west in the trucks that had delivered petrol, and using one tractor to haul three trailers; the flat terrain made this feasible in a large part of the country. So when we had a visit from

Arnold Hofland, one of the Dutch Managing Directors of the Group, we had much to show him. Hofland, who distinguished himself in World War II when he was in charge of fuel supplies to the advancing Allied armies in Europe, was notorious for being a persistent and rigorous asker of questions. Even Puricelli, not normally known for his humour, said in a management meeting, 'That's not a man; that's a machine-gun!'

He had a number of ratios that he used as litmus tests for the efficiency of a marketing company; kilometres run per cubic metre delivered; monthly sales per pump; how many times is a product handled between source and destination, and so on. As a first approximation, many of his ratios were useful yardsticks, but he tended to forget the essential qualification to all such tools: *'All other things being equal'*.

We had a large service station at a busy crossroads about five hundred kilometres west of Buenos Aires, which we had traditionally supplied by a five thousand-litre truck from a rail-fed bulk plant in the same town, and about two kilometres from the station. So Hofland's ratio was 2:5, or 0.4. The rail service was deteriorating, and the freight rate was always going up – the railways thought they had a monopoly – so we switched to direct truck delivery in our three-trailer trucks from Dock Sud, making Hofland's ratio 500:25 or 20. When he saw these figures in my loose-leaf he almost exploded, until I showed him the cost figures, the pesos per cubic metre from refinery to point of sale. He must have been satisfied, because in the next couple of months I got requests from the marketing managers of two or three other marketing companies for details of my system, because they had been told by Hofland that they 'should have the same kind of management information as Ritchie has.'

Though our marketing in general got good marks from

him, Hofland's visit was a disaster in another way. Most of the homes in the better residential suburbs of Buenos Aires had swimming pools, so many of our expatriates enjoyed this amenity. Hofland got to know about this, and told Puricelli that our staff should not have swimming pools. Obviously we did not throw people out of the houses they had, but we were not allowed to rent houses with them for new arrivals. This stupid restriction, together with the salary squeeze and the impossibility of affording a car that I have referred to earlier made Argentina a far from popular posting. It was another case of ignoring the inequality of other things, and should never have happened. But the culture of the Dutch-managed companies of the Group was much more stratified than that of those managed from London. My very good friend Frank McFadzean (later Sir Frank, and then Lord) was sent as Chief Executive of the Group's operations in Indonesia when the Dutch, the ex-colonialists, became *personae non gratae* after independence. He found in his house a list of all the expatriate employees divided according to the drinks they might order at company affairs. A very few at the top could order anything they wanted; the next tranche might order Dutch gin or beer, and the remaining majority – nothing but beer.

But a worse story still is of a fairly junior Dutch employee who was waiting to be repatriated, but got very sick, and was in bed in his home; all the expatriates lived in Company-owned, built and furnished housing. One day the (Dutch) head of Personnel went in to visit this poor man, and sat down on his bed. Suddenly, he leaned over and squeezed the mattress, and said, 'This is a foam rubber mattress! You're only job group four; you're not entitled to a rubber mattress!' and left. Five minutes later two employees arrived with the mattress which corresponded to his grade, lifted him out of bed, took away the rubber mattress, and replaced it with a straw one! Of course

Puricelli should have stood up to Hofland, but he was overawed by rank, and didn't have the self-confidence to argue.

This form of micro-management from the centre was, happily, on its last legs. Sir Henri Deterding, Chairman of Royal Dutch in the early years of the century and architect of the Royal Dutch/Shell Group,[2] was said to have boasted that he knew the whereabouts of every barrel of kerosene in the system, and things changed slowly, though the number of people involved grew. John Loudon, son of Hugo Loudon who succeeded Deterding as head of Royal Dutch, had become a managing director of the Group by the time I joined, and by the mid-Fifties he was in effect the Chief Executive. John, who had been the President of Shell Venezuela (rapidly becoming the Group's major source of

---

[2]The founding of the Group is an interesting story. By the end of the nineteenth century, John D. Rockefeller had formed the Standard Oil Trust, which controlled eighty per cent of the US oil industry, and was trying to create a worldwide monopoly. He tried, first, to acquire Royal Dutch (Het Koninklijke Nederlandsche Maatschappij tot Exploitatie van Petroleum-bronnen in Nederlandse Indien – the Royal Dutch Company for the Exploitation of the Oil Wells in the Netherlands Indies, which was engaged in what its name implies) and then the Shell Transport and Trading Company. This company, again, was involved in what its name implies. It was founded by the Samuel family to import seashells from Asia for the decoration of boxes, mirrors and picture frames which were hugely popular in the later years of Queen Victoria, but then developed a counterflow of packed kerosene to Asia: 'oil for the lamps of China'. Both companies repulsed Rockefeller, but realised that they would be a much stronger competitor if they joined forces, adding Shell's markets to Royal Dutch's production. They agreed to put their assets together into a joint enterprise to be owned fifty-fifty, but before the details could be worked out, personal ambition got in the way. Marcus Samuel decided he wanted to be the first Jewish lord mayor of London, and spent a year lobbying for, and then a year in the post. When his term as lord mayor was over, he went back to Deterding, who told him their deal was off, and Samuel had to accept a combination of assets in which Royal Dutch would have a sixty per cent interest, leaving only forty per cent for Shell.

crude oil) and so had lived at the receiving end of centralised management, came to the conclusion that the thing was becoming too big for this. So, in 1952 he commissioned McKinsey and Co., the most highly regarded of US management consultants, to carry out a major study and devise a new management structure for the Group. The core of McKinsey's recommendations, which were implemented in 1959, was that operating companies should manage themselves, subject to the Group having control of the provision of finance, the supply of crude oil and products, and the right to appoint the senior executives of the operating companies, all to be based on a business plan produced by the companies, and *co-ordinated* but not *managed* by the *central* (no longer *head)* offices. These principles evolved over the years as circumstances in the world oil industry changed, but in essence they lasted until 1995.

Chapter Thirty-Five

Remarriage, and more Argentina

While I was in Cuba, Billie and I had fallen in love, but before I left we accepted that I was married, my duty was with my family, and therefore we would never see one another again. However, my marriage had, over the years, slowly and almost imperceptibly become less and less happy, and after half a year in Argentina I felt I could stand it no longer, and wrote to Billie to ask her whether, if I could arrange a divorce, she would marry me.

Then, in early 1957, as I was beginning to recover from my bad duodenal ulcer, I got the news that I was to be a member of the next 'European General Managers' Program' with Shell Oil in the United States. This was a learning exercise, not unmixed with fun, for senior marketing executives of the non-American companies of the Group to spend six weeks seeing Shell Oil's operations, and learning about the market – the biggest petroleum market in the world by a large margin, and one in which, unlike most of the rest of the world, the market was almost free, and where restrictions were in the main designed to restrain anti-competitive behaviour. Most exciting, though, was the fact that this programme was reserved for people who were expected to go higher in the Group. At the end of these six weeks, Len Abrahamse, Marketing Manager of

Shell Brasil, who was one of the group, paid me a compliment I never forget. 'During all this time, Jock has never been at a loss for a joke – and he never repeated *one*.' My brain sometimes seems to be a storage device for jokes; I have forgotten very few of any that I have ever heard, and can often remember who told me, and where. If only I had been able to use that faculty for more useful things, who knows what I might have achieved?

This programme would keep me away from Buenos Aires from April until July, and I asked Phyllis to go back to England, taking Sarah with her, and told her that I wanted to get a divorce to end our marriage. With the help of a lawyer friend in Buenos Aires I did, and eventually Billie and I were married.

After the end of the Shell Oil programme I went back to Argentina alone, while Billie stayed in Cuba until I was due for my home leave in September. We came back to Buenos Aires by sea, on the RMS *Alcantara*. It was an uneventful trip, except that we won the first prizes for hats representing songs, and that Billie, who wore her hair drawn back into a bun, stuck a rose in it when the Captain invited us to his table for dinner. Among his guests were a Spanish-speaking couple with whom we spoke the occasional sentence or two in Spanish. From these two facts the Captain deduced that Billie must *be* Spanish, and insisted, for the rest of the trip, in speaking to her in that language, of which his command was far from perfect.

The next two years were fairly hectic, but I was helped greatly by the addition of two people to my team. Argentine engineers spent far too much of their time polishing their chairs with the seats of their trousers, and I needed men who would go to where their skills were needed, and since much of our hardware was old, or made in Argentina or both, our maintenance load was heavy. I had come to know well in Cuba a young engineer who had the get-up-and-go mentality that I felt we needed, and Puricelli agreed that we could ask Central Office if Shell Cuba would be prepared to release him for a year or two in Argentina, and I wrote to Julio to make the plea personal. It was agreed, and in early 1958 Nicolás (Nick) Colás joined us, bringing his new wife, Elisa, whom neither Billie nor I had met, with him. He did wonders for the Engineering Department, not without ruffling some feathers, and I felt a little like George III, when they told him that General Wolfe was mad. 'Mad, is he? Then I wish he would bite some of my other generals!' Nick and Elisa became very close friends, and Elisa remains one. Nick, alas, died of brain cancer five years or so ago.

The other came unsought. We received a cable from London asking us to take, to work with me, a man who had joined the Group after serving with the UN Headquarters in New York. A South African, PhD in economics, with a French wife who spoke Spanish, at thirty-six Geoffrey Lumsden was much older than the usual recruit to the Group. He became very valuable to our organisation, because he combines a fine intellect with a real sense of the practical. Geoff and his wife Yvette also became, and remain, very close friends.

Nick proved his worth very early in his time with us. In April 1958 the Uruguay River flooded to an incredible extent. It reached fifty kilometres in width, and inundated two of our bulk storage plants, at Concepción del Uruguay, two hundred and fifty kilometres and Concordia, three hundred and fifty kilometres upstream from Buenos Aires, this latter to a depth of three metres. This plant was surrounded by a chain link wire fence two and a half metres high. All our two hundred-litre drums of lubricating oil floated away from their storage pads; many of them cleared the fence and went sailing downstream, where some of them were recovered a couple of weeks later in the branches of trees. Most of the product tanks were fairly full so that they remained on their bases, except for that holding aviation fuel which floated off its base, but remained anchored by its pipeline, which by a miracle bent, but neither the pipe, nor (which would have been much worse) the valve on the tank fractured. It would have been a horrifying fire hazard to have had a layer of ninety-eight octane aviation gasoline going downstream.

Somehow, we had sporadic telephone contact with Concordia, and as soon as the rain stopped and there was a means of getting there, Nick and I went to see the damage, and start planning to restore operations. The little company plane took us to the nearest airstrip that was usable, and from there we reached the plant by truck and boat. It was an incredible sight: floating oil drums were packed against the fence on the downstream side, and outside the fence was the locomotive that hauled products away by rail. All you could see of it was the top half of its boiler and its cab, looking very forlorn as a little island in the flood. The flood marks round this locomotive, the tanks and buildings showed that the water level was going down, so we decided to stay overnight and leave until the next day a more complete survey of the damage. Nick, however, decided that the aviation fuel tank could not wait, but had to be moved back in place while it was still afloat, and he got to work with all the people there to attach ropes to the tank, and at least get it inside its bund,[1] where it could eventually be got back into its exact place by being emptied so that it floated on the water contained by the bund, then lowered by draining out the water.

By next morning the wheels of the locomotive were visible, and the flood was receding rapidly. So, after a

---

[1]The circle of earth embankment around the tank which would hold all its contents if it leaked.

conference with Nick, the Plant Manager and his assistants, I decided to go back and leave them to it. In the end, our losses were minimal: a dozen or so oil drums were never found, but of the aviation fuel, which was transferred to other tanks while its own was relocated, we lost no more than a few litres, and it was totally uncontaminated by water. As I flew back to the south, the Uruguay in some spots still stretched from horizon to horizon.

This flood affected us personally, too. Julia Garcia (the sister of Elba, our maid) who came to our house and did our ironing, had been working to save some of her family's things, and then gave birth, prematurely, to her first child. She and her baby were taken to the little local hospital, and the baby, Marcelito, was put in the only incubator, clinging desperately to life. A few days later, another premature baby was born, and the hospital's triage system decided that this baby had a better chance of survival than Marcelito, who would have to be taken out of the incubator. By chance Billie was visiting Julia in the hospital when they broke the news to her that she would just have to let her baby die. Billie said no, she wouldn't let that happen. She had my car and driver outside and, having got the doctors to tell her that the baby would have to be kept at body temperature all the time to have a chance of life, she and Julia bundled up the baby and took him out to the car. They put the car heating up to full and drove home, put mother and child to bed in our guest room, turned the house central heating up to maximum, and added a portable kerosene heater in the room to get the temperature still higher. We spent an anxious night, but Marcelito was still alive in the morning.

The doctor came to see him the next day, and then every following day, to give him penicillin to protect against infection. The drug had to be injected into his bottom, which was a pitiful sight – just a fold of loose skin over his bones. Billie and I used to dread the doctor's morning visits, and waited at the bottom of the stairs, hoping, almost against hope, that her news would not be what we feared. But he lived, and gradually put on a little flesh; the doctor's visits became less frequent, and after three months in our do-it-yourself incubator, they were able to go home. Marcelito's only apparent permanent after-effect was poor eyesight, and Julia had three other healthy sons. Her husband developed Parkinson's disease, and became progressively more dependent on help. Then Julia was struck by cancer. She spent her last weeks, never complaining, teaching her sons how to cope with the household, and how to care for their father. She looked like a Spanish madonna, and was one of the noblest women we have ever met.

Julia's and Elba's widowed mother was another victim of the same flood; she lived on an island in the Tigre, the joint delta of the Paraguay and Uruguay rivers, and the beginning of the River Plate. On her little piece of land she kept a cow and chickens, and lived on the proceeds of the sale of their milk and eggs. Her house survived the waters, but cow and chickens were washed away. Billie and I bought her replacements for her livelihood: so cheap were cattle and poultry that this didn't cost us more than the equivalent of about twenty dollars. For as long as we lived in Buenos Aires we had a dozen fresh eggs for our breakfasts every week.

Geoffrey Lumsden took over from Bobby James the provision of our management information, and very quickly we got what we needed, not only routinely but whenever Geoffrey spotted some problem that needed study before it could be fixed. Hugh Dawson had taken my place as Sales Manager, and took care of retail (service stations) heating oil and heavy (industrial) fuel oil, bitumen, chemicals, agriculture and lubricants. Bernard Glover was Operations Manager, with distribution, shipping and engineering as his responsibility. I was the final policy-maker for, and co-ordinator of, the whole, and Geoffrey was my right hand. By mid-1958 we all had become a genuine team, working closely together in pretty good harmony.

The bureaucratic part of my job was immensely eased by my secretary, Ruby Francis. Very capable, unflappable, willing to do anything, she was none the less a very sad person. She had been in the company since she was sixteen, and those who knew her then said she had been beautiful. But she got a severe case of acne, and went to a quack for a cure. He left her face covered with craters, as though she had had smallpox, and Ruby dropped out of the world – except for her job, into which she poured all her energy, and her considerable intelligence and common sense. She lived in a house of her own, accompanied by an aunt, and as far as anyone knew, never went out socially, though she did come to lunch with Billie and me a couple of times.

Of course things don't always go smoothly. In our terminal at Dock Sud alongside the Diadema refinery we loaded and dispatched something like three hundred tank lorries every day, of which a comparatively small number were our own, almost entirely dedicated to petrol, while the great majority were contractors. All were required to have spark-protected electric starters. They were filled underneath a gantry, through articulated filling arms, lowered into the open manhole in the top, to just short of the bottom of the tank. Lorries (except the very smallest) were divided into compartments so that they could carry more than one grade of product, or could deliver to different customers. So when one compartment was filled, the valve to the articulated arm was closed, the arm withdrawn, the cover closed, and the lorry moved on to allow the arm into the next compartment. One morning, a lorry started to move before the arm was withdrawn, and the twist on the arm broke a weld on the supply pipe on the gantry. The crack in the weld sent a horizontal fan-shaped spray of petrol over the gantry and the neighbouring lorries. Most drivers had the sense to jump out and run clear. But one idiot pressed his starter button. His starter was not spark-proof, and set the whole thing on fire. In the blaze, which lasted a matter of tens of seconds before the supply was cut off, four men were killed, and a dozen or more trucks destroyed, some of which went on burning for a long time after the main fire was put out.

Bernard Glover, Bill Stanton and I all went to Dock Sud, where the police, the ambulance service and the trade union were all needing attention, and where we had to get the distribution system back to work again, albeit on a very reduced scale to begin with. It was evening before I got home, had some supper and went thankfully to bed.

At 2 a.m. the telephone beside my bed rang; it was David Nul, our Lubricants Manager, but then doing a stint as Branch Manager in Córdoba. 'Jock,' he said, 'our bulk plant is on fire!' For a moment I thought this might be a joke in very bad taste, but David, hearing the tone of doubt in my voice, said, 'No. I'm serious. We had a terrorist attack on the plant. They cut through the fence and put one bomb on the main petrol tank, and then another on one of the upright tanks. The leaking petrol collected in the bund and caught fire there, so it's boiling the petrol in the tank, and the pressure has caused a fracture at the top of the tank out of which there's a giant jet of blazing vapour. This has set fire to at least one of the houses right outside the fence, and I'm afraid some people there may have been killed. I've informed all the authorities and some of them are here already. The Plant Manager's house [which was in the centre of the plant] hasn't even been scorched, and he and his family are safe.'

It was quite illegal to build anything within fifty metres

of the plant, but shanties just sprouted, many built by our employees, who wanted to live close to the job. But, although the land was ours, we could never get anyone to enforce this. I called Puricelli and told him what had happened, and that I would go as soon as I could get the plane in the morning. He told me I had better take Bruno Piekarski, the Polish-Austrian American citizen head of our Legal Department, with me. So I woke him up, and got hold of our pilot, and by daybreak we were on our way. When we got there the fire was out, but we had lost almost all the tanks and the product they had held. Many of the lubricating oil drums had their ends bellied out as a result of the oil expanding from the heat, and some – a surprising few – had burst and added fuel to the flames. The place was almost a total loss, except for the manager's house, which was surrounded by trees that, though scorched themselves, had acted as a firebreak. The shanties outside though had suffered. The jet of flame had skipped some of the stuff inside the plant, but seemed to have focused on the nearest of the shanties, and a teenage boy had been burned to death.

When the governor of the province of Córdoba heard that I was there, he sent for me to come to his office. He was known to be a left-winger, and was a singularly unattractive man. I saw him on three successive days, and on each he managed to have three days' growth of beard, and a shirt which had perhaps been clean a week ago. He took a very hectoring tone with me, and virtually blamed the foreign oil companies for encouraging terrorism by their very presence, and Shell for allowing the shanties to be built. I hadn't had much sleep the night before, and it took a great effort of self-control for me to count ten before answering him with sweet reasonableness. I expressed our sympathy to the family of the dead boy, and said that I hoped we would be able to count on his support to get the shanties removed to the legal distance to prevent any possible recurrence of the tragedy, and I promised that we would make alternative arrangements so that his province did not lack for supplies. He was quite clearly not prepared to show any sign of reason himself, and we parted politely, but coldly.

The next day the funeral of the young victim took place, and the governor set out to get political capital out of it. Reporters for the local radio station were there with recorders, and the local pressmen with their photographers. The hearse was drawn by six horses with huge nodding plumes of ostrich feathers, and the cortège halted alongside the little chapel just inside the cemetery gate, where Bruno and I and other Shell people waited. The open coffin was carried inside, and the victim's mother, sobbing loudly, was escorted in by the governor, who had neither shaved nor put on a clean shirt for the occasion.

After the brief service the mourners and the governor came out, and followed the coffin – still open – to the site of the tomb. After them came out the priest, who looked as if he had spent his life under a stone: plump and pasty-faced, with scarcely combed black hair, a yellowing surplice of Nottingham lace, and a pair of eyeglasses that had been repaired with insulating tape, but still failed to sit squarely on his nose, so that one lens was a centimetre higher than the other. When Bruno saw him he whispered to me, 'That is a caricature from *Krokodil.*'[2] The 'tomb' was a niche in a tall wall of honeycomb-like cells, each able to accommodate a coffin, which would be sealed with a concrete slab cemented in place, with a space left at the front. Many of these had little decorative brass or wood railings over the lower third of the space, behind which, in the recently occupied niches, were glass vases with flowers; some real,

---

[2]The well-known Russian satirical propaganda magazine.

most artificial. The whole structure stood about three metres high, and this corpse was to go into a space in the second row from the top.

Before the entombment, however, the open coffin was laid on two trestles for friends and relatives to have a last look. The governor beckoned me over, and I had a quick glance. It was a horrible sight; he must have been standing by an open window watching the fire, and been torched by the blast of flame from the top of the tank. His mother was howling, and if she showed signs of calming down, the governor stirred her up again, so that the radio recorders should have full coverage.

When this macabre part of the proceedings was over, the coffin was laid on the ground and its lid screwed on, and a telescopic tower made of steel pipe, on small wheels, was dragged into place in front of the niche. The coffin was put on the top platform of this tower, and the two scruffy undertaker's men started to wind the winch, and the tower unsteadily raised itself to the height of the niche – unsteadily, because its base was no more than two metres by one and a half metres, and the ground was gravel. The two men then climbed up the sides of the tower, and tried to slide the coffin into its niche. But it wouldn't move; from its rest on the ground some bits of gravel had got stuck to its bottom and impeded the sliding. In their struggle to move it, they almost tipped over the whole tower, and the mourners scattered out of the way. The poor mother's howling got louder and louder, and the governor made sure that the radio station had it well and truly recorded. At long last, by dint of one man standing on the opening of three niches down and grabbing the railing of another they finally got it to move, and manoeuvred it into its place, not without a couple more near topples of the tower. The closing slab was cemented in, and a vase of flowers from the family placed on the little shelf. We all walked away; as we left the cemetery Bruno took my elbow and said, in the gloomy voice that was his trademark,[3] 'Well, I've seen it. And I still don't believe it!'

The Shell Group had introduced in most of the countries in which it operated a new formulation of automotive lubricating oil, with the brand name X-100. This was our first multi-grade oil and it had a number of other characteristics which made it a real advance in quality. We blended most of our lubricants, and decided that we could blend X-100 too. So we planned to launch it on to our market with a big splash. In one of our meetings we were lamenting that if only we could offer it in one-litre cans we would have a real winner. But Argentine regulations forbade the use of tinplate for containers for petroleum products smaller than five litres, so our service stations were obliged to use big drums and messy measuring jugs for oil fill-ups. A couple of days later Bernard Glover came to me and told me that there was no restriction on using sheet steel, untinned, for this purpose, and it could be enamel printed on the outside, and lined with epoxy resin. Moreover he had found a company that could make the necessary filling-machines in time for us to fill our initial requirement of cans, and keep us going. We all agreed we should do this, and swore ourselves to secrecy so that we could take our competitors by surprise.

We planned to hold three meetings of our dealers to introduce X-100 to them. We designed their general content and format, and I asked the managers concerned to write up their speeches, for a rehearsal the following week. This was a disaster. Bureaucrat-speak in Argentine Spanish is one of the worst of the breed, based on the principles that you never use the common word for anything if you can

---

[3]After a well-known Austrian song of the time, his nickname was 'Gloomy Sunday – and also Monday to Saturday'.

elaborate, and always use polysyllables as long as possible. My two favourites are for the police: 'Our institution, guardian of the public order.' And for the dustmen: 'The corps of re-collectors of domestic residues', and some of the prepared speeches of my managers were as bad as this. I said it would be boring to the point of soporific, and quite unworthy of the first new product introduction in Shell Argentina for decades. I quickly found that we had a Dale Carnegie Institute ('How to win friends and influence people') in Buenos Aires, which offered a course in public speaking, and over some reluctance I set it up for all those who would have to speak – and I would be the first student. Most of the managers were opposed to this exercise, particularly as we had to have it outside working hours. But Dale Carnegie knew their business, the leader we got was excellent, and by the end of the first evening, everyone was enjoying the fun – for fun it was. And the enthusiasm level was very high.

Once the course was over I asked them all to redo their speeches, and come up with ideas for practical demonstrations of the oil's quality, its adhesion to metal in the presence of steam and smoke, its ability to maintain its viscosity with little variation over a wide range of temperatures and so on, all compared to the old specification oils. We had one final rehearsal, at which all agreed that we had put together a good show. The highlight was in the final part of the presentation, on our proposed pricing, which went: 'In two hundred-litre drums, so much: in five-litre cans, so much – pause – and in *one-litre cans*,' at which words ten or a dozen empty cans were thrown into our audience 'so much.' This was greeted in all three meetings by loud cheering, which went on until we broke up for drinks and dinner. We had really succeeded in getting the dealers on our side, and keeping our competitors in the dark, and the sales results exceeded all our expectations.

The best grazing land in Argentina was subject to a plague, which in its worst years was little short of devastating, a short-flighted form of locust called *tucura.* Eggs are laid in the autumn, and hatched, in waves, in the spring, and the grown insects at a density of about five to the square metre can eat all the grass that grows on the land, leaving bare brown earth, and nothing for cattle. DDT and other insecticides were used, but the cost was too high for large areas to be protected, so cattle had to be driven sometimes hundreds of kilometres to uninfested areas. The insects however never fly more than one hundred metres from where they are born, so if you can clean up one place, you can at least greatly slow down the spread.

In the mid-Fifties the Shell Group had acquired the patents to a class of chlorinated hydrocarbon insecticides with the trade names Aldrin, Dieldrin and Endrin, and had built production facilities in the USA. These insecticides are persistent, and Dieldrin remains active for three months at a very low dosage rate. So they seemed to have promise of being a better anti-*tucura* weapon than others. There was a problem, however, in our trying to develop a market for them: DDT and some other products were manufactured in Argentina, which made the obtaining of import permits nearly impossible. However, we worked closely with the cattle-raisers' organisations, and in 1957 got a permit to import a few – memory suggests fifty – kilograms for a controlled test. So we arranged with an *estanciero* in a badly-affected region to do a test by marking out strips and treating alternate ones by air-spraying. The results were spectacular: treated strips produced a bright green crop of alfalfa, the others were eaten bare. This persuaded the Ministry of Agriculture to give us a permit for twenty tonnes in 1958. We had a difficult task allocating this quantity to customers, all of whom wanted it for their land.

This time we didn't leave test strips between the treated areas, but tried to get the available supply used where it would do most good.

The results were so impressive that we were given an import permit for one thousand tonnes for 1959. Dieldrin itself had to be dissolved in aromatic[4] hydrocarbons to be turned into a usable, transportable product. The common aromatics, benzene, toluene and xylene were expensive in Argentina, and anyway would have to be imported, if we could have got permits. But the chief technologist in Diadema's refinery came to our rescue and produced, in sufficient quantity, an aromatic out of the process of refining lubricants.

To have the maximum effect, the whole quantity would have to be applied in a three- or four-week period in September and October, so a great deal of planning was needed. First, the Dieldrin had to be dissolved and packed in two-hundred litre drums – five thousand of them. To be applied further dilution in a sprayable liquid was required. We needed the aircraft and the pilots; the diluent and the aviation fuel had to be transported to where planes would operate, and that meant airstrips. Many *estancias* had these, in various states of usability. We learned our lesson with X-100, and we repeated the process of meetings, with the owners of the agricultural spraying companies, and of the *estancias* which would be treated, the latter being our customers, and the employers of the planes that would do the work. In the end we organised three hundred airstrips, and distributed to them the Dieldrin solution, the diluent and the fuel. So powerful was Dieldrin that only fifty grams or so were needed per hectare, which meant that we had enough capacity to spray a third of the area of the Pampas.

---

[4]Hydrocarbons with their carbon atoms arranged in rings. They are usually good solvents.

It was hectic, and exciting; we had enthusiastic support from the *estancieros* and the air companies, and the weather did not interfere. And above all, it succeeded: as far as we were aware not a single animal had to be moved to 'pastures new'.

Four tailpieces to this story: not once did Puricelli attend one of our meetings or come to see what we were doing.

The London office now had separate co-ordinators for oil and chemicals: in Shell Argentina both were sold through my organisation, but we were required to report our sales separately: Diadema, until 1959, used to produce twenty thousand tonnes per year of petroleum coke, classified for reporting purposes as a chemical, the major market for which was as domestic fuel, a rival to firewood. As such its price was very low. So when we reported our sales for the year, chemical *volume* was down by the difference between twenty thousand tonnes of coke and one thousand tonnes of Dieldrin, and we got a very sharply worded letter from London, the last gasp of micro-management from the centre, demanding an explanation for this decline. We wrote back (and I hope kept the tone more sorrow than anger) explaining the volume difference, but drawing their attention to the enormous increase in *sales proceeds.*

So successful had this effort been, that Dieldrin sales in 1960 were tiny. And finally, Dieldrin, and all the other chlorinated hydrocarbon insecticides fell victims to emotion generated by the pseudo-science of Rachel Carson's *Silent Spring*, and the world has been deprived of an incredibly valuable resource for public health and cheaper food.

*

In the first days of May 1959 I was in my office, working on the annual appraisals of the department managers under me. I had a persistent dull headache, and felt no enthusiasm for my task. I had all their personal files on my desk, and some papers recording their performance, a blank appraisal form for each and a pencil. I'd been at the job for maybe two hours, and was getting very depressed at my inability to get much done. Suddenly, I wanted to write something but couldn't find my pencil. I knew it was on my desk, under one of the opened files, but I could not summon up the will to look. I folded my arms on the papers, buried my face in them, and burst into tears of frustration. I decided I wanted to end it all by jumping out of the window, but simply could not summon up the energy to get up and walk across the room.

How long I lay here I have no idea, except that the top file was pretty wet. Suddenly Ruby walked in and said, 'Mr Ritchie, what *is* the matter?'

I told her I had no idea, except that I felt awful. Somehow Ruby got me down to my car and sent me home, and arranged for Dr O'Farrell to go there and see me. He at once suspected hepatitis – there was an outbreak of it in Buenos Aires at the time – but he couldn't see any of the tell-tale yellow in the whites of my eyes or anywhere else, so he took a urine sample, gave me a sedative and told Billie just to let me sleep, but make me drink water.

I slept all night and all the next morning, which was Billie's birthday, and woke up feeling not so suicidal. About midday I told Billie I thought I could drink a cup of tea. She brought it up to me, and when I had drunk it I said I'd like a cigarette (though I had given up on O'Farrell's orders for curing ulcers, I had started again – too many people around me smoked). Billie brought me a package of cigarettes, matches and an ashtray. I put a cigarette in my mouth and lit it. It tasted *so* disgusting that I stubbed it out in the ashtray straight away. Even so, the smell of the ashtray was awful, and I asked Billie to take it away. Even then the smell of the open package was more than I could stand, and Billie had to take away that, too. After three weeks I was well enough to go back to work, and when I came home in the evening, I hugged Billie (who still smoked) and said to her, 'You really *stink* of smoke!' She has not smoked since that day, and for years I couldn't see anyone lighting a cigarette without remembering that dreadful taste. There is a Spanish saying: '*No hay mal que por bien no venga* – 'There's no bad that doesn't come for good.' Neither of us has smoked since, though it was not until thirty years later, that, in the course of a check-up at the Mayo Clinic, I learned that a not uncommon side effect of hepatitis is an aversion to tobacco: so the credit for my giving up is not mine!

Chapter Thirty-Six

Break with Puricelli

Most of the lorries in which we delivered petrol to our stations were our own, their drivers on our payroll and members of the trade union. We kept scrupulous records of the efficiency of our own compared to contract transport: we could not contemplate shifting from one to the other because of agreements with the union, who still managed to maintain protection from the government as if Perón and Evita had still been there, but we kept trying to negotiate with the union the right to install time and distance recorders on the front wheels of our lorries, but could never get agreement, on the grounds that it was equivalent to spying on our drivers who, of course, would never waste a minute of their employer's time!

Then, about three o'clock one morning, we were advised by the police that our truck, number so-and-so, had been found abandoned, having run into the railing on the side of the Avellaneda Bridge, which joins the city of Buenos Aires to the industrial suburb of Avellaneda across the Matanza River. It had left the loading gantry in the early afternoon for a delivery that should have taken five hours at the most. The driver did not put in an appearance that day, but we got signed statements from witnesses who had been drinking with him in a bar in Avellaneda in the afternoon and evening, and who had seen the lorry parked outside the bar until about 10 p.m. Puricelli was away on vacation with his wife in a remote place in the south where there was no telephone. Harry Pickett, General Manager of Diadema and next in seniority to Puricelli, was out of the country, so I had no one to take a decision off my shoulders. I consulted the lawyers, our own and our outside counsel, the personnel people, especially Eric Kerr, head of industrial relations, and himself a lawyer, and all my own people concerned, from Bernard Glover on down. We agreed that we had a cast-iron case to dismiss the driver (which we did, without much protest from the union) and the opportunity to get recorders installed. We were fortified in our resolve by the fact that only the previous week the government had begun to take a tough line on worker discipline, and had in fact dismissed some government employees.

Two days later Puricelli came back, and I told him what we had done. He sent for all the people I had consulted, who unanimously confirmed my view that we had done right. He then sent them out of the room, and said to me, 'I accept your decision – but not its consequences.' I argued with him that you cannot separate a decision from its consequences, but he repeated what he had said, and then said, 'Ritchie, I know what you want: you want my job.' I assured him I had no such ambition, and again urged him to change his mind, to no avail. I got all the people who had supported me together, and told them of Puricelli's decision. Eric Kerr (who despite his Scots name was Chilean) burst out, 'That Florentine bastard!' I said that I would resign, and four other people said that if I did, they would too, until Eric, who saw we were all in earnest, begged me not to go and take four others with me, and I cooled down, and agreed to stay. Shortly afterwards, in January 1960, I went on my home leave, and returned in April, only to have my replacement named. I left Argentina on 1st June, before he arrived – Puricelli would not allow an overlap.

I saw Puricelli only once more. Monroe ('Monty') Spaght had been President of Shell Oil Company, and had become a managing director of the Group. Among his areas of special interest and responsibility were the companies in the western hemisphere, and some years later, soon after I became President of Shell Brasil, Monty visited Argentina, and invited the Chief Executives of the larger Shell Companies in South America to meet him in Buenos Aires for short tête-à-tête meetings. On his first night there he gave a small cocktail party in his hotel. Billie and I were in the crowd, and the Puricellis were behind us. Diana, Enrique's wife, suddenly saw us, and said, 'Enrique, look who's here: the Ritchies!' Enrique turned round, caught my eye, and ostentatiously turned his back.

Before leaving Argentina, I should tell something of its cultural joys. The Colón Opera House, one of the great ones of the world, had been used by Perón for political rallies, and had not heard a note of music for almost a decade. But in 1958 we had the great privilege of being at reopening night, with *Aïda*. It was a fine performance, except for one hilarious glitch. The non-singing extras had clearly not had enough rehearsal time, and when the Grand March was due, they were standing in lines, one each side of the stage, with their papier mâché trumpets resting on their toes. When the real trumpets started their *tu-tu-tu-tuu*, one papier mâché one was raised smartly to the horizontal. But seeing himself alone, this man lowered his trumpet, just as some others, started – hesitatingly – to raise theirs, and we had trumpets waving up and down all over, until a stentorian voice from the wings yelled out, '*Arriba! Arriba!*' ('Up! Up!')

We enjoyed many more operas, concerts and ballets at the Colón; tickets to begin with were absurdly cheap, before people began to get used to the idea that Perón had gone, so that opera goers were no longer by definition plutocrats, and thus, per se, enemies of the people. We had a short ballet season with the great Cuban ballerina, Alicia Alonso, with her partner Igor Youskevitch. Alicia was a close acquaintance of Billie's from Havana, and after one performance we asked the two of them for dinner. Billie went backstage and helped rub down Alicia, while I waited in the car by the stage door. After what seemed like an age, but was probably half an hour, Billie came out supporting Alicia by one arm, while Igor held the other. She got into the back of the car, lay back and shut her eyes. I looked at her in the mirror every time we stopped in the traffic, and she never stirred. I had the awful feeling that she had died, or was going to die, in the back of my car. But when we arrived at the door of the restaurant, which was upstairs, she suddenly came to life and scampered up the steps like a cat. She and Igor both ate very hearty meals, and we ordered profiteroles with whipped cream – Alicia's favourite – as our sweet. As she tucked into them, Igor said, 'Hey! Go easy! Remember I have to lift you and catch you, and I don't want any more weight!' Alicia smiled at him, called over the waiter, and ordered a second helping, saying, 'That'll teach you!'

In the summer there were open-air performances, too, in La Boca, the traditional port district of Buenos Aires. There was one pedestrian street, El Caminito, in which all the houses were painted in bright colours, and had lines of equally bright-coloured washing hanging from their balconies. The street was closed by rows of seats with a stage facing them. Simple props, and doors and balconies of the houses alongside provided the staging for brilliant performances of Shakespeare, Molière and other great classics. No absolute ruler can resist the temptation to humble or get rid of groups of people who somehow seem a threat to him, or his ideology, and alas, actors, writers, musicians and those with ideas usually seem to be among them. Franco, in Spain, was no exception, and droves of the artistic and intelligent emigrated, and enormously enriched Argentina.

As well as El Caminito there was a large, wooden-benched amphitheatre for music, including opera. We used to go there with a couple of close friends, Rodolfo and Bobbie Muñoz. Rudi (a career diplomat, and never remotely Peronista by ideology) had been foreign minister of Argentina under Perón, after serving as Argentine ambassador to the United Nations, and was President of the General Assembly in the year of Argentina's turn to hold that office. He had been a Prince of Wales's Scholar in England, and had married an English wife. With the fall of Perón, he was out, and Puricelli (who knew him) took him on as political affairs adviser to Shell Argentina, which is how we came to know him and Bobbie. Rudi was a great tease, while Bobbie was rather serious. In this theatre the four of us attended a performance of Pagliacci and Cavalleria Rusticana, and when the performance ended and the applause started Rudi, clapping enthusiastically, said, in Spanish, and in a voice loud enough to be heard by a dozen neighbours, 'Didn't Tosca sing superbly?'

Bobbie hissed loudly, 'Oh! Rudi, that wasn't Tosca!'

'Oh, wasn't it? What was it then?' Bobbie suddenly realised that he was teasing her, and kissed him.

All these things, as well as food, wine, clothes, household expenses generally and most things manufactured in the country, were very cheap in Argentina, while imports were prohibitive, and accordingly highly regarded. There was a story of a man who had been on a vacation which included a visit to France, and was in a cafe with a group of friends. The conversation went like this:

'Oh! Pepe, Paris must be wonderful, eh?'

'No. The people are very uncivil, everything is very expensive. It's no great shakes.'

'But the wine?'

'It's no better than ours from Mendoza.'

'But didn't you go to Montmartre, to the Moulin Rouge? That really must be something!'

'Yes. we went to the Moulin Rouge, and do you know, even *there* the champagne wasn't imported!'

Chapter Thirty-Seven

Central Offices – London

When I reported to the London office on my arrival, it was made clear to me that I had some mud on my face because of my falling-out with Puricelli. I told my side of the story ('I accept your decision – but not its consequences') and clearly got some sympathy, but Puricelli outranked me, and that was that. So I set out to make the best of whatever job I was put into. And we had to find somewhere to live. We were not well off: two-fifths of my salary went to Phyllis as maintenance, Jeanie was at the Sorbonne in Paris and Sarah was at a boarding school in the Isle of Wight. We found an affordable flat in Richmond, which, though hideous on the outside, was comfortable (after we had put in a lot of work) and Billie made it very attractive inside. Before we left Buenos Aires, she said to me, out of thin air, 'I know how we'll do our flat when we get to London. The soft furniture will be white, the hard, black or dark wood, and the curtains and carpet purple!'

I was horrified, and protested, but Billie was right. We bought a heavy purple Sanderson's fabric for curtains, purple and black tweed-type broadloom carpet from Cyril Lord, the big discount seller, furniture in off-white from G-Plan, we brought a black wrought-iron dining table and chairs from Argentina, and the completed effect was splendid. For two years we could not afford a car (though we rented one for occasional weekends) and it was a year before we really felt we could afford to go to the cinema. But we had Queenie, Billie's cocker spaniel, who took us for long walks in Richmond Park. We were very happy, and glad that Argentina was behind us.

The McKinsey structure of the Group had regional co-ordinators who were responsible to the Managing Directors for all the affairs of one of the regions: Europe, Western, Middle East, East and Australasia, while functional co-ordinators provided Group-wide support in their specialities: supply, planning, marketing, manufacturing and the like. Under the marketing co-ordinator, Pierre Escoffier, were specialists in the various facets of marketing, and a regional marketing co-ordinator for each of the regions, of which I became 'Caribbean, Central and South America'. Our jobs were to help the regional co-ordinator make the McKinsey principles work, by assisting operating companies to put together business plans that would justify the investment they were asking the Group for, by acting as a Group-wide ideas and techniques exchange, and by appraising the quality of their management. This involved a lot of travel, and in two years I visited at least once every market in my region (except one – Puricelli wouldn't have me!) in which Shell operated, and I believe we, the regional marketing co-ordinators, helped get more thought and logic into the process of deciding how much of the Group's available resources should be invested where. Too often the justification for building ten more service stations had been: 'To increase our share of this fast-growing, profitable market.' It was our job to ask the hard questions. At whose expense are you going to increase your market share? If you start trying to outbuild your competitors, are they not going to react? And if they do, isn't that going to increase competition and reduce prices? And we got the local managers to start asking themselves the 'What if…' questions, so that their proposed budgets became the start of reasonable business plans.

One of the issues that the Group did not face with McKinsey was that of transfer pricing – the prices that the Group as central supplier charged the companies that sold to the public. This deprived the marketing companies of a true financial yardstick with which to plan their businesses, and the impression began to pervade the Group that at the well-head not only were gas and water separated from the oil, but also money. 'It doesn't matter whether *we* make a profit, as long as we move the oil, because that's where the Group makes its money' became almost a mindset of marketing people: 'Volume is all; revenue is at best secondary.' There was reason, if not an excuse for this perception of policy.

In all the big oil-producing concessions in the Middle East, the host government at that time received a 'royalty' of twelve and a half per cent of the price, and an income tax of fifty per cent on the companies' profits, to which the royalty was an offset, so that the producing profit was shared between the country and the company fifty-fifty, and this became the name of the system. To assure fairness by establishing a market price, the companies were obliged to 'post' a price at which oil would be sold to all comers. This worked fairly well as long as the number of major oil producers was small enough so that, without any collusion, all producers of the same quality of crude oil posted the same price. Since, in areas like Saudi Arabia, the actual cost of producing a barrel of crude was twenty-five cents, and it sold for over two dollars, the economic rent to be shared between host and concessionaire was large, and snarling over its division was already starting.

By 1955, the USSR had resumed oil exports on a growing scale: in 1956 oil was discovered in Algeria, and a ten-year exploration effort in Nigeria began to bear fruit. These and other new sources of supply started to put pressure on posted prices, but the big attack was yet to come. A growing belief among geologists that Libya might be a large oil province caused the Libyan government to pass, in 1955, an oil law which would not allow one company to have a monopoly, or near monopoly of any oil production, and under which the government's share of the rent would be based on actual selling prices, instead of the increasingly unreal posted prices, so that Libyan oil would be more profitable to the producer than the big Middle East concessions. In 1957 seventeen oil companies bid successfully to explore: in 1959 the first big field was discovered: by 1960 Libya had ten big fields, and had started exporting. Most of the Libyan oil was in the hands of smaller companies, which needed to start generating income quickly to pay for the years of investment. And how do you develop big sales quickly, especially when the USA, which the newcomers had expected to provide a large market for them, suddenly imposes import quotas? You cut prices. This left the traditional 'major' oil companies, like Shell and Esso, in a bind. They could of course cut their prices to match the newcomers, but they were still hooked on paying the host government's share on the (increasingly unrealistic) posted prices.

In 1959, BP, and in August of the following year Esso, cut their posted prices, and with them the revenues of the oil-producing nations. Within five weeks, they reacted. Inspired by two men, Sheikh Abdallah Tariki of Saudi Arabia and Juan Pablo Pérez Alfonso of Venezuela, these two countries joined with Iran, Iraq and Kuwait to form the Organisation of Petroleum Exporting Countries: OPEC. In its first few years this body was not able to achieve much – except that no company would ever again dare to cut a posted price unilaterally. The potential supply of oil greatly exceeded demand, and the countries had only one means of defending their shares of the market: their concessionaire companies. John Loudon, the head of the Shell Group, had described the cuts in the posted price as a fatal move, and Shell, almost alone, began to worry about OPEC and the whole future of the industry.

After two years of regional marketing, I was suddenly invited to take on a new job, nominally working for Fitzgerald, but actually trying to help the Managing Directors of the Group answer two questions. Do we take OPEC seriously? And if so, how do we persuade other major oil companies to do the same? It was a wonderful opportunity, and undoubtedly saved my career from the Puricelli slump. Though I still had one hurdle to overcome: Len Abrahamse, a brilliant South African and a good friend from the 1957 European General Managers' Programme in the USA, had become the marketing co-ordinator and my boss. When I left him, he discussed with me his confidential report on my performance.

'Jock,' he said, 'I don't see you as a leader and motivator of people, but you are brilliant as a back-room boy, and that's where your future should be.' I reminded him of my naval career, over half of which was as a successful leader and motivator, but I don't think I had him fully convinced; and in the end, his opinion did not get in the way.

I started my new job by getting to know some of the brains of the OPEC, and in particular Francisco Parra, then chief economist, later secretary-general, became a good friend. Francisco, a Venezuelan, was born and spent some of his early years in Liverpool, where his father had been consul-general. His English was perfect, and he even still retained some traces of a 'Scouse'[1] accent, about which, when I got to know him very well, I could pull his leg.

OPEC's first, modest, objective was to have the royalty treated as an expense, not as a set-off against income tax.

[1] Liverpudlian.

This would have the effect that fifty-fifty would apply, not to the total profit, but to the profit after deducting the royalty, and on top of this share, the government would get the twelve and a half per cent, thus reducing the company's share by six and a quarter per cent of the posted price. I have called this objective modest, which it was only as compared to their long-term aim – to end the concession system altogether, and regain national sovereignty over the oil reserves. The current conditions of oversupply in the oil market did not suggest that OPEC had a very strong hand at that time, but if its members, who accounted for four-fifths of world oil exports, could remain cohesive, and if they could begin to achieve a system of control over production to tighten prices, then who knew what they might achieve? 'If [they] could remain...' were the key words, and have been OPEC's problem throughout its existence. Only in periods when the balance of supply and demand in the market have been in its favour has OPEC been able to act as if it were a cartel, and hold a price it had set. Professor Morris A. Adelman (of MIT, now emeritus) the acutest observer of oil prices, has always said that every cartel is unstable, because the temptation to cheat is too big, and the risk of cheating is only that others will cheat too. He has called this 'Macpherson's law' after Chief Petty Officer Macpherson, USN, his shipmate during World War II, who stated: 'If you've a friend, trusted and true – screw him quick, before he screws you!' But that truth lay still in the future.

My first steps were to get to know the London representatives of Esso and Mobil (the parent companies, not the local operating companies) which we thought were most likely to perceive the reality of the problem, and of Gulf Oil, fifty per cent owner of Kuwait Oil Company, with which Shell had an agreement (due, optimistically, to expire in 2047!) to market Gulf's half share of Kuwait Oil's production. British Petroleum was naturally easier to reach, since it was in London and I could get to the people specifically concerned.

My message received a generally favourable response from these companies, to the point that the Managing Directors of the Group picked up the baton themselves. Led by John Loudon, the most far-sighted of senior oil company executives of the day, the reality of the OPEC threat began to be appreciated. It was a fascinating experience for me to accompany John Loudon at meetings with the heads of the other major oil companies, in London and in New York, and hear him persuade people who didn't want to hear his story, that yes, we should take OPEC seriously, and be prepared to make concessions when the moment came – when the world glut of oil would give way to tighter supplies and would put the producing countries in the driver's seat. By the time that came about, I was far away.

As the urgency, if not the importance, waned, the responsibility for OPEC affairs was moved from Fitz Fitzgerald to Frank McFadzean, my friend from Egypt days, who was Group Co-ordinator, Supply and Planning. And our financial situation suddenly took a turn for the better: first Fitz recommended a bonus of one thousand pounds for my work on the OPEC issue, and then, when I joined Frank he asked me how much my salary was. When I told him, he said, 'Heavens! That's nowhere near enough.' And I got a salary increase of thirty per cent.

I still spent much of my time with the people of the other major, and less than major oil companies, in the ongoing effort to achieve a general realisation that things would have to change in the relations between oil companies and 'host governments', and that the more we were prepared to take the initiative, the better the outcome we might achieve. We didn't make much headway, because it is difficult, if things are going well for you, to recognise that the party will end some day.

As part of this effort I attended an oil congress held in Germany, and as luck would have it, I shared a room with Morry Adelman (of Macpherson's law), and we spent a lot of time talking about oil, and especially of its price, and he gave me a copy of his book *The Supply and Price of Natural Gas* which, though it dealt specifically with the United States gas market, set forth the whole economic framework of the price of any extractive industry. It opened my eyes to how oil prices were determined, and to the all-important fact that oil is an industry of increasing costs. This does not mean that tomorrow's oil will necessarily be priced higher than today's, but that the lowest marginal cost barrels will always be produced first, and that the cost of finding is always a 'sunk' cost, and once spent cannot influence the day-to-day price. Along with this goes another truth, that any producer will go on producing from a given well as long as what he gets for selling its production exceeds his out-of-pocket costs, regardless of what he may have invested in the well. The lessons were well learned, and in September of 1972, just before the Arab oil embargo, William F. Buckley invited me to debate, on his TV programme *Firing Line*, the oil price issue with Morry himself.

Beyond OPEC Frank asked me to think about the future and to put on paper what I thought were the problems (and their obverse, the opportunities) that the Group would face in the future, and in January, just before moving on to my next assignment, I wrote two papers for him, 'Government Participation' and 'Shell in a Growing Oil World'. An Arab proverb says that 'Those who foretell the future are lying, even if they tell the truth' and few of the proposals these papers contained came to reality, but in hindsight I believe the principles I recommended to Frank influenced the way the Group coped with the dramatic developments of the next decade.

Chapter Thirty-Eight

Marketing Teams

The misleading of strategies in marketing by the 'posted price' distortions has already been mentioned, and as the gap between what the market would pay for crude oil and the posted price widened, so these distortions grew, to the point where virtually no Shell company in Europe made a profit. Not unnaturally, the countries in which these companies operated began to complain that they were being cheated out of the taxes they should have received on these sales, and the Group, and other major oil companies too, faced the prospect that governments in consuming countries could unilaterally fix a notional transfer price on which the local companies would be obliged to calculate their taxable profits, and thus be caught between two prices, neither of which was determined by the market. Moreover the 'volume is all' philosophy had led to many inefficiencies and non-economic planning. Add to these the fact that many of the companies were led by Peter Principle[1] chief executives, and it was clear that something had to be done – and Len Abrahamse was given the task of deciding what.

Len's appraisal of my strengths made me, in his mind, an obvious choice for this assignment, and he asked me and Leslie – now Sir Leslie – Froggatt (whom I knew only as a lunch-room acquaintance, but whose reputation as a

---

[1] See p.378.

thinker and translator into action was very high) to head a team with the task of getting the European 'marketing' – in quotes because most of them were also refining – companies to improve their financial return to their parent, the Shell Group. We were to start together in Switzerland in January 1964, with a finance man, Sandy Dowell, to help with figures, and later split into two groups for smaller countries, spending three to four months in each. Leslie became a very good friend, and no one could have asked for a better companion in a job where, by its very nature, we were (as change agents always are) unpopular and suspect. His toughness in adversity and his humour made life tolerable, and sometimes even fun.

With the proceeds of Fitz's bonus, Billie and I bought ourselves a Hillman Minx convertible, and installed a luggage rack on top of its boot. We packed into suitcases what we thought would see us through two years of a gypsy life, loaded them into, and on to the boot, and the rest of our possessions we put into storage in Kingston, including seven plum puddings, the remains of the batch that Billie had made for the past Christmas. We little guessed that we wouldn't see this stuff until four years later, in New York. We took the car ferry from Dover, and drove to Zürich. There we found ourselves a very modern, small hotel south of the centre of Zürich, on the east shore of the Zürchersee, where we would be able to bring Queenie, our very dear elderly cocker spaniel, on our first opportunity of a visit back to the UK. The tram stopped at the bottom of the hotel's garden, and left me a couple of minutes' walk from the office of Shell Switzerland.

This company was not as big a haemorrhager as some others, but it soon became clear that economic calculation and sensible thought about the future played little part in their decision-making. The management team consisted of a French General Manager, Randel; an expatriate finance manager, and four middle-aged Swiss who ran operations (the physical handling of the products) and the marketing divided into three product groups. The General Manager believed that his job was to maintain morale, and the Operations Manager tended to go to sleep during meetings. About halfway through our work, when we had some inchoate proposals to make to the company, Len decided to pay a visit, and unwittingly proposed a day which had been set aside for the staff skiing competition. We had quickly come to the conclusion that Randel had made his job a very cushy one: he spent a lot of time skiing, and during the week his wife often took the company car and driver – under instructions to keep his mouth and his fly both zipped shut during the trip – to the French Riviera. But neither Leslie nor I would have guessed that his priorities were so inverted that he would tell Len that he would not be able to attend the meeting because he would be in the mountains for the skiing. And he actually went off before getting Len's answer – which, when it came, made Randel abandon his staff skiers and come back to attend Len's meeting, in haste and with obvious bad grace.

The evening before we were due to meet, Len asked Leslie and me to describe to him the people he would be meeting. I commented that the Operations Manager had a short attention span, and would probably go to sleep. 'Oh, Jock! There you go again, exaggerating to make a point,' was Len's comment, but the Operations Manager made my point. He was sitting relaxed, with his chin on his chest, and his eyes in the shadow, when Len asked him, 'Herr Schmidt, what do you think?' With a loud 'schrunk!' of a snore, Schmidt suddenly sat upright, blinked his eyes and asked Len to repeat his question. Len studiously avoided my eyes, and I his, lest we should burst out laughing.

We spent our last couple of weeks writing up our recommendations to Shell Switzerland, and the private ones (new General Manager, new Operations Manager among them) to Len personally. The senior incumbents, almost without exception, opposed our ideas as impractical, while all the younger people with whom we had worked to develop them were in favour. Over a few months they were implemented by the company's new management, and results began to improve. But one day when we were deep in our next project, Leslie happened to be in the bar at Schiphol Airport in Amsterdam, waiting for a plane, when he spotted Randel at the other end of the bar, and 'I walked all the way to the gate for my flight, sideways, with my back against the wall.'

If Switzerland had a somnolent Operations Manager and a Chief Executive who regarded skiing with the staff as more important than attending a meeting with the Group marketing co-ordinator, Germany was fantasy land. It was, however, the only country we visited where we were able to get an apartment of our own. We rented the ground floor and garden of what had been the house of a Hamburg merchant of the Bismarck era, high above the Elbe in the suburb of Blankenese. The corner of the garden with the best view was overgrown, and we had no garden tools. So we spent one weekend cutting the grass with two pairs of scissors until we had a little area of a sort of lawn where we could sit in the sun. The floor above us was occupied by two elderly ladies, Frau ('Mami') Eppmann and Frau Sethe, who watched with amazement our scissors work, and Billie's knitting (she was making a blanket for her grandson, out of little squares on the bias, eventually to be sewn together) which appeared to them to be an ever-increasing pile of *Topfanfassen* (pot holders!). Their curiosity got the better of their natural reticence; they knocked at our door and made themselves known. We became good friends, and kept in touch with Mami Eppmann until she died in the late Sixties, and with Hertha Sethe until ten years later when our Christmas cards were returned marked 'Unknown'.

To Mami Eppmann we owed a special debt of gratitude. When, at the end of our stint, we had to move on to Norway, quarantine meant we could not take Queenie with us, nor could we take her back to the UK. She had already had to have three cancerous nipples extirpated, and she was growing deaf, so very sadly we decided we would have to have her put to sleep. We were on our way to the vet's, both of us in tears, when we met Mami. She asked us why we were so sad, and when we told her, she said, without a moment's hesitation, '*Nein, nein!* You cannot do that: Queenie comes to live with me!' And that chance encounter gave Queenie an extra year of life.

But to business. Our first morning in the office, Barend Scheffer, the Dutch President of Deutsche Shell, sent for us. Randel had already been relieved of his position as General Manager of Shell Switzerland, and word had obviously got around that this team, and the people in Central Offices who were backing them, were something to be reckoned with, so Scheffer tried to dictate to us in advance what we should say in our report on Deutsche Shell. He conceded that some of their practices might look a little strange to us, but we must be aware of the cultural differences involved, and warned us not to be deceived by things we came across which might look odd – they could all be explained, and we must 'write a positive report'.

From this meeting we went to the offices we had been assigned, and I found in my in-tray a memorandum in German, which I could read reasonably well – with occasional help from a dictionary, headed with a polysyllabic German word meaning 'Service-station-location-priority-coefficient', which was a startling example of Scheffer's 'cultural differences'. Before our arrival, the head of marketing economics and market research, Herr

Professor Doktor Bauer, had persuaded himself that it could not be right to leave decisions as to where new service stations should be located to the sales force on the spot (who were in the best position to know local traffic conditions, and so on). Accordingly he set out to devise a scientific method.

The smallest political unit in Germany is the Kreis, and most statistics are available by Kreis. So Dr Bauer and his people developed a formula which, for every Kreis in the country, took as its top line the elements of demand: population, vehicle registrations, consumption of automobile fuels, kilometres of Autobahn and of lesser roads, and so on, each given its own weighting. The resulting figure was divided by supply, the total number of stations of various kinds, each again adjusted by weightings, to produce an 'intermediate'. This was then divided by the number of Shell outlets to give the final priority number. And the rule was that the first new station in any marketing district must be built in that Kreis that had the highest coefficient. But of course there were many Kreisen in which Deutsche Shell had no stations: the divisor was zero. Thus, no matter how small the demand factors might be, the intermediate coefficient divided by zero produced a priority of infinity. This of course was a nonsensical answer, and how could you decide between one infinity and another? So Dr Bauer ordered, in the polysyllabic-titled memorandum, that 'In future, in Deutsche Shell, zero shall be considered as equal to one'! These two, Scheffer's greeting and Dr Bauer's memorandum, were fair warning of what was to come.

The day-to-day management of the company was, by German law, vested in the *Vorstand*, the managing board, which in turn was supervised by the *Aufsichtsrat*, the oversight board. The law held that all members of the Vorstand were jointly and severally accountable, which the directors of Deutsche Shell interpreted to mean that each was entitled to interfere in the management of any part of the business, to the point of taking policy decisions, without even advising his colleague who had the specific responsibility for it. We recorded our concern that Scheffer not only tolerated this, but maybe even encouraged it – perhaps on the principle of divide and conquer. When a conference on trends in the retail market was organised by Shell Oil, and some non-US Group companies were invited to send representatives, Deutsche Shell sent (not, as one would have expected, the Director of Marketing and the Manager of Retail Sales) but Stern, Finance Director, and Baumgarten, Director of Oil Supplies.

The company was riddled with inefficiencies, from the enormous to the ridiculous. Two examples of the former: one of Arnold Hofland's guiding principles was that product transport should, as much as possible, be contracted out, since company-owned trucks tended to be more expensive. The Transport Department of Deutsche Shell had carried out a desk study two years before our visit which persuaded it that to follow the Hofland line would cost it *only six per cent more* than keeping its own vehicles, and we happened to be in Hamburg when the last company-owned truck was given up. Its total transport bill was over DM 30 million per year, so its six per cent voluntarily assumed increase amounted to DM 1.8 million, with no consideration from any executive above the level of Transport Manager.

The company's owners, the Group, every year approved a budget for new service stations, which was based on Deutsche Shell's plans. The execution of these plans took place on the ground, in the divisions and districts. In 1963 the Retail Department in the head office gave Hamburg Division as its target for 1964 these figures:

Company-owned or fringe-financed[2] service stations	20
Filling stations (no lubrication or car wash facilities)	10
Dealer-owned stations	45
Total new stations	75

In January 1964, the number for filling stations was increased to sixteen, and thus the total to eighty-one. No monetary budgets accompanied these targets, which, in February, were passed on to each of the seven districts which comprised the region simply as 'twenty new units', which implied a division total of one hundred and forty. Leslie and I were in Hamburg in June, and spent much time with the managers of two of the districts, Hamburg II and Hanover, the managers of which told us with pride that their plans were to achieve fifty-two new units between them, and that they were well on the way to achieving this – much of it unbeknownst to the division. Extrapolating from these two districts to the whole Division would make the total not eighty-one, but one hundred and eighty-four. We went back to the head office to see how these figures related to the Group-approved budget, and, prodded by us, Deutsche Shell realised that its whole budget would be spent by July, and that even to fulfil the commitments already entered into for the balance of the year would require the Group to approve a ten million-pound increase in expenditure. When Dr Stern, the Finance Director learned this, he said that he could arrange to borrow the money from the banks, and that the Group need not know. It took no little persuading to convince him that a loan of that size to a subsidiary would be impossible without the Group's backing, and in any case would be a total breach of faith to the Group.

Compounding this numbers folly were other policies of

[2]Financed in part by Shell, in part by the dealer.

Deutsche Shell. All their stations were expensively built of brick, with no weather protection over the two pumps which each station was allowed. No provision was made for the sale of diesel fuel – this was left largely to agents – and premium gasoline (with a higher profit margin) was left to play second fiddle to regular, on the grounds that Deutsche Shell's reputation was as a regular grade company! And the pump attendants did not take the money: the driver had to get out and go to the office. Throughput per station was low. In Essen there were two independent stations, Benzin Supermarkt and Moll, on diagonally opposite corners of a heavy traffic crossroads. Each had about twenty pumps, under the cover of a lightly built roof, and their prices were ten pfennigs per litre below Shell's, and between them the two sold as much volume as all the Shell stations in Essen and a neighbouring district. The managers concerned argued that these two must be buying distress product from refineries in the Ruhr. So one day Leslie and I sat in a parked car and watched for a couple of hours. We saw supplies coming in in full truck-and-trailer loads (Shell's trucks made multiple stops, and metered each delivery); we counted the cars and the people working, and saw that the same man filled the car and took the cash. Back in the office we calculated the profitability of these two, and showed quite clearly that they could afford to pay the full refinery price, and still make a handsome profit – after all, if they could not, would they be there?

At the other end of the scale were two examples of chasing the pennies, and letting the pounds go hang. When we had been a short while on the job, we discovered that the company sent a messenger every workday morning to the Dammtor railway station, six or seven minutes' walk from the office, to pick up the foreign newspapers ordered by the company. To take advantage of this, Leslie and I arranged, and paid for, a copy of *The Times* each. Within a week we were sent for by Scheffer, who asked us if we were not aware that only with his personal permission might any employee have a foreign newspaper on company account, and he understood that we had both ordered a copy of *The Times* without his approval.

'But we pay for them,' we said, 'and we had not realised that the President's approval might be necessary for the messenger to carry two more papers.' This, if his suspicion had been well founded, would have been a matter of a very few Deutschmarks a day, subjected to the vigilance of a man who did not know that a decision of his Transport Manager, four levels below him in the hierarchy, was costing his company almost two million Deutschmarks every year, nor that the budget for new retail outlets was already overcommitted to the tune of ten million pounds!

Halfway through our study, Len Abrahamse came to pay a visit, and we arranged a presentation to Grothgar, the Director of Marketing, in Len's presence. One could always arrange for coffee to be served during any meeting, but I had noticed that cookies were served with coffee only when fairly senior people were present, and they were served on this occasion. The waitress who handed them round presented a slip of paper to Grothgar, who interrupted the conversation for a few moments while he went round the table with his eyes, counting those present before signing the paper. This piqued my curiosity, and when I next had a few minutes to spare I asked the young man who was our liaison with Deutsche Shell what this was all about. He directed me to the cookie expense control office, a little back corner room on the top floor. Here I found a young man behind a desk, and at another desk a young woman with a stack of slips and a big ledger. The young man showed me a list of those employees who were entitled to order, and must sign for, cookies served during a meeting. The ledger contained a record of all the occasions, how many cookies were served, which authorised person had signed for them, and how much they had cost, neatly totalled for the month.

'And are you saving money by this?' I asked him.

'Oh yes; before we had this control we were spending at least eighty Deutschmarks a month more than now,' he answered. And when I asked him how much his salary and that of his recording angel totalled, he told me – many times more than the eighty Deutschmarks. 'But it's a matter of principle and discipline!'

No doubt those savings were reported many steps up the organisation, but never in a way that compared them with costs, and nowhere did we find any consciousness of what costs were, despite (no, not 'despite' – almost certainly because of) the flood of computer-generated figures in which the company was choking. The Marketing Director received seventy-nine different returns every month, containing, we calculated, more than fifteen thousand figures. Poor Grothgar not being, like most of the others, a Doktor by education, an ex-officer of the *Wehrmacht*, or an ex-Nazi, was not much respected by his colleagues on the *Vorstand* and so rarely joined them for their daily lunch together, preferring to go home with two bulging briefcases to study his reports. In contrast the district, where most of the sales were made, and many of the variable costs incurred, got twenty returns, not usually passed down to those on the front line who could have used them.

We finished our study, and made a full report of the facts we had found, and a comprehensive package of recommendations, (including detailed proposals for an organisation slimmed down by over five hundred jobs) together with a timetable for the various stages of its implementation, and we wrote (and to ensure security, Billie typed) a personal letter to Scheffer, of which this was the first paragraph:

> We have written our report to you in terms as constructive as possible. We have omitted, except where implication is inevitable, any comment on the way certain things have been or are now being done in Deutsche Shell. Nevertheless we would be failing in our duty to you (and to the Group) if we did not, in this form of a personal letter, record some opinions we have formed, or impressions we have gained on which we believe you may wish to take some action.

Two days later Scheffer wrote a letter to Len, complaining of our report and this letter, and rebutting many of our conclusions as 'sweeping generalisations'. We were able to write a response to Len quoting chapter and verse for what we had written – a task made easier because Scheffer had not even read the key appendices to our report before firing off his blast to Len. And not very long afterwards he ceased to be the President of Deutsche Shell.

After Deutsche Shell Leslie went to the Shell companies in Sweden and Holland, while I took on Norway and Denmark, and we joined forces again for Italy. In general the four smaller companies were better managed than the bigger ones, though the same failures: introspection rather than hard information about the market and the competition; organisation by product rather than type of end use; the tendency to look at average rather than marginal costs and proceeds,[3] and ignorance about how

[3]As an example, Shell Italiana had three general sales outlets for automotive gasoline. In descending order of sales proceeds per litre were company-owned stations, dealer owned, and bulk sales to unbranded outlets. They also had three sources of supply, in ascending order of cost: own crude refined in own refineries, own crude refined by others, and bulk purchases from the open market. If you added up the total costs of all supplies and deducted that from the total sales proceeds, the result

each company was actually contributing to the Group were common. Shell Italiana was in the same league as Deutsche Shell in the sense that its errors were on a large scale, and its President as unwilling as Scheffer to believe that his company was anything but perfectly managed. It had its bright side, none the less. Italian people were much easier to work with than German, and the tension level was much lower. Our liaison with the company was Vittorio Pera, who with his family became good friends. Alas, he died very young, but we still keep Christmas card contact with his widow, Anna, and his daughter Maria Patrizia.

Our living conditions, too, were very pleasant. Shell Italiana recommended to us a hotel, the Savoia-Beeler in Nervi, ten kilometres east of Genoa. Run by a Swiss family, headed by Annie Beeler, it stands in a large pleasant garden, separated from the sea only by a footpath, the Passegiata Anita Garibaldi, and beyond that a large gentle slope of smooth rock from which to swim. The rooms were big and airy, the food superb and the staff very friendly and attentive. The company took a long lunch break, and whenever we were not travelling, or having meetings over lunch, it was easy to drive to Nervi, to eat and even have a quick swim before the afternoon's work. A few kilometres further along the coast were the medieval skyscrapers of Camogli and the resorts of Santa Margherita, Rapallo and Portofino to visit at weekends. In all this travel back and forth we learned an interesting thing about Italian driving: to look at, it's scary, but once you get into it you realise how courteous and considerate the drivers are, and compared with British (and, *a fortiori*, French!) roads, the Italian ones

---

was a profit. But match the unbranded outlets with the bulk purchases, and you have a loss. Therefore, give up all sales which can't make a profit on the most expensive supply. It took a lot of persuasion to get Shell Italiana to be willing to give up any sales volume, and to recast their information system to give marginal figures.

are an order of magnitude less stressful. We had Queenie with us, and although, towards the end, she was getting restless as cancer spread to more of her nipples, and could no longer sleep the night through, she loved the garden and the swimming. She died there, aged fourteen: she is buried in the garden of the Savoia-Beeler, and Annie Beeler planted a bed of lovely flowers over her grave.

There were hazards, however; we were often driven to appointments by Shell Italiana people, in their own cars, and Italians like their cars fast. After one such trip Leslie commented,: 'If these people would only run their business with as much verve as they drive their cars, there wouldn't be much for us to do!' And once we spent a whole afternoon discussing the automotive market with eight or ten people, in a narrow room with marble floor and walls, so that every word echoed. It was exactly as Walter Bedon, Shell Italiana's Advertising Manager and an old friend from several years before, described the typical Italian meeting, 'Ten people sitting round a table, and all twelve talking at once.' When we got out into the fresh air, Leslie said, 'D'you know? I've got a sore throat from just listening!'

As in other companies, the younger employees perceived the sense of, and the necessity for, the changes we were advocating, while the senior people wanted no change, but the hostility so general in Hamburg was commendably absent in Genoa.

This year and a half was a big eye-opener to me. I have already mentioned Shell's propensity to follow the Peter Principle, but the quality of the top managers of most of the companies we had visited, which between them must have been selling well over half of the Group's volume, the United States excluded, was frightening. And ('like master, like man') the quality down the line was in general mediocre at best.

Central offices people, from Managing Directors on

down, were constantly visiting the operating companies. How could it possibly happen that, for years, a company of Deutshe Shell's size could go on running its business without a realistic look at the world outside, at the growth of the market, the views of its customers, the facts about its competitors, and above all without information about its costs? What did all the visitors see? And, to the extent that problems were perceived, who was told about them? And, until Len Abrahamse came on the scene, who had the will and the clout to do anything about them? I have no doubt, however, that our work – Leslie's, mine and that of the half-dozen others who worked with us – had a major impact on the financial health of the Group's marketing operations in Europe.

Three years or so later I received one little pleasant recognition of the success of what we had done. I was in my office in New York, when Dirk de Bruyne, then President of Deutsche Shell, and Norman Bain, President of Shell Italiana, happened to be in the USA at the same time, and came in to see me.

Over a cup of coffee they both expressed their thanks for the work Leslie and I had done – especially in respect of staff numbers and information systems – which was enabling them to begin to turn their companies around. Alas, time would prove that Shell Italiana was in fact beyond salvation – as much the fault of Italy as of Shell.

Top: Concordia Depot: floods receding, April 1959.
Middle: Depot at Concepción del Uruguay, April 1959. THe floods have almost gone, except in the tank bund.
Bottom: On TV: *Firing Line* with Bill Buckley, with Professor Morry Adelman in the centre.

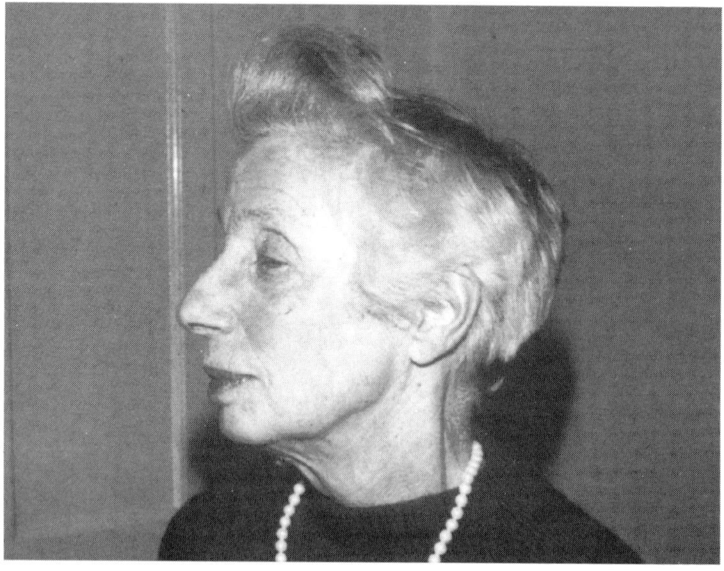

Top: Billie, in 1962.
Bottom: Mother, Elizabeth Helen ('Bessie') Duff.

Clockwise from top left: Great-grandparents George Ritchie ('Waterside Doddie') and Jean ('Jinsie') Walker; Grandparents John Walker and Mary Southern (Father is the solemn little boy with the bow tie); Collieston fishwife: 'Auntie' (really Great-Aunt) Jean Ritchie; Collieston fisherman: Alexander Ritchie ('Cotie') with whom Jock worked as a teenager.

Clockwise from top left: Jock leaving Collieston to join the Navy; MGB 2009: the first ship propelled by a gas turbine; Jock 1998; Billie, the year before our marriage.

Chapter Thirty-Nine

Brazil

I was not able to see the end of the Italian study, though I had participated in all the work that led to our conclusions, leaving Leslie on his own to write up the final recommendations. A couple of weeks before the task would have been completed, I got an urgent summons to visit London, where David Barran, then Chairman of the Committee of Managing Directors, asked me if I would be prepared to go to Brazil as President of Shell Brasil (no, not a typographical error: the 's' is the Brazilian spelling of the country's name). Obviously my experience in Europe was one of the factors influencing my selection, but the one on which most emphasis was placed was that I could speak Spanish, and so should be able to learn Portuguese fairly quickly! I said I would not accept unless Billie was prepared for another uprooting, but I promised an early answer by telephone.

I got back to Genoa late in the day, and Billie and I talked it over until the small hours. It was in fact an easier decision than it might have been, because we had no 'compared with what?' Brazil was, as Argentina had been, deeply nationalistic in so far as the oil industry was concerned, indeed '*O petróleo e nosso*' – the oil is ours – was a flag nailed to the mast of every political party, and an unquestioned assumption. From my days in regional marketing I knew how circumscribed were the operations of the foreign oil companies working there, and how capricious were the rules. The economy was in a mess, and inflation was out of control, so running a business there could not be much fun. On the other hand the making of the offer suggested that Len Abrahamse's appraisal of my future as being in the back room rather than as a leader might be fading, and I would be the Chief Executive of one of the Group's larger marketing companies: and if I said no, what then? About 3 a.m. we agreed that I should accept, but that I should ask for two weeks in Portugal for intensive study of Portuguese beforehand. First thing in the morning I called David Barran and accepted. He conceded a few more days in Italy for Leslie and me to agree on the broad lines of our proposals for Shell Italiana, and then I went to London for a briefing on Shell Brasil – which, had I received it before accepting, might well have made me decide differently.

The outgoing President of the company was Donald Burnet, a close friend from Argentina days. He had got himself into a deal (the details of which I think he didn't really understand) which had resulted in the company losing over one million pounds, and in his senior management becoming demoralised, to the extent that one of his fellow directors resigned from service in the Group. This, and the extreme nationalism of the attitude to foreign enterprises generally, and oil companies in particular, had disillusioned the Group about its stake in Brazil. The value of Shell Brasil on the books of its parent stood at six million pounds. My terms of reference were to make the company earn *and remit* at least one million pounds every year for five years, while we could only invest in the business, other than routine maintenance to keep the assets in working order, after this goal had been met. Not an attractive task to be set! I asked for, and got, a few weeks after arriving in Rio de Janeiro before accepting this remit, or proposing modification of it.

On the bright side, however, Donald's two predecessors had laid the foundations for success in two areas. Harold (now Sir Harold) Atcherley had seen that it was not necessary to have large numbers of expatriates to run the company, and had set out to recruit a score or more of really bright young Brazilians, and had given them training and experience to enable them to take over most of the senior executive positions. Then 'Jonah' Jones (the General Manager of Shell Egypt when I was there) had carried out a study of 'Whither Shell Brasil?' (nicknamed the W papers).

Starting from a thorough analysis of all segments of the business, and recognising that, in inflationary conditions, 'profit' as calculated by conventional accounts is of little meaning, and what matters is cash flow, Jonah proposed to give up all government business – the government never paid on time, and when it did pay, six months later, the money had lost a large part of its value. Other big industrial companies and bus and airlines would be kept strictly to their credit terms, or supply would cease.

I was in regional marketing in London when a cable came in from Jonah reporting the reaction to the first of these moves. The regional co-ordinator to whom it was addressed was Wim Starrenberg, whose career had been spent in exploration and production, and whose familiarity with marketing was minimal. Nor was he familiar with Jonah's custom of writing in what he called 'glorious technicolor', so when he came to words describing the State Railways' reaction to Shell Brasil's new policy 'despite the usual political explosion', he sent for me and asked whether it was within the powers of the president of a marketing company to cause a political explosion. I knew Jonah, and understood what he meant by 'political explosion'. ('But you can't do that, splutter, splutter, you can't bring the railways to a halt' and so on.) I was not able to persuade Wim that Jonah was not risking serious political repercussions, and he cabled Jonah to come to see him in London immediately. The incident probably made it more difficult for Shell Brasil to go as far or as fast in implementing the W papers as it would have liked, but a lot of progress had been made by the time I got there. And there can scarcely be a better set of circumstances for a newly appointed chief executive than to have two predecessors who have prepared the ground for improvement, and an immediate one who has left a mess behind.

After saying goodbye to Shell Italiana and the Peras, and to the Froggatts who had been our comrades-in-arms for eighteen months, we went off to Portugal. We took a room in the Hotel Palácio in Estoril (which a guidebook describes as 'the seaside haunt of fading European aristocrats') and Shell Portuguesa found us a very charming and competent lady to teach us the language. A prior knowledge of Spanish undoubtedly helps; both are, after all, offspring of the Iberian version of late Latin. But the similarities hide many pitfalls: the accent falls on different syllables in *policia* and *farmacia*, and beware of telling your hostess her dinner was exquisite. *Esquisito* means awful! We had an hour-long class each morning and afternoon, and we spent at least three hours each day revising what we had learned, reading and talking with each other, and at the end of our two weeks we could do fairly well. Then in early September 1965 we arrived in Rio de Janeiro, only to find that the Brazilian language was as different from Portuguese as Scots is from Cajun English: different words for lots of common things, and very different pronunciation, and in the Academic Dictionary of the Luso-Brazilian Language, there are twenty thousand words in Brazilian that are not found in Portuguese. So we both started again with an hour a day from a teacher of Brazilian.

We went to live in the Copacabana Palace Hotel until

Billie could find us an apartment, and we were very glad not to have to start housekeeping. The overlap with Donald was very hectic; during the day briefings from him and his senior people, visits to the governor of the State, the National Petroleum Council (the industry's regulatory body) to Petrobrás, the state oil company (and monopoly producer and refiner, and so the supplier from whom we had to buy all the products we sold) and in the evenings cocktail parties to meet politicians, top management of the other oil companies, British, Dutch and American diplomats – the move of all embassies to Brasilia was not yet complete – and influential people in the business community and Rio de Janeiro society. At the first of these functions Billie and I shook almost a thousand hands, and the backs of our right hands were bruised and swollen. Luckily, before that party was over, a member of the British embassy taught us the trick – not to allow the other person to grasp your hand, but to pull it back as soon as contact is made and roll out of the grip all but your finger ends; they are tougher than the back of your hand.

I sensed that Shell Brasil was not a happy company, but it was not until Donald had left that I could start to dig deeper. I was blessed with the help of a wonderful man, and two remarkable women. The Vice-President of the company was Mario Ramos, who had joined the company forty years before as a fifteen-year-old office boy in shorts, and had risen by pure worth. He had learned almost perfect English, not only spoken but written, and he was very contemptuous of people who had not, but still expected to get on in a foreign-owned company, and even more so of people who could not write clearly and elegantly in their own tongue. He and his wife Eth (pronounced in Rio as 'Etchy') were wonderfully hospitable to Billie and me, and became our very dear friends.

My secretary was Marina Brenner, who fifteen years before had been Miss Guanabara,[1] and runner-up for Miss Brasil. She was still a very beautiful woman, but was also extremely able, and had her ear to the ground so that I got a pretty direct reading of people's feelings. I had also an administrative assistant, Edith Goemans, English with a Belgian husband, who had left Europe after the war in search of pastures new. Edith, too, was very good-looking, and always beautifully turned out; she had been with Elizabeth Arden.

From these three and from the other members of my management team, notably our head of personnel, Ivayr Azvedo, who was a dedicated exponent of what I believed in, participative management, I soon learned that all that people knew was that the Treasurer and the Finance Manager had been fired, and that the President was being replaced because of some screw-up which had lost the company a lot of money. It took a day or two to get the full story. It arose from a scheme of the government to encourage exports, under which anyone who managed to export non-traditional products from Brazil could retain the proceeds, free of exchange controls, and which could therefore be used to remit profits to a foreign shareholder, over and above the otherwise minuscule amounts allowed by law.

Two men, Milton Guper and Leon Sragovic, owned a company called Cimportex, which, they claimed, had the potential to export millions of dollars worth of non-traditional products, if only they had the working capital. Shell Brasil agreed to guarantee, over a period, substantial bank loans to Cimportex *in foreign currency terms,* so that the banks ran no exchange risk, and we would in return buy for cruzeiros (Brazilian currency) the proceeds of the new exports in remittable money. The deal required the appro-

---

[1]The state of which Rio is the capital.

val of the Board of Directors of Shell Brasil, and some of them jibbed. Donald told them to remember that they weren't *real* directors, but only heads of departments, subordinate to him. One had the guts to resign rather than agree, but the rest (bamboozled, I believe, by the Finance Manager, and steamrollered by Donald) agreed, and instalments of the bank loans were made to Cimportex. Alas, no monitoring system was set up, and Cimportex gradually drew down all available bank loans and repaid nothing, so that finally the banks called their guarantees, and Shell was left to pay them back in cruzeiros, increased in amount by the intervening depreciation. It had not the funds, and so had to turn to the Group to lend it the necessary £1.3 million.

Clearly my first job was to lay these facts on the table, sweep away the mystery, and say that I would need everybody's help to get the company back on the rails. Then we started between us to make practical plans, and came to the conclusion that if we were firm in sticking to Jonah's W papers, the business could generate the necessary cash. The brightest and best of all the young Brazilians recruited in recent years was Peter Landsberg, who was then working in London; I wanted him back.

We put on paper a rough draft of our plan, and I went off to London to get the blessing of Central Offices, and to persuade Peter that he would have more fun back in Rio than in his job as assistant to the area co-ordinator for India, Pakistan, Burma and Bangladesh. I showed him our embryo plan, and described how we were beginning to think of implementing it. He listened, and said rather sadly, 'It can't be done.' We went out to lunch, and I went over my reasons for thinking that it could be done, and at last he agreed to come back and do his part. That was the beginning of a deep friendship between Peter, his wife, Misé, and Billie and me, which ended only with his tragic death many years later.

There was a sense in Brazil that it was somehow immoral for a company to remit profits to foreign owners: shouldn't all profits *made* in Brazil be *reinvested* there? So the first task I set myself was to try to change this: after all, one could hardly expect Brazilians to be enthusiastic about earning and remitting profits if they thought it immoral. Starting with the example of a local butcher, we argued whether it was right for him to make a profit in the first place. If not, how many butchers would there be? And if he made a profit, should he be obliged to reinvest it in his neighbourhood, or should he be free to buy a butcher's shop, or even an ice cream parlour in São Paulo? Or over the border in Argentina, for that matter? After half a day's discussions we reached, to many people's surprise, the conclusion that, yes, it was right for profits to be remittable – indeed essential if there were to be foreign investment in Brazil. This was a necessary first step in getting to work on what we needed to do. The next was to make clear that everything must be the result of a team effort, so that all had ownership of the plans. The world, I have often argued, is divided into three in its attitude to a new idea. Eighty per cent oppose because it is new; fifteen per cent are in favour because it is new; only five per cent say, 'Well let's think it through, and try it out.' Most Brazilians are in this minority, and it makes them a joy to work with, right down to the level of the illiterate labourer, who will always be in favour of trying a new way to do a task that has always been done the old way.

Now was the time to apply the lessons of Europe. We designed a new organisation to fit the different sectors of the market, automotive, industrial, chemical and so on. Responsibility was pushed down to the level of the salesman, and intermediate levels of management were eliminated. Don Goldie and I devised a planning and information system built up from the bottom, but with the objectives agreed to by the Group as the starting and desired end points. We taught all our salesmen to do discounted cash flow, so that *real* profitability could be worked out at the lowest level of customer contact, and concepts such as 'increasing our share in this fast-growing, profitable market' went out of the window. And we had one big advantage denied to the European companies – we knew what our supplies cost!

Each manager's targets were strictly limited to what he could control – his own sales proceeds and his own costs. Common costs – 'overhead' – were accounted for separately and the responsibility of the appropriate manager, of engineering, legal, finance or personnel, but all the line managers had the right and the opportunity to question these costs, and when they were agreed upon, the money-producing parts of the organisation knew that they had not only to cover their own costs but, collectively, those of the overhead. We laid down strict targets for working capital, in the form of stocks of products and accounts receivable. An interesting little thing came out of this exercise. Shell Brasil prided itself on having the right brand of lubricant for every need of every customer, and to meet the manufacturer's specifications for all the machines he used. This involved something close to two hundred distinct formulations – we blended our own oils – of each of which we had to make at least five two hundred-litre drums. Some of these were only used in tiny quantities by the customers, so we had a large stock with a very slow turnover. We decided to do two things: to persuade our customers to use formulations which, though not exactly what they wanted, would perform just as well, or insist that a customer who demanded exactitude buy the whole batch as it was made. Some protested; a very few went to another company, but enough accepted that we were able to reduce our number of grades to about thirty, with a corresponding reduction in the money tied up in stocks. These decisions were not just handed down as diktats from the top, but worked out by the people responsible, who then owned the idea, and took pride in it.

We had to begin with no planned new investment, except what we could wring out of what we already had. We were required by law to buy from Petrobrás all our products, except those that had to be imported anyway. We got thirty days' credit on our purchases, and we had to do our best to distribute them, and sell them on terms that meant we were paid before the thirty days were up, so as to have minimum capital tied up in stocks and accounts receivable. This was possible in the automotive market, because cash on delivery was the market norm. But in sales to big fuel-consuming industries, like cement manufacturers and bus companies (Brazil had more passenger buses than any other country, even the USA) it was virtually impossible to squeeze less than thirty days' credit, which left the only scope for saving capital in storage and transport. Inflation was running then at around three per cent per month, so that a ten day-reduction in accounts receivable was worth one per cent increase in income.

Our plan for financing new service stations went like this: a would-be dealer came to us with a site in an attractive position, on which he would build the facilities, and pave the needed area. We would install and continue to own the tanks, pumps, servicing hoists and so on. When the site was complete, the owner took over as operator, and we would deliver product, and be paid cash. When we got into our stride, we would have only three or four days' worth of product in our bulk storage and perhaps two more in transit. For a good station our investment in hardware was about two weeks' worth of sales, so we had a total of less than three weeks' investment. Set against our thirty days from Petrobrás, we were in pocket on our automotive fuels business.

Since it was not possible to do this in the industrial market we had to be very vigilant about payment due dates and in reducing the time in storage. All our sales people knew that their feet would be held to the fire on overdue accounts, but they themselves had put the figures into their objectives, and they knew they had to make good.

We had first got our system going in December, when I had been there barely three months, and David Barran came to pay us a managing directorial visit. After we had shown him our plans and the results we were beginning to get, he exclaimed, 'You mean you make money out of inflation? But that's immoral!'

As a basis for our planning, the management team spelled out the broad strategic aims, which we called UPM (Unified Planning for Management). The people in the operations – sales, transport and storage – then worked out what they thought they could achieve with the resources available to them. They could say, 'Give us another three days of working capital, or so much more money to invest, and we could do this much better', and we would try these out, conceptually, to see if their ideas would fit into our plan. Then the proposals were iterated, up and down the organisation, until we had a series of objectives acceptable to management and to the achievement of which the operating units were committed. These were known as APROB (from the Portuguese for evaluation and choice of interfunctional objectives), and from them were derived PROA (Programme of Interfunctional Actions). Matching this, line for line, was COAR (Control and Analysis of Results). Of course, it didn't always come out as planned, but in large measure we avoided both over-optimism and over-caution, and did what we said we would do. In what remained of the calendar year, we repaid the Cimportex loan, and made a small remittable profit. The logic and the simplicity of our plans caught the imagination of our people, and in succeeding years we were able to do better: in my first whole calendar year we remitted two million pounds, and in the next, £3.5 million, though I was no longer there at year-end to gloat!

We changed the company in other ways, too. Brazilian law imposed a system called *estabilidade* (stability) under which no employee who had worked for ten years could be fired. Afraid of how the work habits of *estabilizados* might develop, almost all employers laid off every worker after nine and a half years. My chauffeur, Alberto Coimbra Junior, was a paragon. The only complaints that Billie and I had against him were, on Billie's part that he was over-assiduous in escorting her, and would not allow her out of his sight; and on mine that, when he was waiting to pick me up after an evening function, he would *always* be the first car in line outside the door, with the cars of the governor of the State and the British ambassador behind him. But he was worried: he had eight and a half years of service, and so could expect to be fired in a year or so. I thought this was ridiculous, and first promised Alberto that he would *not* be fired, and then I brought up the subject at our next management meeting. All agreed with me that we probably lost a lot of talent (and enthusiasm in people's ninth and tenth years) and I suggested we find out how big the problem was.

We surveyed all our *estabilizados*, and found only *two* who were not pulling their weight. One had been a salesman, but had become very shy, and the other a woman clerical employee. For the salesman we found a job that people who knew him were convinced he could do, and would not require him to deal with strangers. The woman came to the office every day, but spent her whole time knitting. It was manifestly silly to have her travel to work, occupy a desk, and then have to travel home, and her office mates found her idleness dispiriting. So we agreed she could stay at home and we would continue to pay her as long as the law required. We went on to decide on a new policy, that two years should be a long enough probationary period. After this, we would no longer automatically fire anyone before he or she became *estabilizado*, but we would set up a system of performance appraisal to identify doubtful cases well before the tenth year. We announced our new policy to everyone, and you could almost hear the sigh of relief that went up from our employees. I have always acted on the principle that ninety-nine out of every hundred people are decent, honest, fair and reliable – if you trust them – and Shell Brasil's people didn't disappoint me!

We expected all our senior people to be mobile, to be prepared to go to work in São Paulo, Belo Horizonte or anywhere else we had need of their skills. House prices were out of reach of any normal salaried employee, while rents were controlled, and thus, for tenants who stayed for a number of years, became, by the action of inflation, absurdly cheap. It would have been a real hardship to anyone who had a five-year-old rent in Rio to have to move to São Paulo and start over with the prices of the day, so we charged such employees a percentage of their salaries while the company paid the balance, just as we did for our expatriate staff. Talking with Edith one day it occurred to us that we might be able to use what we paid by way of subsidy to enable at any rate a few senior people to buy their apartments, so they would be building up an equity, while the company was spending no more. We drew up a list of those whom we would expect to be moved around, as well as those who were already enjoying a subsidised rent, and I asked her to discuss the idea with our outside lawyer, Antonio Salgado, and see if we could come up with a workable plan. We could, we did, and we implemented it, much to the delight of the beneficiaries.

We squeezed every cruzeiro we could out of working capital, to the point of delivering our cheque for purchased products to Petrobrás in late afternoon after the banks had closed. We suspended deliveries to industrial customers as soon as their payments were in arrears, and since most of our competitors had begun to copy our methods, we managed not to lose any major customers. We were running risks, but we had done it with our eyes wide open, and only once did we get into trouble, when we hadn't the cash to pay Petrobrás on time. They demanded that, in compensation, they should be allowed to delay payment for crude oil they were buying from Shell Venezuela. Of course we had no power to agree to that: Shell Venezuela was a totally separate corporate entity, and we had to borrow the funds we needed from the Group. They reluctantly agreed, but in a few weeks we were able to clear the debt, and went on to make our targets. This gave us some leeway for investment, and we started to modernise our retail network, and to improve our office space, which needed it badly, though I insisted, to the surprise of many, that the management floor in the office be the last to be tackled. Everyone in Brazil has a nickname, which he or she very rarely learns, and then only by accident. The President of the Republic, who had a very short neck, was 'Giraffe for an apartment'; the rector of the University of Rio was 'Flying saucer' – brilliant, but shallow. Not until a couple of days before I left did I discover mine. I was 'Stale Bread', because nobody was allowed to buy a new loaf until the last crumb of the old was finished.

The road from the southern suburbs into Rio ran along the flat and narrow alluvial plain between the coastal mountains and Guanabara Bay. The municipality of Rio set out to make part of this into a showplace park, Parque Flamengo. The landscaping was designed by Burle Marx,

Brazil's leading designer of gardens and jewellery, and was illuminated at night by 'artificial moonlight' – very bright mercury vapour lights on very high posts. It was to include two or three service stations, and all the oil companies were invited to submit plans. We won this contest with a design that had all the facilities below ground level, and above ground only a glass pavilion which allowed you to see through. We designed special pumps of minimal profile, so that the whole station was very inconspicuous, and the pump attendants were all women, dressed in a strawberry-coloured uniform, who inevitably became known as the *Little Shell Strawberries.* We created quite a splash when we opened the stations, and the sales exceeded our bravest estimates: our problem was going to be to keep up sales when the novelty had worn off.

Our advertising agency had come up with a campaign based on a slogan: 'That little extra that you get from Shell.' Between us and the agency we thought of all sorts of little extras – concrete or in services – that cost very little, but were amusing or practical. In posters, print and on television the slogan was presented by a character created by the agency – *O elefantinho Shell*, the little Shell elephant, a stylised figure of an elephant, dressed and standing erect. He really caught the affection of Brazilians, who love anything *simpático*, to the extent that in the elections for the mayor of Rio (in which you could write in a vote, as well as mark your X for the announced candidates) the elefantinho Shell led the poll! We kept up a steady stream of little give-aways at the Flamengo stations, of which the most successful – so successful that the stations had long waiting lines – was a rose for every woman on Mother's Day, with a label saying: 'That little extra rose that you get from Shell, Mama.'

All our competitors in the market (excluding Petrobrás) were American, and they had become as cautious about investing as Shell, and two, Texaco and Atlantic, had been drawing in their horns for several years, and didn't wake up to the reality that Jonah had put his finger on, that you could still be profitable in difficult conditions. The morale of their station operators was very low, and when they began to find their Shell competitors smiling, many wanted to switch brands and join us. Of course there were contractual arrangements that made this difficult or impossible, but we were able to take over several really first-class operations, and make some modest increases to our market share. I recall one in particular, a Texaco station on one of the main highways. The sun set on it one night, and by dawn it had been transformed into a Shell station – paint, signs and pumps all switched in the hours of darkness. All these things helped get the Cimportex fiasco out of people's minds, and were great spirit raisers.

An amusing little interlude was when Monty Spaght came to visit Shell Brasil. As well as the usual places, we took him out to the state of Mato Grosso, on the vast subtropical Brazilian plateau, where four per cent of Brazil's population live on twenty per cent of the land. Cattle are raised on huge *fazendas* – ranches – and there is a little subsistence farming. The *fazenda* we visited with Monty was measured in millions of hectares, and had no less than five stations on the rail line that crossed it – the only one in the state. We were taken around in a pick-up truck driven by a very solemn five-year-old boy, whose legs didn't reach the pedals. To be able to see out he sat on his father's knees, and he gave monosyllabic orders for the pedals: 'Brake', 'Clutch', 'Fast' or 'Slow'. His father didn't cheat, but did just what he was told. It was fascinating, though we all whitened our knuckles when we came to a bridge across a stream, which consisted of two concrete slabs, each half a metre wide, and separated by the width of the track of a car or pick-up. But, without slackening speed, he steered us across with uncanny accuracy, and delivered us to where we were to have lunch. The inevitable *churasco*, a steak grilled on a steel skewer, was followed by choice of no less than fifteen desserts, mostly based on honey, sugar syrup or avocados. We heard afterwards that no *fazenda* would feel its duty done unless at least a dozen desserts were offered to even a single guest.

Monty asked to see a service station, and the District Manager took us to a very unimpressive one with a driveway of rolled earth, and a little two-storey building; the operator and his family lived upstairs. Monty asked Francisco Garcîa what volume this station sold, and was told two hundred thousand litres a month.

'Two hundred thousand a *year,* you mean, don't you?' Monty asked.

'No, a month,' answered Francisco García, and to Monty's further surprise, added that much of it was to the donkey cart trade. Monty was beginning to look a bit peeved at having his leg pulled, when up drove a donkey cart with a two hundred-litre drum mounted on it, and proceeded to take it. We explained that this was fuel being taken to big agricultural machinery a kilometre or two away. He burst out laughing, and said, 'Wait until I tell my old buddies in Shell Oil about loading two hundred litres into a donkey cart!'

Our systems were working so well that, early in 1967, I was asked if I would accept the invitation of Shell Française to carry out for them the same sort of study that the marketing team had done for other European companies: Leslie Froggatt had in fact started, but was needed elsewhere, and did not speak French. I was, it seemed, the only person in the Group who could both speak French and had the right kind of experience. I was to remain accountable for Shell Brasil, and could fly back for a visit whenever it seemed warranted. Again Billie had to uproot herself, just as she was beginning to find her social feet in Rio, and go back to living in a hotel, with a husband working long hours, and acquiring, because of the personnel savings he and his otherwise all-French team were finding, the sobriquet of *bourreau*: the hangman! But she found plenty to do; she walked almost every day from our hotel near the Etoile to the Louvre, and did some modest shopping in the Rue du Faubourg St Honoré. At weekends Shell Française lent us a car, and with the aid of the *Guide Michelin* we explored a great many of the interesting places within a hundred kilometres of Paris.

Many of Shell Française's problems were similar to those of Deutsche Shell and Shell Italiana, and sprang from the same root cause, the comparing of *average* sales proceeds and costs, instead of *marginal.* In France the problem appeared most clearly in the retail network. Shell had many large, high-volume stations on the highways, but also many Mom-and-Pop stations, often with a single pump, in mountain villages and remote rural areas, all with the same (controlled) prices. Not only prices, but the whole oil industry in France was tightly regulated by law, and the size of permits to refine depended – though not directly – on sales. So Shell Française was very reluctant to shed any outlets, until one of my French colleagues and I did a detailed study of the economics of some of these smaller stations. We discovered that, for many of them, the marginal cost of the paperwork, to say nothing of the delivery cost of small quantities in small trucks over long distances, exceeded the margin between cost of product and sales proceeds. Management was, at length, and not without some difficult persuasion, convinced!

I had to make two trips back to Rio; one in March, when Monty Spaght came for his appraisal of Shell Brasil's performance, and one six weeks later for some minor crisis, the nature of which I have forgotten. Deprived of its

President for four and a half months, except for these two short visits, Shell Brasil was exceeding – modestly but significantly – its financial targets.

We had given up our apartment when we left for Paris; it was not very conveniently located, was not air-conditioned and did not have the space for the sort of entertaining that we had to do, so Edith undertook to find something better while we were away. She excelled herself, and we returned to a magnificent place in Flamengo, on the fifteenth floor, with our back to the Morro da Viuva, a steep rock cliff less than fifty metres away from our bedroom windows, and in front a view across Flamengo Park and beach to the Sugar Loaf and the bay. Alas, our delight was not unalloyed. After I left Paris, I visited Central Offices in London. Apparently what we had done in Shell Brasil had persuaded the Group that maybe I was no longer needed there, and would I please accept reassignment to New York? But keep it under my hat for the time being.

The few months that remained to me in Rio after I had picked up the threads again were busy arranging the handover to my successor. I had told the Group earlier that there were three possible replacements for me: Mario Ramos as a stopgap, and, for the long term, Peter Landsberg, and our Vice-President of Marketing, Francisco García.

This last had an MBA from Harvard, was brilliant in his job and admired by the people who worked for him, but somehow not entirely trusted by others. His lifestyle seemed a little too opulent for his income, and he tended to be contemptuous of those whose education or intellect he thought inferior to his own (including most of his colleagues on the management team).

In due course, the Managing Directors picked Peter, and I announced to the company that I would be leaving and would be succeeded by him. It was a big boost to morale that a Brazilian was to get the top job, but Francisco exploded. He came in to see me and said that he should have the job, his MBA (Peter had been a fighter pilot in the Brazilian Air Force, and then a pilot in a commercial airline) and his record clearly said so. I told Francisco that I recognised his ability and his achievements, but the Managing Directors, on my recommendation, had picked Peter. He got very angry, and burst out, 'Then you don't know Peter, and the Managing Directors don't know what they are doing. And I won't work under Peter.' I told him that I could not tolerate such words, and after fifteen minutes of each repeating our positions, I told him that he left me no alternative but to fire him, and that I would arrange a severance package. In the meanwhile he should clear up his office, and not do any more company business. What he was seriously expecting I don't know; he could not really believe that he would ever be president of a subsidiary of the Shell Group, when he'd said that its Managing Directors didn't know what they were doing, but it was clearly a shock, because he left my office chalk white.

My time in Brazil was best summed up for me when I paid a visit on some other business five years later. Shell Brasil's new management gave a cocktail party for us, in an apartment four floors below our old one in Flamengo, which magnified the nostalgia. When only the hard core of our team was left at the end of the party, I said to Reinaldo Filardi, then Vice-President of Marketing, 'Oh! We had a lot of fun in those days, didn't we?'

He answered me very emphatically, 'No, it wasn't fun that we had: we made a *revolution*!'

I like to remember those words as the best comment upon my service in and contribution to Shell Brasil. Under Peter it never looked back: as the profits and the remittances increased, the Group decided that perhaps Brazil was a country in which it should invest. Peter took over a company the value of which on its shareholder's books was under five million pounds: when he retired several years later, it was half a billion.

Chapter Forty

The United States of America

The company I was to take over was Asiatic Petroleum Corporation, a wholly owned subsidiary of the Group, which operated under the shadow of the Shell Oil Company, the Group's biggest, but not wholly owned, subsidiary; it had a publicly held minority of almost twenty-five per cent. Asiatic's function was to carry out those activities in the oil industry in the United States in which Shell Oil chose not to be involved. Chose not, sometimes for economic reasons, but mostly because of the interests of the minority. US law is very protective of minority shareholdings, and a company is liable to suit by its minority stockholders if they believe that any of its actions give preference to its majority owner, to their prejudice. Asiatic had its origins in the early years of the century, in New York, and antedated Shell Oil, which was established in California, before gradually expanding east. Asiatic's purpose had been to acquire in the United States petroleum products for the Group's markets elsewhere in the world, with no activity in the US domestic market, but this had developed into four separate activities: bulk sales of imported heavy fuel oil and crude oil; the purchase of equipment and materials; purchase and sale of lubricants and chemicals, both these for Group companies outside the United States; and lastly a ragbag of services ranging from keeping contacts with American oil companies to recruiting from American universities non-US nationals for service in places such as Iran and Nigeria, and looking after visiting Managing Directors.

When I started, these businesses neatly amounted to oil sales of two million dollars a day, two million a week between materials, lubricants and chemicals, and two million a year in services. These sound like big numbers, but Asiatic's profit was tiny. The fuel oil came from Shell Venezuela, and the crude from Group central supplies, and our margin was one per cent. We were the actual buyers and sellers – other Group companies could not be selling in the United States without being found to be doing business there, with a consequent big exposure to US tax, and we took the credit risk, so one per cent was not lavish. Our customers were companies which were large resellers of fuel oil, Leon Hess's Hess Oil and Ed Carey's New England Petroleum in New York, and Steuart Petroleum in Washington, for example, as well as electric utility companies and major distributors of furnace fuel in the New York metropolitan area.

The fuel oil market had burgeoned when the production of crude oil, much of it heavy, leaving a large residue of heavy fuel when refined, was developed in Venezuela in the early Fifties. Shell Oil rejected an offer to open a market for oil fuel in what was largely a coal-consuming industry, so the Group set up a company, Shell Caribbean Petroleum, registered in Ontario, specifically for this purpose. Eventually this shared offices and support services in New York with Asiatic, while corporately the two were separate. However, in the mid-Sixties the Group (which always retained the shareholder's right to appoint top managers) set up what anyone ought to have realised was a recipe for trouble. Adam Hulton was President of Asiatic, John Walstrom of Caribbean, and the Group appointed Adam as Vice-President of Caribbean, and John Vice-President of

Asiatic. This raised so many boundary problems that some time before I was appointed, neither would speak to the other, and when John (who was American) heard that another Limey would be coming to replace Adam, he quit, and Adam became President of both companies, and the oil business of Caribbean was merged into Asiatic. John and I had previously met casually, but he refused to meet me all the time I was in New York.

Every expatriate business person knows the phenomenon of culture shock; the need in a strange country to get used, not only to a different language, but to all the differences in law, in customs, in words and gestures that are taboo, in the degree of deference owed to a government official, and lots more. I had been exposed to several such shocks, but found that, after six months, I was over it. Naively, I supposed that the shock of the USA would be easier. Not a bit of it! George Bernard Shaw has said that 'England and America are two countries separated by the same language', and indeed it is so. Many of the differences are well known: sidewalk/pavement, pavement/roadway, gasoline/petrol, kerosene/paraffin, but there are dozens of other, often subtle ones, as 'tabling' an issue in a meeting. In Britain, this means to lay it on the table for discussion now; in the USA it means lay it on the table for discussion some time in the future – to shelve it. To this day, after thirty years, I sometimes find myself mispronouncing, or using a word that is misunderstood. Then there is the attitude to law. The USA has fifteen times as many lawyers per thousand of population as Japan, and you need to take your lawyer's advice far more frequently than in any other country I have worked in. It was two years before this shock was behind me.

Everyone has heard of the American habit of the three Martini lunch, but I had never met it until I started to take over from Adam Hulton. He had arranged a number of lunch parties for me to meet those that I needed to know, from the competitors to the big customers, other British businessmen, and the British Consul-General. This last lunch was very embarrassing: Adam had recently become an American citizen, and halfway through lunch he pulled his British passport out of his pocket and pushed it across the table to the Consul-General, saying, 'I've become an American, so I have no further use for this, and I'd like to return it to you.'

The Consul-General ostentatiously put his hands under the table, and said, very icily, 'You cannot renounce British nationality, and neither I nor anyone else can take your passport from you.' Then, very adroitly, he turned to me and introduced a new subject as if nothing had happened.

On days when we had no guests to entertain, Adam would take me to the 21 Club,[1] three short blocks away, and we had lunch, just the two of us together. Adam started by ordering, and the words came out as if they were a recording, 'A Martini, very dry, very cold, straight up[2] with a twist.' When it came, he picked it up with a hand so shaky that he spilled a quarter of it, drank it in a couple of gulps and ordered another. His hand was now less shaky, he didn't spill much and he took longer to drink it. But it was followed by a third, which he drank slowly and without a tremble.

The 21 had a lounge downstairs with a large-screen television, and when we'd finished lunch Adam would say, 'I've become quite a baseball fan since I've been in this country, and since I'm sure there are lots of files you need to read in the office, I'll stay here and watch today's game.' He would sink into an armchair in front of the TV, and before I was out of the door, he would be snoring. He was

---

[1] A high-class 'speakeasy' in prohibition days.

[2] Without ice.

my first close experience with an alcoholic, and I made up my mind that never would I have more than one drink before lunch, which became easier as the years went by, and the habit moved closer to the three Perrier water lunch.

One problem that Adam had left me was a bad start for me in one of my key relationships, with our biggest customer, Leon Hess. There was some insignificant dispute with him, and just before I arrived, Leon came in to see Adam to make a concession on the issue. He handed a piece of paper to Adam, who, before Leon had even sat down, looked at it, and said, 'I fear the Greeks bearing gifts.' Leon turned on his heel and walked out, and initially I was suspect by association. We became, however, good friends, and the biggest deal I ever did was with him, a few years later. He wanted to buy crude for two of his refineries, and would like to pay in part in sterling instead of dollars. I had the necessary negotiating latitude from the Group and Shell Venezuela, and Leon invited me to lunch at La Caravelle, then his favourite restaurant.

At that time, I carried in my left jacket pocket a bunch of cards, buff manila, the size and shape of playing cards, with my initials in a bottom corner. I used these when I was out to make notes to be dealt with back in the office, transferring active cards from blank by moving them to my right hand pocket. We started to talk and to agree on some points, and as we did so, I made notes on a card. We sat late at the lunch table (not that we had had a large lunch; Leon always had the same, a salade Niçoise). As we progressed we both would make notes on one of my cards, until the complete deal was done. It called for Amerada-Hess, Leon's company, to buy from the Shell Group a quarter of a million dollars worth of crude oil per day – ten thousand dollars per hour – for three years. When I was back in the office I called in Mike Paulli, our Vice-President of Marketing, Bob Koerner, our General Counsel and John

Rochford, the lawyer responsible for commercial matters.

'The deal's done,' I said, and laid five of my cards, half in Leon's handwriting, half in mine, on the table.

'Is that *all* you've got?' asked John, anxiously, and on being told yes, he took the cards down to his office, copied them and locked them in the Legal Department's safe. When he joined us again, I asked him to send a copy of his copies of my cards (with a note from me) to Leon, and to get together with the Amerada-Hess lawyers to draw up formal documents. It says a lot for the degree of confidence that existed in the oil industry of that period (and Hamlet's 'law's delays'!) that it was not until fifteen months later, by which time crude oil worth $120 million had been delivered and paid for, that the formal contracts were executed and exchanged. But I'm jumping ahead.

Asiatic then kept two suites in the Dorset Hotel, six or seven minutes from the office, for the use of visitors, and Billie and I took over the larger of the two and lived there until the end of the year, when we had found an apartment and been able to furnish it with what we had brought from Brazil, and what had been in storage in Kingston from our Richmond days.

After Adam left I began taking stock of Asiatic, and it was pretty daunting. We had acquired a new Vice-President of Marketing, Sidney Goldin, an experienced marketer from Shell Oil, to take the place of John Walstrom, and under Sidney, Mike Paulli was Sales Manager. These two had the most important part of our business pretty well under control, while our legal affairs were in the hands of two senior lawyers. Don Fobes, with long experience of the business of the Shell Group in North America, was General Counsel, and Bob Koerner, whose background was tax, looked after the complications of the relationships between Asiatic, the Group and its shareholding in Shell Oil, all of which were highly charged with possible adverse tax and minority stockholder consequences. Below them were Mike Lorenzo, an intellectual lawyer, and John Rochford, a practical commercial one.

A few days after I was in the chair, I was invited to a meeting to review the company's accounts for the quarter. About a dozen of us sat round a table, and were each handed a copy of the accounts. They were singularly uninformative about the company's business, and our Controller, Bernie Langguth, proceeded to read the figures out to us, line by line, as though we couldn't read, and when we came to accounts receivable, he handed out a back-up sheet to explain a couple of thousand dollars out of a total of many millions. This showed amounts owed to the company by employees who had borrowed from us, widows of deceased employees who had been advanced money for funeral expenses, and other trivial amounts. I asked about our two biggest customers, Hess and Carey, and was told that I could have a statement of those if I really needed it. At the end of the meeting, during which no one but I had asked a single question, Bernie started to collect all the papers. 'Wait a minute,' I said, 'I, and I'm sure others, need to go over these in less of a hurry, so don't take them away.'

'No, the Controller's Department prepares the accounts, and we keep all the copies; it's an accounting matter,' was Bernie's reply, and I had to be pretty firm in telling him that the accounts were a tool for the use of management, and not just a bunch of papers to be filed in accounting.

After the meeting, I went with John Ghents, the Vice-President of Finance, back to his office and explained to him what I wanted to see in the accounts. Quite clearly, John didn't get the point at all, and felt that I was encroaching on his territory, to the point that I had to pull my rank and say that this was the way I wanted it. Some time later I saw, by accident, a detailed statement of an amount which was buried in the total of accounts receivable – the amounts the Group Managing Directors owed Asiatic. It was common practice for some (but not all) to ask Asiatic to book them theatre tickets, buy them this and that, arrange personal travel for them and their families, and 'charge it to my account'. When I saw the statement one of them, who was in fact no longer even a Managing Director, owed twenty-seven thousand dollars, and the total was close to one hundred thousand, which no member of our management but John Ghents ever saw. John owed his position in part to the little favours he was able to do for the MDs, and I had to walk on eggshells. I went to see our auditors, Price Waterhouse, and asked them if I would be right in allowing this practice to continue, and got the answer I wanted – no; and the debts should be settled as soon as possible. I told John, and said that I would take on the most difficult part of the task, the twenty-seven thousand dollars, but he must tackle the others, quoting Price Waterhouse's opinion. Most of the MDs saw the point, and settled pretty quickly, but two wriggled like fish on a hook, and it was four months before the twenty-seven thousand dollars was off our books.

We did at length get marginal improvements to our management accounting, but it was an incredible seven years later, with a new Vice-President of Finance, that we finally got what Shell Brasil had developed in a matter of weeks. Some of this delay was a rearguard action from the old hands, but some was in part justifiable, for Price Waterhouse, whom we had asked to help us setting up the new system, said that our general ledger lacked integrity, and we had to start from scratch to build accounts that would really serve the purpose of guiding management decisions.

Another Augean stable was our Materials Department. It had one hundred and twenty-odd people in it, with at the top four people: the General Manager, and the managers of purchasing, shipping and administration. Most of the business was conducted, initially, by cable, the formal contracts being confirmatory. The General Manager insisted on seeing every cable that came in and was sent out, and so had no time to do anything else in the course of a working day. The purchasing and shipping managers, too, would not allow cables to be sent without their approval, so most of the day there were queues of employees outside their office doors to get their communications initialled. I was walking round the office one day, and seeing all these people waiting made me curious, and I started asking questions.

The Group Materials Co-ordinator in Central Offices was an old friend, Ken Watson, and in many ways he was our customer, so I telephoned him one day and asked how he felt about Asiatic's performance in this field. Ken never minced his words and, in brief, his answer was 'lousy', to the point that he was beginning to explore other ways of procurement in the USA, without risk that the Group as a whole might be 'found', and taxable in the USA. Such a change would inevitably mean duplication of some of our activities, and would be unnecessary if we could get our act in order. I asked the General Manager to come to my office one morning – if I'd gone to his, which I would normally have done, the flood of cables would have kept intruding! I told him that it simply could not be necessary for him to see everything.

'But I'm responsible,' he said, and when I talked about delegation, he said it was just not possible, the quality of his employees was simply not up to it. I said I just could not believe that: I told him of my recent experience in Europe and Brazil, and offered to come and work as a consultant with him for half of every day for a couple of weeks. He was hesitant, and I asked him to go away and think about it, and let me have his answer the next morning. He turned me down, and said he could not do his job any other way. Then his only choice, I said, was to take early retirement. I offered the job to the manager, first of purchasing, and then of shipping, and both turned me down. The Manager of Administration was obviously not of the calibre for the top job, and he indicated, not to me, but to August (Gus) Sand, our General Manager of Personnel, that he would welcome early retirement. I called Ken and asked him if he had any knowledge of other people in the organisation who could take over, and he promptly suggested Alan Gerald, head of the aviation section. Alan accepted the challenge, and in a couple of weeks took over.

He was a great success, and in time increased the volume of the business by a half, and cut his staff by forty per cent. He installed his own departmental computer system, with several terminals available for his people to work on directly. In this he was away ahead of the rest of the company, which, when I arrived had two computers – one of which was in use, and the other a spare, in case of a breakdown. IBM had done a very good sales job – if not a very honest one! Even the one we used did little to enhance our productivity: when I asked what it did for us, the answer was that it served as an accounting machine, and printed the internal telephone directory.

Personnel administration, too, was unsatisfactory, with elementary and uncritical performance appraisals, no feedback to the individual, and no career or succession planning. Many of these problems stemmed from Asiatic's earlier history, when it was no more than a provider of services to Central Offices, and when almost every executive position was held by an expatriate, and Americans (with the notable exception of the lawyers) were hired as clerical workers. New York had been, and in the mid-Sixties still was, an ethnically segregated society, not only between whites and blacks, but between Protestants and Catholics, and within the latter between Irish and Italians. Asiatic's few American senior people were Irish, and as a result almost all the 'other ranks' were Irish too. They happened also to be the cheaper clerical workers, and so we had recruited almost entirely Irish high school graduates: university-educated men were few and far between: women were hired for secretarial and clerical posts only.

Gus Sand was our Personnel Manager. He was not a human resources person in any modern sense, and he had no experience of such things as participative management or individual development. I had been a member of the British Institute of Personnel Management since my time in Egypt, and had come to expect such skills and knowledge in people in the personnel function, like Ivayr Azevedo in Brazil. So after a few months I persuaded Gus, who was in any case close to retirement, to take on a professional, under him to begin with, and then to take his place. After interviewing a small number of what seemed to me rather humdrum applicants there turned up David Sepsenwol, who even by my standards was in the avant-garde. And in time he helped us make some big changes; notably peer review of performance. Instead of the old process of appraisal by the person above in the hierarchy, we began to have everyone's performance of his or her job evaluated by those whose work depended on contributions from the one being appraised. A series of multiple-choice questions were asked, the answers to which defined the extent of help received. There were four levels of satisfaction, all related to our view of the outside market for the relevant skills. They were: If we were recruiting someone to provide you with the support you need in this area, and the person you are reviewing applied, would you: (a) take him or her on without looking further; (b) continue to look, but try to be sure you didn't lose this one; (c) hire, because you need the help, but still keep looking outside, or (d) don't hire; find some other way to get the service?

These criteria were applied to various aspects of service quality: promptness, degree of professional skill, completeness of answers to questions, and so on. This absolutely revolutionised the way we judged performance and fixed remuneration: and a (d) from over half the reviewers meant no salary increase this year, and a second year of the same rating meant *out*!

Gradually we built up a real management team, which became our 'Executive Committee', consisting of the Vice-Presidents of Marketing and Finance, the General Managers of Materials and Personnel and our General Counsel, Don Fobes, with me in the chair. We quickly gave ourselves the acronym Excom, and another committee, of all the department managers, became Mancom. Both met regularly, so we had the means of communicating across the company, up and down, of getting the views of the people concerned (and of others, who though not immediately concerned had ideas to contribute) before a decision was taken, and of the decision and the reasons for it being known beforehand. We also had our Board of Directors (composed of some, but not all, of the members of Excom) which had to vote on those formal matters which the law, or the importance of the issue, required.

One of our biggest customers, as the war in Vietnam heated up, was the Defence Fuels Supply Center, the organisation in Washington that was responsible for procuring all the fuels needed by the US forces, notably, then, in Vietnam. The DFSC could deal only with US corporations, so that in case of trouble the supplier would be found, and sued, in the USA. The Shell Group had a subsidiary in Vietnam – Cong Ty Shell Vietnam – and a big supply centre in Singapore, and so was in a position to be very competitive in this task. So we, Asiatic, entered into contracts for supply with Shell International and Shell Singapore, for transport with Shell International Marine, and for storage and handling inside the country with Shell Vietnam. With this back-up, we contracted with DFSC to supply fuels as it required, in bulk to ocean terminals, down to five-gallon 'ameri-cans'[3] delivered to the front line. DFSC was bound by government regulations designed to protect the interests of the US taxpayer, and was not easy to deal with, and we had a manager, Paul Gallien, dedicated to this business. He was backed up by Frank O'Connor, the manager of our Washington office, whose gift for making friends was scarcely believable, who kept friendly lines of communication open. These two not infrequently needed reinforcement from Sid Goldin and his successors Frank Hunt and then Mike Paulli, and even from me, not that I could add any knowledge to an issue, but for my rank vis-à-vis a general. We were exposed to much suspicion in the press and in Congress of predatory pricing or short weight. Senator William Proxmire of Wisconsin (a dedicated foe of the oil industry) accused us publicly of cheating the US Military because we failed to adjust the price of the five-gallon-can deliveries for the fact that we were delivering product that had expanded in the high temperatures of the front line, while the USA was paying for product at a lower temperature! One wonders if he had ever seen cans being filled, or transported to a line of battle by truck over dirt roads, or even imagined what the process involved. But he was a Senator, and we had to provide answers, without letting it be seen that we thought the question was a silly waste of time!

Having the US government as our customer required that we had a written 'Affirmative Action Program' to

---

[3]'Ameri-cans' on the analogy of 'jerricans'. A common usage in the Armed Forces.

ensure that as a company not only did we not discriminate by race, sex or national origin in our employment, but that we had a programme to redress, in our recruitment practices, any inequalities from the past. Our actions were monitored by the Office of Federal Contract Compliance, and by the New York office of the Equal Employment Opportunity Commission – the EEOC. The general criterion used by the EEOC was the extent to which our personnel matched the population of the area in which we operated. The groups we had to consider were, in addition to black and white, women, Asians and Americans with Spanish last names. We, as I have mentioned, were predominantly white, Roman Catholics, and of Irish origin, so we had work to do, starting with a programme. I called a meeting of our management and all department managers and put the problem to the latter, suggesting that since they would have to live with, and execute, our plan, they had better design one, and submit it to Excom for approval.

When Castro took over Cuba, the then President of Shell Cuba asked for all Cubans seconded to other Group companies to return to Cuba. Accordingly, Nick Colás had left Argentina, but after a few weeks back in Havana found that there was no real job for him, so he and Elisa left for New York, and went back to university, Nick to get his Master's in engineering and Elisa a Bachelor's degree in library management. After they both graduated, Nick got a job in Madrid with an American firm of consulting engineers. When his contract expired and they came back to the States, they made contact with us. He was going to look for a new job, and Asiatic badly needed an engineer with Nick's experience and drive, so I asked him to come and join us. Thus we had an American with a Spanish last name among our managers, and his colleagues elected him their Chairman for this project. Three or four months later, the managers reported to the Board. Their programme was this:

> We are resolved that for the remainder of 1972 and until the company's minority population more closely reflects the minority population of our employment area, Asiatic will give its first consideration to hiring minority group members or women to fill whatever vacancies occur in the organisation. Any departure from this resolution will be reviewed by the Executive Committee in writing before any offer of employment is offered.
>
> Furthermore, the fact that minority group members or women may initially have lower skill levels than other applicants will not preclude their employment.
>
> Furthermore, the company expects its managers to exercise their abilities in training and developing minority staff and women to assure competent and responsible job performance.
>
> The company reaffirms its policy that employees be given every opportunity to capitalize their skills and resources without regard to race, creed, color, national origin, sex or age.

In parallel, David Sepsenwol and his people devised a job-posting plan, which said that, to ensure fairness, we would post every vacancy above the lowest level and below that of department manager, and every employee would have the right to apply for it. Before submitting his or her name as a candidate for any posted opening the employee must have consulted his or her current manager for advice and guidance, *but the manager would have no right to deny the application.* If a candidate were accepted, the present manager might go to Excom and plead serious damage if he were to lose the employee, but might get his way only if he could show that, in the event that the candidate stayed with him, salary and prospects would be as good as in the posted job. The manager of the department posting the job would have the right to choose between offering candidates. While this gave scope to discrimination, it would be out in the open, and could be challenged.

The managers voted fifteen to one in favour of the plan. Ironically, the only 'nay' vote came from the manager of our Technical Department, Mark Levin – Jewish, and so a member of a group discriminated against in the previous generation.

Some time later we were audited by the New York Equal Employment Opportunity Commission, and were told that our plan (which by then was bearing its first fruits) was the best it had seen. And it worked in ways we would never have expected: the job of Assistant Manager, Fuel Oil Sales to (electric generating) Utilities was posted, and a woman who was the senior systems analyst in our computer operations applied. She was interviewed by the managers under whom she would have to work, and, though she had never been in sales nor in anything to do with fuels, she had acquired enough knowledge to show that she understood what the job was all about, and she was picked unanimously. Her old boss protested that she was absolutely indispensable, and that, if she left, our computing plans would be seriously delayed. We reminded him of the saying that the cemeteries are full of indispensables, and suggested that he post the job internally. He found one of his programmers who quickly became a competent systems analyst: the woman, when I last saw her, was Manager of Fuel Procurement at the biggest New York electric utility, Consolidated Edison!

Sidney Goldin was close to retirement age when I joined Asiatic, and in two years or so we had to find a replacement for him. We had a potential candidate in our Sales Manager,

Mike Paulli, but the Group, Shell Venezuela and I all felt that he would be able to do a much better job (and improve the co-operation between us and our suppliers) if he were to spend two years working in Venezuela first. I wanted an American, not an expatriate, in the job, so I approached Shell Oil for the transfer, on loan, of a suitably experienced marketer. They offered, and we accepted, Frank Hunt, who came in first as Sales Manager to replace Mike Paulli when he went to Venezuela, and then took over from Sidney. I liked him immediately, and he went down well with his department, though he caused some amusement by his hypochondria. Margaret Callahan, his secretary, made us all laugh one day by describing all the things he put into his mouth in the space of a couple of minutes. When she went into his office, he was smoking a cigarette and taking his temperature. He put the former down long enough to spray his throat, then take two Tums antacids and two aspirins, and a drink of water to wash them down, put the cigarette back in and began to drink his cup of coffee. It was cruel of us to laugh, because it turned out that Frank had cancer of the lungs, and he died only a couple of years after he left us.

Billie and I got to know Frank and his wife Patricia well, socially, and I often had a vague feeling that I had met Patricia before, though I could never place when nor where, nor did she show any signs of previous acquaintance, until one day when both Frank and I had to go to Washington together on some business with Steuart Petroleum, and decided to take our wives with us. We were all staying in the Watergate Hotel, and in the evening we met in the bar for a drink before dinner. We got to talking, and when my naval background came up, Patricia said she had spent the war in the WRNS.

'Mostly,' she said, 'at Immingham Dock, working on the plot.'

And suddenly, as soon as we could mentally see each

other in uniform, it all came back. And Steuart Petroleum and Asiatic had to take a back seat in the dinner-table conversation to recollections of World War II.

Chapter Forty-One

The NEES Contract

As time went on we began to broaden our customer base from DFSC and large resellers to electric utility companies: Con Edison in New York, Potomac Electric Power in Washington DC and New England Electric System (NEES) in Massachusetts, Rhode Island and New Hampshire. We shared the business of this last with Exxon, and we each supplied fifty per cent of NEES's fuel requirements. The Chief Executive of this system (you may not call it a company; it is in fact a Massachusetts Trust, a form of corporate organisation peculiar to this one state) was Guy Nichols, who worked very hard to keep the cost of his fuel as low as possible, and he kept up pressure on us, to the moment in the late Sixties when we signed a ten-year supply contract with NEES at a price of, I think, $1.69 a barrel for residual fuel oil from Venezuela. Through the Sixties the world's potential supply of oil grew by leaps and bounds, and the number of companies exploring for it, producing it and marketing it grew even faster, and competition became fiercer and prices kept falling. From our point of view it made sense to sew up a long-term customer at a fixed price: from NEES's, security of supply and a predictable cost were worthwhile goals.

A Japanese proverb says 'Speak of the future, and the devil laughs'; *a fortiori*, he laughs even louder when you make plans for the future, based on extrapolation of the past. And the decline of prices which had lasted two decades was coming to an end: low prices and ample supplies had increased the demand for petroleum even faster than the growth of supply. So, suddenly, in the early Seventies OPEC and its members saw their opportunities to start squeezing out higher prices. Qaddafi's Libya started the ball rolling, and by the autumn of 1970 had succeeded in forcing on Occidental (the major producer of Libyan crude) a twenty per cent increase in the Libyan 'take' of royalty and tax together. Iran followed, and won, from the Consortium (of companies that operated in the country) an increase for itself to fifty-five per cent (from the hallowed fifty per cent) of the profits. Not to be outdone, Venezuela, instead of negotiating with its concession holders, simply claimed sovereign rights, and legislated that its share would be sixty per cent, and that moreover it had the right to raise prices unilaterally, without the companies having a right to negotiate.[1] This made our contract with NEES instantly a loss-maker: we claimed *force majeure* and told NEES we were unilaterally increasing our prices by the amount of the additional 'host government take'.

Our contract provided for arbitration in the case of dispute, and we set the process in motion. NEES then took a lawsuit against us, alleging that this was a matter of overriding public interest, and thus not proper for arbitration. We kept on supplying and invoicing at our new price, while NEES continued to pay the old one. Guy Nichols and I met at intervals, and glared at one another over various tables. Guy tried to go over my head to Sir David Barran in Shell in London, by retaining the distinguished solicitor, Lord Goodman, and getting him to arrange a meeting between them. Billie and I were on

---

[1] I am indebted to Daniel Yergin's masterpiece, *The Prize* for jogging my memory about these events.

vacation in London with Billie's grandson, Eric, when Asiatic's Legal Department heard about the meeting, and John Rochford somehow reached me on the telephone at Heathrow, where we were about to take a plane to Paris. He told me this meeting had been set up for the following Friday, and said, in none too polite terms, that I'd better get there, and on time.

On Friday I left Billie and Eric in Paris, got an early flight to London, and went to Shell Centre to meet David. It happened to be his last Friday in the office before he retired: he had clearly had a good lunch with his fellow directors and was in an expansive mood. In his car on the way to Lord Goodman's office I explained the problem to him, but he just wanted to hear what Guy and Lord Goodman had to say. To the latter I took an instant dislike. He was a fat man, sprawling behind his desk, smoking a cigar, with the sleeves of his none too clean shirt loosely rolled up. I said 'hello' to Guy, but then spoke to him only through Lord Goodman. By this time the difference between NEES's and Asiatic's prices on the volumes delivered was almost twenty million dollars, so we were not disputing about peanuts.

Guy argued for the wording of the original contract, and for excluding *force majeure* on the grounds of public interest. I argued that we were facing the acts of a sovereign state, serious enough now, but because Venezuela could in future *legislate* prices, of incalculable effect in coming years. David argued that somehow we should be able to solve the dispute without lawsuits and arbitration, but we got nowhere – Guy and I still just glared at one another, and neither gave an inch. Lord Goodman suddenly said that he believed the way out was friendly arbitration; how 'friendly' differs from the proper legal kind, he didn't explain. He went on to say that he knew a professor at Southampton University, who was well versed in pricing questions, who could arbitrate between us, and asked his secretary to get the professor on the telephone. I said I was in no way empowered to accept such an offer, and certainly not until Asiatic's Board of Directors should agree to a suggestion as unusual as accepting an arbitrator, totally unknown to us, and selected by the solicitor for the adversary party. David Barran made noises of 'Well, I think we could agree to something like that…' I had to cut him short, and remind him that, as he well knew, having himself been President of Asiatic, we were a US corporation, and that no officer or representative of Asiatic's shareholders could agree anything for us without agreement of our Board. That brought the meeting to an awkward end, and I rode back to Shell Centre with David in complete silence. Back in Paris, I arranged for a telephone meeting of Asiatic's Board on the Monday, and Lord Goodman's proposal was turned down unanimously.

We finished our vacation, though I got a blow-by-blow report of the arbitration proceedings every day. And soon after I got back, we got a lucky break. In sworn testimony NEES's Vice-President of Procurement stated that Exxon had undertaken to continue to supply its fifty per cent at the contract price, and we discovered that this was not so – Exxon had committed only to *five* per cent. It struck me that this was perhaps the moment to settle. By now the difference between us was twenty-one million dollars. I dreamed up an offer, and got Asiatic's Board, and Shell Venezuela, *our* supplier, to agree to my trying it on Guy Nichols. I went up to see him in his office in Boston, and started off by saying that, however deep our differences, it didn't seem right for perjury to go unchallenged, but that I had an offer to try out on him, subject to my Board's eventual support. I suggested a price for the period of the dispute which would give NEES eleven of the twenty-one million dollars difference (I did not quote this figure to him – but he could quickly work it out for himself). For the future I offered him a supply commitment for all NEES's uncovered residual fuel requirements, for the balance of our ten-year period, at a price which would be no less than five cents a barrel below Exxon or Hess (who would have been a potential third supplier). In return, we wanted a commitment from NEES that any future increase in host government take would be added to the price automatically.

Guy said that, of course, he would have to get his Board's agreement, but that, subject to his studying the figures more closely, he would recommend Asiatic's offer to them, and he invited me out to lunch. A strange thing had happened that morning: Guy and I had both realised that each one of us was just doing his best for the interests of his shareholders, and that there was nothing personal in the glaring at each other! We suddenly became friends, and our friendship warmed and strengthened over the years. By the time our contract expired, oil prices had more than quadrupled, and Asiatic had received over two hundred million dollars more than the original contract would have allowed. But NEES had never gone short of fuel at a very competitive price.

Chapter Forty-Two

Sprague

One of our larger reseller customers of long standing was C.H. Sprague and Sons Company, which had terminals in New England, centred on Portsmouth, New Hampshire. The last of the Sprague family in the business, Shaw Sprague, was the major stockholder, but he was losing interest in the business in favour of activities involving more fun than work, so the active management had passed to his son-in-law, Robert (Bobbie) Monks, who had taken on board as a junior partner, Dwight Allison. The two of them had come to the conclusion that the market was becoming less and less hospitable for truly independent companies: most of their like competitors had already been acquired by major oil companies. So one day Bobbie and Dwight came to see me and asked if Asiatic would be interested in acquiring Sprague. We already owned a minority in the company in the form of a special class of share, which we had acquired as security for a credit (for supplies) we had given it some years previously.

The possibility was very attractive to us – we had already started to look beyond our traditional boundaries for expansion opportunities, and a direct presence in the retail market would be logical – but for one big difficulty. Shell Oil was, of course, almost wholly in the retail market, and if we were to get into it as well, our market shares added together might be considered an illegal concentration. But

Shell Oil was not present in New England, and Sprague not outside it, so I decided to ask Bill Kenney, Shell Oil's General Counsel, for his personal advice. He, strictly, could not give me *personal* advice, since he was an officer of Shell Oil, and I should not have asked him. But he thought the facts over, and said, 'If I were you, I'd give it a whirl.' With that assurance I persuaded the Group to let us go ahead, and after some second-guessing and nit-picking on the part of Monty Spaght's acolytes in Central Offices, we consummated the deal in early June 1969. The name wasn't changed, and we told the Sprague people that we would disturb their ways as little as possible, but we promised more frequent contact, and all the supplies they needed.

Digression: T-Group

Here I must digress. One of Asiatic's 'service' activities was to keep the Group Personnel function up to date on American developments in personnel management and relations. From my early years in Shell, from Brazil, and from the Navy before that, this field had been, indeed still is, one of my special interests. The job was in the hands of a brilliant and charming person, Donald Leitch, who of course did not keep to himself any ideas and techniques he came across in his gathering of knowledge, but shared them with Asiatic. A process called T-Group was becoming popular in the USA about this time, and Don urged me (and Billie too) to go to one, organised especially for presidents or vice-presidents of corporations, at the Rancho la Costa Resort in California, for which he had provisionally reserved places. Several of my friends had been on T-Groups, and were enthusiastic about them, but none could describe to me of what they consisted. The most articulate answer I managed to get was, 'Well, it's like seeing yourself as if you were another person outside you.'

Not very illuminating, but on Don's assurance that we would both get a lot out of it, we went.

On arrival on Sunday we found ourselves divided into three groups; two, A and B, of eight men each, and the third, C, of the ten wives who had accompanied their husbands. The faculty were all members of National Training Laboratories, a loose network of academics in the field of behavioural science, and especially interpersonal relationships. The top organiser was the doyen of the field, Dr Lee Bradford, and the counsellor of my Group B was a man I came to know very well, Professor Charles ('Chuck') K. Ferguson of the University of Southern California. We dined, all mixed up together, the first night, and on Monday morning, after breakfast, we met together for Lee to tell us what we were going to do. It sounded improbable, even silly. We would, each group in a room, discuss only what was going on in that room, with no format, no agenda, nothing that we had brought with us from back at the office.

With no more than that introduction, we all went off to our rooms. We sat in chairs arranged in a circle, Chuck just one of the circle. He looked rather like Buddha, hands folded over a too-fat tummy, with an inscrutable faint smile on his face. His big head twitched sideways about five degrees every two seconds or so, which was, until one got used to it, a bit unnerving. He told us later that it was caused by a spur on the bones of his neck touching a nerve. But beyond the smile he did, and said, nothing. Nor did we: but silence quickly becomes unbearable.

Suddenly three people started to talk at once, but one triumphed and the other two shut up. 'I'm a medical doctor,' said this man, 'and medicine is a hard science. I just don't believe that there is such a thing as *behavioural* science, and to start from the premise that there can be is a waste of time.'

'Medicine a hard science? Hooey! At best it's a craft based on folklore,' came an instant riposte, and in a general discussion we split into two camps: those who believed there could be a science of behaviour, that from observation you could postulate theories that could be proved by experiment, and from which you could forecast reactions to certain types of behaviour; and those who strongly disbelieved it.

In a pause, when the intensity died down a little, Chuck spoke. He said he would like to comment on two aspects of what we had been saying, from two points of view, *content* and *process* – *what* had been said, *how* it had been said, and how it had been *heard.* He referred back to two particular exchanges, which he was able to re-create almost verbatim, and pointed out that in one, B had not even waited for A to finish before jumping in with an objection which did not even refer to what A had said, and in the other C did not wait for D to finish before he repeated, more loudly and more emphatically, what he had already said before. Were we, he asked, really interested in the other guy's point of view, or just making sure that ours was heard with the highest volume? He spoke quietly, and with no suggestion of the professor in his words, and we were, for a few moments, silenced. I think we all thought about what Chuck had said, and had to accept that he was right. I cannot say that the rest of our discussions were exemplary, but we had all learned one lesson – discussion needs listening, and listening without a closed mind.

By Tuesday evening we had begun to get the feel of what we were learning, and to perceive why this was called a laboratory: we were the substances in the test tube, and we were also the observers of the reaction, and any explosions would be on a test-tube scale, and unlikely to cause much damage. Chuck's occasional comments on process acted as a catalyst and helped us to see how we were coming across to others. We had begun to create trust, and I for one was beginning to see the value of it all. Then, after breakfast on Wednesday Lee Bradford announced, baldly, 'Today, Group A has the obligation and the authority to take over groups B and C, and to decide how we all spend the rest of the day.'

To several of the men, this smelled of the sort of business game they had played before, and began to ask questions, 'What are the rules?', 'Who is the Chief Executive?', 'Are there financial constraints?'

Lee simply repeated, 'Today, Group A... Those are the only rules. But I would suggest that Group A return to their room and decide *how* they are going to take the others over, and then *what* they will do for the rest of the day, while B and C go to their rooms, and imagine what Group A might do, and how they will react. Suppose we give you all an hour, to start with.'

We went back to our room, and asked ourselves what we knew about Group A, and their mini-culture; all that we knew for certain (their room was next to ours) was that they laughed a lot, which was not much to go on. We thought they might perhaps send half their number to join us, and the other half to join the wives, but this would leave them in a minority in each new group. So perhaps they would form us all into one big group, but again they would be in the minority, and though they had the authority to decide on agenda for the rest of the day, it might be difficult if enough of B and C didn't like their ideas. We thought of all kinds of ideas, but none seemed very attractive, and I began to get restive.

'If they try to graft some of themselves – even one or two – on to us we will not be Group B any longer. They will destroy our identity. And I've begun to like Group B. Presumably we shall revert to ourselves tomorrow, anyway, so if I don't like what they suggest, I'm going to take the day off. The weather's lovely, the swimming pool is right out there, and I'll spend the day swimming and having a siesta. They have no sanctions, and they can't compel me to do anything I don't like.' A few of the rest of the group seemed to share my ideas, but most were against me, in words like: 'You can't do that: you can't let our group down.'

'But it won't be *our* group,' I repeated, 'if they try to add or subtract people.'

Group A weren't having an easy time, either, deciding what to do. Through the door that separated our two rooms, we could hear a lot of raised voices, and some angry exchanges. And they exceeded their hour by at least fifteen minutes, until at length the door opened, and a single file of four of Group A came towards us, led by the only person there whom I had already known, Ernst Havemann from Shell Centre in London, and I have seldom felt so much dislike – hate, even – for anyone as for him at that moment. All ideas of swim and siesta vanished; I wouldn't have deserted the group that was *mine* for anything. But they sat down with us, and started to tell us what we were going to do: roughly it was that two of them would join us, and two the wives' group, while their remaining four would be observers to record how groups B and C acted, and what lessons could be learned from that. We said that their presence would change our group, and their group of ten would not be our group of eight.

In the end, we had them convinced, and they agreed to go back and think again. But their other four had convinced the wives to go along, so when they reassembled in their room, one party having convinced their target, and the other having been convinced by theirs, a real storm broke out – we kept hearing words like 'traitors' shouted in angry voices, and it was lunchtime before they calmed down and came back with a new plan – that in the afternoon we should all meet together and discuss something they would propose.

One of the members of Group A was John (now Sir John) Harvey-Jones of ICI, and when we came back after lunch he took the chair. I challenged his right to be there – who had elected him? 'Group A,' he said, but I and others argued that if they were taking us over, surely that gave us some right at least to have a say in who should be boss, in a system which had no bosses. Finally, however, under protest we agreed to hear him out, and to tolerate his chairmanship for the time being. But we totally failed to agree on what we should do.

Sir John Harvey-Jones[1] has written: 'we had spent the entire time in high emotional argument and had achieved no concrete results whatsoever.' But, he continues, 'The lessons were that if you wish to amalgamate two groups you can only do it by actually setting out with the aim of creating an entirely new group, in the composition and design of which both parties are equally involved.'

The rest of the week gave us more opportunities to learn how to communicate, and to appreciate that you can be totally frank in saying difficult things to one another if you have established your sincerity. And we also learned to read the *whole* message, and not only the spoken words, with one splendid example. We had, one day, reached a point where we seemed to have run out of energy, until Chuck invited us to give him some coaching, to tell him how he came across to us, and how he could do better. Most of us were generally positive, but were able to look him in the eye and tell him, without emotion, of whatever we found negative. Until we came to one man, who answered Chuck's 'What do *you* think of me, Charlie?' with '*I hate your guts!*' to which Chuck very calmly replied, 'Which do you mean?'

---

[1]'Making it happen', William Collins, 1988.

'I told you, I hate your guts!' repeated Charlie.

'But you sent me incongruent signals: you *said* you hated my guts, but as you did you laid your hand on my knee, and that's a sign of affection that told me I shouldn't believe your words.'

In the years after Rancho la Costa I was able to get Chuck to work with a number of companies with which I was associated, and always he succeeded in making them better. Almost twenty years later, Chuck's widow, Lois, asked me if I would be one of the eulogists at his memorial.[2] Among other things I said that deep down we all love our fellow men. Chuck's great gift was to bring this to the surface so that communication and co-operation – mutual help – became easier, more natural, more precise and more joyful. And I said that in that one week I had acquired more practical, usable knowledge than in any other week of my life.

Back to Sprague

One thing I had learned was that we had been quite wrong in telling the Sprague people they were on their own. So on the Monday after we returned to New York, I went up to see their top management, and told them we had been wrong. They were now employees of a company of the Royal Dutch/Shell Group, and would be treated as such, with the possibilities of being offered jobs in other companies; in other countries, even. And I invited George Seal, the President, Henry Powers, the Vice-President of Marketing, and Tom Pryor, the Vice-President of Finance, to become members of Asiatic's management team, and said that we would work together on joint future plans, to

---

[2]Sadly, what Chuck thought was a spur on a vertebra turned out to be amyotrophic lateral sclerosis.

get the maximum synergy out of the union. They welcomed this, and all three began to make contributions to Asiatic, and to welcome the ideas we had that might be useful in their business. For two years it was a happy association, and we prospered together.

I soon began to realise that Tom Pryor was a man of unusual abilities, and under his leadership Sprague had better money management and better information and computer systems than Asiatic. John Ghents had, in addition to his job as Asiatic's chief financial officer, the responsibility for stockholder relations in the US for Royal Dutch and Shell Transport and Trading (both traded on the New York Stock Exchange), and I was finding that day-to-day business matters were distracting my attention from what should be my top priority, thinking about and planning for the company's long-term future. So as from 1st December, 1970, we made John Ghents Chairman of Excom, with responsibility for arranging its business, and Tom Pryor his replacement as chief financial officer of Asiatic. We sent Tom off to London and the Hague to begin to get to know the Group, and our close contacts in Central Offices. Tom soon began to show results. Among other things he arranged to invest all our spare cash over the weekend. The interest rate had several zeros after the decimal point, but the amounts involved were large and the earnings were by no means insignificant, and the fact that it could be done made our managers think of other little things that could add up to worthwhile. It was a very sad day when, over lunch in La Caravelle a year and a half later, Tom told me that his wife's health (she had severe thyroid problems) was such that he must resign from Asiatic and return to live in Boston.

Alas, our happy marriage with Sprague did not last long. When the prices of petroleum products started to rise dramatically in 1973, who got the blame? The greedy oil companies, and the Arabs, of course! New England was harder hit than most of the rest of the country: it had no coal of its own, its winters were cold and since it had no natural gas (the price of which had been controlled for decades, so it was, generally, cheap as a fuel for domestic heating) it consumed a lot of domestic oil fuel. Then a conference of state governors sent a telegram to President Nixon urging him to use the antitrust laws more vigorously to help keep oil prices down. He asked his staff to find a suitable case for him to demonstrate action, and they came up with Sprague, taken over by an affiliate of one of the major oil companies – and a foreign one, to boot. And so we became the target of the United States Department of Justice (DJ), which demanded that we and the previous owners of Sprague should simply rescind our deal: undo the sale. This was not a very realistic demand, because the sellers had already invested their proceeds from the sale in other ventures, and they could scarcely be ordered to rescind those, so that Asiatic's acquisition of Sprague could be undone. Nevertheless the DJ maintained its demand for this remedy, and negotiations between its lawyers and ours started. We decided that we would fight the DJ, basing our case on precedent – that both Exxon and Texaco had acquired, without opposition, New England retailers of fuels, almost exact parallels of Sprague, and on the Treaty of Commerce and Friendship between the United States and the Netherlands which guaranteed equal treatment to citizens of the Netherlands as accorded to US citizens. Asiatic's parent was a Netherlands company, and as such entitled to the protection of the treaty. Inexplicably (and in Asiatic's eyes, unforgivably) the Legal Department in Central Offices in the Hague failed to lodge a claim within the time limit, and we lost this chance.

My secretary, Rita Gerhart, used to weed out all the junk mail – invitations to seminars and such – that came addressed to me. One day, however, before the Sprague divestiture had become a problem, I stopped on the way out of the office to say something to Rita, and my eye was caught by a brochure lying on her desk. It had on one cover a paragraph-long quotation from Monty Spaght contrasting the popular notion of how business decisions are made (a corporate bigshot surrounded by telephones, picking up one after the other, barking replies into each) with the reality (the lack of sufficient facts, not enough time to do a thorough analysis, the agonising over choices no one of which is clearly the best – let alone the ideal) and ending with these words: 'Anything that can help in this process must be worthwhile.' The other cover quoted Francis Bacon: 'If a man will begin with certainties, he shall end in doubts; but if he will be content to begin with doubts, he shall end in certainties.' The brochure offered a one-day seminar in Decision Analysis, a discipline for dealing logically with difficult decisions in the face of uncertainty, conducted by Arnold B. Pollard, PhD of SRI (Stanford Research Institute) International. I signed up, had a fascinating (and fun) day during which I learned a great deal about the making of decisions, and made the acquaintance of Arnie Pollard, with whom I have worked closely, off and on, for the last twenty-five years.

Asiatic was clearly faced with a difficult decision of great import, in the face of almost total uncertainty, so I asked Arnie to come and help us. The starting point of Decision Analysis is to draw a 'decision tree', starting with a (square) decision node: should we fight the DJ, or accept the demand and try to negotiate the best terms we could? On each branch comes a (round) node from which branch out the possible outcomes: we win; the Court orders divestiture; or rescission. These branches lead to other decision nodes, until the whole problem is mapped out. Each outcome node shows the estimated probability of each branch – estimated by the focused hard thinking of every one who can contribute – and the value of each possible outcome. Arnie has a whole bag of little games he plays to extract from people numerical values of things they say they can't estimate, and it was fun to watch him get a senior partner in a prestigious New York law firm to estimate the chance of our winning a lawsuit (which he started by characterising as anybody's guess) as between sixty-seven and ninety per cent, by offering him an imaginary reward of one thousand dollars for winning his choice of chances: a spin of Arnie's wheel of fortune (divided into red and blue sectors the proportions of which he could alter) or the lawsuit. Or persuading Mike Paulli, whom we had brought back from Venezuela to participate in this decision, to put a value on our giving up the opportunity of ever expanding by acquisition, by having him imagine a well-dressed stranger coming through the door with a certified cheque, the amount of which can't be seen, and asking how big that cheque would have to be to make the company willing to forego the opportunity.

In the meanwhile, from in-house and published information, Al Ogden, our manager of reseller sales, had identified fifty-four possible acquirers, boiled that list down to five likely contenders, and estimated a net price of fifty million dollars, with a range of uncertainty between thirty-five million and sixty-five million. Each outcome value was multiplied by its probability, and these numbers added together for each branch. We spent several long days exploring the possible shape of the legal processes: first instance, we appeal; DJ appeals; we go as far as the Supreme Court – and estimating the time involved and the costs. Eventually we arrived at a point where the 'fight' branch was worth seventy-five million (it included the present value of Sprague's future earnings, and a value of the synergy we should get from still owning Sprague and having a presence in the retail market, and of the precedent of being permitted to acquire). 'Negotiate' came out at forty-eight million dollars, and the decision seemed clear.

But two voices had not yet been heard. David Sepsenwol told us that we had left out one cost, not easy to quantify but very real. 'If we spend two years in legal proceedings, with the outcome uncertain until the end, what will happen to morale, not only in Sprague, but – since none of us is wholly tolerant of ambiguity – also here in Asiatic? Our management is going to have to spend a big portion of its time on the litigation, to the detriment of our normal business. But I couldn't put a number on it.'

Arnie then pulled out of his hat another trick, his tame Wizard, who, for a price, will make anything happen. How much would David be prepared for the company to pay the Wizard for morale to be unaffected, and to have a clone of top management to handle the litigation while we got on with the business? If the Wizard asked fifty million dollars, would David agree?

'No,' said David, 'but I suppose I'd pay two million. How about the rest of you?'

Arnie told us that his Wizard was insulted by David's offer, and after some discussion we agreed that fifteen million dollars would be a fair price, and we added that to our estimated costs.

Bob Koerner had been almost silent up to this point, he never wasted words, but his face was unhappy. 'Aren't we forgetting the curiosity and cupidity of government lawyers? In the flush of victory or smarting from defeat? They would have had their nose under the flap of our tent for two years, and I'll bet they'd find some other issue on which to challenge us.'

'Like what?' I asked him.

Bob could think of several, but the most important was that we bought almost all our supplies from two affiliated offshore companies. Their interest in the success of our business was considerable, and we met regularly to discuss it. It was perfectly legitimate, and we were always scrupulous to keep our relationships at arm's length. 'But,' said Bob, 'can we be sure that an eager young government lawyer couldn't find in our files enough little pieces of careless wording to build up a mosaic suggesting that our suppliers *were* doing business in the US, through Asiatic as agent, and so liable to US tax – probably on earnings many times ours?' We heard the proverbial pin drop, and got to discussing how much we would pay the Wizard to cure this, and finally agreed on thirty million dollars.

These two 'costs' reduced the value of 'fight' from seventy-five million to thirty million, eighteen million less now than 'negotiate'. Like the others, I had been hoping for a different outcome, and said so, and went on to say that, while I could not fault the logic we had all been through, and all agreed upon, I hated to give up without a fight – it would be a travesty of justice. Arnie jumped down my throat, and said, 'Jock, if you fight in the face of this logic, I put it to you that you would be wasting your shareholders' money to assuage your own sense of outrage – and you just can't do that.'

We all took a copy of the final decision tree with us and broke up for the evening. When we met again at nine the next morning, there were no second thoughts. We agreed to approach the DJ, and do the best deal we could. We went to Washington; we negotiated, we compromised, and arrived at a consent judgement, with eighteen months to complete our divestiture of Sprague, with no mention of rescission.

One of the saddest things I have ever had to do was to go to Sprague and tell the employees of our decision. Many of them were in tears, and I needed all the confidence that the arduous analysis of our decision had given me not to say, 'To hell with it; we'll fight!'

We then set out to negotiate with potential buyers, and with Arnie's help on combining probabilities, we turned down the first offer, and were negotiating with number two, when we got a signal from number three at a much higher figure. We down-valued this price, because we felt that number three might face the same sort of antitrust problems as ourselves, and went back to number two. We used our knowledge of why number three's price was comparatively high to get an offer of fifty-five million dollars from number two; not as high as number three's, but without the risk. So (another lesson from Arnie) by turning down the highest – but not riskless – offer we *assured* ourselves of a very good one.

Chapter Forty-Three

Other Activities

Adam Hulton had been a director of twenty-five or more Bermuda corporations, set up in Bermuda's tax haven to perform various tasks for the Group. I said I could not possibly pay proper attention to twenty-five boards, and Don Fobes agreed. So I stayed, as Chairman, only with two, one a dollar retirement fund for American citizens working outside the dollar area, and the other Shell Overseas Finance, which held part of the Group's central funds outside British tax jurisdiction. Bob Koerner briefed me on what I should do: attend at least three of the four scheduled Board meetings each year, which gave me the opportunity of spending a couple of days in Bermuda – a welcome change from New York's hurly-burly – and make sure that the Board actually discussed the company's business and recorded its decisions in the minutes. In the case of Shell Overseas Finance, this was not always easy, for sometimes there was not even one transaction to report – the portfolio had not changed since the last meeting!

Among the services the Group expected from Asiatic was that I should be the 'Shell' presence in many outside activities, from the International Chamber of Commerce, the British-American Chamber of Commerce, the Council of the Americas, the Conference Board, to the International Road Federation and others. Of most of these I was a trustee or director, and, of some, a vice-president. Some of them invited me to speak at meetings or conferences, and I began to get something of a reputation as a public speaker. I had come to know quite well two of the great gurus of the oil industry: Paul Frankel, founder and Chairman of Petroleum Economics Ltd in London, and Morris A. Adelman, a professor of economics in the Department of Engineering of the Massachusetts Institute of Technology, and the man who, above all others, understood the price of oil and natural gas. Paul invited me to be a member of a panel of speakers, including Morry Adelman, which he chaired, and which provided the introductory two days of an annual seminar on the economics of petroleum at Northwestern University. I kept this up even after my retirement, and participated for twelve years. I was also roped in to lecture at Harvard, Massachusetts Institute of Technology, Princeton and Tulane: these were very enjoyable and stimulating affairs, though they demanded a good deal of preparation, for one was talking to people of intellect, who would not let shoddy logic get by.

For a time we shared a box at the Metropolitan Opera in New York with the manager of Asiatic's Economics Department, Carl Wohlenberg, and a third partner, William F. ('Bill') Buckley, Jr, who had been at Yale with Carl. Bill ran, and still runs, a one-hour programme on Public Television, *Firing Line*, getting together two (or more) people with differing views on topical matters of moment to debate live on television. In September 1972 Bill planned to have Morry Adelman on one side of a debate on the supply and price of oil, and one night at the opera he asked me if I could suggest a suitable adversary. I gave him two names in succession, but both turned him down. The date for Bill's programme was getting uncomfortably close, and finally he asked me if I would be prepared to oppose Morry. I consulted Bob Koerner, because it is illegal in the United States for an alien, unless a Registered Foreign

Agent, which I was not, to attempt to influence US Government policy. And inevitably some changes in policy would be required during the crisis that was inexorably bearing down on the world, but Bob agreed that as long as I did not specifically refer to the US, but confined my words to governments generally, I would be all right. So I accepted, and started to prepare. I like to support numerical arguments – and this would inevitably be one – with graphs, so I got ready some sheets of squared paper and, with Billie playing the role of television camera, practised drawing graphs with thick felt-tips, upside down, over faint pencil lines that would not be visible to the viewer. The programme was timed for 3 p.m. on a day barely two weeks before the Yom Kippur War on 5th October, 1973, and less than a month before the Arab oil embargo, which caused a shortage of supply, and a quadrupling of crude prices in three months. Bill's timing could scarcely have been better!

I was totally unable to eat any lunch that day: the prospect of being on nationwide television dried up my saliva and tied my guts into knots. I had to go to the studio an hour before, to be 'made up' – to have my bald head, my face and the backs of my hands powdered, to prevent reflection, and this was all finished with still another half-hour of waiting, and I began to doubt whether I would be able to talk. With five minutes to go, Bill, Morry and I were placed in our seats on the stage, and we waited for three o'clock, and for the red 'On the Air' lights to go on. Bob Koerner, Mike Lorenzo and John Rochford, Asiatic's full legal team, were in the audience to see whether I transgressed the Foreign Agents Registration Act, or otherwise stepped out of line, and Billie and Carl Wohlenberg were sitting together, willing me moral support. When it was all over, I joked that it had felt like two equal halves – the first five minutes and the remaining fifty-five. And indeed, once you get used to the monitory red lights and warm to the subject, you forget the outside world and argue just as if you were alone in a living room. Morry and I differed on the anatomy of the problem which was already on the horizon, though neither of us would have guessed its magnitude, but we basically agreed on the things that needed to be done in the US; mainly to allow prices to be set by the market, and not go on believing that government-dictated prices would have no effect on both demand and supply. Neither of us forecast the 'gas lines' that would become the most visible and (to the consuming public) infuriating symptom of the United States' policy failure and short-sightedness.

I got a video cassette of the programme, and every now and again I have to get it out to show to friends who say that no one had foreseen the crisis, and to add at the end, 'You see, *I* told you!'

The International Road Federation was the most interesting of the outside bodies with which I was associated, and of which I am still a director for life. It had been founded a couple of decades earlier by Alexander Fraser, the (Scots) President of Shell Oil, to get together companies involved in the design, construction and use of highway systems around the world, outside the USA, to promote better roads, and all that goes with them. (Shell's, and other oil companies' interests were, of course, in the demand for bitumen and the facilitating of road transport.) The International Road Federation was in fact two quite separate corporate entities, with the same name, the same logo and the same mission: IRF Geneva, and IRF Washington DC. The two were often at cross purposes, not to say at daggers drawn, and I was invited to become Vice-Chairman of IRF Washington on the grounds that, though I was resident in the USA and my American company was a member of IRF Washington, I was British, and moreover I could speak some of the languages of the directors of IRF

Geneva. The dual nationality problem was not really solvable, because the two were equal – neither had the last word – but I was able to defuse some of the more contentious issues, and to smooth the ruffled feathers of the two Chief Executives, each in his own way a prima donna, and each afraid that the other had designs on his turf; as an example, should Saudi Arabia be invited to join IRF Geneva or Washington? And the USSR?

We held Regional Meetings and World Congresses periodically in various countries around the world. Two of these were special for me. At a Regional Meeting in Munich in the autumn of 1972 I presented a paper, urging IRF to dedicate more of its resources to 'software'. Our knowledge of how to build the hardware – the roads and bridges, from superhighways to farm-to-market roads – was already of a high standard, but we still could not handle the problems of congested traffic, the use of half of many city streets as parking places for stationary cars rather than as space for movement, and the strains on good temper and civility that these things bring about. I had called my paper: 'I love *my* car; I hate *yours*!' But the German Road Federation (who were our hosts in Munich) judged this inappropriate for a serious meeting, and renamed it (in German) something like: 'Psychological, anthropological and economic aspects of automobile ownership in the United States of America'. I was not consulted, and had no chance to defend my version, but when the moment for my paper came (you didn't read the whole, which the participants received in print, but had five minutes to introduce and summarise it) I said that the title the audience had before it was not my original: I wanted to call it '*Ich liebe meinen Wagen: ich hasse deinen!*' – and I got a big laugh. I had made my point.

A more serious thing was to happen, though. We were in the run-up to the 1972 presidential election, and an organisation with the unfortunate acronym of CREEP[1] was raising funds for Nixon. It is illegal for corporations to contribute to party political funds, but some arm-twisting was going on. IRF's Chairman was Harry Heltzer, the Chairman of the 3M Company, with its headquarters in Minnesota. He was persuaded by Maurice Stans, a millionaire banker, who was Nixon's Secretary of Commerce, to make a contribution of five thousand from his company to CREEP. Many other companies had been persuaded likewise, and the story got out. So, among others, Harry and 3M were accused in court of making illegal political contributions, and the news got to Harry early one evening in Munich. He immediately did the honourable thing: by telephone he told his lawyer to plead him guilty, and he resigned as 3M's Chairman. He booked himself a late flight home, and about dinner time he found me and told me what had happened. 'I'm going home now, and I am resigning, this moment, as Chairman of IRF. So it's all yours now, buddy.' I duly remained, with much enjoyment, and, I like to think, of some use to IRF, as Chairman until the end of Harry's term two years later. Some have glory thrust upon them!

The other was the 1977 World Congress in Tokyo, after I had retired, but had my successor's agreement to attend as Asiatic's representative. A couple of months before the date of the congress, Jerry Wilson, President of IRF Washington, and a good friend, telephoned me and asked if I could make a speech in Japanese. I was in fact studying Japanese at the Berlitz School in New York, and asked my teacher if we could manage this. 'If you stop learning Japanese,' she answered, 'and concentrate on a speech, yes, I think so.'

Jerry suggested a topic, the famous series of woodblock prints of the Japanese painter Hiroshige, the *Fifty-Three*

---

[1]Committee to Re-Elect the President.

Stages of the Tokaido, the five hundred-kilometres highway that linked Osaka, Kyoto and Tokyo. Between Jerry, Steinberg San (my teacher – she was the wife of Mr Steinberg, *Time* Magazine's correspondent in Tokyo for many years) and me, we put together a seven- or eight-minute speech, which I learned by heart, and understood. I made it after a dinner that the Board of IRF Washington gave for the Board of our hosts, the Japan Road Association. It was recorded, and so I have proof that, once upon a time, I could speak some Japanese, and be applauded for it! Alas, I have, for want of practice, forgotten it all.

In these years the Shell Group was widening its direct interests in the US outside the sphere of Shell Oil, and Asiatic acquired a number of subsidiary companies to handle them. AP Shipping Corporation was the owner of two tankers being built in the United States as US-Flag vessels, to be chartered to the Group. Sureflex Elastomers Corporation manufactured components for synthetic rubbers – I have no memory now of how on earth we became involved in such an enterprise! Scallop Coal was a vehicle for acquiring coal production in the United States in which Shell Oil was not interested, but the Group was, for export, and to complete a triangle of supplies of coal, of which the other two corners would be South Africa and Australia.

The name 'Asiatic Petroleum' was historic in the Group. When the combination of the assets of Royal Dutch and Shell Transport and Trading became effective, three operating subsidiaries were formed, Bataafse[2] Petroleum Maatschappij, The Anglo-Saxon Petroleum Company, and Asiatic Petroleum, respectively handling the production of

---

[2]From 1795 to 1806 the (French-controlled) Netherlands was known as the Batavian Republic, and Jakarta, the present capital of Indonesia, was called Batavia.

crude oil, the transport of products, and the sale of products in Asia. This Asiatic had many subsidiaries – Asiatic Petroleum of Hong Kong, of Shanghai and so on – justifying the 'Asiatic'. But after World War II, most of these became 'The Shell Company of...' until when I arrived in New York only two were left, ours and (improbably) the Asiatic Petroleum Company of Texas, which did not last much longer. When we only had a few customers we could live with our outlandish and misleading name, but as we expanded, we needed a new name. 'Shell' was pre-empted by Shell Oil, and so we adopted Scallop, the emblem of the Group, first for the coal company, and then for the most exciting of our ventures, Scallop Nuclear.

This was the Shell Group's half of a partnership with Gulf Oil in General Atomic, set up to develop the high-temperature, gas-cooled nuclear reactor as a steam generator for the production of electricity. The HTGR had many advantages over the light water reactor, which, because it became the standard for naval power plants, was adopted for civilian use. Because the HTGR operates at higher temperature it is more efficient, and if its cooling fails it allows a minimum of eight hours for getting emergency cooling into operation – indeed it is almost certainly self-stabilising – as opposed to a matter of minutes for a LWR. On the other hand it requires a higher concentration of the fissile isotope, U235, of which natural uranium contains just over 0.7%, calling for a more intense enrichment process to produce its fuel.

The Chairman of Scallop Nuclear was 'Tox' Toxopeus, Group Research Co-ordinator, and a scientist, while I was President. We were both members of General Atomic's Partnership Committee, effectively its Board of Directors. General Atomic had already built a demonstration plant of forty megawatts, which was operated by Philadelphia

Electric, and was approaching completion of a larger plant, three hundred megawatts, for Public Service of Colorado at Fort St Vrain. Based on these two trials we had designed a standard 1,100 megawatt plant, for which we had contracts to build three or four, when the 'incident' at Three Mile Island occurred, and effectively brought to an end the US's development of nuclear power for civilian use, a sad example of hysteria getting the better of common sense. There was no release of radiation from Three Mile Island, and the many people who flew in to exploit the situation for the benefit of the anti-nuclear movement exposed themselves to a greater increase of radiation than anything at Three Mile Island by flying, and so thinning the atmospheric shield between themselves and cosmic radiation. Ironically the one serious casualty of the whole situation was Edward Teller, the physicist who led the development of the hydrogen bomb, who had a heart attack from disgust at the overreaction of the public, the politicians and the media to the incident. And of course no one even bothers to think that the United States has many more nuclear reactors in the ships of its navy than in civilian power plants, with hundreds – thousands in the big aircraft carriers – of sailors living in close quarters alongside.

It was a fascinating experience to learn about nuclear reactors, the design problems of the plants, and the economics of nuclear generation of electricity. General Atomic was most interesting, though frustrating in trying to cope with ignorance and its offspring, fear. I do not give up hope that gradually we will come to read the truth about nuclear power, and accept (as have the French) that it is much safer than fossil fuel, and even than hydropower.

⋆

Compañia Shell de Venezuela (CSV) was Asiatic's principal supplier for its fuel oil markets in the US, and from the early Seventies the Venezuelan government began to make clear that it would nationalise the oil industry. Our deal with CSV was a simple one in principle. We would find a potential customer in the US, and ask CSV if it would sell us the oil to cover this contract at a price which gave us a margin of about one per cent, after freight, import duties and similar costs, but not our own operating costs. If it accepted, we made back-to-back contracts with it and our customer. Nationalisation would put an end to this system, but we felt that Asiatic could still offer a valuable service at a very reasonable cost to a state-owned Venezuelan oil company, and we could avoid it having to expose itself to US taxes. So we set out to persuade Petróleos de Venezuela SA (PDVSA) and its subsidiary, Maraven, which would become the successor company to CSV, to work with us in this way. We were dealing with the President of PDVSA, General Rafael Alfonso Ravard, so much of the negotiation required my presence, both from the point of view of protocol and since I spoke better Spanish than other Asiatic employees. It was tempting to ask for a higher margin, but too many of the people on the other side had been in Shell, and so knew what we could live on, and I believe our openness about this made the consummation of the deal easier. Anyway, we – Mike Paulli, Mike Lorenzo and I – did finally consummate it, over a dinner at which I was egged on to tell some of my favourite (translatable) jokes, especially a couple that require simple props, and that I repeatedly climb up on to and down from a chair (representing the Rocky Mountains). This last left me breathless, but our hosts roaring with laughter, and ready to welcome us as a business partner. So on 1st January, 1976, we bought our supplies under a long-term contract with PDVSA.

At first very little changed. Alberto Quirós, who had been President of CSV was President of Maraven, and so on down the line, except that the expatriates were no longer there. But gradually, as the new Venezuelan organisations began to find their feet and their self-confidence, it became clear that they would aim to cut out the middleman and deal direct with the customers. But the old order survived my tenure.

Chapter Forty-Four

Life in New York

Hope springs eternal in the breast of every real-estate broker, and she (or he) will take down in detail what you want, and then show you dozens of places that come scarcely closer to your desideratum than that they have a front door. So it took Billie a couple of months of traipsing round Manhattan before she found an apartment that met what we wanted at 700 Park Avenue. We borrowed the money from the Irving Trust Company (which had been the Shell Group's banker since it moved to the east of the US, so the only security asked for was my signature on a loan agreement – my job was the collateral) and bought it. But this apartment's decoration was appalling, including oak floors stained blood red, and bathrooms with draperies that would grace an Arab prince's tent (but impregnated with heavy scent and talcum powder, so if you touched them you got a shower of grey-white dust) and the cement between the tiles had grown a greenish mildew. It took several weeks to get things ready, to get our furniture from Brazil, and from Richmond before that, out of the warehouse, and to buy the rest of what we needed, and it was 1st January, 1978 before we moved in. Billie's friend of many decades from Cuba, Esperanza Bárcena, was living in Miami, and she came up and stayed with us to help – among other things she scrubbed the cement between the tiles in all the bathrooms with a toothbrush and some cleaning compound and got them all looking like new. We lived there for seven very pleasant years.

For an interesting and varied life, which met the criterion of work – that it must be fun – Asiatic and its offshoots could hardly be bettered, and after office hours Billie and I much enjoyed New York life. As I have written, we shared Carl Wohlenberg's box at the Metropolitan Opera with him, and Bill Buckley and his wife, Patsy. The Buckleys soon dropped out as Bill became busier with his magazine, *National Review*, and for the next seven or eight years we shared the eight seats with Carl. He kept three and we had five, but we worked it so that one week Carl and we each used four; the other, Carl had two and we six. It was a marvellous way to entertain business contacts and friends. We dressed (and by the end we were the only box which still dressed, except on Mondays, when everyone did) and we had two courses of dinner in the corner table of the Grand Tier Restaurant, with dessert, ordered ahead, and ready on the table in the first intermission. We heard many great performances, but none to outdo Joan Sutherland and Luciano Pavarotti in *La Fille du Régiment.* It was Pavarotti's first appearances at the Met, and word had got around that he would sing nine high Cs. As he began his aria, people practically stopped breathing, and you could feel the tension rising, and when the high Cs started, it went up a notch at each, until the last, and the end of the aria, when the whole audience exploded in applause, the like of which we have never heard.

I had a good deal of business entertaining to do, and as well as the opera, we took people to the theatre, or to Carnegie Hall, or just out to dinner. New York had many good restaurants then (more and better it seems than it has now) and we soon settled on a few favourites, especially Le Cygne, whose owners Gérard and Michel became good friends.

Billie's daughter Sylvia Jacobsen and her husband Rafael had bought fifty acres of land in upstate New York, about three hours driving from the city, on which they planned to build a house by the slowest method known to man. Rafael had bought a book called *Pour Yourself a House*, and he was setting out to do just that. You made concrete foundations, and then you prepared wooden forms a foot apart above them. Between them you arranged stones facing the outer side of the form, and propped them in place with smaller stones or with sticks, and poured concrete between them, so that, when the forms were removed you had a stone wall. What the book didn't tell you was how heavy concrete is, and what huge quantities you need to make a house of any size. But when we had a weekend with no other commitments, we would drive up there, stay in a nearby motel, and help. There were a number of trees, not yet very old, but fifteen or twenty centimetres in diameter, which they wanted to clear. They had an axe, and I had learned in the Boy Scouts at Eton how to fell trees, and one weekend I volunteered to start on this task, and felled thirty-five.

It happened that I had arranged for a physical check-up with Asiatic's doctor, Henry Schaffeld, during the following week. Henry gave me a going-over, and then asked me what I did at weekends; what, for example, had I done last weekend? I told him I had felled thirty-five trees with an axe. 'You need to do something like that every weekend: you ought to get some trees of your own to work on, to do some heavy work to make up for all the sedentary weekdays,' he told me.

That started something. I had been a seagoing sailor or an expatriate employee most of my adult life, and Billie had lived in rented apartments, and we yearned to own some land, and to build (but not pour!) a house of our own. We decided that Sylvia's place was too far from the city, so we set ourselves a limit of two hours' drive, and started to look without much success until a casual conversation one day with Andrew Hay, then President of the British-American Chamber of Commerce in New York (of which I was a vice-president). He told me we should see Bill Daron, his real-estate broker in the village of Stone Ridge, just two hours' drive away. We made an appointment to see Bill the next weekend, having told him on the telephone what we were after. He showed us a parcel of nine hectares, back from the road, with a right of way access about four hundred metres long. It was on highish ground, and had lovely hardwood trees as well as pines and hemlocks, and a hunters' cabin with a genuine Lem Putt[1] outhouse, both painted red, with white trim, but no water supply. Bill assured us that we would have no difficulty having a well drilled and finding good water, and we discussed, and agreed on, where we should site a house. We bought the place for eleven thousand pounds. We had offered ten thousand, but the owner said that, no, he had promised his wife a fur coat. He would have taken ten thousand, but he wanted that clear, and he needed the extra thousand to keep his wife happy!

Somehow I had heard of Lindal Cedar Homes, a firm in the state of Washington that sold pre-cut kits of western red cedar; ready-made windows, doors, posts, beams and tongue-and-groove boarding for the walls and roof, complete with nails, hinges and everything for you to build your own house, all for under eight thousand pounds, including shipping. But first you needed a foundation. In Stone Ridge the frost line in winter goes down forty inches, so you had to dig deeper than that, which in practice means you need a basement. Bill put us on to Red Van Demark, the town's superintendent of highways (and as nice a man as one could wish to know) who owned a bulldozer and a

---

[1]See *The Specialist*, by Charles Sale, published by The Bodley Head.

backhoe, and took on jobs like that. We ordered a house, L-shaped, with two bedrooms, bathroom, kitchen and living room, and Red excavated the foundations, poured a concrete slab and built cement-block basement walls seven feet high, their tops eighteen inches above ground at the front, three feet at the back. Meanwhile I bought a petrol-powered chainsaw from Sears, Roebuck, and we cleared trees from the site of the house to be and its driveway: we brought in electricity, which involved installing a number of poles: a well driller came in, and at about forty metres found forty-five litres a minute of clean water, uncontaminated by any trace of iron or sulphur, brought to the surface by a submerged electric pump.

In a very few weeks the kit arrived at Kingston's railroad station, a dozen miles away, and Red arranged to transport it to our land, and covered it with plastic sheets. We drove up the next weekend, which included the Fourth of July holiday of 1968. We arrived in daylight, and saw the pile of raw material. It all seemed in good order, except that a bundle of cedar shingles for the roof had come apart and they were scattered all around. But I took one look at the sheer volume of stuff I would have to assemble, and thought *Oh Lord, I've taken total leave of my senses!*

However, I started to build the next morning. The instructions were clear and simple, and in that one weekend I had actually begun on the walls. The only thing for which I needed help was positioning the two main longitudinal beams – it was a 'post and beam' design – and the beams were six metres long, thirty centimetres wide, eight centimetres thick, and very heavy. We stayed in a motel in the village of High Falls, five miles away, and discovered that the Finnish owner was a carpenter by profession, and had built the motel himself. He offered to come up and help, and between us we got all the beams in place without strained backs, and he gave me one excellent bit of advice.

'Nails are cheap,' he said, 'so never economise on nails; ten too many is always better than one too few.'

By Thanksgiving, the fourth Thursday of November, the house was closed in, and Bill Daron introduced us to another of nature's gentlemen, Dick Stokes, who was electrician, plumber and jack of all trades. Dick and his two helpers (his son-in-law and a friend) wired the house for light, power and heating, did all the plumbing, and obtained the certificates necessary for insurance. Though 'closed in' – it was a weatherproof whole – its interior was unfinished except that it had a bathroom, a free-standing steel fireplace, a cooker and a refrigerator, and the roof had roofing felt, but not yet shingles. We did a little more work inside, mainly stapling fibreglass insulation to the walls, before the winter kept us away.

We suffered a setback the next April. Billie and I had come up over the Easter weekend and started work on the interior, but it began to snow (unforecast!) and so we left to go back to the city while we could. We had, as some sort of protection, a padlocked chain between two trees across the drive. When we arrived the following weekend, the chain was still padlocked around its tree, but in the middle it was cut and hooked together by a piece of wire. Our hearts sank, and when we got to the front door we found it jemmied open, and inside… oh! Oh! There were black footprints across the floor, the fireplace was gone, as were three interior doors that we hadn't hung yet, most of my tools, the cabinets off the kitchen walls (no great loss these – they were old and rusty from the hunters' cabin) three teapots, all our paper plates and Woolworth cutlery, four pairs of Billie's shoes and, most valuable of all, a roll of copper flashing for the roof. But they left behind, and they had to take them out of the kitchen cabinets to do so, about a dozen bars of soap! We were insured, and recovered the cost of much of what had been stolen, but the sense of intrusion, of violation, even, faded only slowly.

We licked our wounds, however, bought a better fireplace, and got to work in earnest on the interior. As domestic help in our apartment we had arranged for Graziela, a young Portuguese woman who had been our housemaid in Brazil, to be admitted as an immigrant, and I did a deal with her that, if she would come and work on the house at weekends, we would pay her fare to Portugal and back in the summer. We also had a part-time Brazilian domestic helper, and my daughter Sarah was working as a nurse in New York. These three came and worked on the shingling of the roof, Billie nailed down the plywood underfloor, I installed the prefinished oak tongue-and-grooved flooring over it, and panelled the walls, cedar in the entrance hall, living room and our bedroom, pre-lacquered plywood (to save money!) in the kitchen and second bedroom. By late spring, it was complete (except that no house is *ever* complete)[2] and it was for ten years our weekend escape from the city. We even kept it open right through some winters, and Red ploughed out the snow so that we could get in and out. I telephoned him one Friday to ask him to clear our drive, and in passing asked him how cold it was.

'When I left home this morning,' he said, 'it was minus thirty.'[3]

When we arrived at the house, the little heat we had left on had been enough to melt some of the snow on the roof, which had formed icicles that reached the ground, and were three inches in diameter at the top and bottom. Spect-acular to look at, but a reminder that Hudson valley winters are *cold*!

---

[2]Billie's Aunt Josie from South Africa came to stay with us one year, and we knew she would only come to the country if she had a bathroom to herself. So out of boards that were surplus from the house, and a set of bathroom pieces bought on sale for $139, I built a bare essentials, but tiled, bathroom off the second bedroom.

[3]Fahrenheit.

Part Five

JDR Consultancy, Inc.

Chapter Forty-Five

Retirement From Shell

For its expatriate staff Shell had a scheme which permitted people who had years of 'tropical' service (not strictly within the Tropics, but in hot climates like Egypt) to retire three months per year of such service earlier than the normal age of sixty, but with a pension calculated as if you had gone on to sixty. This would have made my retirement age fifty-seven, and, though I was no longer an 'expatriate' but a US-based employee, my successor, Keith Doig, was named and began the process of takeover to let me go at about that age. We got as far as selling our apartment to him, while we bought another, cheaper and further away, for ourselves. Keith was an employee of Shell Oil, and the year was 1974 – the peak of the hate-the-oil-companies hysteria. When Cravath Swaine and Moore, our lawyers, heard of the proposed move, they warned us that it would be most unwise, since it would blur the absolute separation between the Group and Shell Oil. So I was asked to stay on, and had to pay Keith back the price he had paid for the apartment. This was a 'co-operative', and an apartment could only belong to a person, so I was still the owner, but Asiatic took effective ownership, in that it paid me back the purchase price, and undertook the sale for its account – just as well, since the Manhattan real-estate market took a nosedive between my deal with Keith and the time when Asiatic found a purchaser. In passing, Asiatic didn't do a good job of this, and I could not interfere since I was an interested party. It kept turning down offers as too low, when next week the market was even lower, and in the event it lost a lot of money. But in return it held on to an experienced president, who worked for another two and a half years. The Group agreed that I could plan on retiring from 31st December, 1976, leaving, to take my accumulated vacation due, at the end of September. I promised Billie that I would not start anything new until the January, and that until then we would take a round-the-world cruise.

In the United States Shell's normal retiring age was sixty-five, but, in order to keep the average age of its top management low, it required everyone in that group to retire at sixty, but compensated them for this by paying a supplementary pension to bring one's total up to what the pension would have been had one stayed on to sixty-five. The pension proper was paid out of a funded pension trust, while the supplement came from the general revenues of the company, so that, in theory, the latter was less secure than the former. One had options for the payment of the funded pension: one could take it for the life of the pensioner only, or convert it to a joint-and-survivor annuity, the pensioner receiving a smaller payment for his life, and a surviving spouse getting half of that amount for life, the different amounts being calculated actuarially.

During the Watergate scandal, André Bénard, who had been President of Shell Française when I was working there in 1967 and was now a Managing Director of the Group, was visiting Shell Oil in Houston, accompanied by his wife, and Billie and I were invited to go along with them. One afternoon Harry Bridges, Shell Oil's President, arranged a golf game for André, Jack Horner (the chief financial officer of Shell Oil), Harry himself and me. After our game we went back to the hotel where we were staying, and found Jacqueline Bénard, Peggy Horner and Billie in front of the television, watching the proceedings of the Senate Select Subcommittee on Presidential Campaign Activities, chaired by Senator Sam Ervin of North Carolina. We four men stood and watched for a couple of minutes, were instantly fascinated, and sat down with our wives. Senator Ervin was doing a superb job of eliciting the facts from his witnesses. He never lost his patience, to say nothing of his temper, and treated all with courtesy, but insistence. When he doubted whether someone was telling him the truth, or the whole truth, he would preface his next question with the words: 'I'm only a country lawyer from North Carolina, but...' and it could not have been clearer if he'd said right out: 'I think you're lying.' We stayed glued to the television until the end of the programme, and I was profoundly moved. Here was a country that was going to get rid of its president (and commander-in-chief of its armed forces) by a calm, civilised judicial process. There were no soldiers in the streets, not a tank in front of the White House, while the Supreme Court ruled that Nixon must provide the special prosecutor with transcripts of the famous missing eighteen minutes of his tape-recordings, which proved his complicity in the Watergate cover-up, and led him to resign before impeachment proceedings against him began. And I thought, *This is a country worth joining.*

Billie and I were beginning to think of my future after retiring, and between us we decided that, after my twenty-eight years (with one short interval) as an expatriate, and soon to be ten years in the US, we did not want to go back to Britain. But I was not yet ready to spend my days lumberjacking in Stone Ridge or playing indifferent golf, but wanted to go on working, as a 'consultant' (without having any more precise idea than that as to what I might do, though I knew that I had acquired a store of knowledge that could be valuable to people in the energy industries). So I asked John Rochford to tell me about the naturalisation process, and he took the task very seriously. First, he explained to me that as an admitted immigrant I had all the rights of a citizen except those of the vote and of serving on a jury, and that therefore it might not seem that I had much to gain by becoming a citizen. But he recommended books I should read, and Bob Koerner joined in by giving me a book, by several authors, called *The National Experience*, unexcelled as a primer in American history. The gem of John's list was *Are we to be a Nation? The Making of the Constitution*,[1] which is the fascinating story of how fifty-five men in Philadelphia answered that question with one of the world's most remarkable and durable of political documents. Incidentally it enabled me, when I was being examined as to my fitness to become an American citizen, to give a smart-alecky answer to what the examiner thought was one of the easiest questions, 'When did the United States declare its independence?' I answered, 'The 2nd July, 1776.' He was just going to give me another chance to give the 'right' answer, the Fourth of July, Independence Day, when he hesitated, and looked enquiringly at me. I reminded him that it was on the *second* day of July that the Continental Congress passed the motion made a month earlier by a delegate from Virginia, Richard Henry Lee, 'that these Colonies are, and of right ought to be, free and independent States'. The splendid document that we know as the Declaration of Independence was drafted by Thomas Jefferson between the 2nd and the 4th, but it is the apologia, the justification, for the Congress's vote – in modern-day terms it is the public relations case for the action, addressed to three audiences: the population of the Colonies (the 'Americans'), Britain, and the powers of Europe for whose active or passive support the new nation

[1]Written by Richard B. Bernstein and Kym S. Rice, Harvard University Press.

would look. And who would deny that Jefferson's superb words are more worthy of celebration than the legal act itself? It is trite to say that we shall not see their like again, but very seldom in history can a group of more remarkable men have come together to create, without historical precedent to work from, a union of independent states, and later to design a mechanism for its government, which has proved strong enough (with relatively few amendments) to guide a small number of agricultural ex-colonies on the road to becoming the strongest – and most decent – power on earth.

The more I read, the more I wanted to belong, and if we were going to make America our home, then let us acquire the right to vote. I was finally sworn in as a citizen on 3rd November, 1976 (the day after Jimmy Carter was elected to the presidency) by Judge Irving Ben Cooper, a little man with a large personality, and a fine judicial mind. He was born in the East End of London, and in his harangue to the newcomers he made much of the contrast between the conditions we had known in our countries of origin and what we could now expect in the land of our new citizenship. He sat behind a bench so high that we could barely see his head, and his voice was hoarse (from years of judicial oratory, I imagined) and he spoke in staccato phrases, separated by pauses. He made a big issue of our obligation never to discriminate against our fellow citizens, and made a totally illegal threat to us: 'and if it is ever reported to me… that any of you… have in any way… discriminated against… your fellow citizens… by reason of race, colour, religion or economic status… you should have your citizenship snatched back from you… and I would sign an order to that effect.'

Before you are admitted as a citizen, you are required to answer a series of questions related to your past life and actions. For example, if you are a woman you are asked,

'Do you intend to practice prostitution?' John Rochford explained to me that the purpose of these was so that, if you were found to have perjured yourself before being sworn in, your citizenship could indeed be 'snatched back from you', whereas it could not be for any offence committed afterwards. So Judge Cooper's menacing words had no foundation in law, and I had for a moment a totally irrational temptation to interrupt and say: 'Your Honour, in view of what you have just said, which I believe would not be legal, and in view of what the electorate decided yesterday, may I withdraw my oath?' However, I behaved myself, and went back to the office, to be met by the whole of my management team with champagne, and a huge wide Stars and Stripes tie for me to put on. After the first glass, Mike Lorenzo asked me if I really had become an American, and when I answered 'Yes', he asked, in a strong New York accent, 'Then how come you still talk so funny?'

Back in June, on the Queen's birthday, I had been appointed a Commander of the British Empire, 'For services to British commercial interests in New York'. For a while I wondered whether I was straddling a fence by remaining a CBE and becoming American, but knowledgeable friends from both sides reassured me, and the Admiralty told me that my new nationality in no way affected my naval rank. In any case, both countries accept the concept of dual nationality. John Rochford's comment was the clincher: 'Only if war were to break out between the United States and the United Kingdom would you have a problem.' Well, that's a risk I'm prepared to take.

Chapter Forty-Six

Four Lunches

One day in the summer of 1976, my old friend from Egypt, Wagih Kotb, was in New York, and invited me to lunch at Le Cygne. He had been the President of Nasr Petroleum, the successor to the nationalised Shell companies in Egypt, but had retired, and joined an oil trading company called Joc Oil, and he wanted me to meet its owner, John Deuss. Wagih had told John that I was due to retire soon, and John asked me if I would like to join him, and become the manager of the First Curaçao International Bank that he had set up to facilitate financing for his oil trading. I said that I didn't think that banking would really be my forte, but we – and back in the office Mike Paulli joined us – ought to see if we could do any trading business together. There was not in fact any scope for that, but John asked me to let him know when I retired, because he would like me to join his company in some capacity or other – Wagih must have done a good sales job! I met John again in his New York office, and he told me about his business: he was taking advantage of the new fluidity in the oil market as the established companies were losing their dominating positions.

I was fascinated, both by John's personality and by the bold and imaginative way he had built a business around the new opportunities, and I agreed I would, after my retirement, join him as a consultant for two days a week after

1st January, 1977, provided I could get Asiatic's blessing.

★

Asiatic had become the principal supplier of fuel oil to NEES, and as such we were in fairly close contact. Guy Nichols used to visit New York, often to make presentations about NEES's business and prospects to groups of security analysts, and on one such occasion he asked me to have lunch with him. We had often discussed the prices and supply of oil, and he was wondering whether the Rotterdam barge market would be a possible source of lower priced oil for NEES. I explained that the barge market dealt only with small quantities, the spot surpluses and shortfalls that arose from short-term imbalances of supply and demand in Europe, whereas what he needed was assured supply at a steady and predictable price, for the large volumes that NEES's operations required. I quoted to him some of recent ups and downs in that market, of which I had read in Platt's *Oilgram*.[1] He told me that NEES needed someone with my kind of knowledge of these questions, and asked me whether, when I retired, I would agree to be a consultant to NEES, giving them one day a week. Moreover, Guy said, NEES was subject to the jurisdictions of four bodies: the Energy Regulatory Commissions of the three States in which they sold electricity, Massachusetts, Rhode Island and New Hampshire, and for its generating and transmission operations, which were interstate, to the Federal Energy Regulatory Commission.[2] 'With your knowledge of supply and price,'

---

[1]The daily newspaper of the oil industry, especially supply and prices.

[2]A system set up as a sort of synthetic substitute for competition, to protect consumers against monopoly suppliers, while allowing these an adequate financial return.

said Guy, 'maybe we can convince some regulators to be more reasonable.' I agreed, on the same conditions as I had asked for from John Deuss, that Asiatic should not object, and that my work for NEES would not involve any conflict of interest with Shell, from whom I would be receiving a pension.

★

When Billie had her annual physical check-up in 1975, Henry Schaffeld noticed too high a level of calcium in her blood and urine, not yet a serious worry, because she showed no signs of bone softening or loose teeth, which is where this condition first shows up. But the next year he told Billie that her calcium excretion was slightly higher than normal, and that while she was not yet in jeopardy, he would send a frozen blood sample for a test 'involving intricate radio-assay techniques' to measure the amount of parathormone (produced by the parathyroid glands, and the regulator of calcium) in her blood.

This test showed that one or more of her parathyroid glands was enlarged, and demanding too much calcium, which it drained from her bones, and she should have surgery to find and remove it – or them. She met the surgeon who would do the operation, who explained what he would have to do, which sounded frightening, involving slitting her neck almost from ear to ear, and finding the rogue gland, which was not always easy. We were booked to go on a short vacation to Bermuda, and both doctors said that there was no immediate urgency, so off we went, agreeing to fix a date on our return. But Billie was worried, and after a few days decided to telephone Henry to ask him to make arrangements for the operation as soon as possible. He called back in a couple of hours to say that she could go into hospital in three days' time if we could get back by then. We left the next day and Billie went into Roosevelt Hospital, where the surgeon removed one parathyroid gland, which he described as the size of a peach stone, when it should have been no bigger than an apple seed.

*

Just before we went to Bermuda I had been contacted by Bill Henderson, a Shell acquaintance who had recently retired after working in Japan for many years. He was totally fluent in Japanese, and had become a consultant to Marubeni, one of the big Japanese General Trading Companies. They had asked him if he could help them find a retired Shell person in the United States to become a consultant to Marubeni America's Petroleum Department, and he suggested my name. The Managing Director of their head office Petroleum Department happened to come to New York while Billie was in hospital. Bill Henderson invited me to lunch to meet the Marubeni people, on the day that Billie was due to be disconnected from the tubes that had been supplying calcium while the three normal glands (which had been having a lazy time while the enlarged one was overdoing things) recovered to pick up the load. Billie's daughter, Sylvia, agreed to go and sit with her while this was done. We had almost finished lunch when I got a telephone call from Sylvia, who had tracked me down through Asiatic, telling me that Billie had become paralysed. I made my excuses and got a taxi to Roosevelt, and found that Billie was now receiving calcium through a tube, and was recovering from the tetany (which is the name for this paralysis) but was very shaken and weak, though relieved that she was not, as she had thought, dying – a belief strengthened by the evident panic of the very young doctor and elderly nurse who discovered what was happening to her.

*

Bill telephoned me the next day to say that, after I had left, they discussed my experience and knowledge as it had emerged in our conversations, and the Managing Director said that, 'with all that softu-ware-u' I should be able to help their profitability, and they would like me to join them as a consultant for one day a week. So I had already four out of five working days a week committed, and I decided to keep the fifth for myself, and for any short-term assignments which might turn up.

Then, just a few days before I retired, Alan Gerald, General Manager of Asiatic's materials business, asked me to lunch to meet a man whose company was the supplier of oilfield tubulars (the steel pipes needed for drilling and then lining oil wells, and for transmission pipelines) for a big contract Asiatic had. He was Henry Zarrow, majority owner and Chairman of his company, Sooner Pipe and Supply in Tulsa, Oklahoma. Over lunch I told Henry of what I was planning to do as a consultant, and offered him my services whenever he thought I could be useful.

As a result of these four lunches at least four days a week of my retirement were committed, and it was time to start planning how this new business was to be run.

*

Just at this time Asiatic was beginning to want to enhance the retirement benefits of its senior people, and by chance Jerry Alexander, who had succeeded me as Chairman of IRF, telephoned to say that he and two associates, L.D. Christiano and Manfred ('Fred') Kieser, had recently set up in business to design plans for doing just this, so I asked them to come and help us. To avoid any apparent conflict of interest, I stipulated that I was not to benefit from anything that was set up as a result of these discussions, and I kept out of the way, except socially. But one day I took the three of them out to lunch, to see how they were progressing, and L.D. (as far as I ever knew, he had no other first name!) asked me about my retirement plans. I told him about my three or four clients-to-be, and he said I ought to make serious structural plans, and asked me about my income, what my pensions would be, how much I expected to earn as a consultant, and suchlike. The next morning he and Fred (who was the actuary and pension expert of the trio) came in to see me, and gave me some advice that has been invaluable – indeed has been the basis for our present degree of financial comfort. We should form a corporation, and set up in it a qualified[3] pension plan, to pay a pension equal to one hundred per cent of my salary from our business, on a joint and survivor basis, with the survivor getting the same amount. I should take my full Shell pension, and cover Billie by giving up my supplementary pension for five years. With these funds Asiatic would buy an insurance policy on my life, which would pay Billie an annuity ample for her to live on if I died before the survivor's pension from our business was big enough. Talking later with Arnie Pollard, who had incorporated his business activities, he gave me the name of his accountant, who had set up his corporation for him, and did his accounting. Thus I became acquainted with Jules Levine, who did the same services for me, and who, with his wife, have become very good friends. We were helped initially by the economic policies of Presidents Nixon, Ford and Carter, which kept interest rates in the US very high. To fund our pension plan in these circumstances required a very large contribution from JDR Consultancy, Inc. (such is the name of our company) – as much as sixty or sixty-five

[3]Acceptable to the Internal Revenue Service.

per cent of my salary, which was by far the largest element of the expenses, but before tax. These sums were invested in a trust fund, and earned the high Carter interest, and so grew rapidly.

In the meantime the Group had been trying to find a successor for me. One name that surfaced was that of Norman Bain, who had been President of Shell Italiana, and had just handled the sale of Shell's business in Italy to the Italian State, because it was just proving impossible to make a decent profit out of it, due to the difficulty of reducing the payroll, and because of strangulation by bureaucratic regulation. Norman came to see us, to 'case the joint', and went back to Italy to think things over. Then someone (I cannot remember who) gave me a bunch of press clippings from Italian newspapers about a judicial investigation into corruption, especially of customs officers who were being bribed by oil companies to facilitate the release of products from bonded storage plants, including a good deal of testimony from Norman. One particularly worrying piece reported Norman's reply to the judge's question as to whether Shell Italiana made payments of this sort to employees of the ministry of finance. 'Yes, of course we did: everyone did. If you didn't play, you could not get the oil in time to supply the customers.' In the current climate of 'Foreign Corrupt Practices', I went to see Roswell Gilpatric, the managing partner of Cravath Swaine and Moore, with translations of the cuttings. He was horrified, and said, 'Tell your people that, if they bring this man here, he will spend half of his time in Washington testifying before one committee or another, to say nothing of the extent to which it will be assumed that this is just the Shell Group's normal kind of behaviour.'

So they started looking again, and proposed Desmond Watkins, head of the Caribbean Regional Centre, which had oversight responsibility for various Shell business activities that had been looked after by Shell Venezuela. Desmond came to look, but turned the job down. Finally John Francis, who had spent much of his career in general management in various Shell Companies in East Africa, but was then in a senior position in Central Offices, accepted the assignment. There was only one problem: John had had tuberculosis, had lost the use of one lung, and could not be available until mid-December. So our round-the-world cruise went on the scrap heap. Moreover, for tax reasons, John did not want to begin his residence in the US until after 1st January, 1977. So he came for ten days before Christmas, returned to the UK, and came back to take over on Sunday, 2nd January. I worked until after 7 p.m. on the Friday, which was New Year's Eve, and at 9 a.m. on Monday I joined Joc Oil, which was John Deuss's US oil trading subsidiary, as a consultant.

Chapter Forty-Seven

Transworld (or Joc) Oil, NEES, Marubeni and Sooner

Over the weekend I had drafted and typed a brief letter agreement with Joc, which I handed to John Deuss when I first got to see him that morning. My copy of that document is still in my files, and it says much about our relations that, although the roles I have played in that organisation, and the remuneration JDR Consultancy received for them, have changed greatly over the intervening twenty years, nothing has ever been formalised on paper. Indeed, although I had been hired for advice on international oil prices and supply, I was, within a week, acting as Joc's Trading Manager for the US, finding buyers for large quantities of heating oil which John had acquired in the USSR and elsewhere. This was a field in which I had no personal experience, but I had many contacts among potential buyers, and I quickly became fairly good at finding this end of potential trades. The name 'Joc Oil', however, caused some confusion: people tended to think that I had gone into the oil trading business for myself!

John was then in his early thirties, and had made a considerable fortune in the days of continually rising prices, and had expanded into a number of businesses, some related to but some, ladies' fashions for example, totally foreign to oil trading. These, and a period of decline in the inflation-adjusted price of oil had made Joc Oil's cash position very tight. In essence the business was like Asiatic's, except that Joc was dealing with spot availabilities, one cargo at a time, for which we traders had to find buyers with spot shortages. Asiatics's time-frames were years, Joc's, hours. John himself bought the cargoes; his father, John Deuss Senior, arranged for the credit necessary to finance the transaction, and I and my counterparts in other markets found the buyers. The trick was to find a seller, who might give one twelve hours to come up with a letter of credit to pay for a cargo, find a buyer who would buy it, and a bank that would give credit on the strength of the buyer's word before the seller's time ran out. It was not the most relaxing thing to have got into immediately after my retirement, but it was undeniably fun! However, I was committed to two other clients for two days of the week, and I found myself doing a lot of Joc's business in the evenings, and on other companies' telephones. We had to find a full-time Trading Manager, and we had, in house, 'wasting his sweetness on the desert air' a man who was excellent at the job. For his abortive entry into the ladies' fashion business, John had hired Max Bernegger, who had worked for the New York fashion house of Bill Blass, and Max took over as trader, while I retreated to part-time Trading Manager. I kept this role for at least two years. I can fix the time because of a meeting of the traders in my office on 16th October, 1978. At the time, Polish jokes were the rage in New York – 'Polish' being the New York equivalent of Irish in England, Belgian in Holland, Corsican in France, Portuguese in Brazil – the Poles were the simpletons. We were deep in matters of sulphur levels, pour points, viscosity and availability dates, and trying to match demand and supply, when our administrative assistant, Halina Lobo, came in and said that my wife needed to speak with me urgently. I went next door, wondering what sort of a crisis Billie was facing, There was a very excited voice on the telephone: '*We have a new Pope: he's Polish!*'

Back next door, I said, 'They've elected a new Pope: he's Polish.' There was a pause until someone said, 'Well... go on!' A reputation as a joker can get in the way of credibility as a bearer of news!

The scope of my services to John soon grew out of pure trading, and I became his general management consultant, working on such things as accounting systems. At my recommendation (which I outlined to him literally on the back of an envelope – at least it was thirty by twenty centimetres) he adopted a system based on Shell Brasil's method of starting at the point of sale, and deducting from the proceeds the cost of goods sold and the direct expenses of the trade, totalling the results across the company, then deducting the next level of overhead for which an identifiable individual was responsible, and so on up to the top: owner's expenses and profit. John is a very quick thinker, and within little over an hour we had my scribble reduced to a workable system, and the first results were on John's desk three days after the end of the month.

A fascinating activity, far removed from trading, was a magazine, *Chief Executive*, brainchild of Henry Dorman, former editor of *National Enquirer*, a supermarket checkout tabloid of the '*if you believe this headline, you'll believe anything*' kind. A complete contrast, *Chief Executive* was a quarterly for, about, and largely written by chief executives, and it was distributed free to qualified subscribers. The aim was to attract advertisers by a readership, certified by the Audit Bureau of Circulation, of above average influence and wealth. The first few issues had presidents of countries, starting with Jimmy Carter, and next the Archbishop of Canterbury, on the covers. Henry Dorman needed more financial resources than he alone could provide, and he sold the enterprise to John Deuss, becoming editor as a salaried employee, with a pretty free hand to produce the magazine, and (except for the profit and loss account) all seemed to be going well for a number of months. But Henry was a strange man; among other things he could not use a lavatory used by anyone else, and had to go home for this purpose. He caught John unawares one day, just as he was about to leave on an overseas trip, and asked if he could have a private bathroom added to his office, to which John agreed, without having any idea of the cost or technical problems involved. Henry's office was in a corner, and all the utilities in the building were in the hollow central core, so the water supply for this bathroom had to run over the ceiling of our nineteenth floor, and the drains between our floor and the ceiling of the eighteenth. This meant that much of the work had to be done while the offices were empty at weekends, thus incurring fifty per cent or one hundred per cent overtime charge, and the final cost was several tens of thousands of dollars. The bathroom had fittings from Sherle Wagner, the most expensive in the New York market, and a little ante-room with a black leather sofa in it. Of course the whole office knew (and most of us were aghast at) what was happening, and there were strong feelings against Henry Dorman's chutzpah,[1] and of regret that John should have been conned into this extravagance, not however untinged with concern that no one had been minding the store for him.

Frank Elias, General Counsel of Transworld Oil (as Joc had now become) began to worry about the costs of *Chief Executive,* which was clearly a long way from becoming profitable, indeed was costing John a great deal of money. One could question why, for example, it was in the interests of the business that the editor should, on a visit to Tokyo, not only stay in the Imperial Hotel, but should

---

[1]Effrontery, shameless audacity (Yiddish).

book the Imperial Suite, and there were other more serious questions. So one Friday afternoon John and Frank had an interview with Henry Dorman, asking for explanations. Alas, nobody thought of locking Henry's office, and on Monday morning all the material for the next issue, the list of subscribers, and all the files and records were gone, except one copy of a telex which had been sent to every subscriber saying: 'The new name of my magazine is *Leaders*. It will be published as usual, and its address is…'

John is one of those people who, in circumstances like this, doesn't waste his time or mental energy in anger, but sets out with cool resolve to rescue the situation.

In very short order he found and hired an experienced publisher, Leda Sanford; a senior editor, Helene Mandelbaum; and an assistant editor, J.P. Donlon, while John himself became editor-in-chief. Senior employees of the trading company became executives of *Chief Executive*, and I became its consultant (and jack of all trades).

In this capacity I went to Buenos Aires in early 1979 to interview the President of Argentina, General Jorge Rafael Videla. He, and the two other members of the military Junta, the heads of the navy and the air force, have been heavily criticised for the political violence which accompanied some degree of economic improvement; at the time of my interview the number of *desaparecidos* – those killed or missing in the military crackdown – was estimated at between four and a half thousand and fifteen thousand. I hold no brief for military suppression of political opposition, but I believe that much of the *post-facto* criticism of the Junta fails to take into account the facts of the time, and the strength of the Argentine tradition of *caudillismo*, government by a leader whose legitimacy is founded not on programme or achievement but on charisma and strong arms, and which the Junta was trying to eliminate.

Leda Sanford was clearly a real professional in her field,

but she shared a characteristic with many others in the same field that I have met – she was too lavish a spender. When she had to go anywhere, she never thought of taking a bus, or even a taxi, but always hired a limousine, and she entertained at the same level. Helene Mandelbaum got across John Deuss, and was unceremoniously fired; and Leda did not long outlast her, with the result that J.P. (no one seems to know what these initials stand for) became managing editor, with an editorial committee to guide him. Although I was the titular chairman of this committee, the professional brains were those of a British journalist who had become a friend of John's, Colin Welch. In one meeting I proposed that we publish a series of articles, not about business as such, but about the kind of recreational facilities of the quality to appeal to senior executives, to have as its title: 'I'm a simple man: the best is good enough for me!', of which the first would be a review of what is (in my opinion, at any rate) the best restaurant in the world, Taillevent in Paris, which I offered to write. The offer to do the work was accepted, but the professionals poured scorn on my proposed title: it had too many words, it lacked punch and so on. I had to bow to their judgement, and unwillingly accepted 'When the best is good enough'. I keep a copy of my article, and every time I look at it (which is usually when I am recommending the restaurant to someone who does not know it) I resent anew the emasculation of my title in favour of a piece of blah! However, the series didn't last long.

As time went on, and the financial haemorrhage was not assuaged, John asked me to think what we might do to improve matters, and I persuaded him that we should get in Arnie Pollard, who was expanding his practice from decision analysis to profitability improvement. Arnie had a number of ideas for new features for the magazine, but John was reluctant to face possible cost increases before results of Arnie's proposals could begin to pay off, and eventually Arnie and a partner agreed to buy *Chief Executive* from him. It is now of genuinely greater use to business, and has turned the financial corner. For some while my name remained on the 'masthead' as a contributing editor, but except for writing a book review published last year, I have contributed nothing for several years, and no longer have any connection with *Chief Executive*, other than as a subscriber with a lively interest in it.

JDR Consultancy is still in existence, but it has only one client left – Transworld Oil, and John Deuss's other ventures. It is not a demanding relationship, but John has recently acquired a one-third interest in a small bank, and he asked me for help in designing employee incentive plans for its employees. Perhaps if I had known as much about banking as I learned from these assignments, I might have accepted his *First Curaçao International Bank* offer.

Along the way I persuaded John that his organisation would be a happier and more productive one if he would get Chuck Ferguson in to help. Once they met, John developed an appreciation of and affection for Chuck, which stood Transworld Oil in good stead. Chuck was to start at a meeting of the trading people in Bermuda, and I had the task of telling them beforehand about Chuck. At the words 'industrial psychologist' there were groans of 'What? You mean a *shrink*?' and the like. But Chuck broke the ice beautifully with a story about a young man who had a glass eye. One day while he bathed his eyelids he was holding the eye in his mouth and swallowed it. The young man rushed to see his doctor, who looked first at where he expected the eye might come out, and there was the eye looking straight at him. 'Son,' he said, 'if you don't trust me, there's no way I can help you.'

He got us all working with his tools – felt-tip markers and pads of newsprint on easels – writing down three words that were positive about Transworld, and three that were negative, and then discussing them. These sessions changed John Deuss's management style completely: by instinct, and, one could almost say, national custom, he had tended to the Prussian manner, but Chuck really got him to see that there are better ways. John has tended to give me credit for much of what was Chuck's doing, to the point of telling people that 'All I know about management I have learned from Jock.' Recently he has modified this to '…from Jock *and my dogs.*' I harbour a little resentment at having to share my credit (however undeserved it may be) with a pair of Old English sheep-dogs.

Always looking for ways to expand his business, in 1985 John acquired the Philadelphia refinery of the Atlantic Richfield Group, together with the marketing assets, including a product pipeline, served by it in Pennsylvania and neighbouring states. It had been a rather stuffy organisation, but John set out to get to know the people, and to listen to the suggestions they had for doing things better, and very quickly the atmosphere changed, the level of enthusiasm rose, and a will to innovate was born. In a very short time, John's understanding of refinery operations and of the possibilities of changing the crude oil feed and the operating parameters had reached a very high level. One evening I was at a reception in Philadelphia for the senior people in the refinery, and I found myself in a group with John and two men who ran the asphalt plant. In a refinery, with a given crude feed, the proportions of the various products can be varied only within limits: if you want more petrol, you have to make less diesel fuel, and then only within a narrow band. Asphalt, used mainly for roads and roofing, has a seasonal demand – you can't work on roads or roofs that are under snow, or when the air is very cold. Moreover it's not cheap to store, since it has to be kept hot to be liquid, and therefore it is usually cracked to produce lighter products, which crowds out other feedstocks from the crackers. The Plant Manager was explaining his current dilemmas, and the restrictions under which he had to work, until John began: 'We have an availability of such-and-such a crude oil. If you could have so many barrels a day of that, couldn't you then do this, that and the other, and get round part of this problem?'

The manager and his number two started to chew this idea over, and in ten minutes they had agreed with John that if he would supply them with a quantity of the crude he had available, then indeed the economics of this part of the refinery could be improved. I have never met anyone who could assimilate esoteric learning as quickly and completely as John, whether in oil refining or magazine publishing. He has made himself a rich man – and deservedly!

Almost ten years ago John got himself into a temporary financial bind, by betting the ranch on the ability of his OPEC friends to make an increase in the price of crude oil stick, and he had a group of us in his house in Bermuda discussing what to do. After all the big potential savings had been brought out on to the table and mostly agreed upon, and the meeting was ending for the day, I suggested to John that he should dispense with the services of JDR Consultancy and he almost snapped: 'Why? Isn't it *fun* any more?' And I had to agree that it was still fun, and that I'd like to go on enjoying it.

NEES

Many in the United States acted, or tried to act, on two false assumptions: that oil, gas and electricity did not obey the laws of supply and demand, so that higher prices would not reduce demand and increase supply; and that in any case federal government regulation could repeal those laws.

There is an inertial effect in the ways the laws work: people still have to drive to work, and they cannot change old 'gas-guzzler' cars for smaller, more efficient ones overnight. It takes time and investment for homeowners to improve the insulation of their ceilings, walls and windows. It takes time for new sources of oil to be found and developed, but a price increase is a powerful incentive, as the OPEC nations began to find, to their chagrin.

Much of my time with NEES was spent on giving seminars to the staff on issues like these, and on the fundamental background of energy. On a couple of occasions NEES asked me to take part in State government organised, or sponsored, conferences with titles like 'The energy crisis and the economy of New England', and on private briefing sessions with State Energy Regulatory Commissioners, so that discussions about prices of electricity to the public could be conducted on a basis of reality, or at least on the assumption that the electricity industry had some facts in its favour.

Gradually these consulting activities began to overlap with my duties as a director of the System, of which more is written later.

Marubeni America

Marubeni America Corporation was the US affiliate of one of the Sogo Shosha, Japan's six 'General Trading Companies'. These are what their names imply, and they handle over half of all Japanese foreign trade, from grains, textiles, electronics to oil and heavy machinery. Each one is represented at some level in almost every country in the world. Their success is due principally to two things: information, and understanding of other cultures. It would not be easy for a lone Japanese entrepreneur to break into any foreign market: very few foreigners speak, and even fewer write Japanese, and the reverse is in part true. So if one company can offer a familiarity with the customs procedures, the shipping documents and the money transfer arrangements, it makes life much easier for the small manufacturer to turn to a huge Sogo Shosha to handle his business for him. And, of course, they do a lot of business for their own account.

It was the Petroleum Department to which I became a consultant. Hiroshi Takagi was the Manager, Koji Tokuda head of Oil Trading and my direct 'client', although Takagi often asked me to write a report for him on wider, often political issues affecting energy. Try explaining to a logical-minded Japanese why the Natural Gas Pricing legislation of 1978 should establish sixteen levels of controlled prices, from as low as nine cents per thousand cubic feet to a dollar or more, while gas from a new well, at a greater distance from an existing well of more than a mile, and deeper than ten thousand feet should be free of control. (It had the effect that anyone should have foreseen. Gas was scarce at the time, and much of the existing supply was tied up in long term contracts, so *marginally available* gas commanded high prices. Accordingly, it came to be said, 'You don't drill for gas; you drill for dollar bills.')

Takagi San's English was serviceable, but not fluent. Koji's (he and I were on first name terms, while to Takagi San I was always Ritchie San) was excellent. He had served in the US before, and one of his daughters was born in California. Only one word regularly gave him trouble: it is well known that most Japanese cannot pronounce 'l' – 'television' turns into 'terebi' – and one of Koji's favourite phrases was 'No plobrem'. He lived in Westchester County, one of the nicest commuter areas north of New York, and played golf and tennis at a country club there. He achieved a very low handicap at golf, and was the club tennis champion. (This made life difficult for him when he was transferred back to Tokyo: golf was totally out of his financial range, and he had to decide between tennis and a car, even though he lived an hour and a half's commute from downtown Tokyo.) He and I became very good friends, and used to go out to lunch together (and talk business) most of the days I was at Marubeni. The Yale Club, of which I was then a member, was just across the street from the building, over Grand Central Station, in which Marubeni had its offices, and if it was my turn to invite, Koji always asked to go there, because he said they made the best hamburgers in New York. If it was Koji's turn, I always asked to go to one of the many Japanese restaurants in the business districts of the city, so that I could indulge my new-found taste for sushi and sashimi.

My agreement with Marubeni called for me to produce at least one report a month. The subject was sometimes asked for by Takagi San or Koji, but mostly it was my choice. There was no shortage of suitable subjects in a period in which the Carter presidency declined into impotence; the Shah of Iran went into exile and Khomeini took over the country; OPEC influence rose to its peak, and had the consuming world very frightened; that saw oil prices almost triple, from thirteen dollars to thirty-four dollars per barrel and then fall to ten dollars in late 1985. High prices had encouraged new production, most of it outside OPEC; when members of OPEC were in open competition with one another, and Iran and Iraq, after Saudi Arabia its second and third largest producers went to war. OPEC had tried to control oil prices, as had the American and many other governments, but 'the market', led by the New York Mercantile Exchange (Nymex) and its trading of contracts for future supplies of oil triumphed, and became the mechanism for setting prices.

Most of my reports, and the discussion they provoked were helpful to, and appreciated by Marubeni, but I had one abject failure. They had a contract with a major American oil company, which simply failed to honour it. They tried persuasion at the highest levels, but got nowhere. They asked me to look through the contract and all the exchanges of messages which had taken place. You didn't have to be a lawyer to realise what the other party was doing – making unscrupulous use of Japanese business culture. To do business you have to establish good relations and mutual trust, and you don't misbehave. A symptom of this is the fact that the United States has fifteen times as many lawyers in proportion to population as does Japan. In Japanese culture it is just not done to go to law against anyone with whom you do business. But this gives an unscrupulous trading partner a chance to wriggle out of a deal that has gone sour, though possibly ending a business relationship. I explained as best I could to the senior Marubeni people that, in this case, they were operating in the United States where the culture was quite different, where going to law was a means of settling differences and not an indication of hostility. I quoted to them Asiatic's difference with NEES, and the happy outcome of that for both parties. In vain. The cultural abhorrence to litigation quite overcame a financial loss, and the knowledge that they had been unfairly treated. And looking around at the abuse of litigation now rife in the United States, who is to say they were wrong?

The Sooner Group

Of the many outstanding people I have met in my life, Henry Zarrow must rank very near the top. He is deceptively modest, but has a brain as sharp as a razor, and a phenomenal memory. His parents were Lithuanian Jews, who came to the United States to escape his father's being conscripted into the army. Initially they settled in Wisconsin, where they had relatives, and father Zarrow peddled women's clothes door-to-door for a living. Henry was born in Milwaukee in 1916, but when he was still a baby a cousin who lived in Nebraska suggested to Henry's father that the two of them should move to Tulsa, where he had heard there were opportunities in one of the typical businesses that Jewish immigrants went into, scrap metal. When Henry was thirteen he decided to set up his own small grocery store, but needed working capital to buy inventory, so he decided to apply for a bank loan. The loan officer lived in a hotel in Tulsa, where Henry went to see him. He found him sitting with another man, J. Paul Getty, whom he knew by sight, but asked for his loan. The bank officer was doubtful about lending money to one so young, but Getty said, 'If he can't raise some money, how will he ever get started?'

The banker was convinced, and wrote out a check for three hundred dollars on no other security than a handshake. Since then, Henry has never banked with any other bank than the one that had faith in him as a very young, totally inexperienced boy, except once when he needed to borrow twenty-five million dollars which was more than his bank could lend to one customer. And he has been a director of the bank for many years.

The grocery opened at 6 a.m., closed at 8.30 a.m. when Henry went to school, to be opened again as soon as school ended for the day and until 8.30 p.m. After high school he went to Oklahoma University, but after one semester he found that his grocery store could not support his tuition payments, so he dropped out. Later he tried again at Tulsa University, but again had to give up, and go to a business college at night. But he wanted wider horizons, and one Sabbath at the synagogue he asked an acquaintance, Harold Manley, a retired senior executive of a small oil company, if he could suggest anything. 'Yes,' said Mr Manley, 'there are hundreds of miles of disused gathering lines[2] all over Oklahoma. Sooner or later the oil companies are going to have to recover them to get them out of the way. You could buy them for next to nothing, and if you lift them, clean them and recondition their couplings, you will have a big market because there are many Mom and Pop wells that can be at best marginally economic, and a saving on the gathering cost may make the difference between making a profit and not being able to produce the oil. All you need is some simple tools, a truck and somewhere to clean the pipe. And I will be your consultant.'

His first real opportunity came when Sun Pipeline wanted to sell several hundred miles of eight-inch pipeline. Gulf Oil wanted the right of way, but not the pipe. So Henry bought, recovered and reconditioned it, and from that small beginning built up the business of Sooner[3] Pipe and Supply until it was the biggest stockist and distributor of oilfield tubulars in the world, in the process making him one of *Fortune* magazine's list of the three hundred richest Americans.

He went on to build up a large oil- and gas-gathering system of his own, because he decided that he would never lift a pipeline if it was the only way for a small operator to get his oil to market. His first purchase was in the city of Barnsdall in Oklahoma, and he was wondering whether to call his yet-to-be-formed company Barnsdall Pipeline, when someone suggested that he take the name that the Osage Indians used for Barnsdall, after one of their chiefs; and Bigheart Pipeline Corporation it became – and a more

---

[2]Small diameter pipelines from individual wells to a central collection storage facility, laid on the surface.

[3]The name derives from the nickname of those white settlers of Oklahoma, who jumped the gun of the famous 'land-run' which started at noon of 22nd April, 1889, on the grounds of 'Sooner, the better'.

appropriate name there could not be for a company belonging to Henry Zarrow. It began by serving small (and not so small) oil and gas fields in Oklahoma, but as it grew it spread through Kansas as far north as Ohio, and south to the Gulf coast of East Texas.

In 1953 Henry acquired a company, TK Valve, that manufactured ball valves to the highest international specifications, and later formed a sister company in Scotland. Later still, in 1986, on the grounds that a valve is only as good as its actuator, he built, also in Scotland, a plant, Prime Actuators, to manufacture valve actuators, from the smallest size to the largest emergency spring-operated shutdown valves in the North Sea.

TK's capabilities were put to the test in 1988, after the disastrous accident when Occidental Petroleum's Piper Alpha platform exploded and caught fire with heavy loss of life. Production not only from the Piper, but also from the Claymore field was shut down, and to restore it many new valves were needed. Occidental asked for bids from a number of suppliers, who quoted delivery times of two to three months and longer. TK persuaded other customers to accept postponed delivery; the Swiss company that forged the steel balls for the biggest valves postponed its annual holidays, which were due in a few days and worked round the clock; the Managing Director of TK persuaded Customs and Excise to allow instant clearance of steel-forging blanks from Scotland to Switzerland and of finished forgings back; and TK swept its worldwide stocks of finished valves from Canada to Singapore, and quoted three weeks. The job was finished in nineteen days.

Henry and his wife Anne live very simply for people of their wealth. Henry drives his own car to and from his office, and their hobby is giving away their money. There is not a worthy charity in Tulsa to which they do not contribute, and Henry gives his time as well as money to many of them, although there are two which are essentially theirs. Zarrow Manor, a complex of sixty apartments for rent, and forty where day and night health care is available, was built by Henry and his brother Jack and given with an endowment to the Jewish community of Tulsa. The other is the Day Care Center for the Homeless, built on land given by Henry. It is managed by the (ecumenical) Tulsa Metropolitan Ministry, and provides a place for homeless people to go by day, to be off the streets and out of the weather, to have showers, to wash their clothes, to have access to a telephone, and to have referrals to potential employers. A sister organisation of more recent foundation is the Shelter for Homeless Women and Children where there are sleeping facilities for a limited number. It was sued recently for having too many people, and Henry told the judge that if more people than allowed by regulation needed to get in out of bitter weather, he wasn't going to stop them, and they could arrest him.

Henry invited me to Tulsa to see what his companies did, meet his senior people, and give a one-day seminar on decision analysis, which clearly interested him. As luck would have it, Bigheart very soon had a question which was ideal for decision analysis, concerning a large quantity of crude oil which it had in stock, at a time when there was a possibility that there might be a substantial increase in the (controlled) price of this oil. Bigheart had to decide whether to sell immediately at the then current price, or hold it for sale at a possibly higher price later. The unknowns were whether there would indeed be an increase in price; if so, when; and how much. All the Sooner people concerned and I met, and started a full-scale decision analysis, pooling all our knowledge, the rumours, and our guesses about the possibilities, using all Arnie's tools and imaginary strangers. After a day and a half we had a decision tree with which we were all satisfied, and we took our recommendations to Henry. He accepted our reasoning, and Sooner did what our analysis had suggested (which was the opposite of what their hunch had been) and made a lot of money.

Over the years since then, the Sooner Group has sought my counsel on a number of issues. Perhaps the most important was several years ago, when Henry invited Billie and me to accompany him and Anne on a trip to Switzerland, so that he and I could discuss the future of his companies and plans for management succession in tranquillity, and without day-to-day business distractions (though I have no doubt but that Henry got up early in the mornings to telephone Tulsa and check that everything was on track). We spent, I think, ten days together, and it was in this time that Henry and I really got to know one another. At the end – indeed in its final version on the plane going back home – I hand wrote, for Henry's eyes only, on a yellow pad,[4] a report of the conclusions we had reached. One of our starting points had been that he, the founder, majority owner and brains of the organisation, and the person that all the big customers knew and were used to doing business with, was nearing the span allotted to us by the Ninetieth Psalm, 'threescore years and ten'. Likewise, many of the company presidents and vice-presidents who were his close contacts were themselves approaching, or entering, retirement. I began my report with verse 8 of the first chapter of Exodus: 'Now there arose a new king over Egypt, that knew not Joseph', and I think these biblical words brought the situation home to Henry more than all earnest persuasion could have done.

[4]The standard pad used by lawyers for manuscript – yellow only because it was cheaper to dye paper yellow than to bleach it white.

Part Six

Director of Public Companies

Chapter Forty-Eight

New England Electric System

Not far into 1977, Guy Nichols was again in New York, and asked me if I would have breakfast with him and Joan Bok, assistant to NEES's President. We met in the Bull and Bear Restaurant of the Waldorf-Astoria, and no sooner was our coffee poured and our breakfast ordered than Guy asked me if I would join the Board of NEES. I was totally surprised, and asked Guy what attributes he thought I had that made him believe I would be a worthy candidate. He said that my understanding of the oil industry, and what he had seen of my negotiating skills in our fight over prices, and what he had learned from others about my interpersonal relationships were enough for him.

I had been, of course, on many boards of directors, but only of Shell subsidiaries, and clearly to be a director of a publicly owned company, the shares of which were quoted on the New York Stock Exchange, would be a very different affair.

But I was flattered, and (though not without some internal qualms about adequacy) I accepted, and at its next meeting the Board of NEES elected me a director until the next annual meeting of the shareholders.

Thus began an association lasting eleven very pleasant years. The System comprised a number of separate wholly owned corporate entities, with a head office in Westborough, Massachusetts, some thirty miles west of Boston.

The retail companies, which sold electricity to the public, and were subject to regulation by state regulatory commissions, were Massachusetts Electric, Narraganset Electric serving Rhode Island, and Granite State Electric in New Hampshire. Because of the importance of relations with state governments, and local customers, these three had outside directors as well as NEES employees on their boards. In no state were we sole suppliers, and our participation in New Hampshire was small. New England Power, which owned and ran the power plants and the transmission and distribution system, was subject to regulation at the federal level.

My fellow directors were a very interesting group of people. Only four were employees; Guy Nichols, the Chairman, Joan Bok, the Vice-Chairman (Joan, who succeeded to the position of chairman when Guy retired, had no tolerance for the feminist correctness of 'chairwoman', 'chairperson' or – my pet abomination – 'chair') Dick Dunn, Vice-President and Secretary, and Leigh FitzGerald, Chief Financial Officer. Outsiders represented insurance, investment management, the law, university professors, manufacturing and one who, starting as a very young man with one bus, developed one of the largest bus lines in the New England/New York area; the President Emerita of Radcliffe College, and a lady who ran a very successful and influential consulting business in Washington. Of course there was a turnover; directors retired and new ones joined the Board, but throughout my eleven years they were all remarkable people.

There were usually four Board meetings every year, of which one followed the annual shareholders' meeting and another included a visit to some interesting part of the System – the hydroelectric plants on the Connecticut River; the enormous dams on La Grande Rivière in James Bay, built and operated by Hydro Québec, and from which

NEES was planning to import power over a purpose-built transmission line; an offshore drilling rig in the Gulf of Mexico during a period when we had our own oil and natural gas production venture,[1] and the Seabrook nuclear plant in New Hampshire of which we owned a minority, but significant, share.

Seabrook was a pathetic example of the ambivalence of the American public's attitude to nuclear power. Its safety record is impeccable: not one death has been caused by it, while a small steam plant in New York City caused a number of fatal casualties, and the breach of a hydroelectric dam could wipe out whole communities. Seabrook was delayed by years, and its cost increased by hundreds of millions of dollars, much of it caused by the Clamshell Alliance, which claimed that the cooling water system would suck in all the remaining colonies of a particular tiny clam. The protesters against this chose a strange way of making their point: they gathered, and threw over the fence around the plant, hundreds of shovelfuls of these poor molluscs – an odd way of declaring one's desire that they be protected. To meet these objections a tunnel costing over a hundred million dollars, and causing months of delay, had to be bored to bring in the cooling water from three miles offshore. And in the event, many other colonies of this clam were found in other places nearby.

The Board had, as is common practice, a number of committees, and at my first meeting I was elected member of one of these. I jibbed, on the grounds that I knew nothing of the workings of the Board, and asked to be allowed to get a little experience first. I was talked out of my objections, and in the course of my service I served on many committees, and as Chairman of at least two, the

---

[1]This was short-lived. A financially risky risk business was an uneasy bedfellow for a regulated industry.

Compensation Committee and the Customer Service Committee. On the first of these I worked closely with Guy and Joan to devise and bring into practice a system – the best I have seen – of performance-related bonuses for the senior executives. (One of our most difficult tasks was to persuade Guy himself to accept the award of a bonus for his superb direction of the whole. He felt that if he were to be one of the beneficiaries of the plan, his objectivity would be compromised, and stuck out for a year or two, until the whole Board virtually had to order him to be appropriately paid.) The Customer Service Committee devised and monitored a system measuring the extent to which we provided our customers with what they wanted, at the lowest possible cost – electricity supply with the minimum of interruptions, and when *force majeure* (for example hurricanes, snow and – worse – ice storms) caused cuts, power restored as quickly as possible.

After every meeting, the Board had lunch in a little room in the office. The menu did not vary much, but it was always an excellent if simple lunch. We started with the best New England clam chowder anywhere, followed by cold seafood, cold meats and salads, and apple pie or something similar for dessert. It gave us an opportunity to talk together informally, and my only reservation about it was that for this purpose it was too short, people were wanting to get home as soon as possible. If I had a criticism of NEES's Board, it was that we didn't give ourselves the opportunity, particularly when there was some delicate issue to discuss, to be able to let our hair down in private before going into the boardroom, and having to talk on the record. But I should not cavil. I believe NEES was as well managed as any public company, and we had remarkably few divisive clashes of opinion.

We did have an opportunity, once a year, for informal discussion: the annual Directors' Seminar, which was held in the early autumn at a resort usually somewhere on the New England coast. All the directors of NEES itself and of the three retail companies were invited, along with all the retired directors, and over a weekend we discussed some issue of serious import to the system – recently, for example, the dramatic change in the industry which deregulation and the opening of supply to virtually all comers was bringing about. These affairs were by no means luxurious, and no spouses were invited so that there should be no distraction from serious business.

The standard of the presentations by the executives was exceptionally high, and if twenty minutes were allowed on the programme for a speaker, in twenty minutes he or she finished. 'She' in this context is important, because NEES was away ahead of most large US corporations in having women in senior level executive positions. And all presentations were enhanced by a very high standard of helpful, usually enlightening charts. It was said (only partly in joke) that you couldn't rise in NEES unless you could produce high-class charts. I attend as many of these meetings as I can to keep up with old acquaintances and with the progress of the system, but unfortunately they often clash with the last weeks of our annual visit to Collieston. In passing, I often find myself comparing NEES people with Collieston folk – the same sincerity, the same seriousness of purpose, the same intellectual honesty and the same care about people, all tinged with humour and courtesy.

When I left the Board, Guy Nichols, who was a director but no longer Chairman, gave me a framed 'testimonial' which hangs on the 'swelled-head' section of my office wall:

Historian, Linguist, Raconteur and Friend –
Businessman of the World, Economist, Woodworker and
Renowned Resolver of Controversy.

★

Confidant of many Managements, and Always
a Believer in working with and within
an organisation to achieve
improvement for all.

★

A husbander of corporate resources, but
always a generous rewarder of those that
help bring success to a corporation.

★

Our System will continue to benefit from
Jock's high standards and we will strive
to make him proud of the organisation
he has helped to build.

I *am* proud of it, and grateful for the opportunities it gave me.

Chapter Forty-Nine
McDermott

One day in the late spring of 1977 I received a telephone call from John Loudon. He asked me if I knew of the engineering and construction company J. Ray McDermott. I answered that, yes, I knew the name of the company, but had a very superficial idea of what it did except that it was involved with the oil industry. He went on to tell me that he had been invited to become a director of the company, but had decided that he could not make the time available from his other commitments. They had then asked him if he could suggest the name of any other person in or retired from the oil industry, especially with an understanding of oil prices, and he had mentioned my name as someone they might consider, subject to my having no objection. I asked him to go ahead, and set out to learn all I could about the company, first by getting a copy of its most recent annual report from Asiatic's Materials Department. Ten days later I had a meeting, in New York, with three of McDermott's directors, Charley Graves, the Chairman, John Morgan (great-grandson of J. Pierpont Morgan) and Doug Carver, both outside directors. I had by then discovered that McDermott's business was the design, building and installing of offshore drilling and production platforms and pipelines worldwide. The likely future demand for, and price of, oil would very obviously affect the demand for McDermott's services, and familiarity with the international oil industry would be useful on its Board of Directors. We talked for perhaps an hour, and somehow got to exchanging jokes, and Charley asked for my agreement for him to put my name forward for election as a director at the next meeting of the Board. I was elected, and joined the Board on 28th July, 1977 at McDermott's office in New Orleans.

The company's business was exciting. It had its origins in Louisiana, building piled foundations for drilling rigs in shallow waters of the Mississippi delta, and had grown to be designer, fabricator and installer of platforms for drilling and then producing oil offshore. As oil deposits are discovered in deeper and deeper water, in the North Sea, the Gulf of Mexico and South-East Asia, platforms have to become bigger and bigger. Just one month before my election to the Board, McDermott had installed the base section of the tallest offshore platform built to date. In 1975 Shell Oil as the operator for a group of eight (and later, fifteen) oil companies discovered a new oil and gas field in over three hundred metres of water off the mouth of the Mississippi. The prospect was named Cognac, and exploratory drilling soon established the probability of reserves of oil and natural gas substantial enough to justify an investment of eight hundred million dollars to bring the reserves to production. McDermott was chosen to build the platform, which, when its two drilling rigs were mounted on its three-storey, eight thousand square-metre deck, was 386 metres tall The drilling rigs could be moved on their bases to enable each to drill thirty-one separate wells.

Nothing of this size had been built before, and it was decided that it would have to be built in sections, the base being fifty-six metres high and over one hundred metres square. This structure was fabricated at Morgan City, loaded on to a barge, and sunk to the sea floor, within six metres of the designed position, where it was anchored by twenty-four steel tube piles, over two metres in diameter, one hundred and ninety metres long and weighing four hundred and twenty tonnes. Fascinatingly these piles penetrated the first fifty metres of the seabed simply by their own weight, and were then driven the remainder of the depth by underwater hammers. A year later the middle and top sections were lowered into position, and all three locked together by ten 'pins', almost two metres in diameter, three hundred metres long and each weighing six hundred and eighty tonnes – some pins!

Two other examples will give some further flavour of McDermott's business, and the enormous sizes involved. *Derrick Barge 23* carries two spools on which are wound almost five kilometres of twenty-five centimetres, or twenty kilometres of ten-centimetres diameter pipe; this is placed continuously on the ocean floor at a rate of thirty metres a minute. This enables the whole length of the pipe to be welded up from the twelve-metre lengths in which it is manufactured, and the joints X-rayed, on shore, under cover. And the barge requires much less time at sea.

Lay Barge 200 is one hundred and eighty metres long, sixty-five metres wide, and its superstructure is supported above water on six steel columns on two submerged hulls, so that it is virtually immune to the effects of high seas. The Statfjord oilfield in the Norwegian sector of the North Sea has large amounts of rich associated gas, which, without transport, had to be re-injected into the productive formation – an inefficient and in the long run prejudicial procedure. Norway wanted to have the gas delivered to its territory, where the liquids could be separated for petrochemical manufacture, and the surplus dry gas delivered to continental Europe by way of an existing gas line to the Enden terminal in Germany. Provision had to be made, too, to connect newly developed fields. In the western half of the North Sea, or in the Gulf of Mexico this would have been a routine job. But between the oilfields and the planned terminal at Karstø, north of Stavanger, lies a formidable obstacle – the three hundred-metre deep Norwegian Trench, particularly its western slope, which is pock-marked with cavities as deep as ten metres and up to one hundred and fifty metres across. To avoid having a length of pipe crossing one of these unsupported required extraordinary accuracy in laying. But in two summer seasons *LB 200* laid almost five hundred kilometres of thirty-six-inch and twenty-eight-inch pipe, all made up on board by welding together twelve-metre lengths, X-raying every weld, and then coating the pipe with up to twelve centimetres of a heavy coating, to ensure negative buoyancy when filled with oil or gas.

Not having to be always looking over its shoulder at regulators, McDermott was able to be somewhat less economical in its Board meetings than NEES, and, as a result we got to know one another better than the latter's directors. For NEES, most of us drove to Westborough in our own cars, arriving just in time for the meeting, and only those who lived some distance away (as did I) spent the night in a nearby motel. McDermott's directors lived as far apart as California, Illinois, North Carolina and New York State, and we were picked up by a company plane. We all dined together, often with senior executives who were not on the Board, and sometimes with an interesting outsider, so we got a chance of meeting and having relaxed conversation with people who might be candidates for top positions in the future, or who had special insight into some issue that could affect our future.

We would, every other meeting or so, visit some part of the company's business, the Morgan City Fabrication Yard for example, where the huge platforms were built, lying on their sides; or the derrick barges which hoisted the three-storey deck (where the work of drilling was done) on to the top of the 'jacket', the steel structure secured to the seabed a thousand feet down by steel piles; or a lay barge, from which sub-sea pipelines were laid. Doug Carver had been in the US navy, and served in destroyers like me. One day when we were visiting *Derrick Barge 100* I said to him, 'Doug, you realise that this derrick could lift one of the destroyers you and I served in out of the water?'

'Yes,' said Doug, 'and could lay it along the deck we're standing on, without any of it hanging over the edge!'

It was not only the size of these barges that was impressive, but the quality of the food that was served to the people who manned them. We often got lunch after a visit, and never have I eaten such fried catfish or pecan pie!

Once a year we held the Board meeting away from New Orleans, in somewhere interesting and relevant to our business: London, where we could entertain our many customers on that side of the Atlantic; Ardesier, on the Moray Firth in Scotland, where we had a big fabrication yard; or Singapore, where we could meet many customers from South-East Asia and visit our yard at Batam Island, Indonesia, only a few miles across the sea from Singapore. On these occasions, spouses were invited, and there was time to play golf or be tourists; indeed, on the visit to Singapore, we were given the option of returning home around the world, so Billie and I chose to go by way of Bangkok, Hong Kong and Japan. The first was a joy, but Hong Kong was a disaster: we stayed in one of the famous hotels, and found it *awful*. Our room was decorated in an unrelieved dark brown wood, and the only closet was not long enough to hang a suit in without the jacket touching the floor, and there was no light, inside or out, to illuminate the contents. And outdoors, it just poured with rain so heavy that one could see nothing. We tried the shopping, but the streets we managed to reach were lined with tourist traps. Billie and I agreed that Woolworth's in the rain would have been more fun, so we changed our reservations and went to spend two more days than we had planned in Japan – Billie's second and my third visit, and very enjoyable. I had not yet quite forgotten all my Japanese, so we were able to get around on our own.

Soon after I joined the Board we decided to expand by acquisition, and made a bid for the Babcock & Wilcox Company, the old-established maker of boilers, turbines, steel pipe and nuclear steam generating plants. United Technologies, the Chairman of which was the redoubtable Harry Gray, who had built up his company by acquisitions, entered the bidding against us, but in the end we were successful, in large part due to the planning and strategising of John Morgan, who had the appropriate skills in his blood. The merger seemed to offer much to both parties; both were essentially heavy engineers – 'bangers and benders of steel' – but culturally they were very different. McDermott was from Louisiana, the only state in the Union with laws based not on the English tradition of common law, but upon the Napoleonic code, and with ethical cultures that reflected that difference, looking to the letter, rather than the spirit of the law. B&W was based in Ohio, in the classical 'Rust Belt' of America. Looking back, we made, in our merger with B&W, the mistake of following neither Machiavelli's advice (his exact words elude my memory, but the gist is, 'When you conquer another principality, kill all the old ruling family') nor Sir John Harvey-Jones's prescription '...if you wish to amalgamate two groups you can only do it by actually setting out with the aim of creating an entirely new group, in the composition and design of which both parties are equally involved.' Even today, my sense is that amalgamation is, almost twenty years later, not yet complete.

One of our outside directors was Graham Mattison, a lawyer who was trustee of the fortune of Barbara Hutton, the heiress of her grandfather, F.W. Woolworth, and of her father, E.F. Hutton, one of the wealthiest men on Wall Street in his time. When I went down to New Orleans for my first Board meeting after my election (not, this time, on a company plane, but a commercial flight) Graham happened to be on the same plane. We were both among the half-dozen in first class, and (from my – indelible – accent, perhaps?) having guessed that I might be on the same flight, Graham recognised who I must be, and came over and introduced himself. We took to each other, and had a very pleasant flight the rest of the way. As in any group, one finds a few individuals with whom one is more comfortable in asking: 'What do you think of this proposal?' or 'Do you think that so-and-so is really the best person for that job?' In my early months in McDermott Graham was, for me, one of those, though I soon began to feel that he lacked profundity, and I tended to prefer to ask Doug Carver, John Morgan (if one could get his head out of his own business) or Jim Hunt.

One of the features of McDermott's ethos had been that the antitrust laws were there to be ignored, if you thought you could safely do so. Then, one day, the explosion happened: we were sued by the Department of Justice for illegally fixing prices and sharing the market with one of our principal competitors, and a subpoena unearthed a log, kept by one of our senior executives, of past jobs bid on, which company did the work, and by comparing the total value of each company's work, establishing whose turn it was to get the next job. The company and the people who had run the scheme all pleaded guilty, and Charley Graves admitted that, while he had not participated, he had been aware of what as going on, for which he was sentenced to a fine, a number of hours of community service and a suspended prison sentence.

Charley had diabetes; his diabetic blindness was beginning seriously to affect his sight, and his retirement date was only two or three years away, and now this penalty was hanging over his head. Under him, in the hierarchy, were two possible successors – Bob Richie, President of the company, and operating head of the marine construction side of our business; and Jim Cunningham, who headed the administrative parts of the organisation, including finance, though he was an engineer by training. Next under Bob Richie was Bill Bailey, who had for years been one of the moving spirits of marine construction. All three of these were members of the Board. Charlie had come to rely on Jim as his link with the operations, and as such Jim was to some degree resented by the operating people. To make matters worse, Charley had indicated to both Bob and Jim that he would succeed to the chairmanship on his, Charley's, departure. There was in fact no official succession plan, and to my knowledge the issue had never been discussed by the Board.

This situation worried me, and I wrote, in pencil on a yellow pad, my thoughts. I argued that Charley's health, eyesight and the suspended sentence hanging over his head scarcely made him fit for the stresses of the chief executive's job, so we must face his imminent retirement. We could appoint Bob Richie or Jim Cunningham in his place, or we could recruit someone from outside. To find and negotiate with a suitable outsider would take several months, and then there would be a further delay before even the smartest man could become intimate with our problems and opportunities, and Bob and Jim's noses would both be out of joint. However, I did not believe that either of them was really of sufficient calibre. So I suggested that we should name one of us outside directors as non-executive Chairman of the Board, and Bob or Jim as President and Chief Executive, to give us time to think, and that we should do this at the next Board meeting. I spoke on the telephone to the directors with whom I had most confidence, and sent them a photocopy of my scribble, with an earnest plea to keep it to themselves until we could bring it up with our colleagues. I should have known better; a secret shared with five others is no longer a secret. And somebody showed a copy to Charley. He telephoned me and angrily said, 'I hear you're trying to hustle me out of my job!' I told him that no, but I did want to prepare him and the company for an event which could not be long delayed, and after ten minutes or so he calmed down, and I think realised that there was nothing personal in it, and that maybe I was right.

Inevitably the insider directors learned that the chairmanship was an issue that the Board would soon have to discuss, and Bob and Bill made an attempt to take over, by telephoning around all of us and urging us to vote at our next meeting for a motion, which they would introduce, appointing Bob as Chairman and Bill as President. They failed to get enough support, and the outside directors agreed we should meet alone for half an hour before the scheduled meeting to discuss my proposals. Well, the half-hour dragged out to three hours, but finally I said that if no one else was willing, I would volunteer. I was the most junior member of the Board, and so the others felt that they should find another candidate, and finally picked on John Morgan. John and I were asked to go and wait in the office next door, while the rest of the Board voted. But John started walking up and down the room, obviously a bit agitated, talking as if to me, but really to himself. 'I've got this to finish, and I've got that to do, and I ought to be giving more time to the other: no, I can't take it on.'

We were called back in, and they announced that they had elected John unanimously: 'Sorry, Jock.' Then John announced that, thinking it over, he had to withdraw, because of other commitments. So, with a little embarrassment, they asked me if my offer still stood, and thus, with zero votes of the nominating committee, I became Chairman, for almost six months, until the next annual shareholders' meeting. The full Board then went on to elect Jim Cunningham President and Chief Executive Officer.

Bob Richie's nose was out of joint, and Bill Bailey was unhappy to say the least, and for a couple of months I did my best (using Chuck Ferguson's methods) to get the three to work together, but failed, and both resigned to join competing companies. Jim accepted my role with, if not a good grace, then at any rate not too ill a one. I had been doubtful about Jim's capacity for the chairmanship, and as I worked with him, my unease did not diminish on, principally, two scores. First, he did not see the virtue of the rule 'stick to the knitting'. In an attempt to lower the cost of the steel we needed for our business, we acquired a Hamburg-based steel-trading company, which turned out to be an expensive and unproductive venture; and Jim proposed that we should go into the business of genetic engineering, on the grounds of 'It's engineering, and we're engineers.' This, luckily, was aborted before we went beyond wasting some of the Chairman's time, and of the attention that our core business needed.

Second was a comment of Peter Landsberg's. McDermott needed contacts and help in Brazil, where offshore production was becoming increasingly important, and I got him to meet Jim. Peter's contacts and standing in Brazil would have been of great help to us, but Peter said that there was no way he would agree to work with Jim. 'During all our conversation,' said Peter, 'he never once used the word "we". It was always "I did this" and "I plan to do that".'

*

Our apartment at that time was on the corner of Park Avenue and 69th Street, and right across the avenue was the Union Club. I was at home one afternoon, when Graham telephoned to say that he was in the Union Club, and could I get across there as soon as possible: he had something very important to tell me. He asked me to promise to keep what he had to tell completely secret, and then he dropped a real bombshell. He had been approached *six months earlier,* he said, by Bill Agee, Chairman of the Bendix Corporation, to say that Bendix would like to acquire McDermott, and that perhaps Graham and I could help him in his approach, and hinted that Bill Agee had suggested that he would make it worth our while. I exploded, and told Graham that he *must* telephone Jim Cunningham at once and tell him, as he should have done six months before – only management could deal with such things. I went back home and immediately telephoned one of the company's New York lawyers, told him the story, and asked what else I should – or could – do. 'Give Graham a couple of hours to call Jim, and then you get him on the telephone to make sure that Graham has informed him of Agee's approach,' was his advice. When I called Jim at the end of the afternoon, he had heard from the lawyers, but not yet from Graham; and he later told me that he, and, he said, some of the other directors to whom he had spoken, had initially wondered whether I, too, had not been sitting on the news in my own interest, which did nothing to endear him to me further.

The Board met soon afterwards, and we agreed that we had no choice but to ask Graham to resign at once. I communicated this to him, and he seemed surprised and started to protest. But I refused to discuss the issue any further, and reminded him that it was he who had told me of Agee's approach, and he should have realised from my reaction then that he should not expect any sympathy from me, and he wrote out a letter of resignation. As he had been on the Board for many years we decided to invite him to a farewell dinner with us, but he never replied. I have since wondered much how a man, comfortably off, if indeed not rich, and a lawyer by profession, could have been so naive as to sit on his news for six months, and then try to make me, the Chairman of the Board, a party to a hole-and-corner approach to a merger between two major corporations.

The annual shareholders' meeting soon came, on 14th August, 1979, and Jim Cunningham was elected Chairman, and I reverted, with no regrets, to being just an ordinary director. While I think that my proposal was right at the time, in that it gave us a breathing space, McDermott needed a full-time Chairman of the Board. Then, at last, after nine more years, all interesting, if not as exciting as mid-1979, I reached the age at which the by-laws of the company mandated my retirement.

Chapter Fifty

Winding Down

After I left Asiatic, but was still busy with consulting and NEES and McDermott, Billie and I began to think about where we should make our permanent home. We used to go to our little house in the woods in Stone Ridge most weekends except in the really cold months, and we were there for the Easter weekend of 1977. On the Sunday we were invited to an Easter egg hunt at the farm of some friends. We set off by a back road and suddenly came upon a cow giving birth to a calf. Her labour had just begun and the head of her baby was barely visible. We stopped to watch – neither of us had ever seen this before – and saw the whole process. When the slimy, long-legged little being was delivered, and lying on the grass in a heap, the cow began to lick it clean and the calf began to straighten its legs, and make attempts, progressively stronger, to lift its head. When she had licked it clean (and rolled it over to do so) she began to nuzzle it to its feet, and after perhaps twenty minutes had got it to stand up, with its legs splayed out rather like a kitchen chair. It tottered, and almost fell several times, but its mother caught it with her nose and gently prodded it to move, until it walked a few wobbly steps, and started to crumple again, to be saved once more by mother's nose. It was a most moving sight, and somehow entirely appropriate to the origins of Easter as the annual beginning of new life.

We must have watched for an hour or more, because when we arrived the egg hunt was over, and lunch was about to start. It was the first time since Christmas (and since I had retired from my full-time job) that we had seen many of the friends who were also there, and after lunch someone asked us where we would be going to live. We said that it would not be in New York City, nor in any of the commuting areas around it, and people started to suggest places – parts of Pennsylvania, the Virginia shore, the Shenandoah valley and other places that were no more than names to us. Finally someone said, 'But why don't you stay in Stone Ridge?'

Billie replied, 'Well, if we could get five acres on Leggett Road, and could build a house on that, maybe we should.' Leggett Road is the poshest street in the village, with a dozen fine houses, including, on an eighty-acre site, that of the Viscount Margesson, grandson of the eponymous Francis Leggett, and Billie did not expect her comment to be taken seriously.

In the middle of the week, however, Bill Daron, our real-estate broker friend, telephoned Billie to ask, 'How would you like five acres on Leggett Road?'

We were very excited, and could hardly wait for the weekend to go and see what Bill had for us. He had persuaded Paul Sturges (another grandson of Francis Leggett) and Magdalena, his wife, to offer to sell us three acres of grass with a small apple orchard, and two acres of woods, all flat land, for ten thousand dollars. We agreed to buy it: the price was a bargain, and the situation was ideal, easy walking distance from the bank, the corner store and petrol station, the hardware store and, a little further away, the post office. The title search, the obtaining of title insurance and the other bureaucratic chores of changing ownership took a long time, and it was October before we became the owners.

It was not time wasted, because in the meanwhile Bill Daron had recommended to us a man to design and build a house on our new land, Robert Filipek, who was neither an architect nor a builder by trade, but a sculptor. This sounded a doubtful bit of advice until Bill showed us some of the houses that Robert had built; and then when Robert himself showed us more, we were convinced. While we were travelling in Europe, we had started to keep a notebook, 'Ideas for new house', in which we noted all the good features we had seen which would help shape the home we intended to build one day. The trouble was that there were so many that the house was going to have to be very big. But we sat down with Robert; we gave him the book and he quizzed us about our ideas and (horrible word) lifestyle, and then started to sketch ideas. His first attempt was ingenious, and in another place might have been successful. It was three separate round buildings with conical roofs, connected by covered passages, and looked, in his drawing, rather like an African kraal. That went on the scrap heap in no time, and Robert started again, from a suggestion of Billie's – that we should build round a central patio in the Spanish (or Roman) style, with the living quarters around it. From that simple idea Robert produced a design that was original, practical and, in its essence, simple. It was based on modules just under five metres square, nine making the main part of the house, with the central one being an atrium under a glass pyramid, raised a metre above the (apparently) flat roof – 'apparently', because it was in fact a series of areas, subtly sloped so that rain would run down to two drainpipes fifteen centimetres in diameter within the house, and then under the ground to a pond. From its back right-hand corner the house extended to make a breeze-way between the garden on one side, and where the swimming pool would be on the other, with a right turn into the guest room, making a sheltered corner for the garden.

On a very cold day in November we walked the land with Robert to place the house, and picked on a corner of the woods close to the right-hand edge of the property, with the front being parallel to Leggett Road. It was not easy driving stakes into the frozen ground, but we managed to get the corners approximately marked, and said goodbye to the project until spring, leaving the winter for Robert to do his drawings and survey his quantities, and us to arrange the cash flow.

Of course the house would have to be built over a basement, to keep the foundations below frost level, so the first job to be done was to bulldoze out the hole. That was when we learned why the village was called Stone Ridge – a ridge of shale rock ran right below where we planned to build, closest to the surface at the front right-hand corner, sloping away back and to the left. Robert's advice was that we should blast out that corner, build the house a metre higher than we had planned, and grade earth up to the new level. Luckily, on the other side of the property there was a marshy area, which Bill Daron jokingly called 'the wildlife refuge'. We decided to deepen this to make it into a pond, and use what was dug out to reach the level we needed around the house. When it was all done, the change in contour was scarcely noticeable, and we had a pond, which in time we filled with fish, and a bedroom at the back of the basement had its own entrance in the form of sliding windows at ground level. And where we had blasted out became our wine cellar, maintaining an almost perfect temperature all year round.

We derived a great deal of enjoyment from working with Robert on the house and shaping its interior spaces. The atrium was an anchor, but other interior walls were not tied to the modules, so we were able to have a kitchen nine metres long with an eating area, and a sitting area in front of a free-standing brick fireplace, the other side of which, in the breeze-way, was a barbecue. On the other side of the house we had a library and a living room, similarly separated by a free-standing chimney breast, with an arch on either side. Talking one day with Doug Carver of McDermott he told me that for his house in California he had bought an antique pine library from Crowthers of Syon Lodge in Isleworth, who recover woodwork from old houses being demolished, and rework it into whatever you want. We went to see them while we were on holiday in England, and ordered a break-front bookcase for one end of the library, with a heavy crown moulding to go round the whole room. In Beauchamp Place we found a (modern) fireplace to match, and ordered from Crowther a marble fireplace from a grand house in Paris for the living room. Interestingly, the George II pine panelling, cabinet doors and moulding cost less than they would have, made in the USA, of new pine! And it was all delivered at the time we wanted it – indeed before Robert was ready to install it, and we had to build a weatherproof shed at the edge of the woods to store it. Crowthers had required the final measurements of the completed space before they would start work, and when Robert came to assemble it in place, he told us that, if it had been one-sixteenth of an inch larger, he would have had to alter the walls.

For the atrium, we ordered white and dark green Carrara marble tiles, arranged in a diagonal chequer-board, with a dark green border. These were cut to Robert's measurements in Queens, New York, and every piece fitted exactly. There are, thank heaven, still some craftsmen left in a world of too much shoddy work!

I had resigned as consultant to Marubeni around my seventieth birthday, and a year later being no longer on the boards of NEES and McDermott, I began to have more leisure, and made good use of my workshop which took up a good slice of the basement. I panelled the open space of the basement, and built a bar at one end, with a twenty centimetre-wide redwood moulding for the elbow rest, and a proper brass foot rail. Billie's niece and goddaughter Patti Sunderland happened to be staying with us, and I cut twenty-five centimetres of the moulding and fitted it to a telescopic stand, which Patti (who is much closer to an average stature for a woman than Billie) tried out with her elbow until we found the right height. With the help of Bill Steenburgh, the teenage son of our housekeeper, Mary Ann Steenburgh, I built a little jetty for the pond, taking advantage of a very dry winter which exposed an almost flat piece of rock on the bottom at a suitable place to serve as a foundation. I worked on clearing the woods of dead trees, and turned them into firewood, and with my motorised chipper, I made cubic metres of mulch for the garden. And in the evenings I had time to read books.

The house was perfect for entertaining, and we let our basement be used for functions in aid of organisations like The Hudson Valley Philharmonic, for whom we had a violin and cello concert. We used it ourselves when we wanted to have dinner parties for more people than we could accommodate upstairs. Every year, on 21st October, we had a Trafalgar Day party. Americans in general know very little about Nelson (except from such movies as *That Hamilton Woman*) despite the fact that one of the best of his biographies was written by an American, Captain A.T. Mahan. Nor do they appreciate the reality of Mahan's words: 'It was those far-off, storm-beaten ships, on which the Grand Army never looked, that stood between it and the dominion of the world.' And which persuaded Napoleon to sell Louisiana to the United States. So I used to make a little speech every year to propose a toast to the immortal memory of Horatio Nelson, and to repair some of the gaps in the education of our guests!

In New York one day I was waiting at a traffic light to cross Fifth Avenue, when John Loudon came along and said, 'Jock, you're just the person I want to see. I want you to take on a job for me. You probably know that I have been active in getting INSEAD[1] going. We want to raise funds in the United States, and a not-for-profit foundation has just been formed. I want you to be its president – and don't be too scared, it won't be too demanding of your time.'

I crossed the street with him and he told me more about the International Management Education Foundation, and I agreed to put myself up for election as a trustee, and then, if the other trustees agreed, as president. I remained President until the annual meeting of 1996, and a trustee for a further year. IMEF was founded to raise contributions for the support of management education outside the USA, though not specifically for INSEAD. US corporations and individuals can make tax-deductible contributions to a US not-for-profit organisation, but this must not become a mere conduit to a foreign entity. So we have to keep at arm's length from INSEAD, to which, however, a large portion of the monies we raise is donated. My main preoccupation as President was to keep INSEAD and IMEF totally separate, and it has not always been easy, since INSEAD has often been too eager to help us.

I was also persuaded, by Denise Bryan, wife of Judge Frederick van Pelt Bryan,[2] and sister of David Farquharson who was the full-time manager of the British–American Chamber of Commerce in New York, and a friend of mine, to become a trustee (and soon President) of the

---

[1]The European business school in Fontainbleau.

[2]It was Judge Bryan who ruled that the artistic merit of *Lady Chatterley's Lover* outweighed the naughtiness, and therefore the book might be read by Americans.

British–American Educational Foundation. This arranged for young Americans, who had finished high school and secured a place in college, to spend a year (or even two) at a British 'public' school. We did not in general help financially, though we solicited contributions to help good candidates whose families could not afford the cost. And now we have a scholarship fund, raised in memory of Judge Bryan. We publicised the scheme in American schools, interviewed and selected young men and women, and then found places for them at schools – and Denise has a genius for making the right match. We provided guide and counselling services, both academic and *in loco parentis*, in the UK, and help with arrangements for holidays and extra-curricular activities. We had a few failures – people who just found the whole thing too strange, or the occasional pot-smoker – but the great majority were most enthusiastic about the experience, and profited from the discipline of A levels, more rigorous and more stretching than the US equivalent. During my tenure we had twenty or two dozen BAEF scholars every year, but recently the increases of school fees in Britain and the softening of the dollar against the pound have substantially reduced the attraction of the scheme. If IMEF was not quite the virtual sinecure that John Loudon promised, it was easygoing: BAEF demanded much more of my time and energy, but what the scholars got out of it made it well worthwhile, and it was only our move to Florida that made me give up.

We also started to do some travelling, mainly on tours organised by the Metropolitan Opera Guild or the Metropolitan Museum of Art. In 1984 we went on an ancient ship, the *Argonaut,* once a very rich man's yacht, to Egypt and Jordan. The two of us decided to have a few days on our own in Israel before joining the ship in Suez. It was fifty years since I had first been in Jerusalem, when I was a cadet in *Frobisher.* We found ourselves an Arab Israeli taxi driver who took us around to Jericho, the Dead Sea, Hebron, Bethlehem, Nazareth, Capernaum and the valley of the Jordan. On our own we walked round Jerusalem and the holy sites within and outside the walls. The city, indeed the whole country, is very moving; even I who am not, in any conventional sense, a religious person could not but be aware of the holiness of the land. Jerusalem is, after all, a holy place to all three of the great monotheistic religions, Judaism, Christianity and Islam. The city was founded by King David, and King Solomon built the Temple, of which the West Wall still stands. This, the Via Dolorosa and the Church of the Holy Sepulchre, and the Dome of the Rock from which Muhammad was carried up to heaven by the Archangel Gabriel in the Night Journey, all stand within a bare square kilometre.

All the passengers were to join the *Argonaut* in Suez, and we hired a taxi from Cairo Airport to take us there. The weather started to worsen before we were out of the airport, as a khamsin wind began to blow, and the air began to darken with blown sand. Our driver first called in at a fruit market, and begged some cardboard boxes with which to cover his headlights, which otherwise would be pitted to the state of ground glass by the sand. (I had personal experience of this: I once had to drive in my car from Cairo to Alexandria by the desert road in a khamsin, and arrived with a windscreen that, at night, simply dazzled, and with the curves of the top of the bonnet and the roof over the windscreen sanded down to bare metal.

We arrived in Suez, and learned that poor visibility had closed the port, that *Argonaut* was anchored outside, and that the rest of the passengers would not arrive until the next day. But we finally found an agent for the ship, who arranged to put us up for the night in the Hotel Summer Palace. This was the worst place Billie and I have ever had to sleep in. The beds had blankets (which had been much used, without ever having been washed) and no sheets. The 'bathroom' had a lavatory of the footprint-hole-in-the-ground variety, and a shower which was just a steel pipe with no shower head, and almost all the tiles had fallen off the walls, so that the underlying concrete (which must have had very little cement content) was eroded away up to ten or fifteen centimetres above the floor, and the space was host to dirt of every conceivable sort. We asked for sheets, and finally got some, washed but grey-brown in colour, and just rolled into a bundle. At least they separated our bodies from the filth of the blankets! In the morning we had cold showers, wearing socks. What we would have done if I had not been able to speak Arabic, I cannot imagine! But eventually the ship arrived, we boarded, settled into our cabin and had long, hot showers.

The tour was worth the wait, however. We visited Petra, Karnak, Luxor, the Valley of the Tombs of The Kings, and Gamal Abdel Nasser's monument to himself, the Aswan High Dam. Nearby are the temples of Abu Simbel, which had been carved into the solid limestone rock. The entrance to the larger is flanked by two seated statues of Ramses II on each side twenty metres high, while the smaller has statues of Ramses and Nefertari, his queen, which are ten metres high. But for an incredible feat of engineering, jointly sponsored by the government of Egypt and UNESCO, and with funds from more than fifty countries, all this would have disappeared beneath the water of Lake Nasser, as it rose behind the High Dam. But they were separated from the parent rock, raised to a safe height above, and moved some distance back from, the new water's edge.

We ended our trip in Cairo, with visits to the recently started excavations of Memphis, and to the pyramids of Giza and Saqqara. The former and the nearby Sphinx impress by their size, and by wonder at how they were built. The Great Pyramid, built as a tomb for King Khufu (or Cheops) four and a half millennia ago, is probably the largest building ever built by man. On a base 230 metres square, it was, before part of its outer casing was stripped off as building material, for example for the Muhammad Ali mosque in the Citadel of Cairo, over 140 metres high. The burial chamber in its heart was made of enormous blocks of granite, and the solid core of the structure of limestone blocks of an average weight of two and a half tonnes: some of the blocks of the outer casing are as big as sixteen tonnes. It was all done to protect the body of the dead king, and the goods buried with him to take to the next world; all in vain: the tomb was plundered bare. One's only reaction to it all can be the words of Ozymandias, King of Kings: 'Look on my works, ye Mighty, and despair!'[3]

When we lived in Cairo, the family used occasionally to go to Saqqara for a picnic on a weekend; there might be another family, but usually we had the place to ourselves. On the *Argonaut* tour, there must have been twenty busloads of people there. But Saqqara is more interesting than Giza. It is the site of first large all-stone building in Egypt, the tomb of King Djoser (or Zoser), one hundred years before Khufu. Originally built as a mastaba, a flat platform, of cut blocks with a core of rubble, with sloping sides, it was added to in stages, by the building of further mastabas, one on top of another, until it became a six-step pyramid. On one side, you can actually see the corner of the original mastaba with its cut side slab disappearing at right angles into the core, and the new side slab two metres further on as it was enlarged to accommodate the next layer. And on one of the higher levels where the side has fallen away there is a small tree trunk buried in the core,

[3]Percy Bysshe Shelley, 'Ozymandias'.

with a metre or so projecting, which apparently was used for a hoist (for tools, or perhaps for men; it would not have supported a stone of any size). Around the pyramid there are many temples, built all of stone, carved to represent palm trunks for ceiling beams, and the walls to simulate brick and reeds, the traditional building materials. Some of these have beautiful wall paintings of everyday life – seed time, harvest, taxpaying, domestic animals, and one of a hippopotamus giving birth. In 1950 there was a watchman there (but usually only one) who was delighted to earn a few piastres by letting you inside, and providing candlelight. Wherever you stopped on the sand to eat your picnic, you could, by sifting the sand through your fingers, find dozens of mummy beads, of glass, about the size of a lentil, with a hole through the middle. One senior manager of the Shell Company of Egypt actually found a tiny – less than a centimetre long – gold hippopotamus. The whole complex had, over the centuries, become buried in (and preserved by) sand, and it was only from aerial photographs taken by the Royal Air Force between the wars that it was identified as a structure and not just a sand hill.

While we were in Cairo, I had a very emotional experience. Wagih Kotb invited us to a party in his apartment in Zamalek (the upmarket residential part of Cairo, on the island of Gezira in the Nile). He had invited all the survivors of those who had been my closest friends and colleagues thirty years before, and their wives, and at my request he also invited my friends from 1940, Ezz-el-Din Atif and his wife Durriyah. Three of the Shell people, including my union 'opponent', Anwar Salama, had been ministers in Gamal Abdel Nasser's government. As soon as Anwar saw me, he came up, hugged me and kissed me on the mouth; what better way of saying 'No hard feelings'?

*

On a trip sponsored by the Metropolitan Opera we heard twelve operas in eleven days, in Paris, Milan, Turin and London, and another (Metropolitan Museum of Art this time) in *Argonaut* – almost on its last legs – took us to the classic sites of ancient civilisations: Athens, Thessaloniki, Istanbul, Troy, Ephesus, Priene in the valley of the river that gave its name to the verb 'meander', Reggio di Calabria, Taormina, Paestum (a Greek city in Italy – then part of Magna Grecia – lost for centuries in the growth of forest) and finally, Rome.

⋆

We had kept up our annual physical check-ups with Henry Schaffeld, and in 1988 he told me that he was hearing a murmur in my heart that he hadn't heard before, and sent me to have an echocardiogram. This disclosed a mitral valve prolapse, with regurgitation; in other words, that my heart was not pumping all of the blood that it should, and that some of every squirt that should have gone into my arteries was leaking back into the atrium. To begin with, this didn't affect me much, but after a few months I started to notice that I soon got out of breath splitting wood, and doing anything else strenuous. Nature was telling me it was time to slow down.

Billie had discovered a Japanese dressmaker in Madison Avenue, who bought her materials in Italy, and whose clothes just suited her, and she had a number of suits and dresses made. Then the lady's lease came to an end, and her landlord demanded an increase of three times her rent for renewal. So she decided to move, and found a shop on Worth Avenue in Palm Beach. A year or two later Billie told me that she needed some new clothes, so would I please take her to Palm Beach. It was February, and bitterly cold and miserable in Stone Ridge, so we booked two weeks in a hotel in Palm Beach. We were very taken by the place; cars stopped to allow you to cross the street, and if there was a Kleenex or a cigarette packet in the street, someone would say: 'Look, there's been a New Yorker here.' In fact I found it – and still do – the best-run municipality (except perhaps for Hamburg) that I had ever known. The hotel, however, was a disaster: it is a fine building in a lovely garden, but had the worst management imaginable. It turned cold one night, and we needed blankets. Billie's bed had one, but mine didn't, so I telephoned the front desk and asked for one. Nothing happened for ten minutes, so I called again, and a quarter of an hour later a Haitian employee came to the room, and offered me a mattress cover, made of non-woven material, ragged, and full of holes. I took this to the front desk, and complained loudly and bitterly, but the lady on duty said they had no more blankets. I asked if there wasn't a room unoccupied in which there might be one. After a lot of humming and hawing, she said that only the bridal suite was not occupied. Very reluctantly, she sent an employee to take me up to the bridal suite, where I (the employee said it was not his job) stripped a blanket off the bed and took it down to our room.

The following year, we tried another hotel – no blanket trouble, but noisy, because our room looked out on to a rooftop parking space. We stayed longer this time, and decided that it would be cheaper to buy a small apartment than spend three winter months in a hotel. After looking with an agent at a number of places we didn't like, and coming with him out of an apartment in West Palm Beach that seemed to be filled with the newspapers of the last five years, and where the owner just sat in a chair surrounded by them, he rather shyly offered to show us his apartment, just along the floor in the same building, which he was selling as he was moving into a house. He opened the door on to a cheerful interior of light colours, and a splendid view of the Intracoastal Waterway through a large window, outside which plants were growing on a balcony big enough for two armchairs and a sofa. We didn't hesitate long, and bought it, though it had only one (but large) bedroom. The building had a good garden, and a big swimming pool, and across the street there was a wide footpath-cum-bicycle track with almost a mile of uninterrupted walking. Every late afternoon if the weather permitted (which, in Florida, was a high percentage of the time) we walked a mile or more along it, often escorted by those most accomplished acrobats, pelicans, which can glide for long distances sustained by an up-current of air, with their wing-tips clearing the top of the concrete seawall by no more than a centimetre.

Gradually I became less and less comfortable living in our big house in Stone Ridge, as my capacity for coping with firewood, snow-ploughing, and just the size of the house diminished. Billie argued that we could hire people to do these things, but the supply of help of this kind in Stone Ridge was shrinking, and I was inwardly afraid that I would get dissatisfied with the way *my* jobs were being done, and try to do too much, and make my heart problem worse. Eventually, however, she gave way, and agreed we should put our lovely home on the market, leave a lot of good friends and move full-time to Florida.

We began a search for an apartment that would not be too much of a comedown from our Leggett Road house. This called for three bedrooms, one *as* a bedroom, one as a library and the third as an office for me. We started in Palm Beach itself, but the norm there seemed to be two beds, two baths, and prices were very high. At last we found what we wanted in a recently built condominium. ('Condominium association' is the Florida legal form for a building in which each apartment is privately owned, while the common areas – the grounds, the lobbies, the lifts, and so on – are owned by an association, of which the apart-ment owners are joint owners. It is managed by a Board of Directors, elected once a year by the owners, which employs a professional manager and the rest of the staff.) We are on Singer Island, the next barrier island[4] north of Palm Beach, which is itself an island. Our apartment is on the seventeenth floor, faces north and west, to avoid the worst of the hot sun, and has a two-metre-wide balcony round the living rooms, and a narrower one around the bedrooms. It is decorated to look as much like our old house as possible, and we had the Syon Lodge bookcase duplicated as closely as we could. It looks out north-east to the Atlantic, and over the Intracoastal Waterway to the west. The building has two swimming pools, heated, so you can swim all year round, and a walkway across the dunes to the beach, where the ocean stays warm enough to swim in most of the year. Our condominium is very secure, and we can just lock the door and leave, to travel, and to spend time in Collieston without worrying. But it has one big drawback: out of 219 apartments three-quarters are owned by 'snow-birds', people who live in the northern states or Canada, and come down only for 'the season'.[5] So while we have a number of acquaintances, we have few *friends*. And of course the peripatetic life we have led has not been conducive to having many old friends.

There are many places worse than Palm Beach county in which to live, especially as one grows older – not for nothing is South Florida known as 'God's waiting room'! Medical care is of a very high standard, we have a good opera company, a first-class symphony orchestra offering

---

[4]Almost from Miami to New York there is a chain of narrow islands just off the east coast of the US.

[5]Roughly from a month before Christmas to a month after Easter.

eight or nine concerts each season, and the Society of the Four Arts. This, during the season plus a little at each end, offers concerts – among them four wonderful musicians are taking us through all the Beethoven string quartets over a few years. Perhaps best of all are the society's Tuesday afternoon lectures; speakers in the last couple of years have included Viscount Norwich, the Baroness Thatcher, and Generals Schwartzkopf and Colin Powell. This last gave a very moving speech, which had half the audience in tears at the end. If he had run for president in 1996, I don't believe he would not have been elected, but several people we have spoken with about him wonder, as we do, if he just has too much distaste for the sleaze of modern American politics ever to throw his hat into the ring. For the sake of America, I hope not.

We bought our apartment just before the developer (or, to be precise, the bank which had foreclosed on its mortgage when the developer ran out of money) turned the property over to the association, and an owner-elected board took office. There was a number of unfinished items for the completion or rectification of which the association had claims against the bank. Negotiations between us and them dragged on for months, until the President of our Board did an unbelievably stupid thing. He had hired an engineer (at any rate, he called himself one) to put into final form our claims. Extrapolating from a totally non-representative example, this man stated that *none* of the penetrations for water pipes and drains through the concrete floors had the required fireproof sealing. He alleged that some of the fire hydrants had not been placed where the plans showed, and listed other defects, of which a few were genuine. He made these claims without bothering to go to the Municipal Department of Buildings to check what the building inspectors had found at the time of construction, nor what changes from the original specifications had been approved by the appropriate authority. He put a cost on all these items, and reached a total claim of over two million and some dollars, down to exact cents. The President opened the next Board meeting by reading a letter he had written to the bank, which stated this claim ('for purposes of negotiation only') and included a totally groundless personal attack on one of his fellow directors, and then he said that he had mailed the letter fifteen minutes earlier – it would not have required a long delay to put the whole Board in the picture! To no one's surprise (except presumably the President's) the bank replied, essentially, 'Negotiations over. See you in court.' This Board (of nine people) had not made itself popular, because it was so evidently two factions – the President and four friends, and four with other (to my mind, wiser) views. By law, all meetings are open to the owners, I had been present at this one, and was vocal in my disapproval of the President's action. An election was coming up soon and I did not need much persuasion to decide to put forward my name. I was not surprised to be elected (my CV was fairly persuasive) but that I got the largest number of votes of any candidate was unexpected. Our new President, Regina King, a lawyer, took the negotiations in hand, brought the bank back to the table, and in the end got for the association all that we could honestly claim – something over three hundred thousand dollars. I served a few months over three years – part of the time as vice-president – and resigned in mid-1996 to have more time to dedicate to this, my present task.

⋆

Tax law requires that JDR Consultancy's pension plan pay out to us, every year, an amount equal to the total value of the corpus of the trust, divided by our joint expectation of life, as determined by actuarial tables. I don't suppose that many people are aware of this number for themselves, but at least once a year we are obliged to, so as to be able to give the investment manager the appropriate instructions. The tables say that it is probable that one of us will still be alive in the year 2008, but of course they do not presume to forecast our physical condition, nor which one of us. But this actuarial guess is a building-block of our plans.

Uncle Douglas died in 1983, and in July of that year there was a memorial service for him in the Kirk (at which Steve asked me to make the eulogy – it caused laughter and tears) before his ashes were buried in his lair[6] in the kirkyard.

The next night Billie and I gave a dinner for all the members of the family who were there. I had sitting next to me Pat Waters, she of the black-lacquered nails, who had inherited the old Collieston bakery, which Uncle Harry had converted into a house, and I asked her to give Billie and me a first refusal if ever she decided to sell. Pat agreed, and a few years later we became 'enfeoffed' of the house and the derelict adjoining tearoom, which surveyors declared unfit for human habitation.

The house needed much work, and I did a deal with my daughter Sarah and her husband Robert, that they could have the use of it if Robert would do the work and I put up the money. The tearoom had, for cheapness, been clad in corrugated iron. Sixty years of exposure to the North Sea, not a hundred metres away, had attacked this from the ends, which were just rust. We were therefore expecting to have to spend quite a sum on demolishing it. But inside it, one day, I noticed that everything was perfectly dry, there was no trace of weather having penetrated. With the help and counsel of an architect living in the village, we planned

---

[6] 'Lair' is the Scots word for a grave site.

to redo the outer walls, and rearrange the interior into an 'owners' cabin' where Billie and I could spend summers, back in the place that, deep down, was to me still home.

We put in central heating, carpeted the floors, and made kitchen and bathroom with pieces and cabinets from the do-it-yourself, so that we have every comfort (except space – to get by the end of the bed in our bedroom, you must walk like a crab!) and it is fine for vacations, but not for a permanent home.

Epilogue

We have hankered after moving back to the UK, to be closer to family and friends, but the weather, the cost of living, the problem of medical insurance, the economic incompetence of some of the big countries of Europe, and our dislike of the bureaucracy that Brussels seems to be determined to impose on every member of the EU discourage us. We are both octogenarians, so we will have to content ourselves with a few more annual visits to Europe while we are still fit to travel, and then count on family and friends from Europe coming to visit us.

Until then, we will return every year to Collieston, the cradle of my forebears. This is where my roots are; this is where my ancestors are buried, and in Collieston's kirkyard there is already a stone recording the dates of birth of Billie and me, with spaces for the final dates. It was here that, as a child, I acquired many practical skills, and I learned how to 'do unto my neighbour as I would he should do unto me'. It equipped me for the wider world.

In October of 1996, various communities in Buchan organised the 'Doric Festival' to help keep alive interest in the dialect, and I was asked to recite, in Collieston, my grandfather's poem 'Geordie Tough's Squeel' ('Tough' pronounced as the German 'Tuch', 'squeel' meaning 'school') in the original Doric.

Done into English, here are some of the lines that I recited:

We'd neither Board nor School Inspectors,
And no newfangled science lectures,
But what was often so much better
He taught us how to write a letter.
And richly trained our hands and minds
To reading books, and readying lines...

We had a kind of examination,
In reading, writing, numeration,
When Reverend Mister Rust came down
With every elder in the town
To test us on our Three-R sessions:
They never asked our other lessons,
Thinking, doubtless, suchlike learning
Was hardly worthy their concerning.
Like many more – and theirs the blame –
They didn't see the simple aim
And end of every education –
To make a working, thinking nation,
To help a man do better work
In labour, commerce, state, or kirk.

Minister Rust was most demanding
About every kind of formal manners,
Bowing and scraping to our elders,
And lifting hats to our superiors.
He quizzed us on the catechism,
And woe betide us if we failed
To answer every single question
From man's chief end to th' tenth commandment.

According to the printed text
With every proof and reason annexed.
We'd to know the date of Adam's fall,
Of Noah's Ark, and Abraham's call
And be able to read, without a falter
The very hardest 'namie' chapter'.[1]

Merchant Willie tried our counting
In long division, compound mounting,
Practice,[2] interest, vulgar fractions,
Rule of three, and root extractions.
He always looked well dressed and trim
In frock coat and prosthetic limb
Of polished wood, all trimmed with brass,
Hobbling about from class to class
Looking o'er the laddies working,
And every slate or paper marking
Fair, or middling, good or ill.
A very clever man was Will
For every week he sold and bought
Enough to fill a fishing boat;
Tea and sugar, soap and treacle,
Forks and spoons and fishing tackle,
Flour and currants, cloth and books,
Worsted nightcaps, thread and hooks,
Curtain fabric, trouser lining,
Yellow cotton, chequered gingham,

---

[1]See, for example, chapter 33 of the Book of Numbers, and many others.
[2]'A compendious way of multiplying quantities, involving several units, by means of aliquot parts' (*Chambers Twentieth Century Dictionary*).

Blue baize coats, and prints for dresses,
Tar, and rope, and leather laces,
And mustard, butter, eggs and honey –
No doubt he made a pretty penny!

Cooper Jamie's field was spellings:
He tried to cure our little failings
In reading and pronouncing words,
For though a man of staves and hoops
(And not a man in all the world
Could mend a tub or make a barrel
And do it better) he was well learned,
And every penny that he earned
Was justly got, and well taken care of.
A deal of poverty and sorrow
Might spare us all if we but heeded
The simple maxims that he pleaded –
Never to spoil, misuse or waste;
Never the maddening drink to taste;
And make our means, with constant care
Supply our wants and something more.

Our writing then was seen by John,
The elder from the Middle town.
Long strokes, and script both large and small,
He looked them over, one and all.
He wrote a bonny hand himsel'
Though he was old and growing frail.
He was as upright and as good a man
As ever God spent breath upon.

Believed in all the country through
For every word he spoke was true.

Preaching Davie came to see us,
And lots of good advice he'd gi'e us
To fear the Lord and seek the Saviour,
And show respect in our behaviour
Towards our neighbours, sisters, brothers,
Obey our fathers, love our mothers.
He was an earnest godly man.
Lived by the labour of his hand –
A fisherman like those of old
By whom the gospel first was told.

But Geordie now is in his grave,
He's gone like all the others have,
But since he's gone God give him rest.

The poem ends with my grandfather's wish for the young men who had been his schoolfellows:

I hope they'll all turn out good men
To take the place of those who've gone.
May God protect their simple lives
And give them honest winsome wives;
The boats be manned by sturdy lads,
And bonnie lasses bear the creels.

There are no fishing boats left in Collieston: the last creel of fish was borne to Ellon on the shoulders of a lassie over half a century ago. Many of the inhabitants are now

Sassenach,[3] and very few Doric-speakers survive, but the people of the village cut the grass on the Braehead, on the slope of the Brae down to the Bog and in the Bog itself. They keep the footpaths gravelled; the children's playground is maintained and improved, and the Bog Well has had a handsome stone basin and wall built around it, with a gravelled path leading to it, all for no other reward than civic pride.

The spirit of Geordie Tough, of the minister and the elders of the kirk, and the people of the village who were his volunteer helpers, which made my grandfather the man he was, and in which in his verses he passed down to succeeding generations, lives on.

Collieston, 3rd August, 1997

[3]English, or at any rate not Scots.